# SITES OF GOVERNANCE

FIELDS OF GOVERNANCE:
POLICY MAKING IN CANADIAN MUNICIPALITIES

Series editor: Robert Young

Policy making in the modern world has become a complex matter. Much policy is formed through negotiations between governments at several different levels, because each has particular resources that can be brought to bear on problems. At the same time, non-governmental organizations make demands about policy and can help in policy formation and implementation. In this context, works in this series explore how policy is made within municipalities through processes of intergovernmental relations and with the involvement of social forces of all kinds.

The Fields of Governance series arises from a large research project, funded mainly by the Social Sciences and Humanities Research Council of Canada, entitled Multilevel Governance and Public Policy in Canadian Municipalities. This project has involved more than eighty scholars and a large number of student assistants. At its core are studies of several policy fields, each of which was examined in a variety of municipalities. Our objectives are not only to account for the nature of the policies but also to assess their quality and to suggest improvements in policy and in the policy-making process.

The Fields of Governance series is designed for scholars, practitioners, and interested readers from many backgrounds and places.

1 *Immigrant Settlement Policy in Canadian Municipalities*
Edited by Erin Tolley
and Robert Young

2 *Urban Aboriginal Policy Making in Canadian Municipalities*
Edited by Evelyn J. Peters

3 *Sites of Governance: Multilevel Governance and Policy Making in Canada's Big Cities*
Edited by Martin Horak
and Robert Young

# Sites of Governance

## Multilevel Governance and Policy Making in Canada's Big Cities

Edited by

MARTIN HORAK AND ROBERT YOUNG

McGill-Queen's University Press
Montreal & Kingston • London • Ithaca

© McGill-Queen's University Press 2012

ISBN 978-0-7735-4001-9 (cloth)
ISBN 978-0-7735-4002-6 (paper)

Legal deposit second quarter 2012
Bibliothèque nationale du Québec

Printed in Canada on acid-free paper that is 100% ancient forest free
(100% post-consumer recycled), processed chlorine free

McGill-Queen's University Press acknowledges the support of the
Canada Council for the Arts for our publishing program. We also
acknowledge the financial support of the Government of Canada
through the Canada Book Fund for our publishing activities.

**Library and Archives Canada Cataloguing in Publication**

Sites of governance: multilevel governance and policy making in Canada's big cities /
edited by Martin Horak and Robert Young.

(Fields of governance; 3)
Includes bibliographical references and index.
ISBN 978-0-7735-4001-9 (bound). – ISBN 978-0-7735-4002-6 (pbk.)

1. Urban policy – Canada – Case studies. 2. Federal-city relations – Canada –
Case studies. 3. Central-local government relations – Canada – Case studies.
4. Municipal government – Canada – Case studies. 5. Public-private sector
cooperation – Canada – Case studies. I. Horak, Martin, 1973–    II. Young,
Robert, 1950–    III. Series: Fields of governance; 3

HT127.S58 2012          307.760971          C2011-908450-3

This book was typeset by Interscript in 10.5/13 Sabon.

# Contents

Foreword   vii

1  Introduction: Multilevel Governance and Its Central Research
Questions in Canadian Cities   3
ROBERT YOUNG

2  Ascending the Main Stage?: Calgary in the Multilevel Governance
Drama   26
BYRON MILLER AND ALAN SMART

3  Charlottetown: A Small, Quiet Seat of Government – No Boom,
No Bust   53
DAVID M. BULGER

4  Submerging the Urban: Halifax in a Multilevel Governance System   73
ROBERT G. FINBOW

5  Overcoming Adversity, or Public Action in the Face of New Urban
Problems: The Example of Montreal   104
LAURENCE BHERER AND PIERRE HAMEL

6  Multilevel Governance and Public Policy in Saint John,
New Brunswick   136
GREG MARQUIS

7  Policy Making in Saskatoon in a Multilevel Context: The Link Between
Good Governance and Good Public Policy   162
JOSEPH GARCEA AND DONALD C. STORY

8  St John's, A City Apart: An Essay in Urban Exceptionalism   198
CHRISTOPHER DUNN AND CECILY PANTIN

9 Multilevel Governance in Toronto: Success and Failure in Canada's Largest City   228
MARTIN HORAK

10 Multilevel Governance and Urban Development: A Vancouver Case Study   263
THOMAS A. HUTTON

11 Multilevel Governance without Municipal Government: Minimalist Government in Winnipeg   299
CHRISTOPHER LEO WITH MARTINE AUGUST, MIKE PYL, AND MATTHEW D. ROGERS

12 Conclusion: Understanding Multilevel Governance in Canada's Cities   339
MARTIN HORAK

Contributors   371

Index   375

# Foreword

This collection about public policy making in the major cities of Canada is long overdue. We are bombarded with messages about the growing importance of cities for national and regional economies, and we have considerable scholarly information about municipal government. But there is not much material available about how the policies that prevail in urban spaces, many of which are not generated by municipalities, actually come about. This is the gap addressed by this book. All of the authors look at concrete policies and analyze them as a function of two major determinants. The first is the complex set of interactions between interested officials and politicians from the federal, provincial, and municipal levels of government. The second is the dense array of organized interests, or "social forces," that articulate various preferences and are involved to various degrees in policy-making processes.

Of course the authors are not confined to this explanatory mission. They understand their cities thoroughly, and they provide fine-grained portraits of their essential character, built on sketches of their history, economy, demography, and political culture, so that the research will be of interest not only to scholars, students, and policy makers but also, we very much hope, to citizens. We also hope that suggestions for improving policy and the policy-making process will bear fruit in improved conditions for citizens.

This collection presents original research that stands alone and makes a significant contribution to our understanding of public policy in cities. But the work is also part of a larger project, Multilevel Governance and Public Policy in Canadian Municipalities. As is explained in the Introduction to this volume, the project has several components. Some involve smaller Canadian municipalities, but all focus on the six policy areas studied by the authors of the chapters about big cities collected here. The overall objectives of the project are to document the policies that exist in many places and to analyze the processes of intergovernmental relations and the pressures of social forces that shaped them. We also aim to draw conclusions about how better policies could be made. More information about the project is available at www.ppm-ppm.ca.

Some acknowledgments are appropriate here. Our first debt is to the authors, who met together on several occasions to coordinate their efforts, and who were willing to undertake the revisions that made this a better book. Andrew Sancton expertly guided some research meetings and helped the project progress. Nothing would have been accomplished, however, without the support of the Social Sciences and Humanities Research Council of Canada through its Major Collaborative Research Initiatives Program. The University of Western Ontario contributed generously to the project, and some other universities have also helped. We thank McGill-Queen's University Press for its continued interest in our work, and we are especially grateful to an anonymous reader who made suggestions that much improved the collection. Ms Kelly McCarthy has served as project manager for the whole research enterprise; with respect to this particular work, she coordinated meetings and conferences and kept track of the many flows of manuscripts, for which we are very grateful. Ms Jen Lajoie helped with making revisions, and she constructed the index. Ms Nicole Wellsbury did the preliminary editing, formatting, and reference checking with skill and professionalism. Finally, we thank Joanne Muzak for her careful and insightful editing.

# SITES OF GOVERNANCE

# Introduction: Multilevel Governance and Its Central Research Questions in Canadian Cities

ROBERT YOUNG

Cities are more vital to Canada than ever before. Increasing proportions of the population live in them. Economically, their weight in the national totals of employment and production steadily increases. They continue to be the centres of cultural life. In most provinces, laws that stipulate the range of their functions have been amended to provide more scope for autonomous political action. Despite all this, we know little about how public policies in Canada's most important urban areas are actually made, and this is the gap that the contributions collected here are designed to fill. This is a book about policy making in Canada's major cities.

Some clarifications are in order at the outset. All of our authors are keenly interested in the cities they have studied. For the most part, they live in them and have observed political behaviour in them for years: they are experts. But these chapters are not primarily about how municipal governments function and the policies that city administrations enact. There are very good general sources about these issues (Sancton 2011; Tindal and Tindal 2009), and some cities – though not enough of them – are the subject of individual monographs.[1] Instead, our interest is in the policies that are enacted in the urban space that particular cities occupy. This is what we mean by the term sites of governance. There are two crucial implications of this focus. First, policies in urban areas are created by governments at the municipal, provincial, and federal levels, which sometimes act autonomously and sometimes in concert. Studying only what city governments do would not capture important policies that shape life in urban areas. So we are interested in all government activity in our cities.

Second, we restrict ourselves to the space that is defined by the boundaries of our cities. We do not look at the entire metropolitan area that
often comes to mind when Canadians think about places like Vancouver
or Toronto. Very few large cities encompass the economic regions that
they dominate. Calgary and Halifax are two such places, but the norm is
to find many other municipalities in the metropolitan zone. We are not
interested exclusively in municipal governments as urban policy makers,
but we are keenly interested in the policy roles of municipal governments. So we have studied the government of the major city itself –
Vancouver, for example, rather than Richmond, Delta, Surrey, New
Westminster, and all the other municipalities that include almost 80 percent of Metro Vancouver's population. We chose to do this because we
are interested in the relations between governments in policy making,
and metropolitan areas generally do not have governments. As well, we
are interested in the role of non-state actors ("social forces") in policy
making, and these are generally organized within municipal boundaries
rather than across metropolitan regions. Consideration of other metropolitan actors is sometimes unavoidable, as in the study of Montreal, but
fully considering how they bear on most policies is beyond the scope of
the research presented here.

Another feature of the studies in this volume is that they are all concerned with multilevel governance. There is a large and growing body of
research being conducted about multilevel governance. The term originated with studies of the European Union (Bache and Flinders 2004a,
1–2), and much work on the EU continues to be conducted under the
rubric of multilevel governance. There is no generally accepted definition
of the term, and scholars even disagree about whether it qualifies as a
"perspective" (Bache and Flinders 2004b, 94) or a theory capable of
generating testable hypotheses (George 2004, 113–18). But it certainly is
a useful guide to the shifting and complex power relationships among
political actors at all levels of the EU.

As for other applications, Hooghe and Marks (2003) attempted to
generalize the concept in an influential article about the migration of
authority from the central state, by drawing a distinction between Type I
and Type II multilevel governance. The first concerns durable jurisdictions with non-intersecting memberships, at a limited number of levels,
that deliver many services (such as in classical federalism, with municipal, provincial, and federal governments). Type II systems involve functionally specific jurisdictions, intersecting memberships, many levels,
and flexible architecture, such as the special districts common in the

United States or the transborder authorities found in Europe. In both cases, the basic problem is the cost of coordinating the activities of several governments (that is, the transaction cost of reaching agreement and collectively implementing policy). Type I systems reduce this cost by limiting the autonomous actors involved to a few general-purpose governments. Type II systems do so by having many functionally specific governing agencies that have only limited interactions.

The study of multilevel governance is in its infancy in Canada (Young and Leuprecht 2006). The studies reported here did not commence from a firm definition of the concept and a uniform set of hypotheses. The state of current research was far too preliminary for that. Instead, we began with a general working definition of the concept, one involving intergovernmental relations and social forces. We also started with a set of policy fields to study, as previous work demonstrates that the patterns of the complex relationships among government actors and social interests vary from sector to sector. We presumed from the outset that the institutional structure and the norms of the provincial-municipal relationship would be important in shaping tripartite and municipal-federal relations because the provinces have complete constitutional authority over their municipalities; hence, our research design maximized this variation by including only one city per province. Finally, we concentrated on a set of theoretical preoccupations about intergovernmental relations and the political involvement of non-state actors; these questions constituted issues to be explored in the various studies. This framework is now described in more detail.[2]

How is the term multilevel governance used in this volume? There are two dimensions to the concept. First, we are concerned with how governments at various levels interact in policy making. Provincial governments and the federal government are active in the urban arena, sometimes in cooperation with each other. They also draw in municipal governments, which have important resources for the formulation and implementation of policy. Moreover, as mentioned, most large cities now have more autonomy in policy making (Garcea and LeSage 2005). There are tendencies in many municipal quarters to undertake new initiatives in many policy areas because of emerging problems and citizen demands, despite the resource constraints that cities face. As a consequence, we suspected that intergovernmenal arrangements would be on the rise in policy making, and there was good preliminary evidence for this (Young and Leuprecht 2006). Vertical interactions between governments are intrinsic to multilevel governance. Since we are examining municipal, provincial, and federal governments in a classic federation, most inter-action involves durable, nested, Type I government architecture. Quite often, however, the researchers have encountered special-purpose, arms-length, Type II governments – special agencies and authorities of various kinds. Their involvement in the policy process can complicate intergov-ernmental coordination; when properly organized and oriented, how-ever, they can facilitate cooperation.

The second dimension is about governance. By governance, we are referring to the involvement of non-governmental actors in the policy process, which is a longstanding phenomenon. To take an extreme example, Canada's famous National Policy tariffs of the nineteenth cen-tury were worked out in detail not by government officials but by manu-facturers themselves, within their collective associations (Forster 1986). Examples of "policy communities" in which organized interests interact with officials and politicians are legion (see Pal 2006, 237–83 for a review). And the relationships in policy making between local govern-ments and what we call social forces (which are more or less organized interests of all kinds) especially business, have long preoccupied scholars interested in cities (Stone 1989). But linkages between the formal instances of the state and social forces seem to be multiplying. On the one hand, citizens in Canada have become less deferential to established elites and elected politicians, and more inclined to demand that their preferences are reflected in public policy (Nevitte 1996). Organized interests have proliferated at the local level. On the other hand, and perhaps more significantly, governments are resource constrained, some-times deliberately so. They need the information and resources that social forces can mobilize in order to design and implement effective policy. Moreover, the widely accepted precepts of New Public Management suggest that networked governance can be more efficient and flexible than traditional bureaucratic administration (Rhodes 1996), and gov-ernments are experimenting along these lines. So governance implies that governments are acting within networks of social forces – organized interests of many different kinds, active at different levels.

In the study of cities, it is very common for analysts to explore the relations between municipal governments and social forces. In particu-lar, the role of business in shaping the policies that city governments pursue is a dominant aspect of the field. It is less common to explore intergovernmental relations – how cities interact with provincial and federal governments in policy making. We have emphasized this dimen-sion for two reasons. First, many cities have gained more legal autonomy and are in a position to take on a broader policy role. Some cities are taking on what we call a "comprehensive" orientation, as opposed to a "minimalist" stance that favours straightforwardly delivering traditional services. Some cities have moved into new areas such as helping with immigrant settlement and trying to deal with urban Aboriginal issues. Such initiatives are likely to bring municipal administrations into greater contact with provincial and federal officials who are active in these areas. Second, pressure from a variety of sources has been rising for some time to have the federal government play a more active role in urban issues (Andrew, Graham and Phillips 2002; Berdahl 2006). This pressure culminated when the government led by Paul Martin embraced his New Deal for cities and communities, which involved tax relief and transfers to municipalities from the federal tax on gasoline. More significant were new infrastructure programs that involved intergovernmental cooperation, and there was also a flurry of new urban development agreements, tripartite arrangements for coordinated interventions into particular problems in several cities. When the Martin government was defeated in 2006, the Conservatives' policy of open federalism strongly suggested that the new government would be much less active on the urban file (Young 2006). But this is a question open to empirical investigation. Our scholars were determined to explore intergovernmental relations and their place in major Canadian cities, which is an innovative feature of this book.

We are interested in public policy in Canadian urban spaces, but we cannot study all policy areas, at least not in the depth required to explore how intergovernmental relations and social forces combine to produce particular policies. There are time constraints on research and space constraints on publications. Consequently, we decided at the outset to focus the research on six policy fields – emergency planning, federal property, municipal image building, immigrant settlement, infrastructure, and urban Aboriginal policy. These policy fields were carefully chosen. We wanted fields where there was some significant probability of intergovernmental relations, especially of city governments with the federal government. So we left aside a substantial part of the day-to-day policy making of municipalities in areas such as land use planning, water and sewers, protective services, recreation, and so on, and we also left out fields where municipalities deliver services under close provincial regulation. We chose our six fields to aim for a representative set. Some involve regulation as the primary instrument and others involve expenditure. Some, such as emergency planning and federal property, are relatively low in public visibility; others generate substantial public interest. Some are areas of federal jurisdiction, some are mixed or contested, and some are mainly municipal. Finally, there is a combination of "hard" policy fields like property and infrastructure and "softer" fields that involve services to people. We do not explore the effect of the nature of the field on the policies that we found, but we did seek representativeness along these dimensions.

The choice of cities was simple. We selected the largest city in each province. Because there is substantial variation across provinces in the structure and functioning of the municipal systems, we wanted at least one case in every province. Because the provincial governments establish the framework within which municipalities operate, it would make little sense to study three or four large cities in a single province while neglecting municipalities in other provinces. With such an approach, we would very likely find little variation within the province and miss differences among provinces. Some of our cities are small in absolute terms, but studying them can still tell us a lot about the play of intergovernmental relations and social forces in policy making. These cities have importance within smaller provinces, and smaller provinces do not act alike in intergovernmental matters. Unfortunately, we were not able to study cities in Yukon, the Northwest Territories, or Nunavut because of insufficient resources; moreover, the federal presence is particularly great in these territories, and the intergovernmental arrangements are fluid.

The policy fields were assigned to cities in advance of commencing the research. First, we allocated fields to provinces to get a representative distribution. The allocation of policy fields also depended on the availability of researchers and their interest in topics. Two fields of the six were allocated to each province as a whole. The remaining four fields were the ones to be studied in the major city of the province. For example, municipal image building was allocated to Prince Edward Island in part because tourism is so important for that province. Since a separate study was done at the provincial level, image building is not discussed in the Charlottetown chapter.[3] Except for Vancouver, each study in this volume covers four of the six policy fields. We have not aimed for full representativeness, but the coverage in any one city is thorough, and we have sufficient coverage across cities that we have confidence in the overall results. We can make generalizations about how policy is formed and about how good it is, as the volume's conclusion demonstrates. Table 1 lays out the fields studied in the various cities.

Table 1
Policy fields studied in the cities

| | Emergency planning | Federal property | Image building | Immigrant settlement | Infra-structure | Urban aboriginal policy |
|---|---|---|---|---|---|---|
| Calgary | | x | x | x | x | |
| Charlottetown | x | x | | x | | x |
| Halifax | | x | x | | x | x |
| Montreal | x | x | x | | | x |
| Saint John | x | | x | x | x | |
| Saskatoon | x | x | | x | x | |
| St John's | | | x | x | x | x |
| Toronto | x | x | x | | x | |
| Vancouver | | | x | | x | |
| Winnipeg | x | x | | x | | x |

The research presented in the chapters that follow was mainly done between 2007 and 2009. Harmonization and polishing of the contributions followed. The chapters here attain a high level of scholarship. Each relies on published and unpublished documents, and this work is thorough. More unusual, however, is the recourse to interviews. Each scholar engaged in interviews with officials and politicians, often from all three levels of government. There was also extensive interviewing with representatives of the social forces involved in each of the policy fields studied. In total, the authors interviewed well over 325 people, which is unprecedented in urban research in Canada.

To various degrees, the authors focus on the six selected policy fields, but each chapter contains much more. The cities are described in a holistic fashion, and readers will get a sense of the history of each place, along with the economic and demographic nature of the city. Moreover, the authors define the essence of their cities, drawing general conclusions about how policy is made and how well the city is faring. A brief overview of the chapters is appropriate here. The chapters are arranged in alphabetical order. Other principles of ordering the studies – by population size, size relative to the provincial population, geographic location, age, degree of involvement in intergovernmental relations – are possible. But objections can be raised to all of these principles, and some lead to less varied and lively orderings. So arrangement alphabetically works best.

The first chapter, on Calgary, opens with an intriguing extended metaphor about the stage on which multilevel governance plays out. The point is that intergovernmental relations where municipalities are concerned often involve complex sets of *bilateral* interactions in a deeply political context; that is, they are played out before the audience. Further, the municipalities tend to be the minor characters, despite much public support for their needs and ambitions. Calgary itself is all about growth. Byron Miller and Alan Smart are blunt: "rapid population and economic growth and its attendant pressures structure everything about contemporary Calgary." Hence, municipal government aims to accommodate growth, and in so doing must confront its attendant consequences – social problems, especially the shortage of low-cost housing – and the infrastructure deficit. The municipal government is learning to cope, often in interaction with the federal and provincial governments. The city's expansion and wealth seem to make it poised to be a new place, but the case study of how its image is constructed reveals conflict about the essence of Calgary. On the intergovernmental front, the authors make some trenchant observations. In particular, their study of the Curry Barracks development challenges "the sweeping generalization that lower levels of government make better decisions in local matters than higher levels of government, and that private developers respond better to consumer demand than a public agency can." It's a strong beginning.

Charlottetown is in many ways the opposite of Calgary. It is old and stable and its issues match its small scale. As David Bulger makes clear, history is very important in the city and on Prince Edward Island generally. The old municipalities of the Maritimes have small populations and large cemeteries, and traces of the past linger. Further, Charlottetown is a capital city, with many functions exercised by the provincial government or under tight provincial supervision. In some ways, the provincial government of PEI is like a metropolitan government. Charlottetown also has a large federal presence, and the many well-paid public servants insulate the city from both boom and bust. Through the case studies about the city, we find the municipal government inactive on files of importance to other cities, notably immigrant settlement and urban Aboriginal policy, while the provincial and federal governments dominate in emergency planning and issues about federal property. Of all the cities explored here, Charlottetown's focus is most "on the delivery of services and not on large policy issues."

The same is not true in Halifax, as Robert Finbow demonstrates. He deals with major decisions about federal property, infrastructure in the form of the sewage treatment plant, the Commonwealth Games bid and its abandonment, and the lack of programming for urban Aboriginal people. The details of these cases are absorbing, but Finbow also draws some general conclusions about their underlying structures. He finds an elitist political culture that is relatively unresponsive to citizens' demands and a highly institutionalized relationship between the Halifax Regional Municipality and local business interests. The provincial government's stance is interventionist but not particularly responsive to genuinely urban issues. And the local political leadership is divided, primarily because in the Halifax Regional Municipality, a vast area amalgamated in the mid-1990s, the interests and voice of the central city have been diluted by the suburban and rural areas. Consequently, the Halifax Regional Municipality is far less effective in multilevel relationships than it should be.

The Montreal chapter presents a lot of intriguing information. We discover, first, how complex the institutional environment is in this big metropolitan region, and how unstable the coalitions of decision makers are across various scales of policy. This effect of complexity and instability is most clear in the discussion of image building, which is an existential policy area because it forces collective identification and a commitment to a vision of the future. In the Montreal region, report Laurence Bherer and Pierre Hamel, "the problem is that no single actor is currently strong enough to convince the others to adhere to a particular vision. The result is, if not a perpetual state of confrontation, at least a series of parallel endeavours with no sign of convergence in the medium term." Another theme here concerns vertical intergovernmental relations. It is not well understood outside Quebec that relations between Montreal and the province have been uneasy for a long time. Bherer and Hamel also explode the myth that in Quebec there are few relations between federal and municipal officials, notably in their description of the Lachine Canal redevelopment. It is true in Quebec that provincial officials oversee every *contract* signed between municipalities and other bodies and the federal government, but there still can be substantial *contact* within parameters established by the province. Indeed, the authors argue that more success in Montreal would be accomplished not only by the achievement of some local consensus but also by a stronger, more continuous federal involvement in urban issues.

The study of Saint John, New Brunswick, cuts to the core of the city's historic position. A port city with a strong base in resources and heavy manufacturing, Saint John has been in a demographic and industrial decline for many years. All policies in the city are dominated by economic imperatives, and Greg Marquis describes a classic "growth coalition," dominated by local business, especially the Irving family interests (which include the local newspaper) and spearheaded by politicians. The influence of its concerns is seen in all of the policies explored in the chapter, especially those about infrastructure. Yet there are tensions. In the economic realm, these tensions occur between heavy industry, with its energy hub strategy, and the service and IT sectors, which actually generate most employment, and tensions are reflected both in the search for a new image for the municipality and in conflicts over infrastructure priorities between environmental concerns and transportation facilities. Finally, in this small place, in a small province, the central role of politicians in the policy process is remarkable, with those at the provincial level largely dominating.

The chapter on Saskatoon depicts a city operating in a very different environment and in a unique policy mode. Over the period studied, Saskatoon experienced an economic boom unparalleled in a century. Perhaps this enabled the successful initiatives in all four of the policy fields studied. More significant though seems to be the unique political culture of the province. Especially where intergovernmental relations are concerned, Saskatchewan evinces smooth, collaborative relations, even when many actors are involved (Garcea and Pontikes 2006). Policy makers are generally competent. They engage in extensive consultation and create committees and networks that include interested actors, and a most unusual tradition of collaboration and compromise pervades the policy process. Joseph Garcea and Donald Story's meticulous description of the organizational mechanisms involved in the four policy areas testifies to the care that Saskatchewan governments devote to the process of policy making. Political considerations are important in all of this, but it is noteworthy that "neither partisan political allegiances nor differing ideological orientations among members of the municipal, provincial, and federal governments had the effect of diminishing the level of collaboration among them." Through careful decision making (and with the aid of the boom), Saskatoon has achieved considerable success in some major initiatives.

The study of St John's focuses on its exceptionalism. The city is apart from the rest of the province of Newfoundland and Labrador, far from the rest of Canada, and distinct in its long history of feeble institutions, weak democracy, and control by the provincial government. It is only since Confederation with Canada in 1949 that the municipality has developed as a city like others, and, though it has greater powers than other Newfoundland municipal governments, it is still under close provincial supervision. St John's is also a petroleum centre, with its unstable traditional economy boosted over the past two decades by oil development and substantial spin-off activity in manufacturing, services, and research. Christopher Dunn traces a new interest in attracting and retaining immigrants, and he shows the rising need for services to urban Aboriginal people. He concentrates most on image building and describes the attempts by many actors to formulate and integrate the components of the image of ocean excellence.

The City of Toronto is Canada's largest and most complicated metropolis, and one that faces a plethora of pressing issues. Hence, as Martin Horak observes, "municipal government in Toronto has tremendously dense and complex interactions with other levels of government and with local societal groups. Multilevel governance in one form or another is omnipresent in Toronto." Horak slices through the complexities in presenting a set of five cogent case studies that are both detailed and succinct and that focus on the coordination problems in multilevel governance – aligning resources and policy agendas. He covers infrastructure funding for the Toronto Transit Commission, federal property in the form of Downsview Park and the central waterfront, the image-building effort of the Tourism Action Plan, and coordination in emergency planning and management. He finds that the policies vary widely in quality, as measured according to whether objectives were met and local stakeholders were satisfied. The quality varies according to whether coordination problems were overcome, which they can be when competent and cohesive administration is supported by sustained political leadership, and actors take advantage of windows of opportunity to advance their projects.

Vancouver, quite appropriately, is set by Tom Hutton in the globalizing economy, which not only requires that action at the municipal level become broader in scope but also offers new opportunities to be realized through intergovernmental coordination and more engagement with social forces – that is, through multilevel governance. He analyzes infrastructure and image building as contributions to economic development, which in Vancouver means a shift from being the centre of a resource-producing periphery to becoming a transnational service-based economy. In transportation, Hutton describes the Asia Pacific Initiative, an extraordinary tri-level enterprise, and also the Canada Line project, where the province's constitutional power was wielded to press the line through to completion. An Olympic bid is very much about the image of the supplicant city. Vancouver has moved from a discourse about "ecotopia" to one about "urban transnationalism" and "sustainability," cemented by the 2010 Olympic process. Mounting an Olympics absolutely demands multilevel governance and the achievement of cohesion among the many actors involved, as was found in VANOC (the Vancouver Organizing Committee). There is a long history of tri-level cooperation in Vancouver, and Hutton intriguingly suggests that repeated experience in such cooperation and learning can, over time, make for smoother and more practiced relations.

Our final study is of Winnipeg. According to Christopher Leo and his colleagues, recent years have seen the orientation of the city's administration change abruptly to an exceedingly minimalist one from one that was highly activist, or, in our terms, a comprehensive conception of the municipal-government role. As a consequence of the change to minimalism, the municipal government is simply absent from many policy areas. This absence is based on ideology, but, structurally, it is also significant that over half of Manitoba's population lives in the city proper, and so the provincial government is particularly attuned to local issues there and is prepared to intervene or supervise closely. In any case, the authors find that "the city functioned, for the most part, neither as a representative of local interests in decision making, nor as a petitioner on behalf of the locality or particular local groups. At most, it served as an administrative agent for another level of government." The authors assess policy according to whether it is effective in achieving its objectives and whether it respects community interests and is informed by local knowledge. In these aspects, the record is mixed. They conclude that "multilevel governance can perform reasonably well in meeting federal government objectives, even without great concern for involvement with and responsiveness to the local community, but that, when such concern is present, much more can be achieved." In this case, surprisingly, good performance was achieved without much involvement by the City of Winnipeg.

Evidently, our chapters are very diverse. They reflect the complexities of Canada's major urban areas and portray intricate and variegated policy making processes. Each is interesting and unique, but we do have broader theoretical interests in the study of multilevel governance and public policy in these municipalities, and these are worth sketching at the outset.

Our first, simple objective is to document the patterns of multilevel policy making. What are the relations between officials and politicians from different levels of government? The primary interest here is in municipal-federal relations, which have been studied very little since the dismantlement of the short-lived Ministry of State for Urban Affairs in the late 1970s (Feldman and Graham 1979). The last attempt at a survey was done long ago (Andrew 1994). More recently, spurred in part by the Martin government's New Deal initiatives, there have been studies of "place-based policy" (Bradford 2005) and of "deep federalism" (Leo 2006). Both of these approaches are similar to the preoccupations of our authors, but our research begins with general agnosticism about the costs and benefits of incorporating municipal governments into policy-making networks, and our coverage of both policy fields and cities is much broader. We are also interested in how provincial governments are inserted into municipal-federal relations, given that they control municipalities and that they are active in many of our policy fields as autonomous agents.

Beyond documenting the state of intergovernmental relations, we have several theoretical preoccupations. Since there is no broad consensus on the meaning and dynamics of multilevel governance, we did not impose a common framework on the authors of the studies. And since so little is known about the shape of multilevel governance in Canada, it was premature to construct a set of precise hypotheses for testing. Instead, we all began with a common interest in a set of theoretical issues that was used to structure the various investigations. These issues concern both intergovernmental relations and social forces.

With respect to intergovernmental relations, we want to explore the relative influence of various governmental actors. In policy making there are several stages (Pal 2006, 97–236). The labels for these stages vary, but we can distinguish agenda setting, problem definition, devising policy alternatives and choosing between them (or policy development and decision making), and implementing policy. It is generally taken for granted that earlier involvement implies greater influence. Actors who implement policy, for example, always have some latitude in applying it, but this is considered less influential than getting an issue onto the policy agenda or actually deciding on a policy from among several alternative courses of action. We are interested in which governments take the initiative in policy fields and which enter the policy arena later, generally as "policy takers."

Influence also varies with the resources that actors bring to the policy-making process. These are of several varieties. In our context, one is jurisdiction; that is, the constitutional control over the policy field (or habitual, *de facto* control). This can legitimize taking a lead role in policy making. Another, obviously, is money. A cursory knowledge of our policy fields and others reveals that the federal government often acts in areas outside of its jurisdiction through its use of the spending power and may take a predominant policy role. Actors may also possess particular expertise and knowledge, and this can work in favour of resource-constrained city governments, which have expertise in areas like land use planning and property. Finally, there are political resources such as electoral weight and legitimacy in public opinion. One of our theoretical objectives is to discover which resources lead to involvement and influence in the policy process.

In documenting intergovernmental relations, the authors pay attention to the fact that actors at all levels consist of both officials and politicians. We are interested in what causes politicians to play an active role in intergovernmental policy files and what the effects of their involvement are. We consider that most policy, most of the time, is the bailiwick of officials, who manage the day-to-day grind of the policy process; but, given how responsible governments work, there is always the possibility for elected politicians to intervene and take the lead. What factors bring politicians into the policy arena and to what effect? Beyond this question, we expect that ideological and programmatic differences between politicians at different levels of government may affect the conduct of intergovernmental relations. We ask, do ideology and partisanship matter and, if so, under what conditions? It is useful to bear in mind here the natural experiment that Canadian federal politics has produced in recent years, with the change from a Liberal federal government that was avowedly interested in urban issues to a Conservative government with little interest in cities, at least from a policy viewpoint. What has been the impact of this change on intergovernmental relations and on policy in municipalities?

A final intergovernmental issue concerns the general orientation of municipal governments. Local governments face pressure to expand their traditional role as service providers and to undertake activities beyond the scope of powers traditionally allocated to them by provincial governments. Some analysts locate this pressure in the evolving global economy, where cities occupy a central position and require greater power and resources (Courchene 2007). Others see it as a consequence of provincial governments loosening control over municipalities, opening the space for them to act with "assertive maturity" (Siegel and Tindal 2006). It can also be seen as a sharpening of the perennial tension between traditional service provision and the vision of cities as deeply political bodies, "the means by which a local community can express and address its collective objectives" (Tindal and Tindal 2009, 7). We distinguish generally between minimalist and comprehensive orientations and seek to understand how multilevel governance is affected by the choice of stance.

The second major theoretical preoccupation that runs through all the studies presented here is the role of social forces. In some ways our interests here run parallel to those concerning intergovernmental relations. We seek first to document what social forces are involved in policy making and also to inquire about those that are not involved but could reasonably be expected to have an interest in a particular policy field. If organized interests do not have a seat at the policy table, their preferences are less likely to be reflected in policy choices (see for example Boyce et al. 2001). As with governments, it is important to know the stage at which they enter the policy process. We know at the outset that in some fields like immigrant settlement and urban Aboriginal policy there are organizations, more or less representative of their clientele, that are involved in delivering policy – that is, in policy implementation (Rekart 1993). And obviously many social forces advocate about issues and attempt to set the policy agenda and define problems. But are they also involved in designing policy and in making choices between alternative courses of action? If so, they have greater influence, and we are keenly interested in the distribution of power among social forces of various kinds.

In particular, we are interested in the relative power of business. There is a very large literature about the connection of business interests with the local state. This is a longstanding area of debate (Hunter 1953; Dahl 1961), and most of the contributions concern American cities, but the core issues remain important. The main point of contention is how constrained municipal governments are to enact policies that promote economic growth. One school of thought holds that municipal governments have few powers, are dependent on the property tax for revenue, and compete for investment; hence they must try to maximize property values and promote development to broaden the tax base. They become "growth machines" (Molotch 1993) and cannot engage in redistributive policies (Peterson 1981). A second view is that cities have more latitude. Political leaders can create "urban regimes" by forging coalitions between segments of the electorate and business and professional groups and can then both engineer growth and deliver benefits, often in the form of jobs (Stone 1989). Finally, there is the view that no business coalition dominates all policy fields toward the single objective of growth; instead, policy making is fragmented, with different networks or policy communities active in different fields (Dowding 2001). Hence, redistributive policy is possible.

Given the nature of our research design, the scholars whose work is collected here cannot definitively pronounce on these theoretical positions in the case of their cities. We are not exploring fiscal issues such as tax competition, and "economic development" is not one of our policy fields, mainly because it is so vast. (Indeed, given the influence of Richard Florida's theories about human capital driving growth and the rise of the "creative class" [2002], the range of policies that can be construed as development-oriented has expanded substantially.) But we are interested in business power, and a major issue in every policy field and every city is the relative influence of business interests. Does policy tend to reflect the preferences of local business?

There is a twist on this issue that is uniquely available in these studies because of their emphasis on intergovernmental relations. If there are many good reasons to expect that business is preponderant in policy making where local government is concerned, does the same hold true when other governments are involved? It could well be that local business power can be mitigated by the policy preferences of the federal and provincial governments. We want to know whether there are signs of this in our case studies. In particular, is it the case that social forces with preferences that differ from those of local business are able to "shift scale" and bring pressure to bear at the federal or provincial level to achieve their objectives? Are such social forces well-organized at other levels through networks or umbrella organizations, so that they can win policy disputes in instances of multilevel governance that they cannot win at the municipal level? We want to explore these issues of power in multilevel governance systems.

The third and final set of issues that these city studies were to explore revolve around the quality of the policies produced by multilevel governance. How good are the policies that emerge from these intergovernmental processes, ones in which social forces are also involved? This is a complex question, to say the least, but it is important to evaluate policies if we aim to improve intergovernmental processes and their policy outputs.

There are many criteria used in the evaluation of policies, and we have tried to be aware of them in the course of research. But first, it should be clear that we hold no preconceived notions about two matters of process. We do not assume that policy is better if it is made by several governments acting together; nor do we assume that policy made by a single government is intrinsically better. Similarly, we do not assume that policy made in concert with social forces or implemented by them is superior ipso facto. These are matters for empirical investigation.

In evaluating policies, we examined some generic features. One is speed. Was the policy created and implemented in good time, or were there delays? Another concerns the scale of the policy – whether it was adequate to address the problems at hand. A third is the coherence of policy. Were policies logically constructed and did they fit with related policies or work at cross-purposes to them? Further, we were concerned with some standard criteria of policy evaluation. The first is effectiveness – that is, whether the policy achieved the goals set out for it. The second is efficiency – that is, whether goals were achieved at a reasonable cost. The third is equity, which has various components, including whether benefits were directed toward those most in need and broadly accessible or narrowly concentrated on certain societal groups. Generally speaking, was the policy fair? Our last criterion is more normative and contestable; it is whether the problem or issue that the policy was designed to address was defined appropriately at the outset. Problem definition can delimit the range of policies that actors contemplate in policy design, and clearly this can be a matter of vigorous debate among politicians, officials, and social forces.

The sources for evaluation were several. The scholars who did these studies interviewed a great many politicians and officials, and these respondents were sometimes quite frank about the strengths and weaknesses of policy initiatives. Obviously, the many representatives of the social forces who were also interviewed, and who can be thought of as stakeholders in the policies, also contributed views about the quality of the policy outputs and outcomes. As well, because we have similar policy fields across many cases, we can compare policies in one city with what has occurred elsewhere to assess relative quality. And finally, researchers and their colleagues have their own expert capacity to evaluate public policies.

While all of these criteria and evaluative techniques were deployed in these studies, two tended to dominate, as Martin Horak explains in the conclusion. The first is effectiveness. Whether the policy achieved its stated objectives is something that can be assessed across all of our policy fields and cities, and it forms the foundation for our judgment about the quality of policy. The second dominant criterion is responsiveness – that is, whether the policies reflected the preferences and opinions of local actors, the local officials and social forces active in the policy field.

Responsiveness is in part an amalgam of problem definition and equity, but it is also a valid indicator of quality because multilevel governance is meant to pool resources and adapt general policy to local conditions (Leo 2006; Leo and August 2009). We therefore privilege the local actors, which is appropriate when studying policy on the ground in Canada's major cities.

Most of the authors evaluate the quality of policy in their cities more or less explicitly. Summary results are found in the conclusion. This is a most impressive chapter. Horak builds on the theoretical framework laid out in his Toronto chapter to make hallmark contributions not only to the scholarship on Canadian cities but also to the study of multilevel governance in general. The essence of multilevel governance, he argues, is the need to coordinate the activities of various authorities. This means cooperation in mobilizing sufficient resources to deal with problems and opportunities and also having an alignment of priorities (or "policy agendas") among governments. Coordinating resources and priorities must also involve non-state actors, or social forces of various kinds. Using the city studies comprehensively, Horak shows that effective policies require coherent administrations – unity of purpose within governments – and, often, sustained political leadership over long periods of time. Effective policy is also more likely when multilevel relationships are institutionalized. For policy to be responsive, it helps when local actors are involved at the stage of policy development and decision making rather than only through advocacy and implementation. This is more likely when the municipal authorities have jurisdiction or a longstanding presence in the field. Financial resources also help to swing the locus of policy making toward the local level, and expertise and information are also important. The electoral weight of the city also contributes to responsiveness, as does administrative capacity. Cities are also taken more seriously by other governmental actors when they conceive of their role in a comprehensive rather than a minimalist manner. Of course, responsiveness to local governments does not necessarily mean responsiveness to local social forces, but the two are more likely when local interests have an established relationship with inclusive municipal governments.

Does business dominate among social forces? Horak's answer is that "multilevel governance as documented in this volume tends to be limited in its responsiveness to local social forces other than business. Enthusiastic promoters of multilevel governance as a responsive mode of policy making would do well to keep this rather sobering conclusion in mind." Horak concludes with suggestions for improving multilevel governance and therefore the policy that flows from it. Cities need greater administrative capacity, social forces need to be better organized at the provincial and federal levels, and provinces should reduce their micromanagement. All in all, Horak has delivered a masterful summary of these cases, an incisive analysis of multilevel policy making, and some sensible suggestions for improving the quality of policy in Canadian municipalities.

But the conclusion ends the book, and we are at the beginning. The chapters that follow contain rich explorations of policy making in Canada's major cities. They portray the history of our cities, their demography and economic challenges, and their governance. There are accounts of the quality of local democracy and of the capacity of cities to chart their own course in the complex world of multilevel governance. We hope and expect that these studies will be interesting to scholars, students, and officials, and to all citizens who are affected by the policy choices that are made in Canadian cities.

NOTES

1   For earlier coverage of six of the cities covered in this book, see Magnusson and Sancton (1983), who provide a good introduction about the development of Canadian city government. Higgins (1986) is dated, but it was comprehensive. Graham and Phillips with Maslove (1998) is a good introduction to urban structures, issues, and the setting of city governments. The book edited by Bunting and Filion (2006) is invaluable, especially from the geographic and planning perspective. Finally, Lightbody (2006) covers political participation and ethics, and has an extensive treatment of metropolitan issues and reforms.

2   The work presented here about Canada's major cities is very substantial, but it is a component of a larger project entitled "Multilevel Governance and Public Policy in Canadian Municipalities." In this enterprise, scholars have investigated public policy, seeking to understand it as a function of (1) the structure of intergovernmental relations through which it was created, and (2) the involvement – or not – of various social forces in the policy making process. This project, largely funded by the Social Sciences and Humanities Research Council of Canada, has involved over eighty researchers and almost as many student assistants. It has produced three other volumes (Young and Leuprecht 2006; Lazar and Leuprecht 2007; Sancton and Young 2009). The first explores municipal-federal-provincial relations in Canada through chapters about the background to multilevel governance, municipal restructuring, multilevel

policies, and the processes of complex intergovernmental relations. The second consists of studies of eight other countries, primarily federations, with the objective of describing how cities fit into the policy process in systems that are very different from the Canadian one. It parallels this book on Canadian cities because the same policy fields are explored in these comparative cases. The third book describes the provincial-municipal system in each of the provinces of Canada, laying out in a carefully systematic manner municipal structures, functions, and finances, with attention to municipalities' demography, political culture, collective organization, and oversight by provincial governments. Several more works on particular policy fields are forthcoming. In the larger project, *Sites of Governance* is absolutely central because it combines many cases and policy fields. On the other hand, it stands alone as a unique contribution to the study of public policy in our major cities.

3 The studies of the policy fields allocated to the provinces were done as follows. For each of the province's two policy fields, researchers studied them in four municipalities of various sizes, including the largest city. For example, image building in Prince Edward Island was studied in St Peters Bay, Wellington, the Resort Municipality, and Charlottetown. Image building was also studied in Manitoba and Saskatchewan. Along with a study of federal policy, this research will be forthcoming in a volume. This and other policy fields are featured in a series published by McGill-Queen's University Press called Fields of Governance: Policy Making in Canadian Municipalities, of which this volume on big cities is an important part.

## REFERENCES

Andrew, Caroline. 1994. "Federal Urban Activity: Intergovernmental Relations in an Age of Constraint." In *The Changing Canadian Metropolis: A Public Policy Perspective*, edited by Frances Frisken, 427–57. Berkeley: Institute of Governmental Studies Press, University of California; Toronto: Canadian Urban Institute.

Andrew, Caroline, Katherine A. Graham, and Susan D. Phillips, eds. 2002. *Urban Affairs: Back on the Policy Agenda*. Montreal and Kingston: McGill-Queen's University Press.

Bache, Ian, and Matthew Flinders. 2004a. "Themes and Issues in Multi-Level Governance." In *Multi-level Governance*, edited by Ian Bache and Matthew Flinders, 1–11. New York: Oxford University Press.

– 2004b. "Multi-level Governance and British Politics." In *Multi-level Governance*, edited by Ian Bache and Matthew Flinders, 93–106. New York: Oxford University Press.

Berdahl, Loleen. 2006. "The Federal Urban Role and Federal-Municipal
    Relations." In *Canada: The State of the Federation, 2004 – Municipal-
    Federal-Provincial Relations in Canada*, edited by Robert Young and
    Christian Leuprecht, 26–43. Montreal and Kingston: McGill-Queen's
    University Press for the Institute of Intergovernmental Relations, Queen's
    University.

Boyce, William, Mary Ann McColl, Mary Tremblay, Jerome Bickenbach, Anne
    Crichton, Steven Andrews, Nancy Gerein, and April D'Aubin. 2001. *A Seat
    at the Table: Persons with Disabilities and Policy Making*. Montreal and
    Kingston: McGill-Queen's University Press.

Bradford, Neil. 2005. *Place-based Public Policy: Towards a New Urban and
    Community Agenda for Canada*. Ottawa: Canadian Policy Research
    Networks, Research Report F/51, Family Network.

Bunting, Trudi, and Pierre Filion, eds. 2006. *Canadian Cities in Transition: Local
    Through Global Perspectives*. Don Mills, ON: Oxford University Press.

Courchene, Thomas J. 2007. "Global Futures for Canada's Global Cities."
    *Policy Matters* 8 (2). Montreal: Institute for Research on Public Policy.

Dahl, Robert. 1961. *Who Governs?* New Haven: Yale University Press.

Dowding, Keith. 2001. "Explaining Urban Regimes." *International Journal of
    Urban and Regional Research* 25 (1):7–19.

Feldman, Lionel D., and Katherine A. Graham. 1979. *Bargaining for Cities*.
    Montreal: Institute for Research on Public Policy.

Florida, Richard. 2002. *The Rise of the Creative Class and How It's Trans-
    forming Work, Leisure, Community and Everyday Life*. New York: Basic
    Books.

Forster, Ben. 1986. *A Conjunction of Interests: Business, Politics and Tariffs
    1825–1879*. Toronto: University of Toronto Press.

Garcea, Joseph, and Edward LeSage Jr., eds. 2005. *Municipal Reform in
    Canada: Reconfiguration, Re-Empowerment, and Rebalancing*. Don Mills,
    ON: Oxford University Press.

Garcea, Joseph, and Ken Pontikes. 2006. "Federal-Municipal-Provincial
    Relations in Saskatchewan: Provincial Roles, Approaches, and Mech-
    anisms." In *Canada: The State of the Federation, 2004 – Municipal-
    Federal-Provincial Relations in Canada*, edited by Robert Young and
    Christian Leuprecht, 333–67. Montreal and Kingston: McGill-Queen's
    University Press for the Institute of Intergovernmental Relations, Queen's
    University.

George, Stephen. 2004. "Multi-level Governance and the European Union." In
    *Multi-level Governance*, edited by Ian Bache and Matthew Flinders, 107–26.
    New York: Oxford University Press.

Graham, Katherine A., and Susan D. Phillips with Allan M. Maslove. 1998. *Urban Governance in Canada: Representation, Resources, and Restructuring*. Toronto: Harcourt Brace.

Hooghe, Liesbet, and Gary Marks. 2003. "Unraveling the Central State, but How? Types of Multi-level Governance." *American Political Science Review* 97 (2):233–43.

Higgins, Donald J.H. 1986. *Local and Urban Politics in Canada*. Toronto: Gage Educational Publishing.

Hunter, Floyd. 1953. *Community Power Structure: A Study of Decision Makers*. Chapel Hill: University of North Carolina Press.

Lazar, Harvey, and Christian Leuprecht, eds. 2007. *Spheres of Governance: Comparative Studies of Cities in Multilevel Governance Systems*. Montreal and Kingston: McGill-Queen's University Press for the Institute of Intergovernmental Relations, Queen's University.

Leo, Christopher. 2006. "Deep Federalism: Respecting Community Difference in National Policy." *Canadian Journal of Political Science* 39 (3):481–506.

Leo, Christopher, and Martine August. 2009. "The Multilevel Governance of Immigration and Settlement: Making Deep Federalism Work." *Canadian Journal of Political Science* 42 (2):491–510.

Lightbody, James. 2006. *City Politics, Canada*. Peterborough, ON: Broadview Press.

Magnusson, Warren, and Andrew Sancton, eds. 1983. *City Politics in Canada*. Toronto: University of Toronto Press.

Molotch, Harvey. 1993. "The Political Economy of Growth Machines." *Journal of Urban Affairs* 15 (1):29–53.

Nevitte, Neil. 1996. *The Decline of Deference: Canadian Value Change in Cross-National Perspective*. Peterborough, ON: Broadview Press.

Pal, Leslie. 2006. *Beyond Policy Analysis*. Toronto: Thomson Nelson.

Peterson, Paul E. 1981. *City Limits*. Chicago: University of Chicago Press.

Rekart, Josephine. 1993. *Public Goods, Private Provision: The Role of the Voluntary Sector*. Vancouver: University of British Columbia Press.

Rhodes, R.A.W. 2006. "The New Governance: Governing without Government." *Political Studies* 44:652–67.

Sancton, Andrew. 2011. *Canadian Local Government: An Urban Perspective*. Don Mills, ON: Oxford University Press.

Sancton, Andrew, and Robert Young, eds. 2009. *Foundations of Governance: Municipal Government in Canada's Provinces*. Toronto: University of Toronto Press and the Institute of Public Administration of Canada.

Siegel, David, and C. Richard Tindal. 2006. "Changing the Municipal Culture: From Comfortable Subordination to Assertive Maturity." Parts I and II. *Municipal World*, (March and April):37–40; 13–17.

Stone, Clarence. 1989. *Regime Politics: Governing Atlanta, 1946–1988.* Lawrence, KS: University Press of Kansas.

Tindal, C. Richard, and Susan Nobes Tindal. 2009. *Local Government in Canada*, 7th ed. Toronto: Nelson.

Young, Robert. 2006. "Open Federalism and Canadian Municipalities." In *Open Federalism: Interpretations, Significance*, edited by Keith G. Banting et al., 7–24. Kingston, ON: Institute of Intergovernmental Relations.

Young, Robert, and Christian Leuprecht, eds. 2006. *Canada: The State of the Federation, 2004 – Municipal-Federal-Provincial Relations in Canada.* Montreal and Kingston: McGill-Queen's University Press for the Institute of Intergovernmental Relations, Queen's University.

# 2

# Ascending the Main Stage?:
# Calgary in the Multilevel Governance Drama

BYRON MILLER AND ALAN SMART

## INTRODUCTION

Multilevel governance (MLG) in Canada is often conceived as a trilateral phenomenon. Instead, our study of municipal policy making and implementation suggests that it could better be seen as a complex mosaic of bilateral relations that occasionally expand into trilateral programs or conflicts. It may be useful to think of multilevel governance as a kind of stage where all three actors – municipal, provincial, and federal – only occasionally appear together. The actor who is absent from the stage may still have a perceptible influence on exchanges between the onstage performers. To complicate matters further, the drama takes place on literal stages with public audiences, except for the partners to the discussions or negotiations and their respective supporting choruses, who are offstage. In the best Shakespearian tradition, however, offstage may simply be an alcove of the main stage where the actors confer in stage whispers. Moreover, the audience for one actor is not necessarily the same as for another, so that the script may be modified to play to different expectations among the listeners. Finally, being "offstage" does not result in the absence of posturing and strutting, but may instead be a set piece for a smaller and more select audience, mostly composed of influential actors in other settings, referred to in this research as "social forces."

Our account so far is too symmetrical because when the city is absent from discussions affecting it, its influence and interests may be more neglected than when the dialogue is between the city and the province, with the federal government standing in the wings. Constitutionally, municipal governments have no independent place on the MLG stage. But the audience – made up of citizens who feel their needs are not being met, academics who argue that cities are the key actors on the rather different stage of the global economy, representatives of the non-profit sector who feel the problems they address cannot be resolved without greater local powers, and business people who feel that without reforms Canada's cities cannot serve as an adequate platform for their global ambitions – is demanding that its favourite bit players be given a starring role (Young and Leuprecht 2006). The critics are for the most part offering negative reviews of the current production, and the actors are all manoeuvring for a better role in the next run. How will the popular acclaim for the bit players influence the rewrite of the governance scenario?

Currently, the rising star among the bit players is Calgary, with fans crowding in. The demands of the throngs are straining its limited resources available through shares from the multilevel play and its own independent productions. Will it move to a better place in the MLG play before its own sets and properties fray too badly to keep its newfound fan base? Metaphors aside, will the remarkable economic and population growth of Calgary in the last decade or so result in a different position in the ongoing negotiations around cities in Canadian governance? Drawing from interviews with municipal, regional, provincial, and federal officials, as well as NGO representatives, we suggest the intense growth pressures Calgary faces may be shared by other large cities, but Calgary in particular has gained a degree of economic and political clout it would not have in the absence of its rapid expansion and growing national and global prominence in fossil fuel production.

While the dramaturgical metaphor may be useful to highlight the dialectic in Canadian multilevel governance between frontstage and backstage actions (Goffman 1959), the positioning on the stage of the different actors, and the peripheral but significant role of the audiences, we should not take it too far. After all, in his analysis of nineteenth-century Bali as a "theatre-state" par excellence, Clifford Geertz (1980, 13) concluded that the elaborate court performances "were not means to political ends; they were the ends themselves, they were what the state was for." Surely we could not conclude the same about Canadian multilevel governance, despite the preponderance of performance over productive results.

CALGARY: COPING WITH THE PRESSURES OF GROWTH

Boom and bust has been the constant rhythm of Calgary's development over the last century, initially focused on cattle ranching, but since 1947 focused on oil and gas and its accompanying finance and headquarters

(Ghitter and Smart 2009). The serious economic recession of the 1980s helped create the problems of the mid 2000s boom through what Edward LeSage and Melville McMillan describe as a "sustained provincial disengagement from the municipal sector" in which cities received greater freedom of action but were "also poorer and saddled with additional responsibilities" (LeSage Jr. and McMillan 2009, 422–3). The most recent boom ran for almost two decades, until 2008, and produced remarkable rates of population and economic growth based primarily on the growth of the fossil fuel industry, moving Calgary to a position on the national and global stage unprecedented in its short history (Hiller 2007). In 1986, when the city was just beginning to recover from its last economic bust, the population of the City of Calgary was 640,645. By 2006 population had increased to 991,759, a 54.8 percent increase. Calgary's economic growth was accelerated by the movement of head offices there, with a 60.3 percent growth in major head offices and a 24.8 percent increase in head office employment between 2002 and 2006. Calgary had the fastest rate of growth of Canada's major cities between 2001 and 2006 (Simmons and Bourne 2007). On a per capita basis, Calgary has the largest concentration of head offices in Canada with 9.8 per 100,000 people, well above that of Toronto at 5.1, Vancouver at 3.6, and Montreal at 2.4. As a result of the economic expansion, per capita income was the highest in the country at $47,178 in 2006, significantly above Toronto at $35,774, and a 25.2 percent increase between 2002 and 2006 (Calgary Economic Development 2007).

This growth has generated huge pressures on every element of infrastructure, so that in the last five years almost every poll asking Calgarians about the main issues facing the city has had infrastructure as the top answer (White 2007, J2). The continuation of the expansion has come to be threatened by pervasive labour shortages and the pressure on living and business costs that they have produced. These shortages are exacerbated by the infrastructure constraints, reflected in an affordable housing crisis with shelter costs that have vaulted past Toronto to be the second most expensive in the country, and increasingly overcrowded transit and road systems. Homelessness is a major concern, with 3,400 people on the street or in shelters in 2006 and the number continuing to rise, and with much higher numbers of people at risk for homelessness due to soaring rents and near zero vacancies. The Vital Signs survey/report card gave Calgary an overall D- for housing and an F for the number of homeless people (Calgary Foundation 2007). It has become harder to attract labour as a result, and while until recently in-migration continued at a high rate, slowing in-migration and out-migration to cheaper parts of the country has emerged as a major concern for businesses. The former CEO of the Calgary Chamber of Commerce has stated that labour shortages have been the greatest concern for Calgary businesses and believes that this situation will continue for many years to come (Douglas 2008). There are widespread feelings that the quality of life in Calgary has deteriorated, and some studies confirm this. A study in the 1990s placed Calgary as having the highest quality of life among thirteen Canadian cities (Giannias 1998). An international survey of fifty cities ranked Calgary twenty-fourth for quality of living, lowest among the five Canadian cities included, although it did rank first for health and sanitation (Mercer Human Resource Consulting 2007).

In all of the policy fields analyzed below, growth and the infrastructure and governance pressures created by growth define the political agenda and the kinds of programs that have been adopted. More importantly, these pressures create awareness of the ways in which intergovernmental relations have not been meeting many needs. While there are some positive accounts of policy responses to the pressures of rapid growth, more commonly the reaction of social forces, ranging from the citizenry to non-profit social agencies to the Chamber of Commerce, has been that not enough has been done to meet the many needs and that many opportunities are being lost.

Calgary has long been a conservative city in a conservative province (Smart 2001; Miller 2007), but the current threats to the continuation of the economic boom are producing some significant shifts in political positions. The Calgary Chamber of Commerce, for example, has been advocating measures to address the growing problem of homelessness and affordable housing more generally and supporting the expansion of public transit and mixed use high density neighbourhoods organized around transit hubs (Calgary Chamber of Commerce 2007). Of course, there is a long history of business interests encouraging government expenditure when it seems to be needed and useful for the expansion of the urban economy. In 1897, a New York urban reformer, Henry de Forest Baldwin argued that "to fail to make an expenditure when good business methods require it, is a sign of inefficient and short-sighted government" (quoted in Revell 2003, 154). Calgary's conservative politics, and the strong influence of the corporate business sector, has meant that NGOs attempting to influence policy making have had to adapt their tactics in order to have any effective impact. We were told that to be effective advocates for social issues in Calgary, NGOs need to make a case that shows that action is in the interests of business, highlighting the benefits for business or the city as a whole, rather than social justice or the needs of particular groups (Interviews 12 and 24). For example, corporations became quite supportive of the Calgary Homeless Foundation after research revealed that a very high percentage of the homeless population were working at full-time jobs. In general, for social program initiatives to have a chance of success in Calgary, a business case needs to demonstrate the returns on social investments and the costs of inaction. The most successful NGOs have been those that can afford to invest resources in research to make strong cases. The NGOs also feel that without corporate support for their initiatives, it is difficult to get sufficient support from city council to move forward. The labour shortage has allowed certain progressive non-profit initiatives to succeed, but the dominance of business interests sets the parameters under which they can be effective. Broader social justice arguments are much less likely to be successful than those that emphasize improving the attractiveness of the city for economic migrants and investors in order to promote further economic growth.

There has long been a sense among many Calgarians that their concerns were not heard in Ottawa, and the longstanding feud between the Alberta government and the federal Liberals has not encouraged close ties between the City of Calgary and the federal government. A senior city official told us that shortly after he started with the city in the 1980s he broached accessing funds through a federal program but was told "we don't do feds here" (Interview 9). Another senior city official noted that before Paul Martin launched the urban agenda the message from federal officials was "very much 'You are a creature of the province, please go talk to the province, the province will come and talk to us'" (Interview 10). City of Calgary officials were equally unprepared to talk to the federal government. The same senior city official noted that within the city "whenever we were saying 'Gee I wonder who in the federal government we should call about this' we'd all go hmmm. They were a faceless entity to us ... the feds were really just this black hole." The response was to create a position devoted to intergovernmental relations, and to launch a joint initiative with the City of Edmonton and the Alberta Federal Council – which facilitates two-way communication between federal departments and agencies and the Alberta regions they serve – to start to build relationships with federal officials, emphasizing civil servants rather than politicians (Interview 10). The electoral success of the Conservative Party in 2006 modified this dynamic by creating more informal channels to Ottawa, but many feel that Stephen Harper has tended to take his base in Alberta for granted.

As discussed in the section on infrastructure below, tensions between the provincial government and Calgary have increased in recent years. A high-profile feud between Mayor Bronconnier and Premier Ed Stelmach dominated headlines for several months in the summer of 2007, with accusations that the premier had reneged on infrastructure commitments. In the context of a looming October 2007 municipal election, with a provincial election to follow in 2008, the mayor was able to extract a new ten-year commitment of $3.3 billion in provincial funds for Calgary in September 2007. This deal caused some anger in Edmonton because it did not receive as much funding. Nonetheless, taking a hard stance against the province seems to have paid considerable political dividends for the mayor (Braid 2007, B1, B4). The political theatre of accusing other levels of government for governance failures is a long and continuing tradition in Calgary, one that frequently parallels the province's rhetoric toward the federal government.

Municipal politics are influenced by the fact that Calgary has the least transparent system of campaign finance among Canada's major cities. Calgary's "wild west" campaign rules (Guttormson 2007, A1) attracted considerable attention during both the 2007 and 2010 municipal elections. The campaign finance system has encouraged the sprawling nature of urban growth (Interviews 1, 5, and 6), given that property developers are among the most important contributors to electoral campaigns (Lorimer 1978). Max Foran has recently argued, however, that despite high levels of developer influence, their clout is at least partially limited by the internal organization of the city administration. The apparent pattern of the development industry getting what it wants, he suggests, is in part a result of consumer demand for spacious detached single-family dwellings. Likewise, an interviewee involved with the development industry contends its influence on patterns of growth is exaggerated and that expansion at the periphery is a result of the market forces. Development industry lobbying, one business association representative claimed, is mostly directed at overcoming obstacles placed in the way of consumer demand (Interview 15). But consumer demand does not arise in a policy vacuum (Miller 2006). It is shaped, in part, by the substantial infrastructure, maintenance, and operating subsidies provided to lower density forms of development (City of Calgary 2009a).

Emphasis on suburban growth at the periphery, rather than an increase in density in the central areas,[1] exacerbates the transportation problems faced by the city. The suburban growth dynamic has proved to be increasingly untenable over the last ten years, with the costs of transportation, water, sewer, and public facility infrastructure, not to mention service provision, outstripping increased revenue to the city from property taxes. The old fiscal model of growth hit its limits, resulting in efforts to change the nature of peripheral expansion while increasing the lot levies charged to property developers. These levies are negotiated with the Urban Development Institute and provide for most of the neighbourhood infrastructure and the costs of connecting to the road network.

Rapid population and economic growth and its attendant pressures structure everything about contemporary Calgary, as our following analysis of the four policy fields will illustrate in greater detail. Growth pressures have resulted in considerable political efforts to obtain resources from other levels of government to deal with these pressures, although critics have argued that there is much that the city could do by modifying its own growth management practices (Couroux et al. 2006).

## IMMIGRATION

While immigration is constitutionally a shared federal and provincial responsibility, the practical realities of responding to the challenges and opportunities created by immigration largely fall on the cities, since the vast majority of migrants are now concentrated in the largest metropolitan areas. Urban administrations vary in the extent to which they are proactively responding to these demands, with Winnipeg and Edmonton, for example, being more proactive in developing immigration policies than Calgary. The City of Calgary has been reluctant to undertake policy development in the area of immigration because there are so many other demands on its resources and because, constitutionally, immigration is not its responsibility. The problem, of course, is that regardless of whose responsibility the issue is, immigration has a major impact on the city and resources are being allocated to deal with its attendant problems. Arguably, a coordinated policy might use the already allocated resources more effectively, efficiently, and equitably. Reluctance to engage this policy field, however, is part of the political theatre discussed in the introduction to this chapter. A municipal official involved in some of the discussions recognized that the absence of a policy created problems, but that the city's approach was to lobby the province and the federal government to "step up to the plate" in terms of their obligations. The adolescent game of "chicken" might be an alternative metaphor (Interview 14).

Immigration has, however, in recent years acquired much higher profile in Calgary because of worries about the growing labour shortage. Calgary's rapid population growth stems more from interprovincial migration than international migration, with net interprovincial migration being twice as large a contributor to the city's population growth as net international migration between 1996 and 2001. In contrast, net interprovincial migration represented just over 8 percent of the net international migration to Toronto in the same period (Hiller 2007). This calculation, however, neglects secondary migration, where immigrants land in one place but move to another later. Secondary migration poses a significant financial problem since the federal grants for immigrant settlement are provided to the municipality where the immigrant lands, even if the period of residence there is short (Interviews 14 and 23). It is widely thought that because of its lower international profile compared to Toronto, Montreal, or Vancouver, but high demand for labour, secondary migration is a larger phenomenon in Calgary than in other Canadian cities (Smart 1994); one informant suggested that secondary migration might account for 20 percent of the immigration stream to Calgary, over and above primary immigration numbers. In 2001, 20.9 percent of the Calgary census metropolitan area (CMA) population was born outside of Canada. The foreign-born population increased by 28 percent by 2006, reaching 23.6 percent of the total CMA population, the fourth largest concentration among metropolitan areas in Canada. The growth of the Temporary Foreign Worker Program in Alberta (see below) further exacerbates the funding shortfall, since temporary foreign workers receive no settlement funding.

Even leaving aside secondary migration, immigration has become relatively more important in Calgary in the new era of pronounced labour shortages. In 2006, Calgary received 4.6 percent of Canada's immigrants, up from 3.9 percent in 2004, for a total number of 11,635. The top sending countries in 2006 were India, China (dropping from first place for the first time in many years), Philippines, Pakistan, and United Kingdom. Economic immigrants accounted for 46.7 percent of the total (dropping from 52.3 percent in 2005) in Calgary, compared to only 28 percent for Canada as a whole (City of Calgary 2007). This difference reflects the economic attractions of Calgary, and various groups, such as the Calgary Chamber of Commerce and Calgary Economic Development, have started to encourage the promotion of higher immigration levels to respond to Calgary's labour shortages (Interviews 16, 17, and 18). However, infrastructure constraints, particularly related to affordable housing, are limiting Calgary's ability to substantially and rapidly increase its labour force. And rising costs are contributing to out-migration, a trend further exacerbated by the campaigns of provinces like Saskatchewan and Newfoundland to entice former residents to return home. The 2007 Vital Signs survey/report card also found that respondents gave Calgary a C- for "valuing diversity" (Calgary Foundation 2007). More effective social integration of migrants, and their better integration into labour markets that still generate wasteful downward mobility among well-qualified migrants, are key challenges for Canada generally and Calgary specifically (Frideres 2008).

Two major intergovernmental policy changes have affected immigrant settlement in Calgary: the signing of an agreement for Canada-Alberta Cooperation on Immigration on 11 May 2007; and the increase in funding for immigrant settlement by the federal government in November 2006. Alberta's settlement funding was projected to increase from $15,940,875 in 2005–06 to $30,591,991 in 2007–08, an increase of 91.9 percent, although from quite low levels (Canada, Citizenship and Immigration 2006). The Canada-Alberta Agreement is not as far-reaching as the Quebec or Ontario agreements and concentrates primarily on achieving a better alignment of migration with Alberta's "particular needs and circumstances," especially its labour requirements, expanding the provincial nominee program, which has largely been employer-driven, facilitating Alberta's own immigration recruitment efforts, and facilitating the entry of temporary foreign workers (Canada, Citizenship and Immigration 2007). An official with Citizenship and Immigration Canada commented that he had never seen the Alberta government as interested in immigration as it has been in the last two years (Interview 23). This heightened interest is primarily spurred by labour shortages, but the creation of an Immigration Ministry has helped because, formerly, the portfolio was split between three departments: employment, immigration, and industry. He also noted that many smaller Albertan centres are putting effort into being seen as welcoming places for immigrants, increasing intermunicipal competition for migrants.

The Temporary Foreign Worker (TFW) Program has grown rapidly and has become the most contested part of efforts to increase immigration to Alberta. Even the Alberta Federation of Labour stresses that "Alberta unions also support immigration. We believe immigration is a key to building a strong and diverse society. In particular, we believe in immigration policies that would allow a broader range of skilled workers into the country. We also believe there is a need for stronger settlement programs for newcomers." However, this statement was given as a preface to their critique of the TFW Program, about which they say:

> The stated purpose of the program is to provide Canadian employers with access to workers when critical labour shortages can be demonstrated. In addition, the program was originally intended to provide access to a pool of workers who would supplement, not replace, the existing pool of Canadian workers. Unfortunately, it has become clear to us that at least some employers are using the program as part of a deliberate effort to drive down wages and working conditions and to bypass unionized Canadian workers. In a sense, the program is being used as a union busting tool. And, by allowing the program to be used in this way, our provincial and federal governments are allowing themselves to become partners in union busting. (Alberta Federation of Labour 2006)

Already in 2005, there were 3,645 new TFWs in Calgary, which equaled half of the new economic immigrants, and the numbers continue to expand rapidly (Calgary Economic Development 2007). In 2006, Alberta processed applications for 40,000 TFWs. In the following year, permits were issued for 41,218 TFWs (Cryderman 2008). Processing these numbers has been a challenge, but the new mechanism of expedited labour market opinions – the process by which Human Resources and Skills Development Canada determines whether employers in Alberta and British Columbia may hire TFWs – has helped to speed up the process. The construction industry had 2,450 applications for Calgary in 2007, and Tim Hortons alone has requests for several hundred TFWs (Interview 23). Given the rapidly expanding numbers of TFWs, the absence of settlement funding for them is creating problems, especially since the work term has been lengthened from one year to two, and many workers arrive with hopes of becoming permanent residents. Exploitative employment situations and terrible housing conditions for TFWs have been regularly raised in the local news media.

The increase in settlement funding since 2005 has reduced pressure on settlement services, which previously had very long waiting lists. Citizenship and Immigration Canada funds language training (80 percent of its total cost) and orientation/adaptation programs. The absence of funding for affordable housing has been criticized as a major gap in settlement arrangements (Tanasescu 2007). Settlement programs are contracted to agencies, primarily non-profits, with co-funding from the provincial government. An evaluation of settlement programs in Calgary in 2001 raised a number of concerns about the lack of coordination, insufficient funding, and high reliance on volunteer labour, up to 29 percent of 428,000 hours of work in sixty programs. The fragmentation and agency-specific nature of the programs made it difficult for immigrants to know what services were available and made it unclear how to access them (Immigrant Sector Council of Calgary 2003). An initiative led by the Calgary Catholic Immigration Society in 2004 called for a better effort to coordinate services "led by a recognized agency or institution;" the absence of coordination had resulted in a situation where "agencies are all in competition for the same funding and duplicating services" (Dowding and Razi 2004, 11). As several people we interviewed pointed out, it is precisely this competition that makes coordination difficult (Interviews 13 and 14). The absence of leadership from the City of Calgary in immigrant settlement issues also contributes to the continuation of problems that were identified years earlier. However, the increasing centrality of immigration to Calgary's continued economic expansion, and the attention of influential social forces such as the Chamber of Commerce and the United Way, will very probably result in more involvement from the city in the future (Interviews 24 and 14).

INFRASTRUCTURE

Infrastructure creates the stage on which all urban activity takes place. Infrastructure itself structures the directions for future urban growth and thus plays a key role in all urbanization process, even if only through the problems caused by its absence or insufficiency (Kaika and Swyngedouw 2002; Davis 2006). However, because infrastructure money is commonly provided by senior governments for new initiatives, one risk is that they do not reflect the central priorities of the cities (Andrew and Morrison 2002). Emphasizing exciting new projects is appealing to senior government officials because they provide a stage for high-profile spending announcements and the political benefits such announcements bring. Thus political self-promotion and legitimation play key roles in MLG.

Given Calgary's extremely rapid growth, it is not surprising that infrastructure issues have been at the centre of Calgary politics for most of the first decade of the new millennium. Indeed, Calgary's former mayor, Dave Bronconnier (2001–10), was elected on a platform of "roads, roads, roads." Bronconnier's initial promise to deal with increasing traffic congestion by narrowly focusing on roads broadened to encompass a much more diverse infrastructure agenda, including the expansion of Calgary's light rail system, recreation facilities, parks, affordable housing, and other projects. Indeed, Calgarians put infrastructure improvements high on their list of municipal priorities. In a 2007 Canada West Foundation survey, Calgary respondents rated several infrastructure issues as "very high" or "high" policy priorities: traffic (79 percent), roads (76 percent), affordable housing (71 percent), transit (70 percent), environment (66 percent), and parks (61 percent) (Berdahl 2007). But Calgary's elected politicians have long been caught between the pressing need for infrastructure investment, the limited fiscal tools and capacity of local government, and an extremely vocal anti-property tax minority. Like most Canadian municipalities, property taxes are a significant part of Calgary's revenue stream, although Calgary's rates are the lowest of Canada's twenty-four largest cities (City of Calgary 2009b). Residential property tax accounts for 38 percent of the city's operating budget for 2009–11, while grants and subsidies from other levels of government account for only 2 percent of the operating budget (City of Calgary 2009b). Calgarians have not traditionally considered property taxes to be a major issue: the Canada West Foundation survey found only 33 percent of Calgarians considered property taxes to be a "very high" or "high" policy priority (Berdahl 2007). But recent hikes in the property tax have made the anti-tax minority even more strident and it continues to exert tremendous pressure on city council to keep property taxes low.

In the 2009–11 $4 billion capital budget, other levels of government and other grants contributed 42 percent compared to only 22 percent in "pay-as-you-go" expenditures (Calgary 2009b). It is widely acknowledged that property tax revenues are insufficient to finance the infrastructure investment needed in a rapidly growing city, and Calgary's infrastructure needs are substantial, especially following low levels of infrastructure investment during the 1990s era of fiscal austerity. The city's 2009–11 capital improvement budget does not include a number of desired infrastructure projects that are simply considered beyond the scope of current possibilities. Calgary's infrastructure deficit is a leading example of what the Federation of Canadian Municipalities considers to be a national crisis: an estimated national municipal infrastructure deficit of $123 billion (Federation of Canadian Municipalities 2007).

While Calgary's revenues are insufficient to meet its infrastructure needs, provincial and federal infrastructure funding for Calgary has increased in recent years. Over the period from 2003 to 2007, the

Infrastructure Canada Program has produced $136 million in infra-
structure spending in Calgary, $39 million of it from the federal govern-
ment, $39 million from the provincial government, $47 million from
the City of Calgary, and $9 million from various partners. The lion's
share of this spending has gone toward water and wastewater systems
(44 percent) and recreational and sports facilities (28 percent). Most
significantly, the agreement on the transfer of federal gas tax revenues to
the city resulted in an additional $141 million in infrastructure invest-
ment over the five year period from 2006 to 2010 – still a small sum
compared to the magnitude of investment needed. The Canada Strategic
Infrastructure Fund has produced another $75 million of federal invest-
ment, plus contributions from the provincial and city governments, to
advance construction of the Calgary Ring Road in the northwest quadrant of the city, while the Canada-Alberta Municipal Rural Infrastructure
Fund produced $32 million of new investment – with $10 million from
the federal government, $10 million from the provincial government,
$10 million from the City of Calgary, and $2 million from partners – in
a downtown Calgary district energy system. The ring road is a good
example of the potential distortion of municipal priorities by project-
based infrastructure funding. A senior planner in the City of Calgary
indicated that the ring road was nowhere near the city's top transportation priority and was very concerned that it would undermine the modest progress that Calgary had made in discouraging low-density
development on the fringe. However, there was also no chance that the
money would be turned down because the road would eventually be
needed (Interview 9).

   Relationships between the City of Calgary and the federal government
have improved since 2002 due to the simultaneous adoption of an urban
agenda by the Martin government and joint efforts of City of Calgary
and City of Edmonton bureaucrats to reach out to federal officials
through the Alberta Federal Council and other channels (Interview 10).
But federal and provincial infrastructure aid is still widely seen as
woefully inadequate. Calgary business leaders have decried the lack of
funding to construct a superfreeway to connect Canadian cities, a second ring road, a new airport, a high speed rail connection between
Calgary and Edmonton, and affordable housing. Moreover, much of the
tax revenue that is generated in Calgary goes to the federal and provincial governments, coming back in lesser amounts and with strings
attached that lock the city into spending programs that are sometimes
poorly suited to local needs. Moreover, the three- to five-year horizon of

most federal and provincial infrastructure funding does not match the longer-term horizon that infrastructure projects typically require.

Not surprisingly, infrastructure funding has been one of the most heated and controversial aspects of Calgary's relationship to the provincial and federal governments. Mayor Bronconnier repeatedly accused the provincial government of ignoring Calgary's infrastructure needs and turned up the heat, especially in the run-ups to elections. Mayor Nenshi, while striking a more conciliatory tone, has continued to advocate for increased provincial funding, as well as for enhanced revenue raising powers for the City. Provincial politicians' need for Calgary's electoral support has its given recent mayors substantial political leverage with the provincial government, paying handsome dividends in 2007 in the form of a ten-year $3.3 billion infrastructure deal with the province. Yet, most of this funding will go to play catch-up after years of infrastructure neglect and rapid growth. Such deals, moreover, illustrate the precarious nature of critical municipal infrastructure funding: in light of the province's projected $4.4 billion deficit for 2009, the provincial government began revisiting municipal infrastructure agreements in fall 2009 (Fekete 2009). One major infrastructure initiative, the $2 billion Green Transit Incentives Program, announced in 2008 as part of the province's climate change action plan, was suspended in 2009. Calgary's 10 Year Plan to End Homelessness, also announced in 2008, will require $3.2 billion of investment. Despite praise from both the provincial and federal governments, and the proven effectiveness of the "housing first" strategy, provincial funding for affordable housing and housing and support programs amounted to only $230 million in the first three years of the 10 Year Plan (Calgary Homeless Foundation 2011).

IMAGE BUILDING

Image building has been a strong refrain in Calgary for years, as it attempts to forge and transmit representations of the world class city that it believes it has become while struggling with the powerful and profitable "cowtown" image of its past. Relatively little of this image-building process involves multilevel governance, but one significant strain has been the impact of plans to expand Stampede Park, which received up to $25 million in matching funds from the federal Department of Transport, Infrastructure, and Communities in 2007. These expansion plans, however, have their roots in prior attempts to project Calgary's image onto a global stage: the 1988 Winter Olympics and the failed Expo 2005 bid.

Twenty years of rapid population and economic growth have strengthened Calgary's position on the national stage, and its role as the oil and
gas capital of Canada increases its importance in a world increasingly
worried about energy shortages and rising gas prices. Calgary has always
been a city whose politics are dominated by boosterism.[2] It shares with
Atlanta, another classic example of urban boosterism that attempted to
translate hosting the Olympics into a more global stature (Rutheiser
1996), the feature of not having a particular reason for existing other
than decisions about the location of railroad infrastructure.

Being a key centre for ranching and stockyards does not carry the
highest profile, but as a result of the Calgary Stampede's success in
attracting hundreds of thousands of tourists from around the world, the
cowtown image is one that cannot easily be discarded. Many Calgarians
feel some degree of discomfort about the Stampede's associations with
"redneck culture" (which some might argue is an oxymoron) and right
wing politics (Pannekoek 2008). It is also an image that has tended to
stereotype Aboriginals, marginalize visible minorities, and accord women
only a subordinate role (Furniss 1998). Yet, whenever "rebranding" exercises (an ironic label given the context) are undertaken by Calgary
Economic Development or other organizations, the conclusion always
seems to be that the existing brand recognition is too useful to be rejected,
even though it interferes with efforts to develop newer images that might
have fewer negative connotations. To return to the theatrical metaphor
in the introduction, if the audience is coming for *Oklahoma*, do you
want to try and sell them *Othello* instead? For example, 1998 was proclaimed the Year of the Cowboy, and editorial efforts were made to
remake the cowboy, rinsing out the redneck and emphasizing entrepreneurialism, independence, and hospitality (Dudley 1998, A1). A similar
exercise can be seen in the widely used, but not official, logo "Heart of
the New West" with a stylized cowboy hat. Calgary's ambivalence
toward the cowboy/Stampede brand has been finessed by running a
"double bill" at the theatre. The city retains its traditional brand, albeit
revised for contemporary tastes, while trying out a series of new ones –
none with quite the same appeal as the old favourite.

In 2003, TD Bank gave Calgary an opportunity to promote an alternative image when it published a report on what it called the "western
tiger," the Calgary-Edmonton corridor. Its description of the region
between and including Alberta's two main cities as "the only urban
agglomeration to enjoy a US-style standard of living with a Canadian
style quality of life" attracted national and some international attention.

Their reassessment of this report in 2007 states that they actually under-estimated the economic expansion that would occur as well as the potential in the rest of the province (TD Economics 2007). However, as impressive as the TD statistics are, an artificial construct based on a corridor stretched over several hundred kilometres does not create a memorable image for a city and does not answer the question for others of what Calgary is, beyond being rich. The Calgary Chamber of Commerce has recently weighed in on this issue by calling for the city to make itself into "Renaissance Calgary." Its "blueprint for a twenty-first-century world-leading capital" notes that 80 percent of the Chamber's members feel that the overall quality of life declined in the three years before 2007; the blueprint proposes a variety of measures that would capture "the spirit of creativity, innovation, competitiveness and cultural vibrancy" of Calgary, leading to "practical actions that enable the city to achieve its potential as a global leader" (Calgary Chamber of Commerce 2007, 5). While many of the initiatives proposed – such as creating vibrant public spaces and increasing density – are very worthy, they also lead in the same direction that many other cities desiring to make the leap to "world class" status seem to be pursuing.

As mentioned above, the only image-building project in Calgary that involves all three orders of government is the Stampede Park expansion. In 2007, the Alberta and federal governments jointly announced that the Stampede Park Western Legacy project would be considered a priority under the Building Canada infrastructure plan. The province and the federal government each committed $15 million to the project, potentially expanding to $25 million from each. As described in the joint official news release, "The Western Legacy Project, estimated at a total of $53 million, consists of reclaiming a 14-acre 'brownfield' to create an inner-city park, the development of a heritage interpretative centre and the relocation of the traditional 'Indian Village' in order to expand the interpretive program and facilitate a cross-cultural exchange with the participation of the Treaty 7 First Nations."

The Calgary Stampede Board has been the strongest voice in maintaining and strengthening the city's association with "Western heritage." The board's website explains the organization's core purpose is to "preserve and promote western heritage and values" and describes the Calgary Stampede as "the community's cradle of western heritage and traditions. As a living embodiment of the western values that bind and build our community, the Calgary Stampede is a gathering place which hosts, educates and entertains the world" (http://corporate.calgarystampede.com/

about/organization/brand.html; see also Calgary Stampede 2007, 1). Despite this emphasis, though, it is intriguing that the title for the expansion plan document is "a gathering place for Calgary and the world," which emphasizes the general Calgary-as-an-emergent-global-city theme more than the western heritage theme. This emphasis may have been useful in obtaining City of Calgary support for the project, which will link in with another urban redevelopment project called "The Rivers," a project intended to link the Bow and Elbow Rivers more effectively into the city centre and to revitalize the east end of the downtown area (Interview 22).

The Western Legacy Project represents the first time in the Stampede's century-long history that it has received federal funds, although provincial funds regularly support the agricultural dimensions of the Stampede. However, federal money was promised for a similar expansion for the Expo 2005 proposal, had it been successful. Success in lobbying for federal support seems to have been in part a result of a strategic plan that addressed multiple sets of interests. One informant indicated that a federal minister became more positive about the Stampede expansion idea when briefed about "the brownfields and the recovery and the environment thing, and the relocation of the Indian village." The change of federal governments also facilitated better ties between members of the Stampede board, their allies, and key federal players (Interview 22).[3]

Although very much updated to fit with other initiatives and priorities, the Western Legacy Project has considerable similarities with the Stampede Park expansion plans associated with the failed Expo 2005 bid. Among the key components were expansion into the adjacent neighbourhood of Victoria Park (Hiller and Moylan 1999) and a new riverbank park, also a key element of the 2009 Stampede master plan. The failure of the 2005 bid was in part a result of the negative associations of the "Western heritage" image. The initial theme selected was "Pioneering the twenty-first century," but it was subsequently discarded when marketers discovered that much of the world did not share the positive associations with pioneers, and instead thought of them as destroying forests and displacing indigenous populations. The theme was later changed to "The land, our common ground."

The history of multilevel support for international events goes back even farther in this case. The expansion of Stampede Park into Victoria Park began with the 1988 Winter Olympics hosted in Calgary (Foran 2008). The Olympics "represented the beginning of a new plan to use tourism as an urban, economic development strategy in which Stampede

Park would play a central role" and which led to a the search for another mega-event, Expo 2005, which would consolidate the shift (Hiller and Moylan 1999, 68). As Kris Olds notes, "The 1988 Winter Olympics represents an important stage in the planned image transformation of this former western Canadian 'cow town' to that of a more international city – a city which presents its inhabitants and visitors with 'world class' recreational activities, high-tech manufacturing opportunities, and tourism thrills" (1998, 17).

The building of Olympic facilities in Victoria Park, adjacent to the Stampede Grounds, initiated the representation of this struggling working-class community as one of inevitable decline rather than possible resurgence. The Stampede Board became a major purchaser of property and allowed it to deteriorate, which created a sense of "fait accompli" around the fate of the neighbourhood (Hiller and Moylan 1999, 69) and ultimately led to the destruction of one of Calgary's largest pockets of market-rate affordable housing. Current multilevel support for Stampede expansion will likely complete a process of urban displacement and transformation that was first set in motion by multilevel support for the Olympic mega-event of the 1980s.

Another aspect of Calgary's contested image that has emerged recently is national media coverage of the contrasts between wealth and deprivation in the city. Increasingly, Calgary is being portrayed as a heartless city, beset by homelessness and inequality (Interview 11). Such imagery can discourage the in-migration of workers that the Calgary economy needs. As a result, concerns about the effects of such images can be used by NGOs to promote philanthropy and social justice. However, our informants stressed that this has to be done carefully. Rather than criticizing funders and government representatives, they need to externalize the imagery, pointing out the costs of such representations and how it would be in their interests to proactively deal with it through projects that the NGO is promoting (Interviews 11, 12, and 24). Handled skilfully, as with the emphasis on the high labour market participation of the homeless population, such concerns do seem to be generating more governmental and private initiatives in the areas of homelessness, affordable housing, poverty reduction, and public transit.

All of these initiatives on the image-building front reflect an intense eagerness to have Calgary take its place on the global stage. The contested question is what its role will be: world-class handsome leading man, the typecast cowboy, or some transcendent combination of the two.

FEDERAL PROPERTY

Federal lands play a relatively small role in Calgary. The airport authority, exercising federal control over landing rights, represents one significant federal function associated with the control of land. Several federal
buildings dot Calgary's downtown as well. But the most significant case
is the role of the Canada Lands Company in Calgary. The Canada Lands
Company, a non-agency Crown corporation, began redeveloping the old
Curry Barracks site – a former Canadian Forces base – in 1995. The
experience of Canada Lands, as a federal land developer in Calgary, was
"very ugly at first" (Interviews 20 and 21). With the federal government
shutting down Curry Barracks while the memory of the National Energy
Program was still fresh in the minds of many, Canada Lands received
very little cooperation from either city administration or other developers for its new development, Garrison Woods. Canada Lands was subject to an approval process that was harder than that faced by most
private developers, and Canada Lands was frequently asked for contributions beyond the norm. However, Canada Lands was, from an administrative standpoint, a difficult developer for the city to work with. It
asked for waivers from many zoning, transportation, and design standards in order to pursue an innovative development plan emphasizing
mixed land uses, higher density, a greater emphasis on pedestrian circu-
lation, and a significant affordable housing component. Deviating from
city standards and regulations added a substantial amount of time to
the development process, time that a private developer could have ill
afforded. But as a federal Crown corporation, Canada Lands had a
mandate to optimize the development rather than maximize profit.
Consequently, Garrison Woods took considerably longer to develop
than it would have if it had been done by a private developer. As a consequence of its innovations it is now widely recognized as a highly successful and desirable "new urbanist" development, one that the City of
Calgary now frequently cites as a leading example of sustainable and
desirable urban development within its boundaries. Ironically, the managers of the project are frequently distracted by requests from the City
to take visiting officials from other cities on site visits (Interview 20).

The development of Garrison Woods and the adjacent developments
of Cyprus Green and Garrison Green involved relations among the
municipal, provincial, and federal governments. An ongoing battle with
the City over planning and design standards was eventually resolved
when city council declared the Curry Barracks area an "innovation

zone," unique in the city. This designation allowed the Canada Lands Company to adopt unconventional planning and design practices. The Canada Lands Company encountered many difficulties, especially from transportation planners who did not want to deviate from standard engineering practice. Ironically, as one planner with Canada Lands told us, the transportation design standards that gave them so much trouble originated with the Canadian federal government, largely based on standards developed in the United States, then legislated by the provincial government (Interview 20). For instance, residential streets are normally designed to carry traffic at fifty kilometres per hour. This speed is considered to be too fast for the safety of pedestrians and especially children. Canada Lands wanted a speed limit of thirty kilometres per hour; after a long dispute, the city and Canada Lands compromised at forty kilometres per hour. The over-engineering of roads, compelled by federal transportation engineering standards and provincial rules (Interview 6), led not only to a more expensive development, but also to a less safe environment.

Nonetheless, other federal and provincial agencies made positive contributions to what has become widely recognized as one of Canada's most desirable new neighbourhoods. Canada Mortgage and Housing Corporation (CMHC) and the Alberta Lottery Board provided money to refurbish sixty-five old homes in Cyprus Green, which were sold at cost to the Calgary Housing Authority to operate as low-income social housing. Some additional units in the yet-to-be-completed Garrison Green development have been sold to the Calgary Housing Authority at cost. Provincial legislation, however, allows condominium associations to prohibit rental units, which limits the capacity of socially concerned developers to develop a stock of dispersed social rental housing.

One of the more interesting and counterintuitive lessons of Garrison Woods is that it took a federal agency, supposedly far removed from the local context, to produce a development considerably more desirable than conventional Calgary developments. Moreover, it took a federal agency to overcome very rigid local regulations that were stifling local innovation. The success of the Canada Lands Company calls into question the sweeping generalization that lower levels of government make better decisions in local matters than higher levels of government and that private developers respond better to consumer demand than a public agency can. Analysis of the Garrison Woods development would appear to reinforce Mark Purcell's (2006) warning against "the local trap" – the assumption that local scales of governance are preferable to other scales.

CONCLUSIONS

Although it is growing in size, wealth, and influence, Calgary has distinct problems coping with that growth. Growth seems to continually threaten to choke itself off, as inadequate facilities discourage the in-movement of the workers needed to maintain economic expansion. As a result, infrastructure project announcements tend to take centre stage in intergovernmental relations, a general tendency in Canada that is only intensified by Calgary's particular situation. The drama of project announcements appeals to senior governments because mundane transfers to operating funds fail to have the public profile that is desired. They also tend, in Calgary and Alberta, to be the only situations in which politicians appear publicly to be cooperating, since mobilization against the depredations of senior governments has long been an effective political legitimation strategy both in the city and in the province. Backstage channels, or informal contacts and understanding, seem to be necessary to generate a "high-road" rather than "low-road" approach to multilevel governance in contexts with a history characterized by conflict more than cooperation (Kratke 1999; Smart and Lin 2004). The question is whether the front-stage dynamics of project launches provide the context in which backstage channels can be developed.

The public performance opportunities afforded by project funding announcements may lead to policies that are less effective in relation to the resources expended and do not match the priorities of cities themselves (Andrew and Morrison 2002). Ring road infrastructure spending is one example of a major expenditure by higher levels of government that was not only not a priority for the City of Calgary, but that may actually undermine some of Calgary's stated priorities. This example also raises the question of the impact of social forces since the intensification of sprawl at the urban fringe may reduce the likelihood that the Chamber of Commerce's vision of a vibrant downtown that attracts talent and investment will come to fruition. Calgary's social forces are clearly dominated by business interests, and those associated with land development play an especially powerful role. In Calgary, any major social force, even social justice NGOs, must make a "business case" if their proposals and projects are to have any likelihood of support and success.

The four policy fields examined here offer distinct perspectives on these questions. The successes of the Canada Lands development of Garrison Woods on a former armed forces base allowed movement beyond the initial conflicts into a situation where this iconic new urbanist project brings city officials into frequent and positive interactions with representatives of other governments, and seems to be stimulating progressive changes in local planning regulations. Immigration probably indicates the clearest example of policies where the needs of Calgary (and Alberta more generally) have had an impact on national policy. The rapid expansion of the Temporary Foreign Worker Program seems to have been intended primarily to help solve some of the labour shortage problems without increasing permanent migration. The mechanism of expedited labour market opinions allows local conditions to influence the number of TFWs that will be permitted. However, there is considerable doubt whether this represents good policy or short-sighted exploitation of workers, instead of encouraging increased permanent migration of people who will have a long-term commitment to the city. In this field, the business and social justice social forces seem to be at odds, with the advantage going to the business interests so far. The image of Calgary seems at risk from this situation, as it is from the shortage of affordable housing, the homelessness crisis, and other signs of a mean-spirited but rich city and province. In some areas relating to image building, however, business interests benefit from promoting more progressive initiatives, and the need to attract labour creates a certain potential overlap in the agendas of social justice and business social forces.

Ultimately, Calgary represents a prototypical boom region economy, with all the attendant political interests and social problems (Markusen 1989). The powerful social and political forces associated with Calgary's rapid economic growth often lack the capacity to address the city's problems in a satisfactory way, so they seek to attract resources and form alliances across multiple levels of governance. Not surprisingly, the success of MLG has been highly uneven across policy fields. Complicating MLG are questions of transparency and democratic accountability at every level. Clearly, inequities in capacity and funding for social and infrastructure needs can wreak havoc in a rapidly growing city, but so can inadequate democratic institutions. Addressing both must be part of any coherent MLG strategy.

## NOTES

1 Calgary's new municipal development plan and transportation plan, known as "Plan-It," passed in 2009 with massive citizen support and strong development industry resistance. It calls for Calgary to become a much denser transit and

pedestrian-oriented city with half of all future development occurring within the existing built footprint of the city. Combined with higher development fees for greenfield development and a meaningful growth management strategy, the City finally appears to be charting a development course not dictated by the development industry.

2 Although Andrew Sancton argues that "Canadian city politics is, above all, about boosterism," a reasonable case could be made that Calgary takes this tendency to an even greater extreme (Sancton 1983, 283).

3 The importance of improved ties with key federal players was demonstrated in the 2011 Department of Canadian Heritage announcement that Calgary would be the 2012 "Cultural Capital of Canada."

### LIST OF INTERVIEWS

1 City alderman, 3 July 2002.
2 City of Calgary planner, 4 July 2002.
3 City of Calgary planner, 25 May 2003.
4 Developer, 7 August 2003.
5 City of Calgary planner, 19 September 2002.
6 City of Calgary planner, 28 April 2006.
7 Regional municipality official, 24 July 2006.
8 Infrastructure planner, 24 July 2006.
9 City of Calgary senior official, 1 June 2006.
10 City of Calgary senior official, 12 March 2007.
11 NGO representative, 14 September 2007.
12 NGO representative, 14 September 2007.
13 NGO representative, 25 July 2007.
14 City of Calgary official, 7 August 2007.
15 Business association representative, 15 August 2007.
16 Business association representative, 15 August 2007.
17 NGO representative, 15 August 2007.
18 NGO representative, 15 August 2007.
19 NGO representative, 19 September 2007.
20 Federal agency official, 20 August 2007.
21 Federal agency official, 20 August 2007.
22 NGO representative, 20 August 2007.
23 Federal immigration official, 12 September 2007.
24 NGO representative, 19 September 2007.
25 Regional agency official, 28 September 2006.
26 Regional agency official, 1 October 2006.
27 Ray Danyluk (Alberta Municipal Affairs Minister), 10 October 2007.

REFERENCES

Alberta Federation of Labour. 2006. AFL Policy Statement on Temporary
  Foreign Workers. Edmonton: Alberta Federation of Labour.
Andrew, Caroline, and Jeff Morrison. 2002. "Infrastructure." In *Urban Policy
  Issues: Canadian Perspectives*, edited by Edmund Fowler and David Siegel,
  237–52. Oxford: Oxford University Press.
Berdahl, Loleen. 2007. *City Views: An Analysis of the 2007 Looking West
  Survey*. Calgary: Canada West Foundation.
Braid, Don. 2007. "Squeaky Mayor gets Provincial Grease." *Calgary Herald*,
  15 September, B1, B4.
Calgary Chamber of Commerce. 2007. "Renaissance Calgary: Blueprint for a
  21st Century World-leading Capital." Calgary: Calgary Chamber of
  Commerce.
City of Calgary. 2006. "Proposed budgets 2006–2008." Calgary: City of
  Calgary.
– 2007. "Calgary and Region Social Outlook." Calgary: City of Calgary.
– 2008. "2005–2008 Financial Fast Facts." Calgary: City of Calgary.
– 2009a. "The Implications of Alternative Growth Patterns on Infrastructure
  Costs." Calgary: City of Calgary.
– 2009b. "2009 to 2011 Financial Fast Facts." Calgary: City of Calgary.
Calgary Economic Development. 2007. "Calgary's Migrants: Origins,
  Destinations, Profiles." Calgary: Calgary Economic Development.
– 2007. "Head Offices." Calgary: Calgary Economic Development.
The Calgary Foundation. 2007. "Calgary's Vital Signs: Taking the Pulse of
  Calgary." Calgary: The Calgary Foundation.
Calgary Homeless Foundation. 2011. *Calgary Homeless Foundation Financial
  Report 2011*. Calgary. http://calgaryhomeless.com/assets/Progress/Year3/
  2011financialreportfinalweb.pdf.
Calgary Stampede. 2007. "Brand Identity Built on Values." *Saddlebag* 6(1): 1.
Canada, Citizenship and Immigration. 2006. "Backgrounder: Settlement
  funding allocations." http://www.cic.gc.ca/English/department/media/
  backgrounders/2006/2006-11-10.asp.
– 2007. "Agreement for Canada-Alberta Cooperation on Immigration." http://
  www.cic.gc.ca/english/department/laws-policy/agreements/alberta/can-alberta-
  agree-2007.asp.
Couroux, David, Noel Keough, Byron Miller, and Jesse Row. 2006. "Toward
  Smart Growth in Calgary." Calgary: Sustainable Calgary Society. http://
  www.sustainablecalgary.ca/files/file/SmartGrowth.pdf.
Cryderman, Kelly. 2008. "Alberta Pursues 41,000 Foreign Workers." *Calgary
  Herald*, 13 April.

Davis, Mike. 2006. *Planet of Slums*. New York: Verso.

Douglas, Heather. 2008. "Time to Combat Wave of Apathy." *Calgary Sun*, 17 January.

Dowding, Jillian, and Farinaz Razi. 2004. "A Call to Action: Leading the Way to Successful Immigrant Integration." Calgary: Innovation in Integration.

Dudley, Wendy. 1998. "Calgary Saddles up Tributes to Cowboy." *Calgary Herald*, 2 January, A1.

Federation of Canadian Municipalities. 2007. "Danger Ahead: The Looming Collapse of Canada's Municipal Infrastructure." Ottawa: Federation of Canadian Municipalities.

Fekete, Jason. 2009. "Tories Revisit Funding to Cities." *Calgary Herald*, 24 September, A1.

Foran, Max. 2008. "More Than Partners: The Calgary Stampede and the City of Calgary." In *Icon, Brand, Myth: The Calgary Stampede*, edited by Max Foran, 147–74. Edmonton: Athabasca University Press.

– 2009. *Expansive Discourses: Urban Sprawl in Calgary, 1945–1978*. Edmonton: Athabasca University Press.

Frideres, James. 2008. "Creating an Inclusive Society: Promoting Social Integration in Canada." In *Immigration and Integration in Canada in the Twenty-first Century*, edited by John Biles, Meyer Burstein, and James Frideres, 77–102. Montreal and Kingston: McGill-Queen's University Press.

Furniss, Elizabeth. 1998. "Cultural Performance as Strategic Essentialism: Negotiating Indianness in a Western Canadian Rodeo Festival." *Humanities Research* 3:23–40.

Geertz, Clifford. 1980. *Negara: The Theatre State in Nineteenth Century Bali*. Princeton: Princeton University Press.

Ghitter, Geoff, and Alan Smart. 2009. "Mad Cows, Regional Governance and Urban Sprawl: Path Dependence and Unintended Consequences in the Calgary Region." *Urban Affairs Review* 44 (5):617–44.

Giannias, Dimitrios A. 1998. "A Quality of Life Based Ranking of Canadian Cities." *Urban Studies* 35 (12):2241–51.

Goffman, Erving. 1959. *The Presentation of Self in Everyday Life*. Garden City, NJ: Doubleday.

Guttormson, Kim. 2007. "Mayor Vows Review of Election Financing." *Calgary Herald*, 17 October, A1.

Hiller, Harry H. 2007. "Gateway Cities and Arriviste Cities: Alberta's Recent Urban Growth in Canadian Context." *Prairie Forum* 1:47–66.

Hiller, Harry H., and Denise Moylan. 1999. "Mega-Events and Community Obsolescence." *Canadian Journal of Urban Research* 8 (1):47–81.

Immigrant Sector Council of Calgary. 2003. "2001–2003 Progress Report and Future Directions." Calgary: Immigrant Sector Council of Calgary.

Kaika, Maria, and Erik Swyngedouw. 2002. "Fetishizing the Modern City: The Phantasmagoria of Urban Technological Networks." *International Journal of Urban and Regional Research* 24 (1):120–38.

Kratke, Stefan. 1999. "Regional Integration or Fragmentation? The German-Polish Border Region in a New Europe." *Regional Studies* 33 (7):631–42.

LeSage Jr., Edward C., and Melville L. McMillan. 2009. "Alberta." In *Foundations of Governance: Municipal Governments in Canada's Provinces*, edited by Andrew Sancton and Robert Young, 384–452. Toronto: University of Toronto Press.

Lorimer, James. 1978. *The Developers*. Toronto: James Lorimer & Company.

Markusen, Ann. 1989. "Industrial Restructuring and Regional Politics." In *Economic Restructuring and Political Response*, edited by Robert Beauregard, 115–47. London: Sage.

Mercer Human Resource Consulting. 2007. "2007 Quality of Living Survey." Mercer Human Resource Consulting.

Miller, Byron. 2006. "Policy Shapes Cities More than You Might Think." *Dialogues* 2 (2): 4–5.

– 2007. "Modes of Governance, Modes of Resistance: Contesting Neoliberalism in Calgary." In *Contesting Neoliberalism: Urban Frontiers*, edited by Helga Leitner, Jamie Peck, and Eric Sheppard, 223–49. New York: Guilford Press.

Olds, Kris. 1998. "Urban Mega-Events, Evictions and Housing Rights: The Canadian case." *Current Issues in Tourism* 1 (1):1–46.

Pannekoek, Frits. 2008. "Cowtown It Ain't: The Stampede and Calgary's Public Monuments." In *Icon, Brand, Myth: The Calgary Stampede*, edited by Max Foran, 251–69. Edmonton: Athabasca University Press.

Purcell, Mark. 2006. "Urban Democracy and the Local Trap." *Urban Studies* 43: 1921–41.

Revell, Kevin David. 2003. *Building Gotham: Civic Culture and Public Policy in New York City, 1898–1938*. Baltimore: Johns Hopkins University Press.

Rutheiser, Charles. 1996. *Imagineering Atlanta: The Politics of Place in the City of Dreams*. London: Verso.

Sancton, Andrew. 1983. "Conclusion: Canadian City Politics in Comparative Perspective." In *City Politics in Canada*, edited by Warren Magnusson and Andrew Sancton, 291–317. Toronto: University of Toronto Press.

Simmons, James, and Larry S. Bourne. 2007. "Living with Population Growth and Decline." *Plan Canada* (Summer):13–21.

Smart, Alan. 2001. "Restructuring in a North American City: Labour Markets and Political Economy in Calgary." In *Plural Globalities in Multiple Localities: New World Borders*, edited by M. Rees and J. Smart, 167–93. Lanham, MD: University Press of America.

Smart, Alan, and George C. S. Lin. 2004. "Border Management and Growth Coalitions in the Hong Kong Transborder Region." *Identities: Global Studies in Culture and Power* 11 (3):377–96.

Smart, Josephine. 1994. "Business Immigration to Canada: Deception and Exploitation." In *Reluctant Exiles? Migration From Hong Kong and the New Overseas Chinese*, edited by Ronald Skeldon, 98–119. New York: M.E. Sharpe.

Tanasescu, Alina. 2007. "Calgary Immigrant and Refugee Housing Needs: A Hidden Homeless Population." Calgary: United Way of Calgary.

TD Economics. 2007. "The Tiger that Roared across Alberta." Toronto: TD Bank.

White, R. 2007. "Shared Vision Needed for Calgary." *Calgary Herald*, 13 October, J2.

Young, Robert, and Christian Leuprecht. 2004. "Introduction: New Work, Background Themes, and Future Research about Municipal-Federal-Provincial Relations in Canada." In *Municipal-Federal-Provincial Relations in Canada*, edited by Robert Young and Christian Leuprecht, 3–22. Montreal and Kingston: McGill-Queen's University Press.

3

# Charlottetown:
# A Small, Quiet Seat of Government –
# No Boom, No Bust

DAVID M. BULGER

## INTRODUCTION

The motto of the City of Charlottetown, as proudly displayed on the city's crest, is "*cunabula foederis*," or "birthplace of Confederation." While this designation may be open to question (Quebec City or London, England could equally claim the title) it is an important part of the city's self-image. Province House, which is the home of the Prince Edward Island (PEI) legislature, is also a national historic site in its alter ego as the meeting place of the so-called "Confederation Conference" in September of 1864. In recent years, during the summer months, actors playing Sir John A. Macdonald, Sir George-Étienne Cartier, Thomas D'Arcy McGee and the like could be seen strolling the streets of Old Charlottetown to both entertain and inform visitors.

This chapter will study the governance of this historic city in general and will couple this with investigations of the city's approach to, and mechanism for dealing with, the following specific policy areas: emergency measures, federal property, immigrant settlement, and urban Aboriginals. Finally, the chapter will suggest that, notwithstanding recent developments in the private sector, Charlottetown remains essentially a "government town," dependent on the presence of both the provincial and federal governments for much of its wealth.

## HISTORY AND GEOGRAPHY

History is an essential element in the make-up of Charlottetown. The city trades on its reputation as the birthplace of Canada. Depending on whether the 1720 founding of the Acadian town of Port LaJoie or the 1764 designation by surveyor Captain Samuel Holland of "Charlotte Town" as a principal city of the king's newly acquired Island of St John is taken as its origin, Charlottetown is the third or fourth oldest capital in Canada. It is also the smallest in population, at 32,174 (Statistics Canada 2008) and was only half that size prior to a 1995 amalgamation (Crossley 2005, 226–9) of the original city of Charlottetown with the suburban municipalities of Sherwood, Parkdale, East and West Royalty, and Winsloe.

Samuel Holland named this "principal city" in honour of Queen Charlotte of Mecklenberg, consort of George III. As a military engineer and surveyor, Holland clearly appreciated the strategic value of the location. Charlottetown has a large harbour, but the entrance from the Northumberland Strait is a relatively narrow and easily defended passage. (It was not defended at all, however, in November 1775, when American privateers swept in, did some looting, and captured, among others, the lieutenant-governor Phillips Callbeck).

The harbour, in large measure, also defines the geography of the town. It is a rough cruciform, formed by the confluence of the Hillsborough (also called the East), West (Elliot) and North (Yorke) rivers, with the fourth arm being the opening to the Northumberland Strait, a north-south passage lying directly opposite the mouth of the North River. Charlottetown itself is a broad peninsula. Like Halifax, the tip of the peninsula is reserved as parkland and the town has grown up from a waterfront, which lies along the Hillsborough River shore.

From the waterfront, the land slopes gently northward. From Peake's Quay, where the Charlottetown Conference delegates landed, Great George Street rises for a short distance and then ends abruptly at the legislative building. Beyond this, a person travelling northward along what was once the continuation of Great George Street and Elm Avenue – now gloriously renamed University Avenue – would not notice any perceptible rise until reaching the area of the "Home Farm" (which will be discussed shortly, in the Federal Properties section). Ahead would be the gentle slope where construction was begun in 1848 for St Dunstan's University, now the site of the University of Prince Edward Island. From there, the land rises a bit more sharply to the northeast until it levels out at the highest point in Charlottetown proper, 160 feet above sea level, at the Charlottetown Airport.

Charlottetown was "designated" by Captain Samuel Holland as the seat of the County of Queens, along with the seats of the other two counties, Georgetown (Kings County) and Princetown (Prince County). There is some question about the extent of Holland's surveying of the townsite. Douglas Boylan suggests that he provided a full survey, down to the four squares, which remain as green spaces today (Boylan 1991, 36). However, Irene Rogers states that the first actual survey was carried out in 1768 by Charles Morris of Nova Scotia, in accordance with Holland's wishes, but that the surveying of "house lots was so scanty" that Governor Walter Patterson commissioned surveyor Thomas Wright to produce a new survey, which is the current plan, and in which, for the first time, the green space squares appear (Rogers 1983, 1–2).

Since there was no significant pre-existing settlement, and therefore no existing streets or by-ways to contend with, the plan is a grid of eleven streets running east to west, starting at the harbour shore, and nine running north and south. Roughly in the centre lies Queens Square, which was set aside for administrative buildings and a church. The other squares are located in each quadrant of the town, Rochford Square in the northwest, Connaught Square in the southwest, Hillsborough Square in the southeast, and Kings Square in the northeast. This plan remains today, though the eleven east-west roads have been reduced to nine.

Charlottetown saw much of the turmoil that characterized other colonial capitals. At the beginning, and in the early decades, it was the scene of faction politics, which saw disputes between followers of individuals rather than arguments about policy. For example, the early decades of Charlottetown's history show one successful petition for the removal of a governor (Walter Patterson) and an unsuccessful attempt to remove another (Edmund Fanning). In addition, many of those who found their way into the public service were second-raters who would not have seen advancement in the mother country, while other players were individuals who had "failed in their circumstances" at home (Holman 1959, 565–9). Added to this mixture was the kind of chicanery and high-handed misbehaviour characteristic of frontier societies. In one instance, the combination of faction politics and fraudulent practice spawned litigation that lasted almost fifty years and saw no fewer than four appeals to King-in-Council during its course (Bulger 2005, 323–56).

Throughout the first 100 years of its existence, the ongoing and divisive political issue was the absentee ownership of the land itself. In his 1764 survey, Samuel Holland had divided the landmass into sixty-five townships, each township containing approximately 20,000 acres. In 1767, the townships were then assigned, by lottery, to pay off a number of creditors of the Crown (e.g., unpaid suppliers and ranking military officers who were owed their wages). For over 100 years, local political groups struggled to lift the burden of absentee ownership in the face of the twin burdens of landlord resistance and an insufficiency of funds to buy them out.

Without any question, the most significant event in Charlottetown's history was the arrival of the *SS Queen Victoria* in the harbour on the morning of 1 September 1864, its hold stuffed with liquor, and its decks awash with political party-crashers. The delegation from the United Province of Canada, impelled by political concerns approaching crisis proportions, had come to "woo" delegates from Nova Scotia, New Brunswick, and PEI (whose official purpose was attendance at a conference on Maritime union) to a larger political marriage.

Charlottetonians could have cared less about the politicians. What had their attention, and the attention of many other islanders, that first day of September, was the Slaymaker and Nichols Olympic Circus, the first circus to visit the island in twenty-one years (Bolger 1991b, 145). Had Charlottetonians fully appreciated the "bill of goods" about to be sold by the Canadian delegation, their attention might have shifted from the big top to the legislative building, or, more properly, to the steamship in the harbour, since on the afternoon and into the evening of Saturday, 3 September, that abundant stock of liquor made its way from the hold to the decks of the *Queen Victoria* where it was consumed, in that same abundance, by the delegates. As George Brown recalled, he and George-Étienne Cartier "made eloquent speeches – of course – and, whether, as a result of our eloquence, of the goodness of our champagne, the ice became completely broken, the tongues of the delegates wagged merrily, and the banns of matrimony between all the provinces of BNA having been formally proclaimed and all manner of persons duly warned then and there to speak or forever hold their tongues – no man appeared to forbid the banns and the union was thereupon formally completed and proclaimed" (Bolger 1991b, 148).

But not "completed and proclaimed" as far as the Island was concerned. Even though Charlottetown clings fiercely to its designation as "birthplace of Confederation," the PEI delegation left the subsequent Quebec Conference without agreeing to join the proposed union, at odds over the issue of an equal and elected senate and upset at the refusal to provide funds to buy out absentee landlords. It was only in 1873, following an economic downturn, and impelled by the same kind of railroad financing and debt that had brought the *SS Queen Victoria* steaming into Charlottetown harbour, that the Island found itself forced into Confederation.

From this point on, Charlottetown receded into a kind of quiet obscurity. Transformed from a colonial to a provincial capital, it closed its customs house and accepted the offices and officers of the federal government housed in Ottawa. Almost coincident with union, the fortunes of the Island, built on wooden ships and transatlantic trade, began to decline. Except for the odd local controversy – the issue of separate schools, for example – the city remained largely a dormant and uneventful place, except, perhaps, for a brief period during the Second World War when it served as an "R and R" destination for Allied airmen stationed at Summerside. Only in 1992 did Charlottetown once again rise to its earlier prominence, as the prime minister and provincial premiers descended on the town to finalize the ill-fated Charlottetown Accord.

## DEMOGRAPHICS AND ECONOMY

In the 2006 census, the population of the City of Charlottetown stood at 32,174 people (Statistics Canada 2008), which represented a decline of seventy-one persons from the 2001 figure, or a loss of 0.2 percent. Part of this decline is probably explained by out-migration into the surrounding bedroom communities that make up the Charlottetown Metropolitan Area. Cornwall, with 4,677 people, and Stratford, with 7,083, had increases in population of 6 percent and 12.2 percent respectively. When other bedroom communities such as Clyde River, Miltonvale Park, Warren Grove, and Covehead are taken into account, the population of the Charlottetown Metropolitan Area settles somewhere in the neighbourhood of 50,000–60,000 persons. By Canadian standards, this figure is well short of the number needed to constitute Charlottetown a "major city."

According to 2006 census figures, the median age of the population was 41.3 years. Some 85.2 percent of the population was over the age of fifteen, while 9,465 persons (29 percent) were in the retirement range of over fifty-five years (Statistics Canada 2008). When it is considered that 4,845 individuals were between the ages of forty-five and fifty-four in 2006, the concerns about an aging population, expressed by a number of politicians in a recent overview of the Island's municipal system, would seem to be borne out (Bulger and Sentance, 2009).

Like PEI as a whole, the population of Charlottetown is remarkably homogeneous, being essentially European in origin. The largest European groups are the Scots, English, Irish, and French, though there has been considerable intermingling through marriage. In 2006, only 1,485 individuals (4.6 percent of the population) were "foreign born," and of that number, better than two thirds (1,025) had immigrated prior to 1991. When ethnicity is considered in terms of the visible minority population, only 965 persons (3 percent) could be placed in that classification (Statistics Canada 2008). Given these figures, it would not be surprising that the city will not place the accommodation of immigrants high on its political agenda.

The scenario is similar with Aboriginal peoples in Charlottetown. Some 450 persons (1.4 percent) made up the "Aboriginal identity" population in 2006. This number represented 26 percent of the 1,730 total "Aboriginal identity" population of Prince Edward Island (which, in turn, was approximately 1 percent of the PEI population of 133,385). Again, while there are urban Aboriginal issues in Charlottetown, as in any Canadian city, the small Aboriginal population tends to preclude these issues from reaching a high place on the political agenda.

The economy of Charlottetown does not rest on manufacturing. The 2006 census indicates that only slightly over 500 persons in Charlottetown and its two major suburbs, Cornwall and Stratford, were involved in "occupations unique to processing, manufacturing and utilities" (principally chemical and bio-chemical manufacturing and metal fabricating). Since there was an equally small number of individuals involved in "agriculture and other resource-based industries," the bulk of the population was involved in retail sales or service industries of some sort (Statistics Canada 2008). Indeed, though at least one new chemical company has taken root, recent growth has been largely in the service sector.

Intuitively, the business of government appears to hold a primary place in the Charlottetown economy. Any person who has watched the provincial government office buildings empty at 4 PM on a summer's afternoon, or who has walked into a coffee shop on University Avenue, just around the corner from Veterans' Affairs Canada, at 10:30 AM, would be forgiven for thinking that the city is dominated by civil servants.

Census statistics do not seem to bear this out, however. For the City of Charlottetown, persons in "government service" were lumped in with persons in "social science, education and religion," for a total of 1,735 individuals out of a workforce of 16,960, or slightly more than 10 percent (Statistics Canada 2008). But the census figures may be misleading. For example, there are occupational categories for managerial personnel and administrators, and it is not impossible that a number of civil servants responded to the census by placing themselves in those categories.

When other statistics for government service are employed, we find that, in 2007, federal government employees on PEI numbered 3,681 individuals, while provincial employees numbered 3,108, not including those persons employed in "health and social services" (4,157) and education (4,258) (Prince Edward Island 2008). In addition, both levels of government maintain business enterprises with workforces, and there are local government workers and the small military contingent of 230 people to be taken into account. The grand total for the public sector is 17,239 persons with a total payroll of $855,702,000 in 2007 (Prince Edward Island 2008). Given that most federal government employees are located in Charlottetown, it is possible to speculate that something approaching two thirds of the 17,239 persons, or upwards of 10,000 individuals, who work in the city and live in the Charlottetown Census Agglomeration Area are employed by government.

Those employed by government significantly exceed other groups in the census, and when income is factored in, the government presence in the economy becomes even more pronounced. While the median income for persons living in Charlottetown was $22,205 in 2005, the average government income in Charlottetown was approximately $49,000, and since most higher-paid senior managerial personnel are likely to be located in Charlottetown, that average may well be higher. When rentals paid on over 15,000 square metres of space leased by the federal government alone are factored in,[1] the government contribution to the local economy is large. Indeed, government appears to be Charlottetown's main business.

### GOVERNANCE

The City of Charlottetown constitutes a single federal riding, called Charlottetown, which coincides with its municipal boundaries. The city incorporates five complete provincial electoral districts, Charlottetown-Sherwood, Charlottetown-Parkdale, Charlottetown-Victoria Park, Charlottetown-Brighton, and Charlottetown-Lewis Point. A sixth electoral district, West Royalty-Springvale, is shared with the municipality of Miltonvale Park, and a seventh, Tracadie-Hillsborough Park, is shared with the municipality of Grand Tracadie and the unincorporated areas east of Charlottetown.

The City of Charlottetown has the general powers of a corporation as provided in section 16 of the Interpretation Act, as well as a specific shopping list of authorized functions as provided by section 21 of the

Charlottetown Area Municipalities Act (Prince Edward Island 1988a
and b). The administration is in the hands of a mayor and ten councillors
(one of whom is deputy mayor) who currently serve four-year terms. The
councillors represent ten different wards.

The day-to-day running of the city is carried on by a chief administrative officer and eleven city departments: Finance, Human Resources,
Parks and Recreation, Fire, Police, Public Works, Tourism and Events,
Urban Beautification and Forestry, Planning and Development, Water
and Sewer, and Environment. The council itself maintains eleven standing committees, which correspond quite closely with the line departments, though mandates may be broader (e.g., Planning/Heritage/Arts
and Culture).

What is obvious from the list above is that Charlottetown has no specific department dedicated to the concerns of two of the policy areas of
this study, immigrant settlement and urban Aboriginals. Likewise, there
is no committee charged with these concerns. Nor is there a specific
department or committee concerned with federal properties (though
Public Works and Parks and Recreation might become involved if federal properties are transferred to the city for use as green spaces.) Only
emergency measures[2] are specifically provided for in the Fire and Emergency Measures committee.

One committee, currently chaired by the mayor, is concerned with
"Executive Policy and Event Attraction." The shift of the chair of this
committee from the deputy mayor to the mayor occurred on 1 January
2009, after research for this chapter was completed. It may reflect a
change in attitude toward policy. Previously, as far as policy making
generally was concerned, the former chair and deputy mayor, Stu
MacFadyen, stated: "I am chair of 'Executive Policy' which is a committee that takes in matters with the provincial government and federal
government and also special events like Labour Day and the Christmas
Day Parade and New Year's in the Park." Direct contact with the federal
government is minimal, he said, "because we are under the umbrella of
the provincial government. In order for us to receive any funding – for
instance there is a 'gas tax' and there is a 'new deal' for municipalities
which was brought through by the federal government – but all that
money goes through the provincial government and the provincial government is responsible to give us our share" (Interview 8). The focus of
Charlottetown's Council is largely on the delivery of services and not on
large policy issues.

## POLICY AREAS

As mentioned in the introduction, the Charlottetown city study will address four policy fields: federal property, emergency management, immigrant settlement, and urban Aboriginal policy.

### 1. Emergency Management

Prince Edward Island in general, and Charlottetown in particular, have been blessed by having very few public emergencies. The rivers are not long and flow easily and directly into the sea, so there is rarely an issue of flooding. While there were serious forest fires in the western part of the Island in the 1940s and 1950s, there hasn't been a repetition in recent decades. Even Hurricane Juan, which caused considerable damage in Halifax in 2003, had a minimal effect on Charlottetown; electricity was out for less than twenty-four hours and some trees were uprooted. The major damage was confined to some personal property, namely boats at the Charlottetown Yacht Club.

Aside from hurricanes and wind storms – and heavy snowstorms – the only other significant weather-related damaging events in recent years have been tidal surges, the result of extreme low pressure systems coinciding with spring tides. However, the damage has been minimal and the people affected few. As this paper was being written, an ice storm had crippled large areas of the Island with lasting power outages. Charlottetown, however, was not significantly bothered. When ice storm damage did affect the transmission line coming into the city, Maritime Electric simply fired up a diesel generator on the waterfront and power was restored to the city and surrounding suburbs within two hours.

Consequently, the need for emergency preparedness is not uppermost in the public mind. This does not, of course, mean that Charlottetown and the Island are immune to disaster. And, indeed, the relatively small number of events may have a lulling effect on the public. As one interviewee stated, "Imagine a situation where [PEI] has a major windstorm in the winter for a couple of days and the [Confederation] bridge is shut down and there is no food supply, and then if you get power outages and there are a lot of different things that can very quickly manifest themselves into a serious situation" (Interview 10).

As already mentioned, the City of Charlottetown has an Emergency Measures Committee, and the Fire Chief, Bill Hogan, is the designated

Emergency Measures Officer for the city. As is the case with many other municipal issues, though, the presence of the provincial government in emergency planning and delivery is very high. As Chief Hogan points out, he is not free to deal directly with federal agencies: "I can't just go and contact Randy Robert out at the RCMP and ask for police officers or phone Fisheries and Oceans and ask for boats, everything has to go through the province" (Interview 5).

This provincial involvement is likely to increase and centralization will grow. On 30 October 2007, the Charlottetown *Guardian* newspaper carried an article entitled "Province Establishing Office of Public Safety." The Community and Cultural Affairs Minister, Carolyn Bertram, announced the creation of the office and stated that it would run joint emergency operations with Public Safety Canada. "Key functions of the office include: 911 administration, provincial fire services, and emergency prevention, preparedness, response and recovery. The provincial fire marshal's office is being moved downtown to join the new operation" (*Guardian*, 30 October 2007).

One of the functions of the office is to help local governments with emergency planning. Again, the high provincial presence in government is characteristic of PEI, and Chief Hogan points out that, in past experience, things have worked out reasonably well: "The only problem I see is that if for some reason there is a catastrophic incident, it could result in the whole process slowing down. Even then, at the very least, I could give them a heads up, informing them that I would need their [federal] resources." He points out that an extreme tidal surge – an unlikely event – flooding the lower half of the city would "certainly be beyond our capability and certainly beyond the province's capability, so it would be nice to be able to say [to the federal authorities] that this request is coming directly from the municipalities and these are the resources we are looking for" (Interview 5). The likelihood of this kind of direct contact between the municipalities and federal authorities would appear to be very small, given the dominance of the provincial governments.

One of the major players in both preparedness and emergency relief is the Canadian Red Cross. On PEI, it has forty-five volunteers who are specifically trained at the emergency response level to provide assistance and services. The Red Cross has contracts with three municipalities – Summerside, Stratford, and Charlottetown – to provide "emergency lodging, emergency clothing, [and] personal services such as religious services" (Interview 10). But, once again, there is extensive involvement with the provincial government; as Tanya Mullally of the Canadian Red Cross noted, "we work quite closely with the Department of Health and EMO, especially around the issue of the pandemic flu for the social services contract we have from EMO and the Department of Health" (Interview 10).

In terms of the organization's collective experience, the Red Cross has been able to provide valuable input for the city's emergency plan. Again, Mullally explains: "If there was an issue regarding the emergency plan in Charlottetown and the city would be calling me. Bill Hogan [Charlottetown Fire Chief] and I would sit down and be discussing what the needs would be" (Interview 10). The Red Cross is the main non-government agency involved in emergency planning, and its role is an influential one.

## 2. Federal Property

The federal government currently owns 1623.37 acres "upland" and 9.61 acres of "waterlot" in the City of Charlottetown (Public Works and Government Services Canada). This constitutes slightly more than 15 percent of the "upland" area of the city, but, when it is considered that 1,465 acres make up the airport, the extent of urban ownership drops sharply. On the other hand, the federal government leases some 15,230 square meters of space in Charlottetown. Expressed in acres, this would add 37.63 to the total. In addition to properties currently owned by the federal government, 248.34 acres of land have been sold to the Canada Lands Company, 59.55 acres to the Charlottetown Harbour Authority, and 1.06 to the Charlottetown Area Development Corporation.

Charlottetown's Chief Administrative Officer Roy Main stated categorically that there has never been any problem with "payments in lieu of taxes" for all of this property (Interview 9). The issues that arise occur when the federal government seeks to divest itself of property or responsibility.

Two very public and well-publicized controversies have involved federal properties in the City of Charlottetown. The first of these concerned the Home Farm, an area of 115 acres, which, since the 1995 amalgamation, is located in the centre of Charlottetown. The Home Farm, also known as the Experimental Farm, or Ravenwood Farm, was used by the Department of Agriculture to test a variety of products, such as fertilizers to pesticides. (If and when the federal government divests itself of the property, there may well be a concern about the responsibility for environmental clean-up in some sections.)

In the mid-1990s, the Department of Agriculture, no longer using the Home Farm for testing purposes, began to explore the possibility of divestment. Coincidentally, with these initiatives, a group of retired Experimental Farm employees formed a grassroots organization in 1996. It was called "Friends of the Farm," and its main goal was to keep the property as green space. Consequently, when there was a proposal in 2001 to build a rink/swimming pool complex on the property, this galvanized a response from the "Friends of the Farm," who circulated a petition that eventually garnered 4,500 signatures and effectively derailed the rink/pool proposal.

But the petition did more than that; it also raised the question of whether the property had ever been transferred to the Canada Lands Company, the federal government's real estate arm that receives and then sells surplus federal property. This much is clear: the petition fuss either prompted Canada Lands to reconvey the farm to Public Works, or "it has never moved to the Canada Lands Corporation [*sic*]." As Laura Lee Howard, a member of "Friends of the Farm" explained, "As a matter of fact, they [Canada Lands] got really scared and they stopped answering our calls" (Interview 6).

The fuss involved active lobbying of municipal and provincial governments and the local member of Parliament. "The city was quite supportive from the start. We had some influential people on our board, so right away the mayor was ready to listen and that helped," remarked Howard. The premier, Pat Binns, was also onside, according to the "Friends" (Interview 6).

What may ultimately have tipped the scales was the announcement, in March 2003, that the Mi'kmaq intended to file an Aboriginal land claim to the property. This announcement probably brought any transfer plans to a grinding halt. Treasury Board policy, which directs Public Works decision making, specifies that "under routine disposals, where the dept[artment] of Indian and Northern Affairs wishes to acquire federal real property on a priority basis to be used for settlements of comprehensive land claims, the dept[artment] must agree to the transfer of administration in writing within 240 days."[3] And for strategic disposals of high value property, "properties are not circulated as in a routine disposal; however, the interest of government agencies should be identified as soon as possible in the process. This would also include First Nations' interest."[4]

Further, a land claim would clearly raise issues beyond the disposal of the parcel itself. Mi'kmaq treaties, unlike the famous "numbered" treaties in central and western Canada, are treaties of "peace and friendship," and do not contain a cession clause releasing title to land. A possible construction that might be placed upon these events is that the pursuit of a land claim might cause considerable difficulties. Whatever the case, as of this writing, the Home Farm still belongs to Public Works Canada.

There is no Aboriginal land claim in the instance of a second property, located in what was formerly the community of West Royalty, on the western extremity of what is now Charlottetown. This is what is known as the Upton Farms. The land was used by the federal Department of Agriculture for crop studies and therefore does not raise concerns about hazardous residue.

This parcel amounts to 248 acres, some of which are wooded and straddle the Trans-Canada highway. By the time development of the Upton Farms came to public notice, the property was already in the hands of the Canada Lands Company. In April 2006, Kirsten Connor wrote to the prime minister objecting to the development of the property: "I got a letter back saying thank you for your interest and we'll send this copy to the minister in charge of Canada Lands … Then about two weeks later, I got a reply from Lawrence Cannon, the minister of transportation. They informed me that they were only policy directors of Canada Lands. Canada Lands is an independent organization that they cannot interfere with under any circumstances" (Interview 3).

By the fall of 2006, Ms Connor had her own signed petition and had established another "Friends" organization, the "Friends of Upton Farms." Her difficulties were greater than those faced by the friends of the Home Farm. Canada Lands already had the property and was in discussion with developers. Further, Charlottetown City Council had approved a rezoning of the property for residential development. Public meetings held by Canada Lands did not address the issue of the possible uses of the land, but rather were presentations of various subdivision proposals: "Canada Lands have said that they have had consultations, but the consultation always was around the fact of the subdivision" (Interview 3).

While there were attempts to lobby the federal government, this group of Friends ultimately found support in the municipality. They appealed to city council "to endorse a freeze on the plans for development." Connor remarked, "Anyway, they made a resolution in council, and they just put it in front of council the other night, and it passed unanimously. And that showed that council had tremendous courage and conviction" (Interview 3). The resolution was forwarded to Canada Lands, to the prime minister, "and everyone that has been involved." The provincial opposition proposed a three-month moratorium on development and MP Shawn Murphy proposed an eighteen-month moratorium. Nonetheless, "it is a bit worrisome that Canada Lands has not stopped – considering that the province and the city are opposed – but we will see" (Interview 3).

The city's "opposition" to Canada Lands' development of the Upton Farms may be an optimistic overstatement on Kirsten Connor's part. The CAO of Charlottetown, Roy Main, denied that development of the Upton Farms had been frozen: "No, no, I don't think that is true. We have an outstanding approval, we have asked them not to proceed, so they have voluntarily opted not to proceed with their development plan" (Interview 9). As to the likelihood that the area will remain green space, Susan Hendricken, director of Parks and Recreation/Open Space, commented that "they're not just going to give it to the city. So they have to get fair market value for that land ... So they are not just going to give the land away, so [we] are trying to find that balance that represents the interests of the citizens and having this green space protected, and still have some profit made off the land"(Interview 4).

CAO Main summarized the situation succinctly: "Given the objectives of the developer, and that we had given the green light, this isn't over until Elvis leaves the building essentially" (Interview 4). How and when Elvis – that is, Canada Lands Company – will leave is an open question at this writing, but this much is clear: part of the parcel has been purchased by the province and will be developed as an industrial park (the BioCommons), specializing in biochemical research and development. As part of the purchase agreement, a significant section has been preserved as green space.

A comparison of these two cases is instructive. What they clearly demonstrate is the difference timing can make. If social forces can become involved *before* federal property is transferred to Canada Lands, there is a greater likelihood of influence over the ultimate disposal, since it remains in the sphere of public demands upon government. Once Canada Lands has title, the issue shifts to a business model; Canada Lands must operate according to commercial principles. In these conditions, bringing public influence and political considerations to bear becomes much more difficult.

### 3. Immigrant Settlement

Given the small numbers of immigrants in Charlottetown identified by the most recent census, it will come as no surprise that the city has neither policy nor administrative provision for dealing with immigrants. It is not that there is any antipathy toward immigrants. On the contrary, when the city has been approached informally, steps have been taken to accommodate the needs of immigrants.

In an interview, Mayor Clifford Lee recounted the following story. The City of Charlottetown has a mainly volunteer fire department. For 150 years, as is the case with many such departments, firefighters had been alerted by the sounding of a powerful air horn. A family of refugees from Kosovo had settled in Charlottetown. In their homeland, such a horn meant an imminent air raid. Lee explains, "they met someone in Charlottetown and told them about their story of the dreaded siren and once we became aware of this development we ceased using it. It was more kind of a history thing, the siren. Most firefighters use a paging system and we use the horn as a back-up system – so if all the paging systems were to fail then we would use the horn, but it is not something you need to use" (Interview 7). As is more generally true of "policy" in Charlottetown and PEI, much is personal and informal.

Mayor Lee was candid about the situation of formal immigrant settlement programs. There is no money for programs specifically directed to immigrants. Lee remarked, "One of the reasons is that it is very difficult for the City of Charlottetown to become as involved as we should be because of the city's limited financial resources." The mayor is sensitive to the presence of immigrants and aware that "we have to find a way to connect people ... with people from the same country" (Interview 7). This point is important because a large proportion of immigrants who initially settle in Charlottetown eventually depart for cities where their ethnic communities are larger.

This view was shared by Kevin Arsenault, executive director of the Association of Newcomers to PEI. However, he noted that the city had not sought funding from "either provincial or federal" sources in order "to address immigration or settlement related matters" (Interview 1). Indeed, in a subsequent interview, he pointed out that, to his knowledge, no municipalities in Atlantic Canada are currently putting any direct funding into "helping and welcoming new immigrants." If so, Charlottetown would not seem to be unusual.

At the provincial level, PEI has a federal-provincial immigration agreement that allows the province to nominate immigrants in four different categories. In 2008, the province nominated 1,800 immigrants. Even so, retention is a major problem. "Even though (the provincial government) may be successful in getting them economically connected to business or whatever else, a lot of times they don't have the quality of life that is sufficient to justify their staying and they end up gravitating towards the bigger metropolises" (Interview 1).

The Association of Newcomers is not likely to pressure the City of Charlottetown into developing policy and procedures for immigrant settlement because they want to see immigrants dispersed throughout the Island. They want "to have the immigrants who are coming in to decide to settle in other areas than Charlottetown, because we're replicating a pattern that is producing itself across the country, that is that immigrants are gravitating towards the large metropolises, even though you can hardly call Charlottetown a large metropolis" (Interview 1).

In the end, then, however sensitive the municipal leadership may be to the issue, the City of Charlottetown can be said to lack an immigrant settlement policy. It has no specific processes for dealing with immigrants and, without an infusion of money earmarked for the purpose, the city is unlikely to develop formal policy and procedure in the near future because, essentially, there is not a publicly perceived need.

## 4. *Urban Aboriginals*

On 5 January 2002, the Charlottetown *Guardian* newspaper carried an article by Jim Day that noted the passing of Charles Patrick Bernard. The same day, an editorial by Gary MacDougall eulogized Bernard; and a letter to the editor by Jake Cullen, dated 19 January 2002, praised Bernard's gentle nature. Public memorial services were announced on 14 and 15 January 2002 (*Guardian*, 5, 14, 15, 19 January 2002). Who was Charles Patrick Bernard to deserve such memorializing? Was he a leader of industry? A prominent politician? A leading professional? No. He was an urban Aboriginal person. Legend has it that he was originally from Maine, that his family perished in a house fire there, and "Charlie," overcome with grief, wandered north until he found the streets of Charlottetown, where he became a fixture, as much a part of the town as those long-ago Fathers of Confederation. He was a gentle alcoholic whose time was divided between the street and jail or the detox centre (to which this writer, as a summer police constable, transported him all too frequently more than a quarter century ago). But, like the town thief in Robert Frost's poem "The Star-Splitter," Charlie belonged to Charlottetown. And the town mourned his passing.

Much in Charlottetown is informal. Certainly, there is no official policy directed toward urban Aboriginal people. If there is little to be said about immigrant settlement in Charlottetown, there is even less to be said about the situation of urban Aboriginals. A prominent provincial Aboriginal leader, Patrick Augustine, believes that in Charlottetown and the surrounding areas, "there's close to eight hundred people who self-identify as Aboriginal or who claim to have Aboriginal ancestry" (Interview 2). This number is at odds with the Statistics Canada census data, which in 2004 showed 450 Aboriginal persons in Charlottetown, sixty in Stratford, and none in Cornwall. The figure of 450 does represent an increase of almost 200 persons over the 280 counted in 2001. Also, the census Aboriginal identity group in 2006 was 26 percent of the total Aboriginal population of PEI, up from 21 percent in 2001, which indicates some possible movement from the reserves to the city (Statistics Canada 2008). But the figure is still well short of 800 persons.

The discrepancy may be explained in two ways. First, people may simply have missed being counted. This writer knows of at least one person of Aboriginal descent who lives in Cornwall, for example, though the census shows no Aboriginals. Second, the Statistics Canada figures may be simply wrong. Augustine pointed out that the number of off-reserve persons claiming Aboriginal identity is 970. Further, the membership in the Native Council amounts to 886 individuals, 198 of whom are status Indians. Further, 123 people are also members of PEI bands, and another 75 are affiliated with PEI bands. Given this intermixing of categories, arriving at accurate figures may present difficulties. It is clear that more Aboriginal persons in PEI live off reserves than on, and it is likely that a large percentage of off-reserve people live in the Charlottetown area.

What is equally clear is that no representative of the city who was interviewed mentioned Aboriginal peoples. Moreover, the Native Council, like the Association of Newcomers, sees its primary relationship to be with the province and the federal government: "We work more closely with the province than the municipal government, we even have a tripartite agreement that has been in place for about twenty-years. It's just the nature of jurisdictions that have been established under the constitution" (Interview 2).

On the other hand, the Council would like to open communication with the city to see whether there are any issues being addressed at the municipal level that impact off-reserve Aboriginal people. One issue, mentioned above, is Aboriginal title to the Home Farm. But there was no specific invitation from the city to meet regarding the matter. Indeed, attempts to open communication have been futile: "We [the Native

Council] have sent correspondence to the mayor here in Charlottetown and expressed that we would like to become more involved with the political process. And we never really received a reply"(Interview 2).

Suffice it to say that urban Aboriginals do not appear on the city's radar; there are no policies directed toward them and no specific processes to engage them. In light of issues like the Home Farm, it would be wise to open lines of communication, but at this writing, there are none. In this case, the informality of policy making in the city results in exclusion.

This does not mean that urban Aboriginals are totally without recourse. On the contrary, there is the Tripartite Agreement between the federal government, the provincial government, and the Native Council of PEI. The Council has a seat on the steering committee set up under the Agreement. As Augustine pointed out, "There is no money per se to actually do Aboriginal housing ... that goes the same for economic development," but the seat on the steering committee "helps with political advocacy" (Interview 2). Even here, though, because of the federal constitutional jurisdiction over "Indians and Indian lands," direct dealings are largely between the Council and the federal government, with the province a bystander. The city would also be a bystander, even with the best will, if this strict constitutional regime is maintained.

## CONCLUSION

Almost twenty years ago, a Charlottetown lawyer remarked to this writer: "You know how it is here: no boom, no bust." That still holds largely true. Charlottetown is a small, quiet city. Small because its population, taken together with those of the surrounding bedroom communities, would fall well short of the cut-off for a census metropolitan area in Canada. Quiet because it is a stable community, with a low crime rate and no obvious racial or cultural tensions. While, like any place large or small, illegal drug use and sales have found their way to Charlottetown, and there have been instances of "enforcement" by drug dealers, these are few and far between. There are no gangs, so there is no gang warfare.

On the law-abiding side of things, there is little in the way of industrial development. While a number of new businesses have started operations in the city in the past few years, (possibly thanks to funding supplied by the Atlantic Canada Opportunities Agency), the real foundation of the city's economy is civil service salaries. In a world of economic fluctuation, there is nothing more stable than the incomes of civil servants.

Consequently, the issues that face Charlottetown City Council will, by and large and probably for some time to come, centre around the delivery of municipal services. There will be no large crises to contend with, no major policy concerns. And even in those policy areas researched in this study, with the exception of federal properties, the City of Charlottetown largely defers to the province. The entire province, after all, has the population of a minor Canadian city, and the provincial government looms large in all policy domains. Furthermore, social forces likewise see themselves relating principally to the province in matters of emergency preparedness, immigrant settlement, and urban Aboriginal issues. This is not surprising. Where each provincial member of the Legislative Assembly represents only 5,000 individuals on average – fewer persons than would be represented by a municipal councillor in many cities – the province is very accessible. Grand policy tends to be made at that level. Charlottetown, the largest city on Prince Edward Island, mirrors other municipalities in keeping its policy sights trained on services.

At the end of the day, Charlottetown is a small, quiet government town that has a good quality of life. There is no boom, and, equally, there is no bust. Perhaps that is as good a summation as any.

## NOTES

1  Ken Kelly, Public Works and Government Services, email response to queries.
2  The City of Charlottetown uses the term "emergency measures." While our overall study has chosen the term "emergency management" to describe this policy area, the city's usage will be followed in the text itself where appropriate.
3  Ken Kelly, Public Works and Government Services, email response to queries.
4  Ken Kelly, Public Works and Government Services, email response to queries.

## LIST OF INTERVIEWS

1  Kevin Arsenault (executive director, Association for Newcomers to PEI), 10 April 2007; 23 April 2008.
2  Patrick Augustine (Native Council of Prince Edward Island), 30 October 2007; 10 April 2008.
3  Kirsten Connor (Friends of Upton Farms), 13 April 2007.
4  Susan Hendriken (Parks and Recreation, City of Charlottetown), 2 November 2007.

5  Bill Hogan (fire chief, City of Charlottetown), 2 November 2007.
6  Laura Lee Howard (Friends of the Farm), 22 October 2007.
7  Clifford Lee (mayor, City of Charlottetown), 15 May 2007.
8  Sterling MacFadyen (deputy mayor, City of Charlottetown), 9 October 2007.
9  Roy Main (chief administrative officer, City of Charlottetown), 2 November 2007.
10 Tanya Mullally (Canadian Red Cross), 10 April 2007.

REFERENCES

Bolger, Francis. 1991a. "Land and Politics, 1787–1824." In *Canada's Smallest Province*, edited by Francis W.P Bolger, 66–94. Halifax: Nimbus Publishing.
– 1999b. "Nation Building at Charlottetown." In *Canada's Smallest Province*, edited by Francis W.P. Bolger, 135–55. Halifax: Nimbus Publishing.
Boylan, Douglas. 1973. "Rule Brittania." In *Canada's Smallest Province*, edited by Francis W.P. Bolger, 33–36. Halifax: Nimbus Publishing.
Bulger, David M. 2005. "Bowley v. Cambridge: A Colonial Jarndyce and Jarndyce." In *Essays in the History of Canadian Law, Volume IX: Two Islands*, edited by Christopher English, 323–56. Toronto: Osgoode Society for Legal History.
Bulger, David M., and James Sentence. 2009. "Prince Edward Island." In *Municipal Government in Canada's Provinces*, edited by Andrew Sancton and Robert Young, 314–44. Toronto: University of Toronto Press.
Crossley, John. 2005. "Municipal Reform in Prince Edward Island: Uneven Capacity and Reforms." In *Municipal Reform in Canada: Reconfiguration, Re-empowerment and Rebalancing*, edited by Joseph Garcea and Edward C. Lesage, 218–41. Toronto: Oxford University Press.
*Federal Real Property and Federal Immovables Act*. 1991. SCC, c.50.
Holman, Harry. 1959. "James Bardin Palmer." In *Dictionary of Canadian Biography*. Vol. 6. Toronto: University of Toronto.
Prince Edward Island. 2008. *34th Annual Statistical Review*. Department of the Provincial Treasury: Economics, Statistics and Federal Fiscal Relations Section, Program Evaluation and Fiscal Relations Division.
– 1988a. *Charlottetown Area Municipalities Act*, R.S.P.E.I. C-4.1, s.3.
– 1988b. *Interpretation Act*, R.S.P.E.I. c. I-8.5.
Rogers, Irene. 1983. *Charlottetown: The Life in its Buildings*, Charlottetown: The Prince Edward Island Museum and Heritage Foundation.
Statistics Canada. 2008. *2006 Census*. www.statcan.gc.ca.

# 4

# Submerging the Urban:
# Halifax in a Multilevel Governance System

ROBERT G. FINBOW

## INTRODUCTION

Halifax presents an interesting case study of the evolving nature of multilevel governance in Canada. Amalgamation and reshuffling of provincial-municipal financing in the 1990s accentuated an enduring gulf in communications between this growing urban region and a province dominated by rural politicians. Fiscal restraint, federal off-loading to provinces, and a neoconservative regime in Ottawa affected Halifax, which has pressing fiscal needs in a politically fragmented, have-not province. Halifax is enmeshed in deepening layers of multilevel governance as it confronts complex challenges on infrastructure, immigration, land management and development, economic competition, and public safety and security. While multilevel systems are often portrayed as equitable partnerships among government and non-governmental sectors (Leuprecht and Lazar 2007), the Halifax experience reveals that such arrangements, however essential, can create problems of coordination and accountability that work against efficient policy, limit public influence, and reduce responsiveness.

This chapter summarizes data collected for four policy areas for the Halifax Regional Municipality (HRM) – infrastructure, federal property, image building, and urban Aboriginal policy. In each policy area, the focus is on major projects and activities. The study is based on interviews with some seventy stakeholders from government, private sector, and non-governmental organizations. The interviews focused on core research questions to determine what forms of intergovernmental interaction and societal input contributed to policy formulation in the HRM. While variations are evident, there are common patterns in the feedback received across policy fields. The findings reveal intergovernmental communication problems in all policy fields and biases in the input process unfavourable to social interests. Poor institutional design in the HRM itself provided a weak framework for effective articulation of policy alternatives suitable to a contemporary metropolitan area. Municipal-provincial tensions, unfunded mandates, and slow provision of federal funds were also primary concerns.

The chapter begins by briefly surveying the history and character of Halifax as the leading metropolis in Nova Scotia and the wider Maritimes. It then addresses the issue of municipal amalgamation, adopted after several false starts in the 1990s. The approach taken to amalgamation in the Halifax Regional Municipality produced enduring distortions in tri-level interactions. In particular, the incorporation of sizeable rural regions with interests far removed from the urban core – essentially submerging the urban in a largely rural municipality – created challenges for responsiveness and accountability in a province dominated by rurally-oriented provincial governments. The chapter then explores the four issue areas in turn, focusing on the implications of multilevel governance for policy development, with an emphasis on key recent high profile cases. In each area, key decisions reveal problems of responsiveness and coordination, which produce suboptimal policies or missed opportunities. In federal property, promising proposals for multimodal transport nodes and recreational facilities on surplus defence lands were derailed, while federal goals of promoting social housing were entirely neglected. In infrastructure, the centerpiece policy of cleaning the harbour was delayed and eventually used an outmoded technology that sometimes does not work properly; meanwhile, rural and suburban interests pushed transport projects detrimental to neighbourhoods in the urban core. On image building, the high profile bid for the Commonwealth Games was abandoned amidst intergovernmental miscommunication and discord; efforts to balance heritage and development were undermined by provincial interference favouring skyscrapers and downtown concentration that threatens historic streetscapes. Finally, urban Aboriginal policy is underdeveloped and requires substantial additional support from federal and provincial actors to meet Aboriginal needs. The chapter concludes by assessing the implications of this record of reversals and ineffectiveness for multilevel governance in this province and by outlining potential changes to restore a genuine urban government structure for Halifax.

## FROM HISTORIC COMMUNITY
## TO CONTEMPORARY METROPOLIS

An historic community facing contemporary challenges, Halifax is a distinctive blend of traditional and contemporary economic, architectural, and cultural forms. Founded in 1749 as a British naval outpost, Halifax developed around the port and citadel, and it long remained an important military outpost and node for transatlantic shipping. Halifax pioneered in Canadian journalism, finance, and education before losing status to larger centres. Based on British Caribbean commerce in the mid 1800s, Halifax experienced diversification into sail-based shipbuilding and processing. The era of rail and steel undermined Halifax, and the early 1900s saw corporate consolidation, political marginalization, and economic stagnation (Acheson 1977). Consolidation of finance, transport, and industry in central Canada hampered adjustment to demobilization and economic change. Halifax did not recover much during World War II, as federal military and industrial policy favoured other regions even in shipbuilding. Regional leaders challenged federal policies, designed for electorally-dominant central Canada, which worsened economic weakness (Forbes 1979). Post-war alterations in federal policy like equalization and regional development, despite imperfections, made Halifax into a centre of administration and commerce for the Atlantic provinces.

Originally covering the core peninsula between the Harbour and the Northwest Arm, Halifax annexed several smaller entities in the early 1970s. Suburbs grew across the harbour in Dartmouth after construction of bridges in 1955 and 1970 and later in Bedford and Sackville. Since the 1970s, the downtown area has blossomed, with restoration, new construction, and improved access to dockside, which have drawn citizens and tourists alike. Current projects threaten to crowd out some historic districts as demand for office space increases; heritage preservation remains a constant source of controversy. Though based around public institutions and governance, Halifax developed a self-sustaining economy with sufficient critical mass to attract significant private investment in retail, industrial, and new service sectors (Macdonald 2006, 18). The harbour remains crucial: shipping now approaches six million metric tons annually, one-third containerized (Greater Halifax Partnership 2007).

Halifax's metropolitan population increased 26 percent between 1971 and 2001, from 264,421 to 360,000 inhabitants (Halifax Regional

Municipality, 2006c). Its economy produces 47 per cent of Nova Scotia's and 20 percent of Atlantic Canada's GDP (*Chronicle Herald*, 12 February 2007, A6). Unemployment rates are below national averages at 4.5 percent in 2006–07, with 70 percent labour force participation. Twenty-five thousand post-secondary students add to the vibrancy of the city. Populated by the British, Halifax gradually and uncomfortably dealt with diversity. From Edward Cornwallis's notorious bounty on Mi'kmaq scalps, to Halifax's role in the expulsion of the Acadians, to the relocation of the black community from Africville in the 1960s (Clairmont and Magill 1973), Halifax has experienced racial tension. Alongside Indigenous and African Canadian populations, a Lebanese community emerged from the 1800s. Karma Dzong Buddhists transplanted their headquarters from Colorado in 1985; 800 professionals from this community brought new cultural and business ventures (Jones 1991, F1). Immigrants are drawn by a healthy economy as Halifax outpaces the rest of the Maritimes in growth and diversity.

## MUNICIPAL AMALGAMATION: SUBMERGING THE URBAN

By the 1990s, four municipalities governed the Halifax region: Halifax, Dartmouth, the Town of Bedford, and Halifax County, a sprawling rural area. To rationalize costs, the province experimented with transregional entities like Metro Transit, but it soon adopted a "consolidationist" approach to create a "stronger and more accountable municipal government, greater efficiency in the provision of services and more fairness in allocating costs to residents" (Sancton 2002, 35).

In 1996, the provincial Liberals arranged a forced merger of Metropolitan Halifax, including the entire county, urban and rural. The government predicted savings of $18 million annually, with reduced taxes and increased economic activity (Canadian Press Newswire 1994). The unilateral approach resembled mergers elsewhere in Canada, with no plebiscite to gauge support or provide legitimacy (Feldman and Graham 1981, 167). Efficiencies and cost savings were the stated objectives (Sancton 2001, 548). The new Halifax Regional Municipality incorporated vast districts from the former county that will not urbanize in the foreseeable future, which created long-term challenges of "serving both urban and rural residents simultaneously" (Sancton 2002, 64). Amalgamation essentially submerged urban areas in an oversized, rural-based entity that is unable to effectively advocate for urban interests. In essence, there is no city, only a municipality, which is not conducive to promotion of urban interests.

The HRM merger reflected the shifting character of multilevel government in Canada, in an era of fiscal restraint and federal off-loading of costs to provinces, which had to reorganize municipal finances to compensate. In Igor Vojnovic's words

The new surge in the municipal consolidation advocacy is linked with political and fiscal trends common to all the provinces. As the federal government shifts a greater portion of the financial burden on the provinces, the provinces readjust their own finances by placing greater fiscal responsibility for local governance on the municipalities. In this process of fiscal reorganization, the provinces want to promote the rationalization of municipal functions by attempting to improve municipal efficiency, hence the push for consolidation. (Vojnovic 2000b, 412)

The province viewed amalgamation as a solution to crushing debt (Stewart 2000, 205), but the "forced" merger bred "resentment" between levels of government (Vojnovic 2000b, 412).

The HRM covers 5,577 square kilometers, which is larger than Prince Edward Island. It includes 200 communities, mostly rural. HRM has twenty-three municipal districts, represented by regional councillors. The mayor is elected-at-large. The municipality is governed by the council and chief administrative officer (CAO). HRM "assigns all administrative responsibility to the CAO, who reports directly to the elected council" (Halifax Regional Municipality, 2006c). The mixed public responses on HRM's tenth anniversary indicated persisting disparate interests and loyalties. The conurbation is diverse, with 70 percent of residents crowded into 5 percent of the municipality near Halifax Harbour; the huge rural areas contain only 30 percent of the population (Vojnovic 2000a, 65). Planners suggest that the "unique blend of urban and rural geography is a defining characteristic. It is our strength, not our weakness." The blend is said to be "one of interdependence rather than irreconcilable differences" (Halifax Regional Municipality 2005, 6). However, urban-rural divisions have created intramunicipal tension, as issues like highways, taxes and landfills, heritage conservation, and specific transit and recreation projects pit rural and suburban councillors against those from the urban core.

The existence of such deep intramunicipal tensions has intensified what many respondents see as a political system with a democratic deficit, in which accountability is not a priority for city officials. This has been dramatically demonstrated by some recent high profile confrontations over infrastructure projects. Divided votes on road expansion and high-rise projects give the impression that residents in the urban core have been disenfranchised, outvoted by suburban and rural councillors. Notably, the use of police force and multiple arrests at protests against the Chebucto Road widening project in 2008 suggests a willingness to use coercion to impose measures developed by officials and consultants, with minimal popular input. In-camera meetings on development and zoning enhance the perception that the city is out of touch, notwithstanding high-profile consultation in the regional planning process. In addition, further undermining accountability to urban voters, the provincial Utilities and Review Board (URB) can overrule city decisions on zoning, planning, and development (Myrden 2009).

The four policy areas examined in this chapter will be assessed with a focus on the quality of policy and the health of democracy in the HRM. Democracy for this author refers to a system of accountability in which citizen interests are at the forefront. Of particular importance in this context are the municipal administration's responsiveness to both citizens and council, and council's responsiveness to a diversity of preferences and interests in the amalgamated city. The cases, which provide further evidence of Halifax's democratic deficit, will assess whether this deficit can be attributed to the complexities of multilevel governance, and whether responsiveness can be improved by reconfiguring collaboration among levels of government. The cases reveal tensions between the three levels of government, which often act at cross-purposes. And they indicate a rift between citizens and municipal decision makers in a social setting that favours inputs by selected interests and is compounded by tensions between urban and rural interests in the outsized HRM.

FEDERAL PROPERTY

The immense public sector in this capital city and regional governance centre makes the disposal of public lands and buildings significant. "Publicly-owned property in the Capital District makes up approximately 50 percent of the land area," encompassing transport, defence and port facilities as well as administrative buildings and Crown lands. "A strategy around the disposal and development of public lands is needed to ensure the region benefits long-term" (Halifax Regional Municipality Regional Planning Project 2003, 3). The cases of federal property disposal and conversion discussed here indicate that an effective strategy has yet to be implemented. Respondents suggested that Halifax has a passive approach and is not proactive in seeking uses for federal property, particularly for social housing. These cases of federal property dispersion illustrate the halting, uncoordinated nature of the process.

Halifax has been affected by the downsizing of defence properties, notably the Shearwater airbase near Dartmouth in the 1990s. Most of this large base was turned over to Canada Lands Corporation (CLC). CLC serves "as a real estate agent when it resells some these properties ... as a developer servicing lots for sale to home builders and as serviced industrial sites," or as a service provider, "building/owning/managing business and industrial parks" (Watson 2003). CLC is mandated to seek commercial value for surplus properties. The Department of National Defence (DND) kept one quarter of the site for helicopter operations but transferred fixed-wing aircraft to Greenwood. DND is a major employer, and its bases have been economic mainstays in HRM. An official noted, "We have a long history with DND and the closing of Shearwater was a huge hit for us, although any reduction of DND's sizeable and very valuable presence for the municipality is always a concern" (Watson 2003, 34).

To preserve economic activity, base closures must be handled effectively and sustainable uses found for the properties. However, delays in redeveloping Shearwater illustrate how personal and partisan agendas complicate the process. With well-developed runways, Shearwater is proximate to rail, highway, and port facilities – perfect for an intermodal transport node. Business leaders suggested the base, which also had extensive land for commercial development, could be expanded to handle post-Panamax container ships, which are too large to pass though the Panama Canal. It could also become a site for just-in-time manufacturing, with no peer on the eastern seaboard (Macdonald 2000). A private group, Shearwater Development Corporation (SDC), received $2.5 million to attract business, including air cargo ventures, but the company went out of business in 1999 and was sued by creditors and the city for unpaid taxes (*Chronicle Herald*, 24 August 1999, A5). The corporation blamed DND for not ceding valuable waterfront properties or providing links between buildings. DND did not even turn over a full runway (the middle was retained for military use). The province accused Ottawa of overcharging for land and refused to bail out SDC without a right of first refusal on land use, which CLC rules prohibited since federal agencies had first choice (*Daily News*, 8 February 1999, 5). After the collapse of the Shearwater Development Corporation, DND sold 373.12 hectares to the CLC, though later swapping some hectares to meet changing requirements. DND's decision to upgrade the helicopter contingent and convert Shearwater to a heliport (DND Backgrounder 2007), remove old runways, and continue naval use permitted only limited commercial, light industrial and residential development. Hence, a lucrative opportunity for intermodal port development was missed in part due to intergovernmental infighting. But some stakeholders argued that renewed DND investment in the heliport and commitment to its continuance provided the best alternative for the site (Interview 70).

Shannon Park, a downsized base in Dartmouth with highway and coastal access, brought together all four policy areas: federal property, infrastructure, image building, and urban Aboriginals. The Shannon Park site was mired in bureaucratic uncertainty involving DND, Canada Lands Company, First Nations communities, and municipal actors, which delayed redevelopment of boarded-up military housing. The local school provided French immersion and the community sought to ensure its viability. DND gave the school to the school board but held on to the rest of the site. A successful land claim was made on a portion of the property by a Mi'kmaq community, which had earlier been relocated to Millbrook (*The Coast*, 29 January 2004). This claim then influenced subsequent debates over use of this surplus DND land.

Social groups like the Affordable Housing Association of Nova Scotia (AHANS) proposed making buildings available quickly for affordable housing, which was in short supply. Residents of this high-density district, which has many low-cost apartment complexes, feared social housing would compound existing social problems. Opposition to affordable housing was led by the District 9 Citizens' group and by high profile political figures, one of whom declared, "Shannon Park will not be more social housing while I am alive – should not, will not and shall not happen while I am alive!" (Interview 17). AHANS believed that community resistance was based on "misconceptions" (Interview 18). Delays caused a loss of potential funds from the National Housing Initiative (NHI), a Canada Mortgage and Housing Corporation program to help fund low-cost homes. Social actors suggested that HRM's disinterest in affordable housing contributed to this missed opportunity. Compared to other similarly-sized cities, Halifax did not maximize potential contributions from the NHI. A federal MP suggested that the problems with property disposal reflected bureaucratic conflicts and politicians' desire to leave a legacy; despite federal policy promoting social housing, the stigma made conversion contentious (Interview 4).

Plans for social housing at Shannon Park were pushed aside by the Commonwealth Games bid after 2005, which is discussed in detail below. Commonwealth Park, with a new stadium, aquatic centre, and field house, was to help attract sporting events and franchises in professional soccer or football and leave a legacy to the HRM. Environmentally-friendly housing at the 6,000-bed athletes' village would provide a residential component, with "a marina, ferry terminal, and walking trails" (Smulders 2005). The collapse of the games bid in March 2007 again left the Shannon site mired in uncertainty, though new proposals for sports complexes, social housing, and ferry connections have surfaced (Taylor 2009). The site remains fallow as of 2011, but has been proposed as the location for a stadium designed to attract the 2015 Women's Soccer World Cup to the city, as the booster coalition tries a new approach to gain taxpayer support for a sports stadium.

These cases demonstrate the uncoordinated character of multilevel interaction on federal property. Inter-jurisdictional and inter-agency rivalries limit efforts to ensure best use; at the same time, the lure of profit and property taxes links city and developers and limits influence by social forces, helping to marginalize social concerns and sideline proposals for social housing.

INFRASTRUCTURE PROGRAMS

Infrastructure development is crucial to urban development and is often subject to intense political debate (Andrew and Morrison 2002, 237–9). Several federal infrastructure initiatives have contributed to funding HRM projects, including rural and suburban sewer and water upgrades, recreation and sports facilities, and community centres. The Municipal Rural Infrastructure Fund has been used to construct rural fire stations and provide well upgrades. City officials express awareness of constitutional constraints, as dealings with Ottawa must respect provincial priorities; but federal-municipal and tri-level interactions on infrastructure are nonetheless evident in this field. Despite helpful changes in attitudes, some provincial agencies remain inflexible and "difficult" (Interview 10). The city has ambitious plans for infrastructure – a high-speed ferry, arterial roadways, modernized storm water and wastewater piping, rural broadband expansion, recreation facilities, and suburban services. The key problem is the province's and city's lack of financing, which makes federal contributions essential (Halifax Regional Municipality 2006a, 1–2, 7–8).

One project dominated multilevel infrastructure debates for years – the much-delayed Halifax harbour cleanup. Although the harbour provides much of the city's ambience, its waters have been spoiled by the continual dumping of untreated sewage. Ottawa's assistance was essential for the ambitious Harbour Solutions Project, which aimed to channel sewage through water treatment facilities. The need was evident for years, with loss of recreational use and embarrassing odours and beach refuse plaguing citizens and tourists. The city raised charges on municipal water bills for years, with some funds used for sewer upgrades. Amalgamation complicated matters as some communities treated sewage prior to joining HRM and disputed whether it was fair for all residents to pay a surcharge. A surplus, accumulated from the surcharge, committed the city to the project before it had secured federal or provincial funding. On its own, HRM sought bids for construction and operation of the treatment system (Flinn 1999, 7). Yet proposals were debated for three decades while sewage volume rose to 100 million litres per day (Jackson 2000, A10). The long history of this project demonstrates the problems of communication, political and partisan tension, and fiscal pressures affecting multilevel governance in HRM.

In the late 1990s, after a tri-level agreement on funding the harbour cleanup had collapsed, city officials proposed a public-private partnership, which would allow a private consortium to run the sewage treatment plants for thirty years. However, a consultative exercise recommended in favour of a public utility. "The area of greatest concern is that of ensuring that the community's dependence on a service as important as sewage treatment is reflected in guarantees that the service is driven by public priorities as opposed to private sector priorities. Ultimately, the safeguard is public ownership and control of the facilities" (Harbour Solutions Advisory Committee 1998, 26). Some councillors felt the city could run the plants more economically, while others feared pressure from a private operator for surcharges to boost profits (Simpson 2000, A1). Business leaders and think tanks supported the public-private option. The Chamber of Commerce declared the private-public partnership (P3) option was in the "interests of taxpayers" by blending the "public interest" with the "discipline" and "efficiency" of the market (Doig 2000, A2). This approach eventually gained the support of the mayor and top city officials.

While council called for a "shadow bid" to price the costs of going it alone, the private sector preferred a "reference bid," which private bidders could review and match. Officials opted for the latter approach. Critical councillors claimed bureaucrats ignored council and rigged the process to favour private firms. One councillor suggested, "I shouldn't use the word sham but this exercise to produce a dummy bid ... I'll bet you the first $100 that comes out of my pocket it comes back and recommends a private-sector approach" (Maich 2000, A1). The "reference bid" was supervised by a firm that had already reported in favour of a public-private system. A local editorial noted, "The call for proposals went out during a two-week council break with the mayor and some councillors out of town at a conference; even as a coincidence the appearances are murky" (*Daily News*, 5 June 2000, 10).

Officials proceeded with the public-private approach advocated by the Chamber of Commerce. Critics claimed this indicated that business interests had distorted the bid process. A spokesperson for environmental NGOs noted that, when input was sought, most public participants agreed that a private sector approach was the least desirable option. Nonetheless, it quickly became dominant, suggesting that public input was ignored. Exclusion of environmental and community groups from policy design and implementation resulted in a policy that was not in the public interest; outside consultants, managers, and engineers took precedence over the public (Interview 15). Also worrisome were conditions in the tender that barred parties from revealing details about their bids or the city's process for deciding among them. Unions expressed concerns about secrecy, hidden costs, lack of input, and loss of jobs. A CUPE leader declared, "for it not to be done out in the open in a transparent way with citizens being able to have input is, frankly, an abomination as far as democracy is concerned" (Power and Schneidereit 2000, A10).

While critics pressed for the process to be a core election issue, little changed after Peter Kelly, an opponent of the P3 approach, was elected mayor in 2000. In 2002, a private consortium, the Halifax Regional Environmental Partnership, received a sixty-year contract (twice the initial proposed term), conditional on receipt of funds from other levels of government (Moar 2003, 3). Critics condemned the share of the costs to be borne by regressive municipal taxes and noted that one consortium partner had been fined for environmental infractions on European projects (Mcdonough 2002, B2). Tension emerged between the city and the province over how to manage relations with Ottawa in seeking funds for the project. Premier John Hamm initially requested Canada Strategic Infrastructure funds only for highways (electorally useful for a rural-based government) and assumed that other federal dollars would be provided for the harbour project. Mayor Kelly felt that this threatened the project. Some councillors and MLAs criticized the mayor's "interference," which could do "substantial damage" to provincial-federal relations (Flinn 2002, 4).

There was a shortfall in funds when Ottawa said it would only match Nova Scotia's $30 million pledge, threatening to delay or derail the project. Eventually, Ottawa settled on a contribution of $60 million for the cleanup (Infrastructure Canada 2004), but it expected the city to fund $30 million in other projects as a condition (Interview 6). The city planned to raise $210 million from water surcharges. The extended bickering revealed significant partisan and ideological divisions across levels of government. And taxpayers faced hikes in pollution control charges, which had increased over the years; while $71 million had been accumulated since 1974 on the pollution control charges, council allowed some to be spent on related works (Interview 6). One commentator summed up public frustration: "taxpayers are the losers in the harbour mess, victims of three levels of government playing politics with an important matter of public policy" (Rodenhiser 2002; Simpson 2002, A1).

Ultimately, the public-private partnership proved untenable. A report from the Canadian Environmental Assessment Agency complicated matters, suggesting that the proposed primary treatment technology inadequately screened industrial waste from dairies or breweries and could leave water quality below environmental mandates. In 2003, HRM dissolved its contract with the Halifax Regional Environmental Partnership in a dispute over who would pay fines for inadequate water quality. The city portrayed this as a cost-saving approach, which freed it to pursue better options. Environmental interests sought to implement newer green technologies like solar aquatics. Instead, the city turned to a local construction partner to proceed with the primary treatment system. Critics decried the secrecy around these decisions and the impression of ineffectiveness surrounding the city's handling of the project was high (Howe 2003, 18). African Canadian leaders took HRM to the Human Rights Commission when one plant was located in a poor, predominately black neighborhood in the north end. The commission ruled that the choice had not been discriminatory, but the community believed the city had ignored the impact on the neighbourhood (*Daily News*, 15 September 2005, 11.) The city held consultations and the Department of Municipal Affairs gave money for a Community Integration Fund to integrate the plants into communities (Interview 6).

In the implementation period, a working committee representing all three levels of government coordinated regularly and major changes were discussed in private prior to public announcements. The province used its control of approvals to influence the project and did not allow decision making by Ottawa and the city bilaterally. Local politicians complained that political interference, driven by electoral priorities outside HRM, prevented a constructive provincial role (Interview 8). The city had difficulty managing its contacts with the many federal agencies involved in the project – Fisheries and Oceans, Defence, Environment, Parks Canada, etc. It did not help that provincial and federal contributions were inadequate, which forced HRM to choose a less effective system (Interview 15). The confused consultations and protracted process suggest serious problems of partisanship, jurisdictional jealousy, and financial constraint, which do not bode well for future major infrastructure commitments.

Despite some technical problems in the rocky terrain, construction of the pipelines and plants proceeded on schedule. Officials state that technical considerations eventually overrode political ones (Interview 6). Environmental activists disagree; they suggest that sustainable, effective options were neglected because of business influence. In 2008, two oceanfront beaches were declared safe for swimming after contaminants measured below harmful levels – at least when heavy rains did not flush runoff into the harbour. Yet, mechanical problems after power outages remained troublesome (Smith 2009). Openness and accountability were also questioned. In 2009, one of the plants went offline indefinitely, forcing removal of some filter screens and a return of odours and floating sewage just in time for a global tall ships celebration; council discussed the problems in secret session (*Chronicle Herald*, 2 June 2009). Since then, the system has functioned, though water quality is often lower after major rainstorms.

IMAGE BUILDING AND ECONOMIC PROMOTION

Halifax banks on its image as a modern city with ecological, historical, and cultural amenities, including a burgeoning alternative music scene and a plethora of theatre, arts, and literary festivals. Halifax has moved away from its sleepy image as a conservative seaport; downtown is vibrant, especially in summer. HRM capitalizes on these impressions by presenting Halifax as a "smart city" with its educational, medical, administrative, and research venues, lively student life, and cultural

diversity. Led by the Greater Halifax Partnership, the approach draws
on conceptions of the "learning city" since "urban contexts that support
the growth and development of the creative class will be best positioned
to reap the full benefits of the knowledge economy" (Plumb, Leverman,
and McGray 2007, 43). Promotions emphasize the competitive advantages of a city with triple the national level of post-secondary graduates
per capita. Critics argue that this coerces citizens to support a corporate
competitiveness agenda: "Haligonians are left with the niggling feeling
that, if they do not get learning to get on board the knowledge economy,
they might end up in serious social, cultural, and economic trouble"
(Plumb, Leverman, and McGray 2007, 43).

Efforts to change the reputation of Halifax as a staid centre governed
by traditional elites have met with success. High profile events like the
G-7 summit in 1995 raised the city's profile. Hosting of national finals
in college basketball and world championships in figure skating and
hockey instilled confidence that the city could punch above its weight in
such visible ventures. John DeMont argues that "while everyone's eyes
were elsewhere, Halifax was reinventing itself as a buoyant, forward-
looking place to do business" (DeMont 2005, 35). It is now the largest
magnet for immigrants east of Quebec, and it boasts an increasingly
diverse community with many recent arrivals in business and professional circles. The economy has reduced its dependence on government
and military activity as new industries like biotechnology, offshore
energy, and information technology have emerged (DeMont 2004, 26).
Investments in harbour boardwalks, museums, a cruise ship facility and
casino have attracted tourists; the city has emphasized both heritage
(like the Titanic connection) and contemporary cultural events and amenities. Halifax has emerged as a major tourist destination.

After amalgamation, accelerating economic and cultural change
prompted the city to rethink its image and priorities. A comprehensive
regional plan was developed in a process that the city believed provided
ample opportunity for popular input. While interviewees suggest it
reached preconceived conclusions based on staff and consultants
reports, the report claimed that the

   public consultation process used in developing this plan ensured all
   citizens had an opportunity to participate and to provide input, and
   emphasized information sharing and collaboration. It involved region-
   wide, large-scale participatory approaches including public information meetings, open houses, focus groups, surveys, workbooks, and

smaller more informal initiatives such as one-on-one meetings, local community meetings, fairs and events, and meetings with various community groups. A key goal of the consultation process was to target and engage those who might not normally participate in a planning process. (Halifax Regional Municipality 2006b)

The ambitious plan set guidelines for future development and expansion in HRM based on an optimistic vision of the city's future prospects, as a centre with sufficient agglomerative capacity to face the challenges of changing technology, demography, and global competition. It emphasized sustainable growth, balancing heritage and ecology with economic dynamism. The plan set guidelines for integrated land use and planning that focused on growth in compact zones to permit ecological preservation alongside dynamic economic nodes, efficiently connected by infrastructure (HRM, Regional Municipal Planning Strategy Halifax 2006).

Yet the most prominent recent image-building venture occurred outside this planning process – the failed bid to bring the 2014 Commonwealth Games to Halifax. After disappointing losses in bids to host the 1994 and 2010 games, Halifax secured the support of Commonwealth Games Canada and was Canada's official bid city for this prestigious sporting event. As David Black indicates, Halifax's repeated bids demonstrate the role of "a persistent 'booster coalition' that has doggedly pursued an events-based strategy for enhancing Halifax's profile, identity, and development on a global stage, with a strong focus on promoting the important tourism industry of the city and region" (Black 2008, 474–6). The ambitious proposal had implications for infrastructure and renewal of federal property at Shannon Park, to be renamed Commonwealth Park. The bid committee proposed construction of a stadium that could host professional franchises and amateur sports events, athletes' housing that could be used for residential purposes, and a multisport facility. A stadium had long been sought by the "booster coalition" to attract a professional football or soccer franchise. The stadium "would have been HRM's new venue for large, open-air cultural and spectator events. With a permanent seating capacity of 25,000, it would have offered numerous hosting opportunities for the municipality" (Halifax 2014 n.d.).

The province and city appeared to coordinate well in the bidding process and stressed the contribution of the project to Halifax's image. The mayor and premier jointly declared that the Commonwealth Games "represent an opportunity to showcase our people, our history, and our accomplishments to the world. Indeed, if these Games are awarded to

Canada – with HRM as host city – the event will leave a legacy that would pay dividends to the municipality, the province, the region, and the nation for generations to come." This legacy was to be built on "the remarkable co-operation" among the city, province, business, sports associations, other Atlantic provinces and cultural communities "that characterized our successful domestic bid" (Hamm and Kelly 2006, A7). The bid was supported by a coalition representing business, including media and energy companies and athletic and sports associations who sought upgraded facilities. Supporters accused critics of "resisting progress" and hindering Halifax's move from "quaintness" to "dynamism" ("As Halifax Fades from View" 2007).

At an advanced stage in the process, however, the bid was abandoned after the province and city withdrew funding out of concern over escalating costs. A consultant suggested that the proposed $1.36 billion budget was a "floor" that did not preclude escalating costs. The province decided not to fund the games, and the city joined in announcing the abandonment of the bid. Despite extensive lobbying by the mayor and premier, failure to secure increased federal support beyond $400 million cemented this decision (Dooley 2007, 5). Bid officials argued that they were still trying to reduce the cost when the plug was pulled. There was a $425 million gap between what the city and province believed they could raise and what the games would require, if costs did not escalate. Business sought to keep the plan alive, to reap the economic benefits that government consultants had allegedly neglected (Fraser 2007, A1).

Despite behind-the-scenes efforts, there was no change in Ottawa's contribution. Councillors criticized Ottawa's lack of interest, since its $400 million limit was set before detailed costing was ready. The mix of cash and property and other in-kind federal contributions remained unclear. The bid also suffered from a change of federal regime to the new Conservatives under Stephen Harper, who held a different view on municipal-federal relations, preferring to defer to provinces. Liberal critics argued their contribution would have been twice as high as the Harper government's maximum, but cost overruns on the 2010 Vancouver Winter Olympics made Ottawa reluctant to support another such project.

According to interviewees, there were also local problems with the bid process. Some councillors noted the local organizer's tendency to complete elaborate plans, insist on secrecy and then come to council for ratification and funding, which undermined council's trust and eroded public support. A "more transparent, accountable, and forthright" process, with stronger direction by the city could avoid such an embarrassing fiasco in future (Interview 7). Bid organizers countered that the province and municipal levels handled the process poorly. There was "a disconnect between the committee and the regional council, as well as the provincial cabinet" (Interview 7), resulting from council and cabinet reluctance to accept full briefings from the bid committee. Bid organizers even claimed that the mayor (who was skeptical of the games bid from the start) made the decision to pull out without consulting council, which was allegedly illegal.

Games supporters suggest that public servants focused on governmental or political responsibilities and did not assess the bid on its merits. The province ignored its own finance officials who determined that the city and province could run the games without a deficit, with costs of $1.3–1.7 billion, "if every homeowner in HRM were to pay $2 additional property tax per month for 7 years" (Interview 1). The mayor and premier focused on residents on fixed incomes who feared tax hikes. According to bid officials, the politicians ignored economic spinoffs, which organizers estimated at $2.3 billion in revenues, 18,000 jobs, and a one million dollar increase in GDP. Overall, the "provincial and municipal governments were working at cross-purposes" and chose a "shortsighted" approach based on political survival. "Real leaders" would try to "inspire people to be a part of something ... something that we can do together ... something that the working class can cheer for and be a part of, and which would boost the mental and physical well-being required for a well-functioning society and economy" (Interview 1).

Not all local actors mourned the demise of the bid. Some suggested that the process was driven by an "old boys' network" of local business interests (Bousequet 2008) and that the collapse of the bid was beneficial, as experience elsewhere demonstrates the long run legacy of the games would most likely be debt (Mosher 2007, C4).

In addition, the demise of the bid refocused attention on the development and implementation of the new regional plan. The plan called for development approaches that spread growth across the region and avoided concentration downtown. The plan also noted that "the Regional Centre's vibrancy, animation and economic health will be strengthened through the cultivation of a compact, civic inspired and human-scaled urban fabric of streets, blocks and buildings" (Halifax Regional Municipality – Urban Design Vision Statement 2007).

Yet the city's commitment to the guidelines elaborated in the plan is unclear, since both provincial officials and local business actors favor downtown intensification. As of 2011, new downtown high-rise projects are under construction, with provincial government support, as part of an effort to build a concentrated financial services sector. One observer suggests some projects were intentionally rushed into place before the implementation of HRMbyDesign guidelines, which streamline development applications and provide for citizen input on heritage protection. This quick action allowed permits to be issued for office towers alongside some of the best heritage streetscapes in the city (Fraser 2008). The provincially-sponsored convention centre, announced in 2011, has also been criticized for threatening the few remaining views of the harbour from Citadel Hill. The province has also considered a paved road through the railway cut from west end to downtown (which has been proposed as an urban "greenway") to move trucks to the central container port. Such actions suggest the province may work to support business and employment goals over those of heritage preservation and community consultation. The image of Halifax could be much different in future if implementation of many such projects proceeds, lucrative to contractors yet destructive of the ambience.

## URBAN ABORIGINAL POLICY

Halifax has a limited Aboriginal presence. Some 1 percent of HRM's population, around 5,320 persons, reported Aboriginal background in the 2006 census. This number was up from 0.6 percent in 1996. The small population has resulted in limited application of federal policies to HRM. A federal website with an Urban Directory of Programs and Services does not provide information for any Atlantic municipality, listing only cities in western Canada (Aboriginal Canada Portal 2007). The Urban Aboriginal Strategy, a national initiative funded by Indian and Northern Affairs Canada, designed to reduce the level of disparity between urban Aboriginal peoples and other Canadians, is not being implemented in HRM. The Homelessness Partnership Initiative is also not enacted there.

A Nova Scotia Framework Agreement on Aboriginal Treaty Rights/ Umbrella Agreement was signed on 7 June 2002 between the Canadian government, province of Nova Scotia, and Mi'kmaq people. Nova Scotia has created an Office of Aboriginal Affairs to promote coordination within the provincial government. Its mandate is to "represent Nova Scotia's interests effectively in intergovernmental, bilateral, and trilateral initiatives and negotiations; promote Aboriginal economic development and community capacity building across Nova Scotia; and enhance the awareness of Aboriginal heritage and culture within government" (Sterling

Research 2000, 2). This agreement could provide an institutional node for involving the province and the city in urban Aboriginal issues, but many respondents reported limited visibility to date.

Some local urban Aboriginal initiatives do exist in Halifax. The city is home to the Mi'kmaq Friendship Centre, which receives federal funding as well as tax breaks and grants from HRM. The centre provides "structured, social-based programming for Urban Aboriginal Peoples, while serving as a focal point for gathering, community functions and events" (Interview 16). Local revenues were recently provided to assess the condition of the current building and to evaluate alternative properties for the Friendship Centre; centre leaders also met with municipal officials in an unsuccessful bid to seek space in a vacated HRM building. HRM community grant programs have provided project-specific grants to support organizations like "Nations in a Circle," which organizes First Nations' arts exhibits.

However, the HRM Regional Plan, which makes reference to cultural diversity, does not refer explicitly to First Nations concerns. Cultural programs, heritage protections, and the like seem to exclude sites and events of importance to First Nations. The First Nations community lacks visibility, though construction of a new friendship centre in the urban core could increase this profile. An annual powwow on the Halifax Commons in summer has become high profile and popular. But jurisdictional rivalries, political infighting, and poor communication have limited the scope of effective policy. Notably, the province has not pressed for inclusion in the Urban Aboriginal Strategy. Exclusion of municipal decision makers from intergovernmental policy discussions has hampered comprehensive responses to the complex problems faced by urban Aboriginal peoples (Interview 11).

Given this dearth of activity, it is not surprising that most of those interviewed spoke of unmet needs. For instance, one respondent noted a gap in health care for off-reserve versus on-reserve persons. Urban Aboriginals use the same health care system as other citizens, with limited provision for translation services via the Confederacy of Mainland Mi'kmaq. As noted above, urban governments have confined their activities to cultural events and multicultural and race relations policies, not First Nation-specific initiatives. Federal and provincial initiatives have focused mostly on reserve-based services, even though one-third of Aboriginal peoples in the province reside in HRM. This leaves unaddressed gaps in cultural awareness, sensitivity, and access to core services like health care and post-secondary education (Interview 5).

One way in which the federal government has a presence in Aboriginal affairs in the region is via the Aboriginal Business Services Network (ABSN). With support from the Atlantic Canada Opportunities Agency (ACOA) and working with Canadian business service centres, the ABSN is a point of contact and information source for Aboriginal business interests. It partners with thirteen Aboriginal communities and two Aboriginal organizations in Nova Scotia. It provides no-fee information on starting a business, growing a business, writing a business plan, and marketing strategies. This initiative coordinates the activities of ACOA and other federal departments that support First Nations business initiatives, but there is no local or provincial collaboration; coordination occurs between ACOA, ABSN, and First Nations leaders. While ABSN officials saw many opportunities for action, they have so little engagement with city government that they are uncertain what role the municipality could play in this field (Interview 14). Another initiative, Aboriginal Business Canada, run by Indian and Northern Affairs, collaborates with ACOA only, focuses on individual First Nations citizens, both rural and urban, and sees no need for involvement by municipal officials (Interview 13).

Leaders of Aboriginal organizations in the province assert that they have no relationship and few contacts with municipal officers or agencies. The province is beginning to reach out, and some programs are being extended for off-reserve populations in the housing field, for instance. As more gaps are identified, more consultation with urban communities might develop (Interview 5). Nonetheless, some of the excellent initiatives pioneered in western Canadian cities like Winnipeg have yet to be emulated in the east. Halifax could benefit from adult education initiatives, for example, which have integrated Native Canadians into the workforce in other cities (Silver, Klyne, and Simard 2003). Existing consultative mechanisms, such as the tripartite forum, did not include municipal representatives, though they did improve federal and provincial collaboration with First Nations groups. One observer suggested the local government did little beyond cultural celebrations, only occasionally attending special events at the Friendship Centre. City support remained limited even though some of the Friendship Centre's programs, like the needle exchange, served many clients, including non-Aboriginals.

As more First Nations people live in cities, they will not have access to on-reserve benefits and services. HRM's small Aboriginal population may make the problems less visible, but no less real for those Aboriginals cut off from necessary support. The unique character of multilevel governance in this area will clearly require distinct arrangements, which may never be fully extended to cities with small First Nations populations. Respondents were pessimistic that much would change in this respect. There is neither the demand from the community, nor the will from government to extend such arrangements beyond limited measures respecting cultural awareness and sensitivity. Respondents suggested that meaningful municipal involvement was unlikely to emerge in the near future, which means that important needs will go unmet.

Across Canada, there is intensive rethinking of urban Aboriginal policy development and implementation. Even in regions where policy is more developed, there are calls for better institutionalization of federal-provincial and municipal involvement in this field (Hanselmann 2003, 8). As Francis Abele suggests, it may take time for a new model that incorporates provincial, city, and Aboriginal governmental and "para-state" organizations in meaningful "partnerships" to emerge and overcome "dysfunctional" relationships with the state across Canada (Abele 2004, 26–7). Whether Nova Scotia's Office of Aboriginal Affairs can help coordinate such institutionalization of links remains to be seen. HRM's intergovernmental capacity would need a significant boost before the city could be a viable participant in such collaborations.

### SUMMARY OF FINDINGS: POLICY PROBLEMS
### AND DEMOCRATIC DEFICITS

The cases investigated here suggest that multilevel governance in Halifax is performing inadequately and the quality, pace, and delivery of policy is seriously affected. Specific successes have occurred in cost sharing on some issues, like urban walkways and wilderness protection. But many respondents reported delays, distorted policy choices, and unfilled needs resulting from poor communications, jurisdictional rivalries, inadequate funding, and partisan conflict. In most fields, it is not that institutional structures at any one level of government are underdeveloped. Rather, it is ineffective consultation and lack of coordination that rankles many in the relevant policy communities. One actor in the urban Aboriginal field, for instance, complained that there "is lots of governance, too much governance, but so much competition between levels of government. There is a lack of communication and collaboration, and government tends to be driven by self interest rather than what is easiest for customers [and] ... everything gets all tangled up, when the municipality is totally excluded from federal programs. The municipality is not at the table; we need more say in water, housing, service issues. Lack of participation almost makes initiatives fail because [cities] are excluded" (Interview 11).

It is not the case that this region and its partner governments are incapable of collaborating. For example, when the provincial government created the Halifax Regional Development Agency, it switched its regional development strategy from attraction of investment to development of local entrepreneurs. Legislative frameworks and financial support were redirected in a sustainable fashion, with arguably positive benefits for the local economy. Since amalgamation, public-private collaboration between HRM and the Chamber of Commerce via the Greater Halifax Partnership has similarly energized aspects of economic and development policy. There are close and open ties between city and provincial bureaucrats and business sector actors on major infrastructure and development initiatives (Halifax Gateway Council 2008).

Nonetheless, the frequent concerns expressed by the respondents about poor communication, interjurisdictional jealousy, political games, and exclusion of social interests presents long-term challenges for multilevel governance in the Halifax region, and Nova Scotia more generally, with implications for the effectiveness and responsiveness of urban public policy. These problems are compounded by the insulation of local policy processes from public opinion. The failure of the current regional governance model to clearly separate urban and rural interests has produced chronic policy tensions within HRM, which have been dealt with in part by removing major development decisions from public scrutiny. Despite high profile planning and consultation exercises, Halifax seems to exemplify what Christopher Leo calls a "disconnect between the bureaucratic and legal theory of planning and the reality on the street." Involvement "in the process of city planning often induces a feeling akin to our experience when we watch a film with excellent special effects. It all looks so real, yet we know it is not" (Leo 2002, 215).

City officials claim that public opinion remains paramount, that "the guy down the street really makes a difference in councilors' opinions" (Interview 10). Yet, social forces interviewed gave conflicting accounts. Some business groups suggested that, "in Nova Scotia, the level of collaboration between the public and private sector is remarkable. I get the sense that, in Nova Scotia, there is probably a better working relationship between the private sector and the provincial, federal, and municipal levels of government than in any other province" (Interview 12). However, other social forces suggested that the city was closed to their views, frequently operated in secret, and marginalized their concerns. One interviewee noted the importance of connecting with city government but remarked, "if I wanted to work more with the province or the city, I wouldn't even know who to approach" (Interview 14). The imbalance in access was reflected in the debates over HRMbyDesign when participants in the HRMbyDesign process were canvassed: "The business community and those who would like to find jobs with them said during the public hearing that they feel their voices have been heard. But large numbers of citizens who have tried to participate in the process feel their voices have not been heard" (Bosquet 2009).

The problems of accountability in Halifax's governance system reflect not only the complexity of intergovernmentalism, or the political power of business, but also a widely perceived elitist culture of top-down decision making at the local level. They reflect traditional biases in decisions and expenditure towards wealthier districts and an aloofness among officials, consultants, and planners. These actors keep their bureaucratic vision of what a modern city should look like paramount, even in the face of popular discontent. There is also a disconnect between urban areas and rural regions, which produces intra-municipal tensions and creates contradictions, like that between traffic inflow and a sustainable urban core. Social constituencies like urban Aboriginals, African Canadians, environmentalists, conservationists, the poor and homeless, and those in need of social housing find their voices marginalized. In the view of many respondents, amalgamation has the illusion of an integrated democratic unit, but the reality is an unaccountable administration and a lack of financial resources to respond to popular demands and community needs.

### CONCLUSIONS: RESTORING URBAN GOVERNANCE?

Halifax is celebrated as birthplace of responsible government in Canada, but, in the opinion of many of those interviewed, HRM appears to suffer from a lack of accountability and democratic deficits. Frequent complaints about closed-door decisions give the appearance of avoidance of accountability. And when the city is disposed to listen to public opinion, it finds itself overridden by provincial priorities and interventions, as in disputes between mayor and premier on downtown development (Smith 2008) or provincial proposals for truck roadways, which may undermine urban greenway initiatives (Lightstone 2009). Weak constituencies like urban Aboriginals or less affluent neighbourhoods have little hope of promoting their concerns and defending their interests. In 2008, on the 250th anniversary of responsible government at Halifax, it was hardly a ringing endorsement of democracy when the sole remaining daily newspaper, in the context of the Chebucto road widening, commented, "Resistance is futile" (Muise and Lightstone 2008).

Improvements might be obtained by clarifying the structures of multilevel governance. First, the federal government must clarify its role in urban affairs to ensure continuity of dialogue and sustainable funding. In addition, clearer, more collegial relationships between provincial and municipal actors, with less political and ideological conflicts could be helpful. The inability of municipal leaders to engage consistently with federal agencies appears to constrain potentially beneficial policy making. The province must embrace more constructive engagement with Ottawa in municipal affairs, given the need for federal leadership, expertise, and funds. The province must become a facilitator and advocate of federal-municipal collaboration; the province needs to be less disruptive and not focused on its own political priorities. Provinces in Canada have significant leeway to rewrite urban charters and organize governance to be more locally responsive, to create a "provincially supervised public participation process" (Leo 2002, 233); but the province must also be proactive to ensure that specific interests with substantial power and resources do not overwhelm councils and work with urban bureaucracies against the larger community, and that multilevel interactions do provide more responsive, transparent governance.

Such changes will need to be both underpinned and supported by governance change at the local level. Greater transparency in the HRM Charter and tighter reins of accountability for urban bureaucrats are essential to ensure council has a meaningful policy role, since some of those interviewed claim the recent increase in discretion for officials has produced undemocratic practices in pursuit of specific development projects. However, simply returning power from technical experts to council will not be sufficient. The oversized nature of HRM and the incorporation of rural districts mean that council does not effectively represent the interests of citizens in the urban core; some of the more contentious recent decisions on infrastructure and development have been taken with enthusiastic support of rural councillors (Bosquet 2009a).

Thus, a true urban centre must be restored in the capital region of Nova Scotia, separate from rural areas. An urban-focused City of Halifax must be recreated in place of the ineffective, unresponsive urban-rural hybrid, which – in conjunction with rural dominance of the legislature

– essentially robs residents of a true urban political voice. There is, in other words, an urgent need to shrink HRM to rational boundaries to produce a council responsive to urban interests. Instead, in 2011 the URB, which clashed with council on some zoning and development matters, imposed a reduction from twenty-three to sixteen councillors without reducing HRM's boundaries, in the name of efficiency. If councillors are overburdened in future, officials may face even less scrutiny, which could prove more problematic for democratic accountability.

Changing relationships with Ottawa and the province, as well as (once again) changing the boundaries of HRM, are both complex and difficult undertakings. But without such changes, Halifax could face policy distortions that favour suburban and developer interests at the expense of social constituencies and local communities. It will likely encounter prolonged conflict-ridden policy processes that result in sub-optimal policies, as seen in many of the cases discussed in this chapter. Halifax's interactions with Ottawa are likely to continue to be constrained unless pressure from electorally influential metropoles elsewhere produces rationalized tri-level relations nationwide, putting pressure on politicians in Nova Scotia to follow suit. Given the dominance of provincial government by rural and development interests as documented in the interviews, as well as limited media scrutiny, reforms to city boundaries and relations with the province are unlikely to occur soon. Nonetheless, the restoration of a genuine urban City of Halifax is necessary to make governance accountable to the interests of residents in this dynamic urban community.

## LIST OF INTERVIEWS

1  Commonwealth Games bid official, 6 August 2007.
2  Commonwealth Games opponent, 2 August 2007.
3  Cultural group consultant, 16 August 2006.
4  Federal MP, August 2 2006.
5  Mi'kmaq policy group advisor, 18 July 2007.
6  Harbour Solutions project official, 25 July 2006.
7  Municipal councillor, 10 July 2007.
8  Municipal councillor, 4 August 2006.
9  Municipal councillor, 11 July 2007.
10  Intergovernmental officials, HRM, 11 July 2006.
11  Municipal finance official 13 August 2007.

12 Business advisory group official, 20 July 2006.
13 Mi'kmaq business group official, 10 September 2007.
14 Mi'kmaq social sector official, 15 August 2007.
15 Environmental group official, 23 July 2006.
16 Mi'kmaq community service officer, 10 August 2007.
17 Retired provincial MLA, 20 July 2006.
18 Social movement official, 6 July 2006.
19 Federal official, 7 July 2006.
20 Municipal official, 17 August 2006.
21 Senior municipal official, 19 July 2006.
22 Business group official, 20 July 1996.
23 Municipal councillor, 27 July 2007.
24 Interest group leader, 2 August 2007.
25 Provincial official, 21 July 2006.
26 Social movement official, 24 July 2006.
27 Senior municipal official, 11 July 2006.
28 Municipal official, 25 July 2006.
29 Mi'kmaq community leader, 18 July 2007.
30 Mi'kmaq community official, 18 July 2007.
31 Mi'kmaq community official, 18 July 2007.
32 Municipal councillor, 11 July 2007.
33 Environmental lobby group leader, 21 July 2006.
34 Business group leader, 6 August 2007.
35 Aboriginal group leader, 15 August 2007.
36 Provincial official, 13 August 2007.
37 Mi'kmaq business group official, 10 September 2007.
38 Business group leader, 18 September 2007.
39 Business group leader, 21 September 2007.
40 Business group leader, 19 September 2007.
41 Federal official, 21 August 2006.
42 Federal Member of Parliament, August 2006.
43 Federal official, September 2006.
44 Federal official, 23 August 2006.
45 Municipal official, 25 August 2006.
46 Municipal official, 25 August 2006.
47 Provincial official, 26 July 2006.
48 Municipal official, 13 July 2006.
49 NGO official, 13 July 2006.
50 Public sector union official, August 2006.
51 Federal official (retired), 16 September 2006.

52 Federal official, 10 October 2006.
53 Provincial official, September 2006.
54 NGO official, September 2006.
55 Provincial official, August 2007.
56 Business lobbyist, August 2006.
57 Municipal official, August 2006.
58 Aboriginal group official, July 2007.
59 Business advisory group official, July 2006.
60 Municipal official, May 2007.
61 Municipal official, May 2007.
62 Provincial official, August 2007.
63 Federal official, 21 August, 2006.
64 Business lobbyist, by email 20 July 2007.
65 Environmental group officer, by email, March 2009.
66 Social movement activist, August 2006.
67 Social historian, by email, April 2009.
68 Higher education official, by email, April 2009.
69 Public housing advocate, September 2007.
70 Business lobbyist, by email, July 2007.

REFERENCES

Abele, Francis. 2004. "Urgent Need, Serious Opportunity: Towards a New Social Model for Canada's Aboriginal Peoples Canadian Policy Research Networks." Ottawa: CPRN Social Architecture Papers Research Report, F 39.
Aboriginal Canada Portal. 2007. "Urban Directory of Aboriginal Programs and Services." Accessed September 2009. http://www.Aboriginalcanada.gc.ca/urban/site.nsf/en/ao31919.html.
Acheson, T.W. 1977. "The Maritimes and 'Empire Canada.'" In *Canada and the Burden of Unity*, edited by D.J. Bercuson, 87–114. Toronto: Gage.
Andrew, Caroline, and Jeff Morrison. 2002. "Infrastructure." In *Urban Policy Issues: Canadian Perspectives*, 2nd ed., edited by Edmund Fowler and David Seigel, 237–50. Don Mills, ON: Oxford University Press.
Black, David. 2008. "Dreaming Big: The Pursuit of 'Second Order' Games as a Strategic Response to Globalization." *Sport in Society* 11 (4):474–6.
Bousequet, Tim. 2008. "Public Money, Private players." *The Coast*, 13 March. http://www.thecoast.ca/Articles-i-2008-03-13-151783.114125_Public_money_private_players.html.
*Canadian Press NewsWire*. 1994. "Super-city Plan Creates Political Storm (Halifax Metropolitan Area)," 27 October.

*Chronicle Herald*. 1999. "City Sues Shearwater Development Corp." 24 August, A5.

– 2007. "Hub Cities Key to our Future." 12 February, A6.

– 2009. "Floatables Discussion Should be Open – Group." 2 June. http:// thechronicleherald.ca/Metro/1125154.html.

Clairmont, Donald H., and Dennis W. Magill. 1973. "Africville Relocation Report Supplement." Halifax: Institute of Public Affairs. http://www.library. dal.ca/ebooks/africville/.

*Daily News*. 1999. "Preparing to Take Off: Shearwater Development Corp. Faces Eviction Today." 8 February, 5.

– 2000. "Council Bypassed in Harbour project." 5 June, 10.

– 2005. "Sewage Plant Site Raises Questions." 15 September, 11.

DeMont, John. 2004. "A Surging Tide of Creative Energy." *Maclean's*, 19 January, 26.

– 2005. "Maritimes Magnet." *Canadian Business* 78, 6 (14 March): 35.

DND Backgrounder. 2007. "Shearwater Construction Projects BG – 07.014." 11 May. http://www.forces.gc.ca/site/newsroom/view_news_e.asp?id=2284.

Doig, Peter. 2000. "Public Private Harbour Solution the Right Way to Go." *Chronicle Herald*, 6 April, D2.

Dooley, Richard. 2007. "Commonwealth Games Support Down Months Before End, Committee Told." *Daily News*, 29 March, 5.

Feldman, Lionel, and Katherine Graham. 1981. "Local Government Reform in Canada." In *Local Government Reform and Reorganization*, edited by Arthur B. Gunlicks, 151–68. New York: Kennikat Press.

Flinn, Brian. 1999. "City Mulls Water-bill Hike." *Daily News*, 30 March, 7.

– 2002. "MP: No Other Money Coming: Nova Scotia's Cabinet Representative Scratches Head Over Hamm Letter." *Daily News*, 31 August, 4.

Forbes, E.R. 1979. *The Maritime Rights Movement, 1919–1927*. Montreal and Kingston: McGill-Queen's University Press.

Fraser, Amy Pugsley. 2007. "So you thought it was over … ; Commonwealth Games Boosters Trying to Resuscitate Halifax Bid." *Chronicle Herald*, 30 March, A1.

– 2008. "Flurry of Projects Surprises Official." *Chronicle Herald*, 3 July, C1.

Greater Halifax Partnership. 2007. "Greater Halifax Economic Snapshot, Second Quarter 2007." http://www.greaterhalifax.com/site-ghp2/media/ greaterhalifax/Economic_Snapshot_2007_Q2.pdf.

Halifax 2014, n.d. "Commonwealth Park." Accessed April 2007. http:// www.2014halifax.com/bidplan/commonwealthPark.aspx.

"As Halifax Fades from View …" 2007. Accessed August 2007. http:// supportthehrmgames.com/.

Halifax Gateway Council. 2008. "Members List." Accessed October 2009. http://www.halifaxgateway.com/members.htm.

Halifax Regional Municipality. 2003. *Regional Planning Project – Capital District Case Study.* June. http://www.halifax.ca/capitaldistrict/Publications/CDcaseStudy/CDcaseStudy.pdf.

– 2005. "Strategies for Success: Halifax Regional Municipality's Economic Development Strategy, 2010–2050." Halifax, 6.

– 2006a. "HRM Initiatives." Summer, Halifax, 1–2, 7–8.

– 2006b. *Regional Municipal Planning Strategy.* August. http://www.halifax.ca/regionalplanning/documents/Regional_MPS.pdf.

– 2006c. "HRM Region." Accessed July 2007. http://www.halifax.ca/regionalplanning/Region/region.html.

– 2007. "Urban Design Vision Statement." Approved by HRM Regional Council on 27 February. http://www.halifax.ca/capitaldistrict/HRMbyDESIGN-VisionPrinciples.html.

– 2008. "Principles Goals and Objectives." Accessed October 2009. http://www.halifax.ca/regionalplanning/RegionalPlanning/GoalsObject.html.

Hamm, John, and Peter Kelly. 2006. "The Commonwealth Games: Moving Forward Together." *Chronicle Herald*, 26 January, A7.

Hanselmann, Calvin. 2003. *Shared Responsibility: Final Report and Recommendations of the Urban Aboriginal Initiative.* Calgary: Canada West Foundation.

Harbour Solutions Advisory Committee. 1998. "Final Report to Council." Halifax Regional Municipality, 25 March. http://www.halifax.ca/harboursol/documents/final_sac_report_001.pdf.

Howe, Rick. 2003. "Mayor's Honeymoon Over: The Feisty Fighter we Elected has Become Part of the Mundane City Hall Gang." *Daily News*, 4 July, 18.

Infrastructure Canada. 2004. "Federal Government Investment of $60 Million for Treatment Plants." March 19. http://www.infrastructure.gc.ca/csif/publication/newsreleases/2004/20040319halifax_e.shtml.

Jackson, David. 2000. "MLAs Dislike Harbour Cleanup Price; City Asks Province To Find $52.5m for $315m Sewage Treatment Project." *Chronicle Herald*, 12 January, A10.

Jones, Deborah. 1991. "The Buddhists of Halifax: Eastern Philosophy, Western Lifestyle." *The Globe and Mail*, 11 May, F1.

"Land of Dreams: Millbrook Mi'kmaq Have Big Plans For Land Once Lost." *The Coast*, 29 January, 4 February 2004, 11, 34.

Leo, Christopher. 2002. "Urban Development: Planning Aspirations and Political Realities." In *Urban Policy Issues: Canadian Perspectives*, 2nd ed., edited by Edmund Fowler and David Seigel, 215–36. Don Mills, ON: Oxford University Press, 2002.

Leuprecht, Christian, and Harvey Lazar. 2007. "From Multilevel to 'Multiorder' Governance?" In *Spheres of Governance: Comparative Studies of Cities in Multilevel Governance Systems,* edited by Harvey Lazar and Christian Leuprecht. Montreal and Kingston: McGill-Queen's University Press.

Lightstone, Michael. 2009. "Residents Voice Off Against Widening Plan; Wisdom of Paving Rail cut Challenged." *Chronicle Herald,* 15 January, B2.

MacDonald, Michael J. 2000. "A Brief Submission to Canada Transportation Act Review." 20 November. http://www.reviewcta-examenltc.gc.ca/ Submissions-Soumissions/Txt/Greater percent2oHalifax percent2oPartnership. txt.

MacDonald, Andrea. 2006. "Halifax Rate at Nearly 20-year Low." *Daily News,* 2 December, 18.

Maich, Steve. 2000. "Harbour Bid Process Irks Councillors; Odds Stacked in Favour of Private Cleanup – Kelly." *Chronicle Herald,* 2 June, A1.

Mcdonough, Alexa. 2002. "NDP Doesn't Owe Apology for Position on Harbour Cleanup." *Chronicle Herald,* 26 September, B2.

Moar, Kim. 2002. "Council OK's $465m Sewage Deal: Taxpayers Get to See Contract for First Time." *Daily News,* 10 July, 3.

Mosher, Monty. 2007. "Our Field of Dreams; With Halifax's Bid for the 2014 Commonwealth Games Gone, Is a Big Owe Still Necessary?" *Chronicle Herald,* 1 May, C4.

Muise, Monique, and Michael Lightstone. 2008. "Resistance is Futile." *Chronicle Herald,* 28 June. http://www.thechronicleherald.ca/Front/1064567. html.

Myrden, Judy. 2009. "Unelected, Unknown and In Charge; With the Broadest Mandate of any Regulator in Canada, Some Fear the N.S. Utility and Review Board has too Much Clout," *Chronicle Herald,* May 19, A1.

Plumb, Donovan, Andrew Leverman, and Robert McGray. 2007. "The Learning City in a 'Planet of Slums.'" *Studies in Continuing Education* 29 (1): 37–50.

Power, Bill, and Paul Schneidereit. 2000. "CUPE Wants Harbour Cleanup Considered 'Top' Election Issue; Union Fears Jobs Would be Lost." *Chronicle Herald,* 13 October, A10.

Rodenhiser, David. 2002. "Tweedledee, Tweedledum: Kelly Should Resign, Hamm Should Apologize for Debacle." *Daily News,* 22 September, 2.

Sancton Andrew. 2001. "Canadian Cities and the New Regionalism." *Journal of Urban Affairs* 23 (5):543–55.

– 2002. "Metropolitan and Regional Governance." In *Urban Policy Issues: Canadian Perspectives,* 2nd ed., edited by Edmund Fowler and David Seigel, 54–68. Don Mills, ON: Oxford University Press.

Silver, Jim, Darlene Klyne, and Freeman Simard. 2003. "Adult Learning Centres Deserve Top Marks for Aboriginal Education: Fast Facts." *Canadian Centre for Policy Alternatives: Manitoba, Winnipeg,* 27 June.

Simpson, Jeffrey. 2000. "Council Split on Plan to Privatize Sewage." *Chronicle Herald,* 11 February, A1.

– 2002. "'Small Price' for a Clean Harbour; City Staff Recommends $64 Hike in Water Bills Over 5-Year Period." *Chronicle Herald,* 22 October, A1.

Smith, Amy. 2008. "Premier Watching Project Appeal; Macdonald Wants Downtown Halifax Development to go Ahead." *Chronicle Herald,* 15 November, B4.

– 2009. "Shutdown 'Disappointing', but Sewage Plant No Lemon – Kelly." *Chronicle Herald,* 18 January, A3.

Smulders, Marilyn. 2005. "Shannon Plan a Winning Idea: Proposed Sports Park Swayed Committee." *Daily News,* 17 December, 5.

Stewart, Ian. 2000. "The Dangers of Municipal Reform in Nova Scotia." In *The Savage Years: The Perils of Reinventing Government in Nova Scotia,* edited by Peter Clancy, James Bickerton, Rodney Haddow, and Ian Stewart, 199–227. Halifax: Formac.

Taylor, Roger. 2009. "No Shortage of Ideas for Recession-Era Cures." *Chronicle Herald,* 10 January, C1.

Vojnovic, Igor. 2000a. "Municipal Consolidation, Regional Planning and Fiscal Accountability: The Recent Experience in Two Maritime Provinces." *Canadian Journal of Regional Studies* 23 (1):49–72.

– 2000b. "The Transitional Impacts of Municipal Amalgamations." *Journal of Urban Affairs* 22 (4):385–417.

Watson, Albert. 2003. "The Great Military Base Sell-Off." *Building* 53 (2):32–6.

# 5

# Overcoming Adversity, or Public Action in the Face of New Urban Problems: The Example of Montreal

LAURENCE BHERER AND PIERRE HAMEL

## INTRODUCTION

Taking as its point of departure four areas of public policy – emergency preparedness and crisis management, image building, urban Aboriginal peoples, and federal property management – this chapter is based on the premise that urban issues do not begin and end with municipal affairs. In other words, cities' problems are rarely solved by municipalities alone. The city should be seen as a place shaped by conflict as well as by public policy from a variety of sources. To study municipal politics requires examination not just of the initiatives and programs municipalities develop, but also those developed by other economic and social actors at work both in and on the city. In Quebec and throughout Canada, the role of provincial and federal governments in shaping cities has often been underestimated. Moreover, the study of their actions too often limits itself to official policy and neglects the influence of various forms of higher levels of government and their effect on urban development. Though some studies have tried to bring perspective to urban problems in Canada (see notably Graham, Phillips, and Maslove 1998; Bunting and Filion 2000; Lightbody 2006; Lorinc 2006), the interrelations between various levels of government policy and their impact on urban planning and development have tended to be neglected by researchers.

Based on the case of Montreal, this chapter undertakes to look beyond traditional urban questions and thus is distinct from studies that focus too narrowly on municipal politics. We will see, for example, that local autonomy is not a significant variable in determining outcomes in the four areas under study. Likewise, the idea that the Government of Quebec rejects any form of relationship between municipalities and the federal government is also not a viable foundation for analysis. From a pragmatic point of view, the reality is considerably more complex. The notion that municipal structures are the primary determinants of urban public action seems to us reductionist in the extreme. Thus, the municipal reorganization that has so profoundly marked Montreal since 2000 has had a relatively minor effect on the four areas of this study. A better hypothesis is to look instead at the way these areas of public policy have become institutionalized in more recent times; the various levels of government have tinkered, groping about in the dark, to create new policy areas as they seek to impose their values and priorities in the public sphere. The logic of urban action has thus been driven more by trial and error, particularly provincial government action, but also that of municipalities. The result is a series of temporary measures continually interrupted by new initiatives and new projects that require previous alliances to be constantly rethought.

The fact that the areas of activity in this study are all of relatively recent vintage is no accident – emergency preparedness, image building, urban Aboriginal people, and federal property management are new policy areas, emerging because of new needs engendered by tensions specific to the urban setting in a world of increased globalization. With uncontrolled metropolitanization and increasing competition between urban areas for investment and business, urban agglomerations are often led by unstable regimes that have little or no success in meeting the contrary objectives of growth and economic development on the one hand and social solidarity on the other. Government action has of necessity had to proceed by developing a territorially based public policy with urban tunnel vision.

Before considering governance in the four selected categories of public action, the first section will set out the broad contours of Montreal urban governance past and present. Analysis is based on a thorough review of the literature as well as forty interviews of local and government officials as well as a certain number of civil society actors involved in various ways in Montreal's urban and metropolitan governance.

## GOVERNANCE OF MONTREAL

On the Canadian level, Montreal no longer has the lustre it enjoyed at the end of the nineteenth century. Then undisputedly Canada's leading city thanks in part to its strategic location at a juncture in the St Lawrence River, it suffered from a westward shift in economic activity combined with a change in economic leadership over the course of the twentieth century. As an international city both economically and industrially, Montreal is now resolutely engaged in a repositioning process.

At once a city and a region, Montreal remains the undisputed economic and cultural engine of Quebec. Eighty-two municipalities make up the metropolitan area, grouped together under the umbrella of the Montreal Metropolitan Community (CMM). The City of Montreal covers most of the island with its more than 1.8 million inhabitants, bookended by two other major centres – Laval to the north and Longueuil to the south – with a population of over 350,000 people each. Montreal generates 49 percent of Quebec's jobs while its economy accounts for 50 percent of Quebec's GDP (Montreal Metropolitan Community 2005). The population of the metropolitan area is over 3.4 million people spread over a 4,360 square kilometre area, although 58 percent of the land remains protected for agricultural purposes (Montreal Metropolitan Community 2005).

An old trading and industrial city whose British Empire connections fuelled expansion through the nineteenth century, Montreal felt the after effects of that empire's decline and the corresponding rise of the United States, which gave Toronto a geographic edge (Léveillée 1987, 7). Of course, other social, economic, and political factors can also explain Montreal's relative decline in the twentieth century (Higgins 1986). The gradual shift from an English-speaking to a French-speaking elite at the head of Quebec and Montreal businesses (Levine 1990) came at a certain price, namely the reconstitution of business networks. Added to these changes has been the relatively slow response to the demands of modernization by Montreal-area industry since the 1950s and 1960s. Moving from a Fordist economic and industrial paradigm to a post-Fordist economy dominated by services has proven difficult. While certain sectors of the new economy met with particular success in Montreal – for example, new information technologies and biopharmaceutical research and development – this has not been enough to make up for the job losses in older industrial sectors.

The fate of cities, urban agglomerations, and metropolitan areas is not built into their DNA such that we can merely unlock some code to find out what lies ahead. Rather, the future is constructed in response to changes in the local and world economy and market forces. It thus depends on compromises that social and economic agents arrive at and also on the political choices of local authorities and the ability of governments to win support for urban projects that will shape the agglomeration's development.

In the case of Montreal, the processes underway are contradictory and difficult to untangle. While the agglomeration does show a general lack of economic vitality according to standard indicators when compared to other North American metropolitan areas (OECD 2004) – revealed among other things by its difficulty in retaining immigrants – it must also be acknowledged that Montreal's civil society shows remarkable energy and resilience. This antinomy between weak business productivity growth and investment on the one hand and the commitment, capacity for innovation, and even creativity of civil society on the other sounds a cautionary note for anyone wishing to clearly identify the determinants of urban policies. As Erik H. Monkkonen states, it is still a difficult challenge to clearly establish who is in position among economic and political actors for "directing urban policy" (1998, 217). It might be added that it is no easy task to measure the relative impact of urban policy on a city or agglomeration's development. In hindsight, it may be possible to identify trends that certain circumstances or political choices can influence. Yet, ultimately, between such contextual influences as markets and intergovernmental support and political factors (along with their sources in local culture and democratic expression) occur adjustments and adaptations based on highly variable interactions that are determined by the bargaining capacity of local communities (Savitch and Kantor 2002).

In the case of Montreal, given the uncertainty that has characterized its political leadership on the local level since the 1990s, governance arrangements have proved to be not only very turbulent but also quite ephemeral. In part, this unsettled situation can be explained by weak political leadership. The standing of Montreal's local government in the provincial context has also been a factor.

Montreal is not a capital city. Unlike other large cities, the municipality does not receive the publicly-funded benefits that typically accrue to a capital. Furthermore, due to the city's demographic and economic weight on the provincial level, the provincial government prefers not to accord Montreal too great a share of public resources. Nor does the province allow it to become a political focus in the Canadian federal system; given the continuing jockeying for position between the provincial and federal governments, allowing Montreal to gain in political importance would tend to weaken the position of Quebec vis-à-vis the federal government. The result is a series of provincial initiatives and institutional reforms aimed at Montreal that are quite simply contradictory. While the government seeks to strengthen Montreal in its role as developmental engine, it simultaneously keeps it politically fragmented, dividing up power, organizational responsibility, and decision-making authority.

This ambivalence is something Montreal political observers are all too familiar with. Beginning in the 1990s, however, when the Parti Québécois government decided to undertake a major reform of Montreal's metropolitan governance by creating a megacity and forcing the island's edge cities into amalgamation, this ambivalence assumed hitherto unparalleled proportions (Hamel 2006).

The proliferation of stakeholders, levels, and areas of jurisdiction arising out of the urban and metropolitan reform of the late 1990s did not facilitate cooperation and coordinated efforts among local actors (LeBlanc 2006). Neither did it help assuage the tensions and conflicts that had characterized relations between Montreal and some of the cities on the island's periphery, or between the central city and the cities of the northern and southern suburbs, or even between the southern suburban cities themselves. For the provincial government, one of the reform's objectives was to increase the demographic weight of Longueuil relative to Laval and Montreal in order to establish a kind of trilateral balance. Reality, however, has failed to bend to the reformers' wishes.

By adding new layers and actors, the reform disrupted existing alliances. It also created new management and communications problems for city services given the multiple levels involved, as we will see in examining the four urban policy areas considered here.

## EMERGENCY PREPAREDNESS AND CRISIS MANAGEMENT

Emergency preparedness is a relatively new field of public action in Quebec. Although legislative measures have been in place since the 1960s, the first framework legislation, the Civil Security Act, was only adopted in December 2001. While public enquiries on a flurry of tragic events in the early 1980s revealed some of the weaknesses of Quebec's emergency preparedness model, it was the infamous ice storm of 1998 that spurred Quebec to develop a crisis management policy. The new legislation profoundly changed the way governments operated, particularly at the municipal level. In Montreal, several initiatives undertaken in the late 1990s were consolidated after the 2001 reform.

## The Ice Storm and New Emergency
## Preparedness Measures in Quebec

The January 1998 ice storm was unprecedented in terms of the number of people and the area affected. Heavy rain was followed by intense cold, causing electrical towers, traffic lights, street signs, and trees to collapse under the weight of the ice. The population of Greater Montreal, where most homes are heated electrically, found itself without power at the coldest time of the year. To investigate this unusual occurrence, the government created the Technical and Scientific Commission for Analysis of the Events Surrounding the Ice Storm of 5 to 9 January 1998, also known as the Nicolet Commission. Its main conclusion was that emergency preparedness remained neglected in Quebec due to an inadequately developed culture of civic safety. As evidence of this neglect, the commission pointed to the failure to follow the procedures designating the municipalities the lynchpin of the emergency preparedness system (Government of Quebec [Nicolet Commission] 1999; see also Gagnon and Dufresne 1999). During the ice storm, the government quickly took a centralized approach to management, preferring to act by sector rather than municipality (Gagnon and Dufresne 1999). This meant that at the height of the crisis, many municipalities were left to deal with the situation in their territories.

In Montreal, management was less rudimentary thanks to the existence of a supramunicipal body, then known as the Montreal Urban Community (MUC). The MUC had a head start because it had its own police force and had been designated in its constitution as the coordinating agency for emergency measures on the Island of Montreal. It had established a centre for emergency planning and expertise called the Emergency Measures Bureau (EMB), which proved relatively effective during the ice storm.

In the wake of the commission's recommendations, in 2001, the government adopted a new policy whose main purpose was to highlight the most important emergency preparedness issues and better distribute roles among the various players. The principle of subsidiarity was applied to risk management; that is, municipal governments were reconfirmed as the primary actors, with the provincial government called in only if the demands of a situation exceeded municipalities' ability to cope. Eight years after the adoption of this act, emergency preparedness officials are working to establish better emergency management systems. Compared to other municipal territories in Quebec, changes to Montreal's system have been less significant because some of the previous activities initiated by the Emergency Measures Bureau, however rudimentary, had paved the way for further developments.

## Current Emergency Practices in Montreal

It would be premature to draw conclusions about how Montreal's emergency preparedness system might function, given the newness of the system, the numerous recent changes to Montreal's institutional structure, and the non-occurrence of a major event that might have put the new model to the test. There is still a spirit of excitement and freshness from the recent reforms. Nevertheless, our study has been able to outline the basic features of Montreal's emergency preparedness model.

One peculiarity of the system is the high level of knowledge and resources of the municipality. This is because of the coordinating organization, the City of Montreal Civil Security Centre (CMCSC), which was created in 2001 to continue the work begun by the Emergency Measures Bureau in the 1990s. The CMCSC is the main resource for emergency preparedness expertise, investigation, networking, and planning on the island. It is responsible for the prevention and preparation levels of the City of Montreal's central and borough services, as well as those of the island's other municipalities. The CMCSC has recycled and systematized a number of other measures initiated by the EMB before the municipal mergers (CMCSC 2007, 5).

One of Montreal's contributions to the new Quebec emergency management model is its committee structure, inherited from the EMB. Since 2001, existing committees have been strengthened and new ones have been formed to bring together all those involved in specific aspects of emergency preparedness. The Montreal actors we spoke to tell us that this system has been chosen because, in an emergency, it is critical to know who is involved in each area in order to gauge what resources are available. Committee work is thus a sign of willingness to be proactive and prepared. In this spirit, the new act also calls for a municipal emergency preparedness committee to be formed. In Montreal, this committee comprises civil security officials, service providers (Hydro-Québec, Bell, etc.), and provincial-level institutions such as the Public Health Branch and school boards.

Our respondents state that the partnership approach characterized by regular meetings, networking, information sharing, and collaborative development of emergency preparedness documents has helped each participant clarify its role. For example, this mode of operation has enabled community organizations to determine how they should contribute to the crisis management system, as the Nicolet report recommended. After the ice storm, the EMB formed the Emergency Measures Humanitarian and Community Organizations Committee (EMHCOC) to raise awareness and help plan and prepare emergency procedures. Still the only institution of its kind in Quebec, the EMHCOC now comprises twelve groups, the main ones being the Red Cross, the Sun Youth Organization, the Saint Vincent de Paul Society, Moisson Montréal, and the Salvation Army. The EMHCOC is primarily concerned with agency training, networking, and agreements to provide front-line support if the city so requests. These kinds of agreements help organizations prepare and recruit volunteers and clarify roles. As one respondent explained, "Concertation groups allow us to get to know each other's roles, which is very helpful in a major emergency. When we were involved in Operation Lebanon or the housing shortage, everyone's role was really clear. The point is to keep to your role and do what's needed. Even if there's an earthquake in Montreal, we won't just send people into the field, we'll wait till we're called" (Interview 4, our translation).

Another Montreal innovation was the formation of a mixed municipal-industry committee (MMIC) for the prevention and management of industrial risks. The MMICs are volunteer groups (i.e., jointly initiated by a high-risk industry and a municipality) made up of municipal and industry representatives, individuals delegated by three provincial ministries (Environment, Public Safety, and Health), and private citizens. The MMIC certification process specifically requires that citizens be included and kept informed. This policy can be traced back to the first MMIC, created in 1995 in Montreal's east end around the petrochemical industry (Frattolillo and Boutin 2005). In 2009, we found around twelve MMICs in Quebec, four of which are on the Island of Montreal. The Civil Security Act encourages these initiatives by giving municipalities the power to require industries to publicize the risk of major events, bring in protective measures, and inform the public.

In all, networking activities and regular meetings have helped clarify the respective responsibilities of provincial and municipal governments. This territorial rather than sectoral division of responsibilities has also favoured the development of a bottom-up chain of responsibilities, from the municipal to the provincial level. Municipalities retain front-line responsibility for emergency measures, leaving the provincial government to take a supporting and coordinating role. This operational mode is particularly functional in Montreal, where the city's expertise and extensive civil safety resources significantly reduce its dependence on the provincial government, resulting in a more equal partnership.

The 2001 reform thus led to a horizontally and vertically integrated emergency response system in Quebec. Given this interlocking and integrated system within the province, the federal government has been little involved in the various emergency preparedness structures. The rule of thumb is that the federal government will only step in as a last resort if and when a province declares itself unable to respond alone with its own resources, regardless of the nature of the disaster (except in the case of an external threat). However, the federal government remains involved through work with various emergency respondents, including provincial and municipal governments. Its primary contribution is in the formulation of new Canadian standards. For example, in response to the risk of an influenza pandemic, the federal government required its partners to make preparations, leading the CMCSC to revise its procedures and develop an influenza pandemic plan. In other areas, such as the environment or national security, the federal government collaborates closely with the other levels of government, notably by forming specific committees; the Montreal antiterrorism advisory committee is one such example. This openness is no accident. According to those involved, emerging risk management concerns have brought the three levels of government together as they have come to understand the benefits of working jointly. Those involved in emergency preparedness highly value networking and coordination, which contributes to this openness. Several of our respondents expressed the hope that discussions involving the three political levels would help clarify emergency response roles in areas where roles and jurisdictions are less well-defined and not always easy to agree on, either between political levels or fields of expertise.

> Last week, there was a ship leaking toxic fumes in the Port of Montreal. As long as the ship remained out in the river, it was Canada's responsibility, but when the fumes reached the Island of Montreal, it became a provincial, then municipal issue, so we all had to work together. You have different regulations, different jurisdictions ... there are environmental regulations, quarantine regulations, and civil security regulations. We have to know all the regulations very well because the question will arise – "Is it our job or their job? Who's responsible for all this?" Then whoever's responsible is in charge and asks for help from the others. (Interview 12, our translation)

The confusion in jurisdiction and roles is particularly the case for environmental emergencies because federal and provincial responsibilities in this area are not well defined. The two governments also have different philosophies: the provincial government feels that the federal regulations about environmental emergencies do not permit effective control of high-risk operations. Moreover, the Quebec government prefers a bottom-up approach in which the municipalities are in control and the provincial government coordinates emergency measures. At the federal level, this is reversed, and the approach is more centralized and top-down. According to our respondents, meetings between the three levels of government can lead to an accommodation of these diametrically opposed approaches.

## IMAGE BUILDING

Using images to promote the development of big cities is not a new idea. It is an approach that can be associated either with planning or urban policy. Whenever elites need to convince local populations to go along with their plans, they have had recourse to representations and images to obtain the necessary financial resources and to circumvent institutional, social, or cultural obstacles that stand in their way. These images and representations remain active parts of any form of political discourse. They contribute dynamically to the establishment and extension of hegemony.

In Montreal in the late 1950s, Mayor Jean Drapeau explicitly embarked on image building in order to convince political decision makers at higher levels of government, economic elites, his own political base – small business people and homeowners – as well as the population in general to support his ventures (Paul 2004). His successes are well-known, as are some of the less fortunate results of his grandiose ideas. In that respect, his "modern" vision of Montreal was converging with an unbridled capitalist type of urban development completely blind to the social and physical integrity of urban popular neighbourhoods.

Mayor Drapeau experienced many political victories. He managed to hold on to power for more than twenty-five years. His charisma, allied with an ability to construct and promote powerful images around Montreal's international stature, allowed him to conceal the economic transformations that were taking place (Léveillée 1987). For at least two decades, megaprojects like the 1967 International and Universal Exposition (Expo '67) or the 1976 Summer Olympics and their associated images created an illusion of progress, making the return to reality particularly painful during the 1980s and 1990s. Despite the unquestionable vitality of several sectors, the city has never made up the ground lost during that period or, to put it more positively, managed to carve out its own distinctive place in the North American economic zone.

At the turn of the millennium, the City of Montreal could not really be said to be in better shape than it had been two decades earlier.[1] Nevertheless, an economic recovery – manifested particularly in real estate – helped dispel some of the gloom of the period between the late 1970s and the late 1990s.

Of course, as the 1990s came to a close, the economic context had changed. International competition had made tremendous inroads. The transition to the new economy was complete. With this reality came a new image of Montreal communicated through urban projects aimed at attracting private investment for urban renewal. Various neighbourhoods were selected to be shrines to the new economy or at least to be associated with its clientele, among them notably the Old Port and the Lachine Canal, as well as Cité Multimédia and Cité du commerce électronique (Poitras 2003). For each of these sites, a strategy was put forward to create for Montreal an image as a dynamic city thoroughly oriented toward the new economy thanks to the initiative and the participation of the two upper levels of government.

Since 2005 Montreal has not wanted for images: "City of Knowledge, Creativity, and Innovation," "Avant-Garde Metropolis of Culture," "City of Design," or "City of the World." These images are somewhat similar to those in use since at least the end of the 1950s by the city's political and economic elites. Three things, however, have changed. First, the panoply of images has never been so great. Second, images have – in some cases – spilled over the borders of Montreal proper to encompass the entire metropolitan region. Third, the role of higher levels of government has been different from in the past.

*A Profusion of Images*

Following the 2002 Montreal Summit organized by Mayor Gérald Tremblay after his election, city officials began formulating a series of challenges, projects, and sectoral plans. These were summarized in the document *Imagine. Achieve. Montréal 2025. A World of Creativity and Possibilities* (City of Montreal 2005). They are mapped out around five "strategic areas" that bring together a number of interest groups and economic stakeholders in order to increase the city's "prosperity" and improve citizens' quality of life.

However, this process has not succeeded in unifying the multiple images and representations that continue to proliferate. Neither within the five areas, nor between them, has a single comprehensive image of Montreal emerged. A large majority of the representatives of both the city administration and the main economic sectors with whom we met agree that, for the moment, the city lacks a single representative image: "Each group puts forward its own vision, understanding, and hopes for Montreal. All are well intentioned. All of them have constructed their own narrative of Montreal, but often they are not coherent" (Interview 18, our translation).

This point of view was qualified, however, by one city official who maintained that there was no incompatibility between the various images. Whether Montreal is thought of as a centre for design, project management, or cultural festival organization, or with regard to knowledge and innovation, all of these representations can converge provided the focus is on the search for quality: "There isn't necessarily one common image. But in any case, that's part of the reality of a city. Cities possess a number of features that allow them to stand out against the competition from other cities. There's no incompatibility between the various images of Montreal (design, project management, festival, or knowledge city). What we need to aim for is excellence in several cutting-edge fields. The common point should be that focus on quality, on the search for excellence" (Interview 14, our translation). Still, if there is no agreement on what Montreal's image ought to be, there is general agreement on the urgency of formulating an image that can position the city among other leading cities, as a City of Montreal official pointed out (Interview 20).

While several people mentioned the idea of creativity as the iconic image that should evoke Montreal's strengths – creativity manifested as much in festivals as in industrial clusters, in new technologies as in life sciences or aerospace research – others felt attention should be drawn more to the kinds of activities to which this creativity gives rise. For these respondents, connecting creativity to industrial clusters, for example, is not a particularly good idea because it appeals to too narrow a clientele. Their preference would be to address clienteles and activities with a broader reach, such as culture. Cultural branding, defined implicitly and vaguely as the promotion of the image of a city where culture is valued, is a more inclusive notion. This idea of a city of culture is being promoted by a coalition made up of several partners, including the City of Montreal, Culture Montréal, Board of Trade of Metropolitan Montreal, Government of Quebec, and Government of Canada.

However, tourism, economic development, and cultural development officials do not share a single understanding of culture. Big differences exist between them, as was apparent in the heated controversy surrounding the establishment of a entertainment district in the middle of the 2000s. Its promoters advanced a cultural concept centred on cultural consumption, thereby marginalizing certain categories of artists, cultural producers, and audiences whose cultural activities and experience run along lines other than that of mass culture.

Alongside the City of Montreal, Culture Montréal, a non-profit organization working in partnership with the City of Montreal and Quebec's Ministry of Culture, Communications, and the Status of Women, also brings together those who strive to "promote culture as an essential element in Montreal's development." Culture Montréal has become one of the biggest promoters of culture in the public forum. Its objectives are threefold: (1) "to promote the right to, access to, and participation in culture for all citizens of Montreal"; (2) "to assert the role of culture in Montreal's development, especially by encouraging the cultural community to actively participate in city life"; and (3) "to contribute to strengthening Montreal's position as a cultural metropolis through the enhancement of its creativity, cultural diversity, and national and international prominence" (Culture Montréal 2008).

Culture Montréal was one of the main organizers of the colloquium "Rendez-Vous November 2007 – Montreal, Cultural Metropolis" where a plan of action was put together to improve Montreal's "international cultural prominence" and promote the development of its character as "a cultural metropolis." The establishment of a downtown show district was one of the means selected.

## Images for the Metropolitan Region

The battle over image building is not confined to the city, but has now spread to the entire metropolitan region. Actors less present on the central city stage – notably the north and south shore municipalities, including Laval and Longueuil – play an important role in this regard, as do the higher levels of government, whose actions play out differently at the metropolitan level than that of the central city. However, it is the actions of the Montreal Metropolitan Community (CMM) that speak loudest at this level. As we know, the CMM is entirely dedicated to the management, development, and promotion of the metropolitan region.

Since its inception, the CMM has undertaken a number of initiatives directly or indirectly linked to the image question. In fall 2006, CMM determined that a branding operation was not only essential, but that it had to be metropolitan in scope and target an international audience. A massive public consultation was launched to survey the region's main socioeconomic, political, and cultural stakeholders as well as its residents with a view to developing a Greater Montreal brand. The main goal of the operation was to develop a brand image that achieved consensus among all economic stakeholders while at the same time resonating with residents: "The brand we choose must convey a clear, uniform, and distinctive message for all stakeholders with international activities. It must also reflect a unifying metropolitan vision in which residents of all the region's municipalities can identify themselves" (CMM 2008, our translation).

For the moment, the image of Montreal as a cultural metropolis appears to be the favourite with CMM officials. But the definition of culture underlying this notion has a strong innovation and creativity component. The fact that Montreal was named a UNESCO City of Design in June 2006 lends credence to this vision, as do investments in the multimedia industry, a view shared with us by a CMM official.[2] From this standpoint, culture is not viewed as anathema to business and economic development, but rather as a contributing factor.

Although the public consultation process launched by CMM was designed first and foremost to win over foreign investors, it also sought to bring residents and elected officials from Greater Montreal's northern and southern suburbs on side. It is an open secret that suburban residents and officials do not automatically support the investment and development projects promoted by the central city.

To what extent, then, will the CMM's initiative garner widespread support, building the legitimacy needed to mobilize the private and public resources required to create a community at a city region scale? How can the image of the metropolitan region be reconciled with images constructed to promote the central city? Is a branding initiative alone enough to overcome the cleavages in interest?

### Image and Multilevel Governance

Along with initiatives specifically aimed at developing a brand capable of overcoming differences and building consensus around a shared representation, as the CMM consultation seeks to do, there are numerous other efforts, initiatives, and projects that can help transform the representations, culture, and image – or images – of a city or metropolitan region.

Since the 1990s, there has been an increase in the number of planning, management, and intervention bodies in the Montreal area. The powers these bodies exercise are shifting, and all of them attempt, to varying degrees, to influence the decision-making processes. To this end, they promote a certain vision of Montreal's urban development and future, contributing in their own way to the construction of an image of the metropolis. The problem is that no single actor is currently strong enough to convince the others to adhere to a particular vision. The result is, if not a perpetual state of confrontation, at least a series of parallel endeavours with no sign of convergence in the medium term.

This does not mean that the three levels of government and their private partners are in a perpetual state of trench warfare. However, alliances tend to be formed on an ad hoc basis and are constantly being reassessed and renegotiated. This inevitably adds to the difficulty of building a strong consensus around an image that all share. A telling illustration of this difficulty of building consensus around an image was the April 2008 decision by Public Works and Government Services Canada to withdraw funding from Montreal International (MI), after having annually contributed $2 million. Montreal International is a non-profit organization built in 1996 through a public-private partnership for supporting the economic development of metropolitan Montreal and increasing its international influence. The idea of reinforcing the economic attraction of Montreal was shared by all the public and private actors involved in MI. At the outset, the values and representation shared by all the members of MI are orientated towards a dynamic business environment where competitiveness is strongly encouraged, even though life quality specific to Montreal is also part of the general picture. The move followed on the fall 2007 decision by the Quebec minister responsible for the province's economic development agency to "no longer fund non-profit organizations in order to prioritize direct assistance to businesses" (Canadian Press 2008, our translation).

As we can see, the Montreal region faces challenges that other metropolitan areas do not face due to its controversial position inside the Quebec geographical and political zone, but also due to the internal tensions proper to the metropolitan community itself. Since at least the end of the 1990s, the federal government has generally opted to play a low-key role, even though this role still can be of vital importance to Montreal's development in some areas. We do not fully subscribe to the views of one of our respondents, who believes that Ottawa will adopt an accommodating position: "These days, the message the federal government often sends is that it supports projects that dovetail with the priorities of Quebec City and Montreal. You could call it a sort of 'win-win' form of interference, not to impose projects from the top down, but to support projects that all three levels of government can agree on. This forces governments in Quebec City and the Montreal area to get their priorities in order" (Interview 14, our translation). However, we can say that the federal government must now negotiate with more stakeholders than in the past and increasingly accepts the principle of multilevel governance.

URBAN ABORIGINAL PEOPLES

Despite Montreal's growing Aboriginal population, the city's Aboriginal community has been little studied, no doubt because of the obstacles researchers face. First, the population is hard to measure, which tends to make the community an "invisible" one. Second, because Aboriginal peoples living on reserve fall under federal jurisdiction, determining responsibility for urban Aboriginals is not so simple. In short, Montreal's Aboriginal community remains largely ignored. The few measures we identified reveal only the most rudimentary form of recognition in this policy area.

*Montreal's Aboriginal Population: An Invisible Community?*

The most recent Statistics Canada data shows that in 2006, the Aboriginal population of the Montreal census metropolitan area (CMA) was 17,685 (Statistics Canada 2007). Just under half that number (7,600) lived within Montreal city limits. The data show a significant increase over the 2001 census, which counted an Aboriginal population of 11,090, of which 3,555 lived in Montreal proper. This increase corresponds to the increase in Canada's Aboriginal population, which grew by 45 percent between 1996 and 2006 (Statistics Canada 2008).

These figures should be treated with caution and are disputed by a number of Montreal sources. The Native Friendship Centre of Montreal, for example, estimates the population at around 45,000 in the CMA.[3] According to our respondents and the sources we consulted, the urban Aboriginal reality in Montreal is hard to grasp and is systematically underestimated, as it is elsewhere in Canada. In addition, the issue of Aboriginal identity, like all identity issues, comes with its own share of ambiguity. For example, in Montreal, among those who declared themselves to be of Aboriginal origin, only 18 percent reported an Aboriginal identity. In contrast, 86 percent and 83 percent of the population of Aboriginal origin in Regina and Saskatoon reported their identity as Aboriginal (Siggner 2003). It should also be noted that population surveys conducted by the communities themselves are rare. Those that do exist do not count members of the Montreal Aboriginal population who are originally from communities outside Quebec. There is also a very high rate of refusal to participate in the Canadian census among Aboriginal communities. In the Montreal metropolitan region, for example, inhabitants of the Kahnawake and Kanesatake reserves did not participate in Statistics Canada's 2006 census survey.

The proximity of Indian reserves to Montreal also raises questions as to very definition of "urban Aboriginal people." There are two Mohawk communities within the boundaries of the Montreal Metropolitan Community, which overlap those of the CMA. This proximity may have an impact on the urban Aboriginal experience (Lévesque 2003). For example, the presence of the Mohawk reserves and of Aboriginals from communities whose members' first or second language is English (Cree and Inuit) explains why most of the Montreal organizations that work with the Aboriginal population are anglophone (Regroupement des centres d'amitié autochtone du Québec 2008, 44). This situation poses challenges with respect to services because of linguistic incompatibility between Aboriginal organizations that operate solely in English and certain provincial civil servants who are unilingual francophone.

From an institutional perspective, the very concept of "urban Aboriginal" conflicts with how jurisdiction is divided between levels of government. The federal government is responsible for First Nations living on reserve, whereas the Government of Quebec tends to be responsible (with some exceptions) for various services provided to Inuit and First Nations people living off reserve, which includes urban Aboriginals. The urban Aboriginal category applies in equal measure to Aboriginals who make their homes in small towns near their communities (La Tuque, Val d'Or, Sept-Îles) and to those living in Montreal. While it is easier to identify and recognize the Aboriginal population in small towns, it is harder in a culturally diverse city like Montreal. As an agent of the Centre for Native Education remarked, "We tend to ignore the needs of people living in the city. I think it has a lot to do with the fact that Aboriginal people aren't concentrated in one area. We're scattered throughout the city, which makes it very hard to identify us. Especially in a multicultural city like Montreal where there are people from many different nations and cultures" (Interview 34, our translation). Moreover, the notion of urban Aboriginal runs counter to current practice in Aboriginal Affairs, which is to structure programs based on the needs of reserves and Aboriginal communities. Urban Aboriginals often have a more complex identity. They may come from one of the Quebec's eleven Aboriginal nations or from elsewhere in Canada. The trend among policy makers to view Aboriginals on the basis of their attachment to a community or their membership in an Indian band seems justified from the viewpoint of government-to-government relations, but has little traction in an urban setting. As one respondent explained, "One of the biggest problems is the funding part. Because we're off-reserve, we don't have a council, we don't have chiefs. We don't have a system where the government can give funding to and it would be disbursed. Each organization has to fight for its own funding" (Interview 32). Another respondent echoed these ideas: "The priorities are established for people living on reserve. Obviously we get funding as an organization, too, but it's nothing compared to what goes to the reserves" (Interview 34, our translation). The corollary to this lack of visibility is the virtual absence of urban Aboriginals (and, especially, Montreal Aboriginals) in public policy at all levels of government.

### Scattered Initiatives for Montreal's Urban Aboriginals

For the moment, the rare measures implemented in Montreal are the result of scattered initiatives on the part of a handful of Aboriginal organizations that struggle to bring urban Aboriginal issues to the attention of the various levels of government, including on-reserve Aboriginal governments. The absence of dialogue and cooperation between the three levels of government indicates how far they still have to go. We will limit ourselves here to analyzing the logic behind the behaviour of the three levels.

At the federal level, the main program for urban Aboriginal peoples does not apply to Montreal. The Urban Aboriginal Strategy, which aims to reduce inequalities between urban Aboriginals and other Canadians, targets twelve cities outside Quebec. Since its beginning in 1998, the Urban Aboriginal Homelessness component of the National Homelessness Initiative did not extend to Montreal. However, in the new version, the Aboriginal funding stream of the Homelessness Partnership Initiative does include Montreal. Other federal programs specifically or partially targeted at urban Aboriginals have also been extended to Montreal, notably the Aboriginal Friendship Centre Program, the Urban Multi-purpose Aboriginal Youth Centre Initiative, and Aboriginal Head Start. Most of these programs are managed by the Native Friendship Centre of Montreal, which ends up providing front-line services even though its mandate is to build bridges between Aboriginal and non-Aboriginal cultures.

Provincially, the Quebec government does not provide for special Aboriginal programs, but rather for specific delivery methods for its universal programs. Each provincial department has a head of Aboriginal affairs in charge of implementing these universal programs in collaboration with Aboriginal communities. However, these specific measures target the Aboriginal communities, while measures for urban Aboriginals remain very much in their infancy.

In the field of housing, for example, the Quebec government subsidizes a single Montreal organization that provides some thirty social housing units adapted for Aboriginal needs. Emergency shelters exist for Aboriginal women (largely funded by the United Way), but not for men. In terms of child care, the universal program for all Quebec families is in place in Quebec's Aboriginal communities. However, there is an exception in the Quebec urban context, and it is Montreal. Since 2010 Montreal has an Aboriginal child care services in the Verdun neighborhood. Interestingly, the development of Aboriginal child care services is the only area of provincial early childhood policy where the Quebec government has not sought an outright transfer of federal funds. Instead, after a federal-provincial negotiations, the Quebec government obtains that the federal government should be an equal partner.

Provincial officials, whether they have links to Montreal's Aboriginal community or not, face the same obstacles to understanding the needs of urban Aboriginals: the absence of dialogue partners, lack of familiarity with Montreal's Aboriginal community, and the impossibility of providing culturally sensitive services. As one respondent put it, "Unfortunately, aside from [one organization], we don't really have anyone we can talk to right now. Nobody seems interested in developing projects in that community. Maybe they're not aware of the possibilities either. I don't have a list of organizations that we could work with in Montreal" (Interview 30, our translation).

One area where the lack of connections between levels of government and Aboriginal organizations is visible is in the cultural arena, where funds are available for projects related to Aboriginal culture, but few

Aboriginal organizations apply. As for the City of Montreal, it has no programs specifically designed for Aboriginal residents. Nor does it deal directly with the city's Aboriginal organizations (except to fund the First Peoples' Festival, organized by the organization Land Insights). As at the provincial level, municipal programs are universal and Aboriginals are therefore eligible. Unlike the Quebec government, however, the city has no special measures for Aboriginals.

The recognition deficit that Montreal's Aboriginal community suffers at the hands of public institutions is also fuelled by the absence of representative bodies specifically for Aboriginals. Without a representative forum, Montreal's Aboriginals cannot lay claim to their dual Aboriginal/ urban identity. The provincial association – the Assembly of First Nations of Quebec and Labrador (AFNQL) – defends the interests of Quebec's forty-three band councils, but not its urban Aboriginals. Urban Aboriginals are represented by civil society organizations like the Regroupement des centres d'amitié autochtone du Québec (RCAAQ), which is a non-voting member of AFNQL, and the association Quebec Native Women. However, these associations operate at the provincial level, which leaves the local arena to Aboriginal organizations who are tasked with providing front-line services. With their limited resources, they cannot act as political representatives.

The anonymity of Montreal's Aboriginal organizations is also reflected in the uncertainty as to their actual number. An RCAAQ survey identified fifty-one groups encompassing everything from private companies (like Air Inuit) to university research groups and Aboriginal affairs coordinators within a variety of organizations (Regroupement des centres d'amitié autochtone du Québec 2008). The people we interviewed, Aboriginal and non-Aboriginal alike, concurred that there are few specifically Aboriginal organizations in Montreal. Those that do exist remain isolated because there is no collaboration between them or with other Montreal associations. In the housing field, for example, Aboriginal organizations have no links with established advocacy groups like the Front d'action populaire en réaménagement urbain. This isolation is further accentuated by provincial government practices: the Habitat Métis du Nord housing corporation, which serves Aboriginals, and Société d'habitation de Montréal, which manages the social housing stock in Montreal, are considered as two separate partners by the provincial government, rather than as stakeholders with a common interest in Montreal housing issues.

In light of this situation, a number of respondents with Aboriginal organizations and from other backgrounds acknowledged the need for urban Aboriginals to establish representative bodies. In the same vein, a recent RCAAQ report called for the creation of a Montreal Aboriginal community centre to foster a sense of belonging among Montreal's Aboriginal population (2008). A place for gathering, socializing, and learning, the centre would serve as a single-window access point for Aboriginals and also as a means to raise the community's profile with political institutions and reach out to the general public.

## FEDERAL PROPERTY MANAGEMENT
## AND URBAN DEVELOPMENT

Federal property management represents a special case among the four sectors selected for the Montreal study because it is not strictly speaking a public policy field. Federal property comprises buildings, facilities, and land belonging to the federal government and its agencies. Given how much of it there is, it was impossible to do a comprehensive analysis of federal property management in Montreal. Instead, we took a case study approach that demonstrates the value of looking at federal properties from an urban standpoint – that is, at their location and how their management affects urban development. The Lachine Canal revitalization project is a particularly interesting example because it meets the three conditions that qualify it as a model of multilevel governance: accessible budgets, unusual alliances between the three levels of government, and a logic of collaboration and networking.

### Federal Property in Montreal

Federal property occupies nearly 5 percent of the Island of Montreal (23.17 km²).[4] Many of these properties are in the city centre where most federal offices are found (Place Bonaventure, the Guy Favreau Complex, the Montreal Stock Exchange Tower, Place de la Cathédrale, and the World Trade Centre) and where the St Lawrence River port facilities and federal bridges, such as the Jacques Cartier and Champlain bridges, are located.

The concentration of federal property in the heart of the island testifies to the critical role that the federal government plays in Montreal's urban development. Unlike in Quebec City and Ottawa-Gatineau, this is less the result of historical and political factors and more a matter of

Montreal's special geographical setting. As an island bordered by the St Lawrence River to the south, the agglomeration has several characteristics that make it subject it to federal government jurisdiction over port management and the river. Along the river, the federal government owns a huge swath of property between the Jacques Cartier and Honoré Mercier bridges (Société du Havre 2004, 6–7) totalling 10 km² and extending along 31 km of shoreline. This includes very important federal infrastructure like the wharves and facilities in the Old Port, the CN and VIA Rail marshalling yards, Canada Post properties, the Lachine Canal, and the St Lawrence Seaway. A number of other actors are present in this highly coveted area: the provincial government, the City of Montreal, businesses, civil society actors, and residents. Since 1978, this area has been the subject of several revitalization plans. Its strategic location and potential (large portions are vacant) has whetted developers' appetites and inspired all nature of schemes. However, the presence of highways, railways, port facilities, and numerous industries makes access to the area and to the river difficult. Redeveloping it would require huge investments and collaboration by numerous partners. Since 1978 redevelopment has thus proceeded section by section, notably with the Lachine Canal revitalization project. The canal occupies a straight and narrow strip of land stretching 14 kilometres between Lake St Louis and Montreal's Old Port.

### The Lachine Canal Revitalization Project

In the late 1990s, the federal government undertook a vast revitalization program to reopen the Lachine Canal for pleasure boating and to transform it into a recreation and tourism area (Piché 2003). Once a waterway serving the industries that lined its banks, the canal fell into disuse after being closed to local navigation in 1970. In the 1980s, three events testified to renewed interest from the three levels of government in the St Lawrence River and its shoreline. The first of these was the signing of the Canada-Quebec Agreement on the St Lawrence (subsequently named the St Lawrence Action Plan). The plan sought to improve environmental management of the river and its surroundings; its priorities included sediment management and decontamination of the Lachine Canal.[5]

In the wake of this bipartite agreement, a joint federal-provincial environmental assessment panel was formed in 1989 to study decontamination of the Lachine Canal. The panel and the St Lawrence Action Plan demonstrated that the federal and provincial governments were prepared to work together, which boded well for subsequent progress. Municipal governments were also engaged. Montreal and its neighbours had been lobbying since the 1970s to have Ottawa and Quebec recognize the strategic value of the Island of Montreal river system. The redevelopment of Montreal's Old Port into a major recreational and heritage attraction at the turn of the 1980s is an example of the spirit of collaboration that prevailed between the three levels of government. The public also had an opportunity to express its support for this new vision of the port area, with access to the river, through public consultations about Old Port redevelopment that were held in 1978–79 and 1985–86.

It was in this favourable context that Montreal's mayor at the time, Pierre Bourque, succeeded in forming Grand Montréal Bleu, a coalition of municipalities at the metropolitan scale whose goal was to protect and enhance the region's waterways. Building on this support, Bourque presented federal authorities with a variety of the coalition's projects, including the Lachine Canal revitalization. The mayor obtained promises of funding. From this point on, events accelerated, with the federal government giving clear signs of its determination to get the project underway. These included a full-scale revision of the canal management plan and the creation of Pôle des Rapides, a non-profit corporation for local tourism development, that was composed of the partner governments, associations, and businesses involved in the Lachine Canal project. Corporation members elect a board of directors every two years. In 1995, consultations were initiated with all stakeholders concerned by the revitalization project, around 200 in all, according to Piché. An agreement between the federal government and the municipalities along the canal was officially announced in April 1997 and led to major work that was completed in 2003.

### Money, Cooperation, and Government Alliances: The Benefits of Successful Multilevel Governance

The revitalization of the Lachine Canal was not only a project initiated and implemented almost exclusively by the state, but was also the result of joint action by three levels of government (Michel and Sénécal 2002). The ideal conditions in which the revitalization was carried out make the project a model of multilevel governance. Of course, there were tensions as to the nature of the project during the planning phase, but these did not hamper the process. All three government actors shared the same determination to proceed. What explains their cooperation? According to our study, three factors helped promote consensus around the Lachine Canal revitalization: the availability of funding, ad hoc government alliances, and ongoing collaboration and dialogue between all stakeholders involved in the project.

One of the keys to the revitalization project was the money that the federal agreement agreed to invest in the 1990s. The success of the mayor of Montreal in mobilizing local political support, and Ottawa and Quebec City's cooperative St Lawrence River enhancement initiatives, convinced federal authorities to allocate the resources to launch the project. Although municipal investments in the project were actually greater ($60 million from Montreal and Lachine vs. $37 million from the federal government), federal funding was doubly significant. By signing on, Ottawa was not only agreeing to contribute financially, but also was allowing federal properties to be included in a broader urban redevelopment project. The involvement of civil servants from Parks Canada and Economic Development Canada for Quebec regions, along with federal members of Parliament from the electoral districts along the Lachine Canal (including then-Finance Minister Paul Martin) helped cement the deal. As a result, Parks Canada officials in Montreal inherited a budget the likes of which they had never seen before, along with an exciting project to work on.

The division of responsibilities between governments was quite straightforward. The federal government was tasked with handling the heritage component of the revitalization project – that is, restoring and enhancing the canal's immediate surroundings. The municipalities (especially Montreal and Lachine) were responsible for the urban development component – updating zoning and encouraging housing and other real estate developments along the canal. The Quebec government's role was a very minor one, limited to heritage and cultural oversight. Normally in Quebec, federal and municipal authorities work together only if the Quebec government and the federal government sign an agreement allowing them to do so. In the Lachine Canal case, a draft agreement was drawn up but was never finalized because the responsible federal and provincial ministers failed to agree. Nevertheless, the federal government and the municipalities did work together. For those involved, this was seen as evidence of the pragmatism of which the three levels of government were capable when a project met with broad support. In another departure from standard practice in Quebec-federal intergovernmental relations, both governments also struck an unusual alliance to oppose certain aspects of the development vision that were championed

by the municipalities involved in the project. Given the heritage significance of the Lachine Canal site, Parks Canada sought the Quebec government's help in convincing Montreal city officials to make the canal's
industrial history one of the centre points of the project. The municipal
team in place had been leaning toward a project similar to the Rideau
Canal project in Ottawa, which focused solely on real estate development (Michel and Sénécal 2002, 162). "We [the Quebec government]
had a good working relationship with Parks Canada. We often backed
the federal viewpoint against the municipal one and teamed with federal
authorities against the municipal government. It happened that way
more often than the other way around" (Interview 36, our translation).

Collaboration was also evident in intergovernmental loans or leases of
land and infrastructure: the patchwork of federal, municipal, and provincial properties in this part of the city made it necessary for authorities
to concede pieces of land to each other in order to complete specific
projects or redevelopment initiatives.

The third key factor in the Lachine Canal revitalization project was
the ongoing dialogue and networking by project leaders, and notably by
Parks Canada. A number of committees were set up to bring together all
actors with a direct or indirect stake in the project (Michel and Sénécal
2002). These included intergovernmental committees, forums for dialogue with local residents, neighbourhood groups, and business people,
and more formal mechanisms of public consultation. Dialogue and
consultation were particularly important because many groups had
expressed concerns about the possible gentrification of the area. Compromises were worked out through consultation with organizations that
were more closely tied to the government, notably by placing limits
on residential development and reaffirming the area's working class and
industrial history (Michel and Sénécal 2002). Committee work was
complemented by ongoing networking whose aim was to keep partners
informed about the progress of the project.

Phase I of the revitalization was completed in 2003. Subsequent difficulties in initiating the next phase of revitalization show that the initial
favourable conditions no longer exist, even though stakeholders did make
a commitment to pursuing urban redevelopment at the Montreal Summit
in 2002. The federal government is not prepared to invest the funds needed to kick start a new phase. In light of this situation, the City of Montreal
has launched a new lobbying and awareness campaign similar to the one
conducted under the auspices of Grand Montréal Bleu in the early 1990s.
The city has spurred the creation of a non-profit organization – the Société

du Havre – whose goal is to promote the revitalization of the area down-stream from the Lachine Canal. In 2011, the Société du Havre was still seeking partners for the revitalization project.

### CONCLUSION

Since 2000, urban policy in Montreal, while functioning at multiple levels and various territorial scales, has generally borrowed the idea of governance. This does not at all mean that there is in place a successful, stable urban management system. In fact, it primarily bears witness to the challenges that public officials face in responding to contradictory economic and social demands. Results at the end of 2008 have been less than satisfactory; at least this is the conclusion to which we have arrived after examining four understudied public policy areas in Montreal.

Much of our conclusion can undoubtedly be explained by the fact that (federal property management aside) the public policy areas we examined are relatively new – at least in the form they have taken in recent years, image building being a good example. Indeed, in the first three fields we looked at, the policies and programs derive from new economic and social concerns related to various contemporary forms of metropolitanization. Whether the issue is public security, branding the city or metropolitan area for promotional purposes, or the urban Aboriginal presence, we are dealing in each case with a situation strongly impacted either by structural change – including an urban development context increasingly influenced by investment and trade processes linked with the new economy and globalization – or by cultural or political changes that reflect growing concern and openness on the part of civil and political society about the recognition of minorities.

The relative newness of these public policy fields may explain, at least in part, the management problems that we observed and that our respondents reported. It is true that expertise in these areas is still emerging. But this factor alone is not enough to explain the difficulties or problems that the local and metropolitan governments have been unable to resolve. Disagreements between political and social actors and resistance from certain groups to the orientation of implementation of public policies transcend questions of know-how, learning, and expertise. Deep divisions remain between different categories of actors, and between different visions or conceptions of public management. There are also divisions with respect to priority setting for development and related issues in Montreal. Numerous controversies in our policy fields in Montreal in recent years point to the lack of consensus in both political circles and civil society. So the absence of clear and strong policy directions in these areas comes as no surprise.

This finding clearly ties in with the multiple levels of government concerned with these policy fields and, by the same token, with the multiplicity of actors involved. Generally, we find actors attached to three levels of government involved. Moreover, even though the three levels of jurisdiction (federal, provincial, municipal) could in principle be expected to play complementary and sometimes hierarchical roles, this is not what we observed. The role of each government varies depending upon the problem, sector of activity, and the existence of a tradition of intervention, rather than upon the constitutionally recognized prerogatives proper to each. The provincial government sometimes plays a secondary role, notably when dealing with federal property management or certain public security issues. The municipality has little if any involvement in managing the integration of Aboriginal peoples. And the federal government, for its part, tends to get involved on an ad hoc basis for a certain period, then to withdraw, as occurred with respect to the management and promotion of a Montreal brand.

In short, Montreal is characterized by a highly flexible form of multilevel governance, with "variable geometry" that is also quite unstable and not very durable. This observation testifies to the uncertainty typical of the logic of urban action, which is deployed across a range of geographical scales. This pattern was confirmed by many of the respondents we interviewed.

Municipal autonomy proves to be highly relative. In our four policy fields, this is shown by the multitude of economic, social, and political actors that the municipal government must deal with when it seeks to take action. Urban policies address complex, multidimensional problems. So the actors involved in the formulation never fall exclusively under municipal jurisdiction. Sometimes, as is the case with Aboriginal people, the municipal government's involvement is minimal.

It is noteworthy that the urban and metropolitan reforms implemented at the turn of the millennium hardly affected the predominant modes of cooperation between the various levels of government in the four policy fields studied. For example, the metropolitan government still lacks sufficient legitimacy to play a significant role – that is, to be able to modify the configuration of conflictual and cooperative relationships that prevails between the federal, provincial, and municipal governments.

On this point one might consider that there has been a transition period that endures, given the structural adjustments arising from the resistance to the municipal reform by political elites and citizens in suburbs both on and off the island. The conflicts over institutions and local identities strongly channelled the engagement of civil society. But this did not prevent more or less intense mobilization around other issues such as urban development and transit projects and the environment.

What can be done to improve the conduct of urban policy in the fields studied here and in the urban policy field at large, based on the results of our analysis? As we have seen, it remains difficult within the framework of Canadian federalism to coordinate effective public responses to urban problems by the various levels of government. We must reiterate what others have already noted in this regard: there is an absence of a comprehensive federal policy on urban development and planning (Sgro 2002). Canadian cities lack the resources necessary to meet the needs of their residents. This is due in part to the lack of appropriate federal policies in areas such as urban transportation, infrastructure, and housing. But it is also due to the prevailing tensions between the three levels of government and the challenge of building a shared vision of priorities in light of these tensions. Even if there is no ready-made pathway to a solution, we can postulate that no progress will be made unless two conditions are met. First, the federal government must commit to taking urban issues seriously. Second, there must be built a consensus or strong hegemony that can increase the capacity for action on the part of all actors involved in the urban public policy field.

## NOTES

1 In a study comparing twenty-six metropolitan areas in Canada and the United States, Montreal fares poorly in several areas, with low productivity, lower education levels than elsewhere, and a low GDP. Of these twenty-six regions, the Montreal Metropolitan Area was in last place, with a per capita GDP of only $26,000 USD (Montreal Metropolitan Community, 2002: 27).

2 "Everybody is always talking about innovation and creativity, and that is often expressed in culture. It is also expressed in video games. Montréal is recognized for this. It's the creative and innovative side of Montreal that makes the city such a trend setter" (Interview 15, Manager, CMM, our translation).

3 Native Friendship Centre of Montreal, www.nfcm.org, retrieved June 9, 2008.

4 This and subsequent data are from the *Directory of Federal Real Property*, consulted on 16 July 16 2008. The conversion from hectares to km² is ours.

5 *St Lawrence Plan*, modified 26 August 2011, www.planstlaurent.qc.ca.

## LIST OF INTERVIEWS

1 Civil servant (Service de sécurité incendie de Montréal), 6 July 2007.

2 Civil servant (Saint-Laurent borough, City of Montreal), 4 May 2007.

3 Civil servant (Centre de sécurité civile, City of Montreal), 12 April 2007.

4 Agent (Quebec Division of the Red Cross), 9 May 2007.

5 Civil servant (Public Safety Canada), 4 April 2007.

6 Civil servant (Environment Canada), 18 July 2007.

7 Agent (Association des industriels de l'Est de Montréal), 10 July 2007.

8 Civil servants (Ministère de la Sécurité publique du Québec), 12 July 2007.

9 Civil servant (Services Québec – Mesures d'urgence), 19 June 2007.

10 Civil servant (Environnement Québec, Direction régionale du centre de contrôle environnemental de Montréal, de Laval, de Lanaudière et des Laurentides), 13 June 2007.

11 Civil servant (Ministère de la Sécurité publique du Québec), 20 April 2007.

12 Official (Montreal Health and Social Services Agency), 19 April 2007.

13 Business community representative, Montreal, 17 April 2007.

14 Private promoter, Montreal, 17 April 2007.

15 Civil servant (Communauté métropolitaine de Montréal), Montreal, 18 April 2007.

16 Civil servant (Ministère des Affaires municipales et des Régions du Québec), Montreal, 20 April 2007.

17 Civil servant (Ministère des Affaires municipales et des Régions du Québec), Montreal, 3 May 2007.

18 Business community representative, Montreal, 4 May 2007.

19 Agent (Conférence régionale des élus), Montreal, 8 May 2007.

20 Official (City of Montreal), Montreal, 9 May 2007.

21 Manager (Quartier International), Montreal, 15 May 2007.

22 Manager (Montréal International), Montreal, 17 May 2007.

23 Manager (Conférence régionale des élus), Montreal, 18 May 2007.

24 Civil servant (Ministère de la culture), Montreal, 23 May 2007.

25 Manager (Chambre de Commerce du Montréal Métropolitain), Montreal, 24 May 2007.

26 Manager (Comité aviseur de développement économique Canada pour l'île de Montréal), Montreal, 24 May 2007.

27 Manager (Culture Montréal), Montreal, 7 June 2007.

28 Agent (Société de l'Habitation du Québec), Montreal, 3 April 2007.
29 Aboriginal civil servants (Ministère de la Famille et des Aînés du Québec), Montreal, 26 April 2007.
30 Civil servant (Ministère de la Culture du Québec, direction régionale de Montréal), Montreal, 11 April 2007.
31 Coordinator (Habitat Métis du Nord/Corporation Waskahegen), Montreal, 23 May 2007.
32 Community worker (Native Women's Shelter of Montreal), Montreal, 1 May 2007.
33 Agent (Femmes autochtones du Québec), Montreal, 10 May 2007.
34 Agent (Center for Native Education), Montreal, 29 May 2007.
35 Civil servant (Intergovernmental Affairs Canada), Montreal, 12 April 2007.
36 Civil servant (Ministère de la Culture du Québec), Montreal, 13 June 2007.
37 Civil servant (Parks Canada), Montreal, 19 June 2007.
38 Civil servant (Ministère de la Culture du Québec), Montreal, 5 June 2007.
39 Civil servant (Service des Parcs, City of Montreal), Montreal, 5 June 2007.
40 Civil servant (Lachine borough, City of Montreal), Montreal, 19 June 2007.

## REFERENCES

Bunting, Trudi, and Pierre Filion, eds. 2000. *Canadian Cities in Transition: The Twenty-first Century*. Don Mills, ON: Oxford University Press.

The Canadian Press. "Québec vient en aide à Montréal International." 2 May 2008. http://lapresseaffaires.cyberpresse.ca/.

Centre de sécurité civile de Montréal (CSCM). 2007. *Le Lien: Bulletin de liaison du Centre de sécurité civile de la Ville de Montréal* 13, no. 3, Fall.

City of Montreal. 2005. *Imaginer. Réaliser Montréal 2025: Un monde de créativité et de possibilités*. Montreal: City of Montreal. http://www2.ville.montreal.qc.ca/ocpm/pdf/P37/6e.pdf.

Culture Montréal. 2008. "Culture Montréal." http://www.culturemontreal.ca/cult_mtl/culture.htm.

Frattolillo, Pietro, and Stéphane Boutin. 2005. "Le projet de communication des risques industriels dans l'Est de Montréal." In *La communication des risques: Un nouveau défi*, edited by Danielle Maisonneuve, 135–46. Sainte-Foy: Presses de l'Université du Québec.

Gagnon, Alain-G., and Guy Dufresne. 1999. "La gouverne dans la tempête du verglas: Le volet politico-administratif d'un sinistre." *Administration publique du Canada* 42(3): 349–70.

Government of Quebec [Nicolet Commission]. 1999a. "Pour affronter l'imprévisible: les enseignements du verglas de 98." *Rapport de la Commission scientifique et technique chargée d'analyser les événements relatifs à la tempête de verglas survenue du 5 au 9 janvier 1998.* Sainte-Foy: Les Publications du Québec.

Graham, Katherine A., Susan D. Phillips, and Allan M. Maslove. 1998. *Urban Governance in Canada: Representation, Resources and Restructuring.* Toronto: Harcourt Brace.

Hamel, Pierre. 2006. "Institutional Changes and Metropolitan Governance: Can De-amalgamation be Amalgamation? The Case of Montreal." In *Metropolitan Governing: Canadian Cases, Comparative Lessons,* edited by Eran Razin and Patrick J. Smith, 95–120. Jerusalem: The Hebrew University Magnes Press.

Higgins, Benjamin. 1986. *The Rise and Fall? of Montreal: A Case Study of Urban Growth, Regional Economic Expansion and National Development.* Moncton, NB: Canadian Institute for Research on Regional Development.

LeBlanc, Marie-France. 2006. *Des communautés plus ou moins civiques: Le capital social et la gouvernance métropolitaine au Canada et aux États-Unis.* Quebec City: Presses de l'Université Laval.

Léveillée, Jacques. 1987. "L'action économique de la ville de Montréal." In *L'action des grandes villes en France et à l'étranger,* edited by Jean Bouinot, 7–31. Paris: Économica.

Lévesque, Carole. 2003. "La présence des Autochtones dans les villes du Québec: mouvements pluriels, enjeux diversifiés." In *Des gens d'ici: les autochtones en milieu urbain,* edited by David Newhouse and Evelyn Peters, 25–37. Ottawa: Government of Canada, Projet de recherche sur les politiques.

Levine, Marc V. 1990. *The Reconquest of Montreal: Language Policy and Social Change in a Bilingual City.* Philadelphia: Temple University Press.

Lightbody, James. 2006. *City Politics, Canada.* Peterborough, ON: Broadview Press.

Lorinc, John. 2006. *The New City: How The Crisis In Canada's Urban Centres Is Reshaping The Nation.* Toronto: Penguin Canada.

Michel, Gildas, and Gilles Sénécal. 2002. "Le réaménagement de la zone du canal Lachine à Montréal: un grand projet sous tension." In *Grands projets urbains et requalification,* edited by Gilles Sénécal, Jacques Malézieux, and Claude Manzagol, 157–69. Quebec City: Presses de l'Université du Québec.

Monkkonen, Eric H. 1988. *America Becomes Urban (The Development of U.S. Cities & Towns, 1780–1980).* Berkeley: University of California Press.

Montreal Metropolitan Community. 2002. *La Communauté métropolitaine de Montréal: Vision stratégique. Document déclencheur (Tome 1. Diagnostic).* Montreal : Communauté métropolitaine de Montréal.

– 2005. *Cap sur le monde: pour une région métropolitaine de Montréal compétitive.* Montreal: Communauté métropolitaine de Montréal.

– 2008. *Site officiel de la Communauté métropolitaine de Montréal.* http:// www.cmm.qc.ca/.

OCDE. 2004. *Examens territoriaux de l'OCDE: Montréal.* Paris: Publications OCDE.

Paul, Darel E. 2004. "World Cities as Hegemonic Projects: The Politics of Global Imagineering in Montreal." *Political Geography* 23(5):571–96.

Piché, Claude-Armand. 2003. "Lieu historique national du Canada du canal de Lachine: Bilan du projet de revitalisation, première phase 1997–2003." Personal notes.

Poitras, Claire. 2003. "La nouvelle économie à la rescousse des métropoles industrielles: Analyse comparée des stratégies publiques à Montréal et à Glasgow." *International Journal of Canadian Studies/ Revue internationale d'études canadiennes* 27:149–71.

Regroupement des centres d'amitié autochtones du Québec (RCAAQ). 2008. *Évaluation des besoins des autochtones qui composent avec la réalité urbaine de Montréal.* Wendake: RCAAQ.

Savitch, Hank V., and Paul Kantor. 2002. *Cities in the International Marketplace. The Political Economy of Urban Development in North America and Western Europe.* Princeton: Princeton University Press.

Sgro, Judy. 2002. *La stratégie urbaine du Canada: une vision pour le XXIe siècle.* Ottawa: Government of Canada.

Siggner, Andrew J. 2003. "Populations autochtones urbaines: Mise à jour d'après les données du recensement de 2001." In *Des gens d'ici: les autochtones en milieu urbain,* edited by David Newhouse and Evelyn Peters, 17–22. Ottawa: Government of Canada, Projet de recherche sur les politiques.

Société du Havre. 2004. *Le Havre de Montréal, Vision 2025: La ville et son fleuve – une proposition pour l'avenir.*

Statistics Canada. 2008. "Peuples autochtones du Canada en 2006: Inuits, Métis et Premières nations, Recensement de 2006." *Le Quotidien,* 15 January.

6

# Multilevel Governance and Public Policy in Saint John, New Brunswick

GREG MARQUIS

Saint John, once one of the leading urban centres in the dominion, is one of Canada's smallest CMA cities. Together with its location in an outlying hinterland, this makes Saint John and its problems relatively unknown in Ottawa. In the perceptive words of one person interviewed for this project, "It is at the bottom of the urban agenda" (Interview 13). The population of the city began to decline in the early 1970s as more families and homeowners moved to surrounding suburban municipalities, which, in terms of per capita income, are some of the most prosperous in New Brunswick. Partly because of the skyline and the concentration of industrial enterprise, Saint John has been mistakenly labeled an industrial city. The community, since the mid-twentieth century, has suffered from a negative reputation as politically conservative, poor, polluted, shabby in appearance, and lacking middle-class amenities and culture (Marquis 2005, 2007). Recently, for example, the Conference Board of Canada rated the Saint John CMA as "the second least attractive" in Canada for immigrants (*Telegraph Journal* 2007a).

In Saint John, a mid-sized Canadian city with a limited tax base and mounting governance challenges, development since the last third of the twentieth century has depended on large companies or the provincial and federal governments. Each level of politics is dominated by the question of economic development.[1] This chapter examines multilevel governance (MLG) in Saint John with a focus on four policy areas: image building, immigration, federal-provincial infrastructure programs, and emergency planning.[2] In terms of relations among the three levels of government, residents think not in terms of multilevel governance, but in terms of funding agreements and job creation. In 2007, for example, the three levels of government announced a federal government commitment of up to $8.1 million from the Public Transit Capital Trust for a municipal transit operations centre. The announcement photograph includes Saint John's mayor, a local member of the provincial Liberal caucus, and two Conservative MPS from outside of Saint John, which in 2007 was represented federally by a Liberal. In a mid-sized city in a "have not" region, partisan squabbling can coexist with non-partisan cooperation and deal-making involving the three levels of government.

## BACKGROUND

The population of the City of Saint John in 2001 was 69,661, or 56.8 percent of the total CMA. Between 1976 and 2001 the city lost 22.6 percent of its population. By 2006, the total had fallen to 68,043. Saint John contains significant pockets of poverty, especially involving single-parent families, and lacks affordable housing. One quarter of all families are lone-parent, usually headed by a woman. Almost half of the dwelling units are rented, in contrast with bedroom communities in nearby Kings county where the median family income in 2001 was 58 percent higher than in the city. Despite Saint John's smokestack image, the five largest manufacturing or processing companies, all located within city limits, accounted for less than 4 percent of the employed workforce in 2001. Roughly three-fifths of workers in the CMA belonged to the business, finance, administration, management, sales and service sectors. Within the sales and service sector, several thousand people work in information technology (IT) and telemarketing and communications. Provincial politicians and local boosters promoted IT and call centres in the 1990s as a way to bring Saint John into the new economy and away from a reliance on large cyclical construction projects such as the multibillion dollar frigate contract won by Saint John Shipbuilding. As of 2001, a year after the shipyard was mothballed, Saint John was home to 40 percent of the province's IT workforce and had been anointed by *Time* magazine as one of the top IT cities in Canada. Education, health care, and government services also employed several thousands in the CMA. Between 1996 and 2007, although the CMA's population remained stagnant, the number of persons employed grew by almost one third, and the unemployment rate fell to under 6 percent (McMackin 2001; Enterprise Saint John 2007a, 2007b). Until the May 2008 election, which introduced a modified at-large/ward system of representation, the mayor and council were elected at-large.

Municipal and provincial politics in greater Saint John operate in the shadow of the powerful Irving family interests whose newspaper, the *Telegraph Journal*, traditionally has been an important part of a growth coalition that has included politicians and "community leaders" who are tied in to the Liberal and Conservative parties, the Board of Trade, the construction sector and organized labour.[3] The growth coalition is both constrained and motivated by the fact that New Brunswick lacks a dominant city; in 2006, the Saint John and Moncton CMAs and the Fredericton Census Agglomeration constituted of 16.7 percent, 17.3 percent, and 11.7 percent of the province's population respectively (Interview 13; Statistics Canada 2006). The language of development resonates with the competitive spirit of nineteenth-century boosterism, with Saint John's interests usually pitted against those of rivals Fredericton and greater Moncton.[4] Much of the Irving industrial empire is located within city limits and includes an oil refinery, two pulp mills, and a new liquefied natural gas (LNG) terminal (LNG is natural gas imported via tanker to be "regasified" and exported by pipeline, in this case to the United States). By 2008, despite the launch in 2005 of a more balanced True Growth economic development strategy, business and political leaders embraced a more narrow energy hub strategy.[5] This economic development strategy was based on the existing energy base as well as a controversial LNG pipeline to New England, a proposed second refinery, and a refurbished nuclear power plant at nearby Point Lepreau. The proposed refinery, which like much of the energy hub would focus on exports to the United States, represented a potential investment of several billion dollars and 1,000 new jobs (Enterprise Saint John 2007a). In 2009, Irving announced that the second oil refinery would not be constructed.

It is difficult to find any public official, labour leader, or organization opposed to the energy hub. Energy projects are being promoted by the Atlantica Centre for Energy, based in Saint John, an industry-funded "independent voice" that portrays opponents of energy industrialization as follows: "Public discussion is often impeded by highly vocal posturing of confrontational anti-development groups who oppose any and all new energy developments in their community. Oftentimes these groups are motivated by rigid attitudes and ideologies about private sector-led development. They often seem to be more interested in 'opposing' than in 'understanding and critiquing' a potential project or development" (Curry, n.d.).[6] This quotation hints at the challenges faced by citizens and social forces that oppose or question aspects of the energy hub, a situation compounded by the monopolization of the province's print media by the Irving interests. The energy hub was supported not only by the five area municipalities, but also by the Liberal provincial government, which saw Saint John's re-industrialization as the key to its self-sufficiency agenda, and by the Conservative federal government. The local Liberal MP supported not only the energy hub, but also the provincial government's decision to hire Atomic Energy of Canada Limited to conduct a feasibility study for a second nuclear reactor in the greater Saint John area. Simply put, energy in the period 2007–09 was "the gorilla in the room," influencing even the province's post-secondary education agenda. An important aspect of this focus on energy as the salvation for not only Saint John but also the province was its emphasis not on government, but on private capital (Zed 2007).[7] The non-partisan appeal of the energy hub helped to explain the virtual absence of public resistance to the environmental approval of the Irving-Repsol YPF LNG terminal near Saint John in 2004, in contrast to the active opposition from the New Brunswick public, environmental organizations, and politicians to similar facilities planned for the American side of Passamaquoddy Bay. Similarly, the decision by NB Power to convert its Coleson Cove plant to burn Venezuelan orimulsion, a dirtier fuel than petroleum, was widely applauded by the growth coalition because it provided construction jobs (McMullin 2007).

When research for this chapter began in 2006, New Brunswick had a Conservative provincial government led by Bernard Lord, with several members of the legislative assembly (MLAs) in the Saint John area, and Canada had a Liberal government. Saint John, up to the 2004 federal election, had been represented for nearly a dozen years by Progressive Conservative MP (and former mayor) Elsie Wayne. The result of the 2004 contest was the election of a Liberal, who was flanked on the east and west in rural and suburban ridings by Conservatives. The same pattern held with the January 2006 federal election, which produced the Harper minority Conservative government. Prior to the 2006 provincial election, which defeated Lord's Conservative government, the Saint John area had been represented by four Progressive Conservatives, three Liberals, and a lone NDP MLA. The election involved a Liberal sweep in the Saint John area; a lone Tory member remained in the city itself, surrounded by six Liberals and two Conservatives in the city and area (Elections Canada 2006; Elections New Brunswick 2006). Although there are no official party slates in municipal politics, partisanship is a longstanding factor in public affairs. Many candidates for provincial and federal office have served as city councillors or on public boards and agencies and hail from the business and legal sectors. Party operatives and staff are recruited from various boards and the leadership of voluntary organizations. The impact of the two-party system, combined with the economic power of local industrialists, limits the extent and influence of social forces in the community and, according to some, silences dissent. In the city, as in the province as a whole, there is much overlap between the provincial and federal parties, which most often is apparent in electioneering. For example, following the "second announcement" of federal infrastructure funding for a highway project in Saint John, the local Liberal MP, who had assisted in the election campaign of the provincial Liberal government, praised Premier Graham "for being aggressive and finalizing this agreement" (Mazerolle 2007). On the other hand, political leaders in the growth coalition also resort to the language of nonpartisanship, such as "Team Saint John." The team concept usually relates to lobbying directed at the federal government and its senior officials (Zed 2005).

## IMAGE BUILDING

In the late-twentieth century, boosters in Saint John, as elsewhere, became convinced that selling the city's image was as important, or more important, than providing modern infrastructure and competitive business conditions (Trueman 2001). It was first necessary to fashion a new image. The beginning of Saint John's negative image coincided with its relative economic decline in the decade following World War I, when the Maritime region as a whole experienced an economic downturn. Starting in the late 1950s, a growth coalition promoted three policies that affected the city's image: industrial development based mainly on resource processing; transportation infrastructure centred on the federally-owned port, and urban redevelopment based on slum clearance and urban renewal in and around the central business district (CBD). The existence of two pulp mills by the 1960s the prominence of rail and port facilities, the construction of an oil refinery, and the expansion of the Irving shipyard and dry dock and oil tanker docking facilities in Courtenay Bay produced a smoke stack skyline and added to Saint John's reputation as a polluted blue collar community. The stereotype surrounding the city was that it was "notoriously dirty, smelly and awash with pollution" (Carson 2002). The two senior levels of government contributed to this so-called lunch bucket image by employing relatively few civil servants in the area.

One attempt in the early 1980s at countering this negative image, and revitalizing the declining CBD, was the creation of Trinity Royal, a heritage preservation district of late Victorian brick and stone buildings, many of them residential properties, that has featured prominently in tourism promotion. Positive image building was hampered by decades of expert, media, and NGO advocacy on issues such as housing and income that bolstered an image of Saint John as poverty city. A recent statistical report by Vibrant Communities and the Saint John Human Development Council,[8] for example, is entitled *Poverty amid Plenty*. The 2001 census revealed that 10.3 percent of the population and 30.9 percent of low-income persons lived in high poverty neighbourhoods. The averages for all Canadian CMAs were 4.6 percent and 11.9 percent respectively (Peacock 2005; Marquis 2007). Other NGOs have emerged to work on the poverty and housing issues, including ONE Change and the Business Community Anti-Poverty Initiative. One Liberal MLA who was interviewed expressed concern over the large number of "working poor" in the city and their exclusion from many of the benefits of urban development (Interview 9). The negative image pertained to more than social deprivation; during the 1990s, the assessed value of property in the CBD fell by one quarter, there was little construction activity, and the fringes of the area displayed signs of urban disinvestment (Mullin 2007). A representative of the local economic development agency acknowledged the negative impact of poverty on Saint John's image but explained that "growing urban centres always have problems" (Interview 9).

Although the federal and provincial governments are responsible for most social program spending, the economic and demographic structure of the city, with its large population of poor families and persons on fixed income, together with a less than robust municipal revenue situation, and the power of provincial governments to freeze or cut taxes on local industries, restricts the ability of the municipal government to assist vulnerable neighbourhoods.[9] Complicating this situation is decades-old pressure from major industries and groups such as the Board of Trade to cut municipal taxes and services and the growth coalition focus on the CBD to the neglect of vulnerable neighbourhoods. New Brunswick cities, which carry the third highest per capita debt load in the nation, depend on property assessments and provincial unconditional grants for their own budgets. Throughout the 1990s, those grants declined by 29 percent, prompting protests from the Cities of New Brunswick Association. The provincial budget (20 percent of which consists of transfer payments) is sensitive to federal government spending fluctuations. Provincial officials have cited a lack of flexibility in acquiring and spending federal funds in cities; municipal officials in turn complain about provincial government barriers to fixing urban problems (*Telegraph Journal* 1999; Klager 2002a; MacKinnon 2004).

In 1991, the City of Saint John and the Board of Trade (the major business organization) conducted a survey of Saint John CMA residents. A majority of those surveyed rated the area as a good place to live and believed that conditions had improved over the past several years. The most notable pattern was the high proportion of respondents who identified pollution as a major problem compared to other cities in Atlantic Canada. The survey indicated a demographic split in that younger, better-educated residents were less satisfied with broader "quality of life" issues and exhibited less attachment to the community (Corporate Research Associates Inc. 1991). Although environmental issues were a high priority, Saint John, as a result of provincial and federal legislation and industry efforts, had taken important steps towards improving its air quality starting in the late 1970s. The general public, according to the findings of an on-going municipal visioning effort, continues to prioritize environmental remediation and protection and preservation of green space. Opposition in 2007 to the route of a natural gas pipeline, owned by the Emera Brunswick Pipeline Company, indicates that social forces in Saint John have the capacity to periodically challenge, if not seriously hamper, the growth coalition (Young 2004).

For many, the closure of the Saint John Shipyard and the disappearance of its 4,000 highly-paid jobs signaled the end of an era; former Premier Frank McKenna spoke of shipbuilding as "a sunset industry" and urged business leaders to embrace the new economy (Roik 2003).[10] The growth strategy developed in 2003 by the regional development agency, funded in part by Ottawa and adopted in 2005 by Saint John and four neighbouring municipalities, highlighted tourism as a key economic engine for future growth. As a result of business lobbying, most of the attention in terms of tourism has been on the "uptown" area, part of the CBD and on cruise ship traffic. As with other cities, attempts to spruce up the CBD and to improve the quality of life have led to periodic attempts to address street begging. At a growth strategy meeting in 2003, business and political leaders discussed the need for the city to "define itself" and attract people by upgrading its "blue collar image."

A journalist reported what the census statistics had revealed for years, that Saint John was no longer an industrial city. The mayor at that time even suggested that the iconic "Loyalist man," a tourism promotion image that tapped into the city's eighteenth-century roots but had existed only since the early 1960s, be updated (Kerr 2003; City of Saint John 2007). To the consternation of traditionalists, these discussions produced, with the help of an outside consultant, a new logo and motto for the "Loyalist" city: a generic "explorer person," peering through a telescope, which supposedly paid tribute to the city's entrepreneurial spirit. The new motto was "Explore Our Past. Discover Your Future." The growth strategy and the new logo were an attempt to provide a city with a negative outside reputation and an uncertain economic future with a positive brand (Trueman 2003b; Urquhart 2003).

An important project that has affected Saint John's image in the past several years is Harbour Passage, a waterfront trail designed to bring the public back to the harbour area. The project was spearheaded by the Saint John Development Corporation, formed in 1980, mainly to advance the Market Square development project near the CBD. It is managed by a business-heavy Waterfront Development Partnership composed of the City of Saint John, the Province of New Brunswick, Uptown Saint John Inc., Enterprise Saint John Inc., Saint John Board of Trade, and the Saint John Port Authority. The first phase was completed in 2003 and attracted considerable public support. As with Camden, New Jersey's waterfront development, Harbour Passage is about improving the city's image as much as creating tourism and small business spin-offs (Gillette 2005). The first stage envisioned a plan for the inner harbour that would enhance the value of waterfront properties and promote tourism, recreation, and culture with a low-impact trail that interpreted the city's natural and human history. One of the chief rationales behind the project is the use of public resources – land and money – to leverage private investment. The general manager of the Saint John Waterfront Development Partnership has estimated that Harbour Passage, over a period of fifteen years, will create more than $240 million in private investment and an increased tax base for the city (Chillibeck 2006a).

In terms of funding, waterfront development has been mainly a municipal-provincial issue, although the Atlantic Canada Opportunities Agency (ACOA) and the Port Authority have made contributions and other federal agencies and departments are consulted (Interview 1). The federal government is involved in this policy area because it owns and operates the Port of Saint John, which controls access to the water, as well as Partridge Island, a neglected heritage site. The senior level of government also owned a strategic waterfront property known as the Coast Guard site, which both private and public developers have eyed for a decade or more. The basic mission of the Port Authority is to maximize traffic and revenues for the port, which provides for more than 3,000 direct and indirect jobs and a $10 million payroll, according to the head of the Authority. Statistically, Saint John by the late 1990s was one of the busiest ports in Canada, but in reality most of the tonnage shipped constituted petroleum products handled by private Irving facilities. Despite this, port officials and International Longshoremen's Association Local 273 have opposed changing traditional inner harbour land use away from cargo handling exclusively towards tourism and recreation. One exception is support for the development of a multimillion dollar cruise ship terminal on the east side of the harbour, which will cost up to $12 million. The former president of the Waterfront Development Partnership resigned when the Port Authority permitted the ongoing open storage of limestone, which many considered unsightly and a barrier to future development of condos and other amenities (Davis 2002; Urban Strategies 2003; Williams 2005).

Most of the interviewees were positive about how the three levels of government interacted in the area of city image building, although direct federal government contributions to this policy area were not easily identified. One elected official, MLA 2, stated that the energy hub was a positive contribution to the city's image, and also believed that the city would benefit from the Graham government's polices on population growth, postsecondary education, self-sufficiency, and health (Interview 8). MLA 3 explained that Saint John had been associated with "multiple images" for many years; one of these was that the city was a "labour town." A new economic prosperity, including the lowest unemployment rate in history, was supposedly channeling these conflicting images into a single positive image (Interview 9). A prominent arts community member was generally optimistic that Saint John was projecting a "revived image" as a vibrant, liveable community, and that politicians and business leaders were appreciative of the social and economic contributions of the arts. He also pointed to the CBD's rich stock of Victorian buildings as a genuine asset (Interview 15).

One social forces interviewee questioned the impact of the energy hub focus on Saint John's image; with its emphasis on heavy industry, the energy hub focus seems to conflict with the type of quality of life and new economy development promoted in other cities. A controversial tax break on the LNG project had split the community and damaged the city's reputation by reviving accusations that Saint John was an Irving company town. There was a "perception" in the community that those with economic power enjoyed special influence and that regulatory and other policy decisions were characterized by "too much political discretion." This interviewee opined that non-elected bodies such as Enterprise Saint John, the Board of Trade, and Uptown Saint John,[11] had the biggest impact on the city's "official" image (Interview 3). A second NGO representative was positive about the quality of life promises of True Growth, but questioned whether the current economic boom was actually helping the poor (Interview 4). A third stated that based on the poor state of the immigration policy field (see below), city image was suffering (Interview 6). The representative of a fourth NGO described its mission as ensuring that development does not ignore social issues (Interview 5). A fifth, commenting on business-driven city image making, asked rhetorically whether you can "wish a better city" into being. For this interviewee, the energy hub is simply an old idea – heavy industry megaprojects and the boom-bust economy – dressed up in new clothes (Interview 13). The labour representative interviewed was enthusiastic about the investment and employment promises of the expected boom, but worried that large companies exerted too much power in the community. He feared that members of the municipal government were too closely identified with the Irving interests (Interview 16).

A representative of the Board of Trade described the True Growth strategy as innovative but in need of more attention. All polices under discussion were described as equitable and "attuned to meet all needs." The board itself was described as "proactive" in its various activities affecting city image, operating within a consensus framework and mostly successful in its activities (Interview 4). One example of Board of Trade activity was lobbying to secure additional airlines servicing the federally-owned Saint John airport. The Board of Trade, and its several hundred individual members, were described as playing a "huge" role in the city image field (Interview 4). Part of the True Growth Strategy was reclaiming the waterfront area for both leisure and other commercial purposes. A representative of the Waterfront Development Partnership, which enjoys support from the business community, described Harbour Passage as a "catalyst for development" and a positive use of public space that signaled the community's "confidence" in its future (Interview 1).

IMMIGRATION

Compared to other provinces, New Brunswick attracts few immigrants. It also suffers from outmigration; between 2001 and 2006, it experienced a net loss of more than 10,000 people. Saint John, and the province as a whole, is missing out on mainstream immigration. In 2006, immigrants were less than five percent of the city's population. Given that urban population growth in Canada depends on immigration, this places Saint John at a decided disadvantage. In New Brunswick, an immigrant is more likely to be from the United States, Great Britain, Germany, or the Netherlands than Latin America, Africa, or Asia (Linke 2007a; Statistics Canada 2006). Business leaders are promoting increased immigration not as a social reform or human rights issue, but as tool for economic development. Newcomers are seen as a way to counter the province's shrinking population (and workforce) and its poorly-educated (as defined by the business sector) workforce. The True Growth Strategy, for example, identified attracting former residents and immigrants as a high priority (Kerr 2005).

The provincial government, initially working through a Population Growth Secretariat reporting to the Minister of Business, has been attempting to reverse population decline by boosting provincial immigration to 5,000 a year by 2015. A minister in the Liberal government identified immigration, in the context of the provincial self-sufficiency agenda, as a top priority. ACOA, the federal regional development agency, has been involved in promoting the region as a destination for immigrants. In addition, the regional development agency, Enterprise Saint John, has been working with Moncton and Fredericton to bring a facility to the city that would assist immigrants in the broader Maritime region, a project also promoted by Saint John's MP (Interview 8). Most landed immigrants arrive as part of the provincial nominee program, which focuses on wealthy newcomers. The average nominee arrives with $400,000 to invest in a business. At present, despite hopes for a regional immigration centre, Saint John is competing with both Moncton and Fredericton for immigrants. Between 2001 and 2006, the CMA attracted only 920 landed immigrants, with a noticeable increase of families from South Korea. Recently, the provincial business minister spoke of a "disconnect" between New Brunswick's immigration requirements and the role of the federal government (Trueman 2005; Linke 2007b).[12] Earlier, another minister expressed frustration at Ottawa's control of immigration, and suggested that the Martin government expend part of its large surplus on infrastructure and services for immigrants to the Maritime provinces (McGinnis 2002).

Immigration recruitment and retention was identified by all interviewees who spoke on the topic as a weak policy area for Saint John, in terms of its scale, timeliness, and support from government (Interviews 2, 4, 9, and 10). Opinion polls suggest that residents of the city, one of the least diverse in Canada, are not all convinced of the economic benefits of immigration. One MLA and a union official spoke of a feeling in the community that it was important to help local residents first and newcomers second (Interviews 9 and 16). Interviews with immigrants, and with organizations that work with them, indicated the employment is the single most important challenge in both attracting and retaining newcomers. Retention rates are a particular problem in Saint John; many immigrant families leave the area within five years of arriving (Maclean 2006; Linke 2005). Lack of both fulfilling jobs and cultural pluralism are not the only barriers. In 2004, a national report gave New Brunswick a rating of F for settlement services and C for immigrant language services (Friesen and Hyndman 2005).

Representatives of social forces spoke of the need for the community to be more accepting of diversity and reflective of the broader Canadian experience. They stress immigration recruitment and retention as part of the "inclusion agenda," not strictly an economic development strategy (Interview 5). Like business and political representatives, they stressed a lack of coherence and funding in this policy area, which, in the words of one informant, has produced "huge delays" in implementation. Saint John's immigration strategy was deemed to be inclusive, balanced, and well-planned, but stalled (Interview 5). Population decline – the very issue driving business interest in immigration – was mentioned as a detrimental factor influencing immigrant recruitment and retention: "Can a city of 60,000 sustain the social services we think we deserve?" (Interview 5). Another social forces representative doubted that greater Saint John could attract significant intraprovincial migration; immigration is the only possible source of new population, yet the modern immigrant wants to live in Montreal, Toronto, and Vancouver. He pointed to the business orientation of immigration policy – evidenced by the presence of immigration consultants – as lacking balance (Interview 13).

The main point of contact for newcomers in the city is the Immigrant and Refugee Support Centre, operated by the YM-YWCA. Its key informant spoke of obstacles to program delivery, such as a shortage of staff and resources for language training. Overall, policy is shaped by federal officials in Ottawa, who supply the funds; the NGO acts as contractor. The lack of a mandate to provide services to refugees, who are a growing presence in the greater Saint John community and have links with various churches, was identified as a problem. Although the city lacks an active multicultural association, the informant for the YM-YWCA cited the role of other organizations, such as the University of New Brunswick Saint John, the New Brunswick Community College, Enterprise Saint John, the Human Development Council, and the Chinese Cultural Centre, in supporting immigration recruitment and retention (Interview 6). According to a community activist, one of several reasons why the Saint John branch of the University of New Brunswick was vital to the community's future was its role in attracting international students (Interview 14).

A Board of Trade official confirmed the interest of the business community in immigration, particularly in terms of workforce needs. Its representative described as unfortunate a decision to cut funding for Avantage Saint John Advantage, a program the promoted bilingualism in the business sector. It had been supported by both the provincial and federal governments. The Board of Trade also cited the need for someone to spearhead the immigration file (Interview 5). According to MLA 2, who was also a cabinet member, immigration had emerged as a "defined policy" only in 2007 (Interview 7). MLA 3 described the federal government as "control oriented" and "a bit rigid" on the immigration file, but believed that Ottawa was "listening" now that New Brunswick had formed a Population Growth Secretariat (Interview 8).

FEDERAL-PROVINCIAL INFRASTRUCTURE PROGRAMS

Lobbying efforts for cost-shared infrastructure in Saint John traditionally have emphasized two arguments: practical requirements and the business community's desire to attract and retain "residents and wealth" (Trueman 2003). With a declining population in the city, and growing suburban municipalities nearby, Saint John cannot use population growth as a justification for infrastructure. Yet, there remains an obsession with "putting up buildings" (Interview 14). The growth coalition sometimes nurtures certain projects for decades until they come into being, often much modified from their original plan because of political complications or the need to bring other parties into the deal. Other projects are embraced for short-term political reasons. As late as 2003, for example, the Board of Trade and large industries benefiting from special water rates, warned that the city's ambitious water and waste-water modernization plan would raise taxes and place businesses at a competitive disadvantage. Yet, a few years later most business boosters were publicly supporting "harbour clean-up," which had become a top priority with the public and an issue of interest to the federal and provincial parties during election campaigns (Malik 2006). According to a labour spokesperson, infrastructure announcements are timed for election purposes (Interview 16).

Starting with its port and rail facilities in the late nineteenth century, Saint John looked to the federal government for assistance with large infrastructure projects. The trend continued under various urban renewal and development schemes starting in the late 1950s, which also involved the provincial government. Since the 1960s, many major public projects have been planned on the basis of "33 cent dollars," tripartite cost-sharing by the three levels of government (Marquis 2005b). During the years when the city was represented by a Conservative MP in opposition to a Liberal national government, there was a feeling that "federal dollars" were bypassing the city. By the early twenty-first century, municipalities in New Brunswick, like those elsewhere in Canada, were looking to Ottawa for a substantial cash infusion to repair crumbling infrastructure (White 2002). In 2004, the mayor (a former provincial Conservative cabinet minister) and the new Liberal MP revived an approach from the 1970s: "Team Saint John," a nonpartisan lobbying effort based on trips to and communications with federal officials in Ottawa. The team (which does not include provincial MLAS) "wins" when it secures funding from Ottawa, such as ACOA financial assistance to the ailing Saint John-to-Digby, Nova Scotia ferry service or money for the Saint John Transit Commission (Mullin 2004).

The business community has continued to push for traditional transportation infrastructure that supposedly assists economic development. Since the early 1990s, for example, the Board of Trade has advocated the construction of the "One-Mile House Interchange," an elevated connector road to divert heavy truck traffic connecting with the industrial park and oil refinery away from the city centre. In June 2007, the federal and provincial governments announced a cost-sharing agreement to complete the project (Mazerolle 2007; Interview 12). Typically, boosters regard each new publicly-funded project, zoning change, tax concession, or environmental approval as a necessary precondition to the city's entire future prosperity. Rather than a simple – but expensive – traffic engineering project, the president of the Board of Trade describes the

One-Mile House project as "leveraging $7 billion in investment in the new refinery" (Malik 2007).

Harbour cleanup is one infrastructure project that has been both a victim and a product of politics. Promoted by environmental organizations such as the Atlantic Coastal Action Program (ACAP) Saint John,[13] the multimillion dollar project is not so much a cleanup as source-control pollution prevention. Because of a failure to upgrade infrastructure, by the early twenty-first century almost half of Saint John's municipal sewage was being pumped untreated into the harbour, in violation of provincial environmental regulations. Municipal officials hoped that the city's wastewater treatment plan would receive funding from the provincial and federal governments, as was the case with Halifax and St John's. ACAP's education and awareness efforts helped push sewage treatment to the centre of the stage. It also dovetailed nicely with the push for waterfront development, a prominent civic issue. Partisan disputes and electioneering delayed cooperation between the two senior levels of government until 2006, following the election of the Graham provincial government, which made harbour cleanup one of its first priorities. In 2007, after a false start, Stephen Harper's Conservative government also made a formal commitment of $26.6 million to the project. The federal commitment was made under the Canada Strategic Infrastructure Fund (Klager 2002; New Brunswick 2007a).[14]

Most of the officials interviewed wanted to discuss infrastructure in general and not the specific programs that are the focus of the MLG project. The Canada-New Brunswick Municipal Rural Infrastructure Fund, announced in 2003, involves ACOA, the provincial government and participating municipalities. Cash-strapped municipalities were optimistic in 2003 when the Martin government appointed Fredericton MP Andy Scott as minister of state for infrastructure. The Canada-New Brunswick Infrastructure Program (CNBIP) agreement was signed in 2004. The maximum total federal contribution for New Brunswick was to be $54 million and the emphasis was to be on "green," local government infrastructure. A minimum 40 percent of project funding was earmarked for rural communities, including Local Service Districts. Municipalities could apply to the provincial Capital Borrowing Board to help fund their contributions. By 2008, the CNBIP had provided funding for Saint John to build two new water towers (Infrastructure Canada 2004; Chiarelli 2003). Saint John also is benefiting from the federal gas-tax rebate, an initiative developed by the Martin Liberal government as part of its New Deal for Cities and Communities and honoured by the

Conservatives. The nearly $15 million earmarked to assist Saint John in repairing water mains, roads, and bridges in the period 2007–12 is channeled through the provincial government, which requires municipalities to develop capital investment plans. Municipalities feel shortchanged under this agreement (*Telegraph Journal* 2007b).[15]

A business representative concluded that infrastructure projects had been delayed partly because of the bureaucratic process and partly because of "a lack of vision." This informant declared that it was important to make a "business case" for specific projects (Interview 4). The social forces representatives interviewed accept the need for basic infrastructure investment, such as water and sewage modernization, and agree that other projects benefit the community. But they expressed concern that the emphasis on infrastructure to aid industry indicates a growing divide between "haves and have-nots" (Interview 5). Everyone agreed that Saint John has aging infrastructure, but planning, in the opinion of one NGO spokesperson, was characterized by insufficient "critical thinking" and too much competition among communities (Interview 13). A labour official expressed concern about the growing popularity in policy discussions of public-private partnerships (Interview 16). In the view of MLA 3, tripartite infrastructure projects benefit the entire community – not simply one economic class. This representative, in a 2007 interview, hinted at forthcoming Liberal initiatives and repeated the importance of supporting programs for the poor and underemployed and funding NGOs such as AIDS Saint John (Interview 8). Yet one veteran community activist believed that the economic planning agenda, largely because of the absence of a strong municipal presence, was driven by the business sector (Interview 14).

EMERGENCY PLANNING

As a major port and industrial centre, Saint John has experienced a number of natural and human-made disasters, such as flooding, the 1998 ice storm, and various industrial accidents. The presence of an oil refinery close to the central city, railroad rolling stock carrying hazardous materials, and the new LNG terminal and pipeline make local officials and neighbourhoods highly conscious of industrial emergencies. The existing oil refinery is less than two kilometres from the city's major shopping mall area. In 1998, for example, an explosion and fire in a boiler killed one worker before it was contained by refinery emergency crews. The surrounding community was apprehensive about how the situation was handled. Recent deliberations by the Common Council (the name of the city council) and hearings by the National Energy Board over the route of a natural gas pipeline through the city prompted Saint John's fire chief to state his concerns to the municipal government about the company's proposed route, which he believed was dangerously close to the oil refinery, manufacturing plants with hazardous materials, an electrical substation, and a radio tower used by the police and fire departments. He also cited a lack of proper training and equipment in dealing with large industrial accidents (Kinnear 2003).

Under the New Brunswick Emergency Measures Act, each municipality must maintain an emergency measures organization and prepare emergency measures plans. Provincially, emergency planning and preparedness is coordinated by the NB Emergency Measures Organization (EMO). The Saint John EMO, which reports to the Common Council, works with a variety of community partners. Most of the agencies and organizations involved in planning and responding to emergency situations are municipal or provincial, such as Saint John Energy (the electrical utility), the Atlantic Health Sciences Corporation (in charge of local hospitals), the police, fire, and emergency medical services, the municipal water and works departments, New Brunswick EMO, or nongovernmental organizations such as the Red Cross, St John Ambulance, and the Salvation Army. The major federal agency involved is the Saint John Port Authority (Saint John Emergency Management Organization 2007).[16] Other than voluntary organizations that are part of the emergency measures network, few social forces are involved in this policy area, although environmental advocates have raised the issue of climate change and its impact on flooding, storm events, and coastal erosion. One exception is the Board of Trade, which, through its periodic attacks on municipal taxation and expenditure, has demanded cutbacks in fire and policing services (Editorial 2001).

The main person interviewed on the subject of disaster planning was the Saint John fire chief, who was also the director of the Saint John EMO. Chief Robert Simonds was professional and informative. Although he was in regular communication with the local MP, and reported that federal initiatives were on the horizon, his main point of contact was with the provincial government and provincial officials, such as the director of the New Brunswick EMO. The province is also involved in the federal Joint Emergency Preparedness Program, a shared-cost program that funds equipment for mobile command posts, telecommunications, and emergency operations centres. The federal government's role in the emergency measures policy field was limited to a helping and educational capacity. A committee of the Saint John Common Council is also involved and all plans and policies are approved by the municipal level. According to the chief, Saint John has a limited number of potential hazards, but there is neighbourhood sensitivity to various risks, as evidenced in the 2006 hearings and media discussion on LNG safety (Interview 11). The Saint John EMO is supported by a single full-time employee. The chief spoke of a high level of coordination in the provision of emergency services in greater Saint John; emergency management was not as well coordinated but this is likely to change. Both Saint John and the neighbouring towns of Rothesay and Quispamsis in the Kennebecasis valley maintain separate emergency operations centres (EOCs). The Saint John EOC also involves specific industrial representatives. The chief was in favour of greater cooperation and coordination because "emergencies do not respect municipal boundaries" (Interview 11).

### GOVERNANCE RELATIONSHIPS

The public face of urban policy, as presented in the media, is that the mayor, Common Council, and municipal bureaucrats are responsible for successes and failures. Interviews with five elected officials revealed a more complex reality, and one that transcended political partisanship. Mayor McFarlane reported constant communication between municipal officials and the provincial government, "from the premier on down" (Interview 2). He identified the senior government MLA for the Saint John area as the key contact and stressed the need for cooperation among the five municipalities of the greater Saint John region in areas such as economic development, image building, emergency planning, and the attraction and retention of immigrants. Municipal officials working on infrastructure and other projects also deal with the local MP, the regional minister in the federal cabinet, and other federal ministers (Interview 2). The three Liberal government MLAs interviewed spoke in general terms of the need for all three levels of government to cooperate; they stressed, however, that Ottawa's most important role was not in policy evolution or specific projects but in funding. The MLAs also acknowledged the government's need to be seen as treating all regions of the province, and towns and cities, on equal terms (Interviews 7, 8, and 9).

At the time of the interviews (2007–08), the Saint John business community was focused on the promises of the energy hub, with its projections of massive private sector investments and labour force shortages.

The business representatives, speaking on behalf of "the community," saw their projects and policy goals as consensus-driven and non-controversial. The interviews with the three business organization representatives suggested the importance of continuity and persistence in promoting municipal, provincial, and federal cooperation and funding of infrastructure and other projects. Non-elected individuals – politicians' staff and public servants – were identified by the Enterprise Saint John and the Waterfront Development Partnership spokespersons as important in the multilevel governance process (Interviews 1, 4, and 10).

The interviewees from the non-governmental and non-business sector were more critical of MLG relationships in Saint John and in the province in general. Successful outcomes for NGOs depended on grassroots support and organizational needs coinciding with provincial and federal policies and the ups and downs of electoral politics. Personal contacts – with the mayor and Common Council, the regional caucus of the provincial ruling party, and the local MP – were identified as crucial. Criticisms included that the federal government's regional development policies were focused on rural areas at the expense of cities, that the provincial government lacked any substantial "urban policy," and that the "corporate voice" was increasingly powerful in municipal and provincial policies affecting Saint John. Interviewees pointed out that many of the business and community leaders who exert a strong influence on the city, its image, its budget, and its services live not in Saint John but in nearby middle- and upper-class residential communities with few fiscal and infrastructure challenges. The business elite, aided by the private media, have managed to exclude organized labour from much of its historic community role and portray it as a "special interest" (Interviews 2, 5, 6, 13, 14, 15, and 16).

CONCLUSION

Although conservative think tanks such as the Atlantic Institute of Market Studies question traditional regional development and government aid to business, both business and the general public in Saint John continue to value politicians who can turn on the tap of federal government assistance. Given the limited resources of the municipal government, the role of the senior levels, for example, in helping to engineer the closure of the local shipyard, in not subjecting the LNG terminal project to full environmental review, in subsidizing call centre jobs or recruiting immigrant entrepreneurs, is crucial. A survey conducted in 2006 suggested that "what people expect now are big projects to improve their community" (Chilibeck 2006). Those people, it should be noted, had been prepared by hegemonic messages by the growth coalition. The state's role in the energy hub is not that of funder, but enabler, and the rewards are political. The Saint John growth coalition continues to plan, lobby, organize, and involve politicians, and public money, in its agenda. A recent organized effort was the Benefits Blueprint, a public-private planning process announced in late 2007. The official goal was to promote collaboration between the two sectors, in order, in the words of a Conservative MP, to "provide opportunities for economic growth throughout the province." The effort was managed by Enterprise Saint John, chaired by a former president of the Board of Trade and funded equally by ACOA, the provincial government and Irving Oil. The latter company described the refining and export of non-renewable carbon-based energy as the basis of "sustainable growth." Planning identified seven key areas – apparently extending beyond Saint John but all based on a second oil refinery that was then planned for near the city: community interests, training and education, business and supplier development, infrastructure, workforce expansion, housing, and arts and culture (Moore 2007; Irving Oil 2007). The lure of economic development, with its necessary private-public sector cooperation, is especially potent in a city that has lost not only population and political influence, but prestige. Traditionally, Saint John saw itself as competing with Halifax; now it is reduced to competing within the province with Fredericton and Moncton. As the May 2008 civic elections demonstrated, organized labour is capable of exerting influence in Saint John, but its social responsibility mission is compromised by its practical need to support the politics of growth.[17] The provincial government's need to promote economic growth, which under the Graham government (2006–10) was pursued by a committee of deputy ministers, will likely also continue to influence three of the policy areas discussed in this chapter: city image, infrastructure, and immigration. In this climate, the challenge for government and the other sectors shaping the four policy areas, will be to protect the interests of "all citizens, not just business" (Interview 16).

## ACKNOWLEDGMENTS

I wish to thank Gay Fanjoy and Wren Crandall for research assistance and the various parties who agreed to be interviewed. I also wish to thank Christopher Leo, Daniel Bourgeois, and Kurt Peacock for comments made on a previous version of this chapter.

NOTES

1 In the words of one representative of a NGO, "The economy is the driving factor." See Interview 4.

2 The key primary research for this project consists of interviews with Saint John's mayor prior to June 2008, the fire chief, three local Liberal MLAs, the local Liberal MP, representatives of the Board of Trade, the local regional development agency and the waterfront development agency, a prominent lawyer with connections to the political and business communities, a prominent member of the arts community, and representatives from NGOs working in the areas of environment, organized labour, housing, anti-poverty, and immigrant settlement.

3 For growth coalitions in the American experience, see Teaford 1990 and Schuyler 2002. Academic studies of the Irving empire are few. For accounts by journalists see Hunt and Campbell 1973 and DeMont 1991.

4 The need to compete with Moncton has been highlighted by the fact that the Moncton CMA is now larger than the Saint John CMA, and that the population of the Moncton CMA and Fredericton CMA have increased by 6.5 percent and 5.3 percent between 2001 and 2006, but the Saint John CMA by only 0.2 percent.

5 The True Growth Strategy, named in 2005, was an initiative of five municipalities in the greater Saint John area; the strategy advocated economic diversification that included information technology, tourism, health sciences research, energy related development, and immigration. It also stressed quality of life and adopted the marketing strategy "Life on Your Terms."

6 The centre takes its name from another high-profile and controversial business effort, Atlantica, an attempt by business interests to lower trade and investment barriers and create a cross-border economic zone based on New England and Canada's Atlantic provinces. New Brunswick is affected because 90 percent of its exports go to the United States. See Atlantica, http://atlantica/org.

7 For the self-sufficiency agenda, which aimed to wean New Brunswick off federal transfer payments, see New Brunswick 2006a. For federal government support of the provincial agenda, see Linke 2005, 2007b.

8 The Human Development Council, which grew out of the United Way and the Social Services Council, was created in the 1970s to research, advocate, and coordinate programs dealing with poverty and housing issues.

9 In 2001, for example, the Lord government, by freezing assessments on industries denied the City of Saint John $2 million in revenue. Saint John's annual operating budget at the time was $90 million. See Klager 2001.

10 In return for agreeing never to build or repair vessels on the site again, the Irving interests were given funding by the federal government to convert the

site into an industrial park and to diversify operations either in Saint John or elsewhere in the province.

11 Uptown Saint John is a CBD commercial property owners' organization dedicated to promoting shopping, tourism, heritage, and investment.

12 The Provincial Nominee Program, signed in 1999 between the federal and provincial governments, attracted only one immigrant during the first year (Morris, 2004). The emphasis is on skilled immigrants and entrepreneurs.

13 ACAP Saint John, formed in the early 1990s, is one of more than a dozen ACAP sites in the Atlantic region. Although viewed by Environment Canada as one of its programs, ACAP obtains most of its funding from the provincial government and has broad representation from the community.

14 The harbour cleanup issue was characterized by a degree of brinkmanship. The author attended a meeting where the provincial environment minister stated that her government would not commit funding until the federal government made its commitment.

15 Total gas-tax spending in the province will exceed $140 million. The Cities of NB Association in 2005 opposed involvement by the provincial government in gas-tax negotiations with the federal government. The Lord government was insisting that gas-tax rebate revenues be allocated on a per capita basis, including to local service districts.

16 The Saint John fire department, responding to federal and provincial funding available to standardize and enhance responses to hazardous materials accidents, is contracted by the province to respond to emergencies of this type in the southeastern New Brunswick region (New Brunswick 2004).

17 The election of Mayor Ivan Court was widely interpreted as a victory of labour and residential taxpayers against candidates who were identified with business and strongly supported by the Irving newspaper.

## LIST OF INTERVIEWS

1 Saint John Waterfront Partnership representative, 4 June 2007.
2 Norm McFarlane (former mayor of Saint John), 14 August 2007.
3 Non-governmental organization representative, Saint John, 14 August 2007.
4 Board of Trade representative, Saint John, 15 August 2007.
5 Non-governmental organization representative, Saint John, 15 August 2007.
6 Non-governmental organization representative, Saint John, 16 August 2007.
7 MLA 1, Saint John, 20 August 2007.
8 MLA 2, Saint John, 20 August 2007.
9 MLA 3, Saint John, 20 August 2007.
10 Enterprise Saint John representative, Saint John, 27 August 2007.

11 Rob Simonds (fire chief, Saint John), 28 August 2007.
12 Paul Zed (member of Parliament, Saint John), 8 September 2007.
13 Non-governmental organization representative, Saint John, 15 January 2008.
14 Community leader, Saint John, 7 February 2008.
15 Non-governmental organization representative, 20 February 2008.
16 Organized labour representative, 12 March 2008.

## REFERENCES

Atlantica. 2007. http://atlantica/org.

Carlson, Andrew. 2002. "Saint John Making Headway Environmentally, say Experts." *Telegraph Journal*, 26 June, A9.

Chiarelli, Nina. 2003. "Saint John Will Get Two New Water Towers at Cost $2.5 Million." *Telegraph Journal*, 21 January, A4.

Chilibeck, John. 2006a. "Construction Cranes About to Reappear on City Skyline after 13-Year Absence." *2006 Progress Report, Telegraph Journal*, 18 May, 3–4.

– 2006b. "Desire to make It Happen." *Telegraph Journal*, 22 July, B1.

City of Saint John. 2007a. "Saint John Emergency Management Organization." City of Saint John. http://www.cityofsaintjohn.com/services_emo.cfm.

– 2007b. "Vision 2015." Accessed 30 June 2008. http://www.saintjohn.ca/vision2015-index.cfm.

Curry, Tim. n.d. "Recommendations for Mutual Engagement." Atlantica Centre for Energy. Accessed 30 June 2008. http://atlanticaenergy.org/information_resources.php.

Davis, Sandra. 2002. "Group Set Up to Unveil Long-Term Plan for Harbour." *Telegraph Journal*, 12 September, A11.

DeMont, John. 1991. *Citizens Irving: K.C. Irving and His Legacy: The Story of Canada's Wealthiest Family*. Toronto: Doubleday.

Editorial. 1999. *Telegraph Journal*. 12 November, A4.

Editorial. 2001. *Evening Times Globe*, 31 January, D6.

Elections Canada. 2006. Accessed 30 June 2008. http://www.elections.ca.scripts/OVR2006/default.html.

Elections New Brunswick. 2006. Accessed 30 June 2008. http://www.gnb.ca/elections/06prov/06provgeninfo-easp.

Enterprise Saint John. 2007a. *True Growth Economic Update*, Issue 3, Winter.

– 2007b. *Brief to Population Growth Secretariat*. Government of New Brunswick. Accessed 30 June 2008. http://www2.gnb.ca/.

Friesen, C., and J. Hyndman. 2005. "A System in Crisis: 2004 Interprovincial Report Card on Language and Settlement Services in Canada." Accessed 30 June 2008. http://www.immigrantsandrefugees.ca/.

Gillette, Howard. 2005. *Camden After the Fall: Decline and Renewal in a Post-Industrial City*. Philadelphia: University of Pennsylvania Press.

Hunt, Russell, and Robert Campbell. 1973. *The Art of the Industrialist*. Toronto: McClelland and Stewart.

Irving Oil. 2007. "Governments of Canada and New Brunswick Support Benefits Blueprint Plan for Sustainable Growth." Accessed 30 June 2008. http://irvingoil.com.community.news1.asp?newsid=170.

Kerr, Grant. 2003. "City Has to Define Itself, Say Leaders." *Telegraph Journal*, 27 January, A1, A8.

– 2005. "Growth Strategy Makes the Grade." *Telegraph Journal*, 8 January, A4.

Kinnear, Leanne. 2003. *Saint John Disasters*. Saint John: Saint John Public Library.

Klager, Bob. 2001. "Making Ends Meet." *Telegraph Journal*, 29 December, A1.

– 2002a. "Government Needs to Invest in Cities, Says NB Official." *Telegraph Journal*, 29 March, A11.

– 2002b. "A $200M Pipe Dream." *Telegraph Journal*, 27 September, A1.

Linke, Rob. 2005. "Attracting, Keeping Arrivals is Crucial: Study." *Telegraph Journal*, 15 October, A1, A3.

– 2007a. "10,605 Residents Left Province Between 2005–06, Census Says." *Telegraph Journal*, 5 December, A1, A5.

– 2007b. "Foreign Content." *Telegraph Journal*, 5 December, C1–2.

MacKinnon, Bobbi-Jean. 2003. "Full Steam Ahead on Harbour Project." *Telegraph Journal*, 12 June, A1.

– 2004. "No Word yet on NB's Grant to the City." *Telegraph Journal*, 22 October, A1, A6.

Maclean, Candace. 2006. "Immigration: 'Fear of the Unknown.'" *Telegraph Journal*, 26 June, B2.

Malik, Khalid. 2006. "Saint John's Team 'Alive' and Well." *Telegraph Journal*, 22 May, B1.

– 2007. "One Mile Depends on Ottawa." *Telegraph Journal*, 10 April, C1.

Marquis, Greg. 2005a. "Saint John: How Bad Was/Is It? Problematizing the City, 1961–2001." Paper delivered at the Forging Social Futures: Canadian Council on Social Development Conference, Fredericton, NB.

– 2005b. "Rebuilding Saint John: 1945–85." Unpublished paper.

– 2007. "Re-Imag[in]ing the Post Industrial City: Contemporary Saint John." Paper delivered at the Town and Country: Exploring Urban and Rural Issues in New Brunswick, St Thomas University.

Mazerolle, John. 2007. "One Mile a Done Deal." *Telegraph Journal*, 26 June, C3.

McGinnis, Sarah. 2002. "Minister Defends NB's Approach." *Telegraph Journal*, 28 January, A6.

McMackin, Bill. 2001. "Coming: A Fresh Way for Everybody to Sell Greater
    Saint John." *Telegraph Journal*, 19 October, A9.
McMullin, Roy. 2007. "Birds of a Feather All Flock Together." *Telegraph
    Journal*, 11 June, A5.
Moore, Rob. 2007. "Rob Moore Announces Funding for Benefits Blueprint."
    Accessed 30 June 2008. http://www.robmooremp.com/110807_01.htm.
Morris, Chris. 2004. "Province Wants More Help on Immigration." *Telegraph
    Journal*, 21 January, A3.
Mullen, Mike. 2004. "Priorities." *Telegraph Journal*, 16 November, A8.
– 2007. "Economic Engine is beginning to Rev: MP." *Telegraph Journal*,
    2 January, C1.
New Brunswick. 2004. "Communications New Brunswick." News Release.
    5 November.
– 2006. "Our Action Plan to be Self-Sufficient in New Brunswick." Accessed
    30 June 200. http://www.gnb.ca/2026/OSSPDF/report-Epdf.
– 2007a. "Governments Commit Funding to Harbour Cleanup." Office
    of the Premier. News Release. 16 March. http://www.gnb.ca/cnb/news/
    pre/2007e0336pr.htm.
– 2007b. "MOU Signed to develop Atlantic gateway strategy." Communica-
    tions New Brunswick. News Release. 15 October.
Peacock, Kurt. 2005. *Poverty and Plenty: A Statistical Snapshot of the Quality
    of Life in Greater Saint John*. Saint John: Vibrant Communities Saint John/
    Saint John Human Development Council.
Roik, Richard. 2003. "City May get More Federal Cash in Wake of Shipyard
    Announcement." *Telegraph Journal*, 28 June, A4.
Schuyler, David. 2002. *A City Transformed: Redevelopment, Race and
    Suburbanization in Lancaster, Pennsylvania*. University Park: University of
    Pennsylvania Press.
Statistics Canada. 2006. "Community Profiles." "Saint John." http://www12.
    statcan.ca/english/census06/data/profiles/community/Index.cfm?Lang=E.
Teaford, Jon C. 1990. *The Rough Road to Renaissance: Urban Revitalization
    in America, 1940–1985*. Baltimore: Johns Hopkins University Press.
*Telegraph Journal*. 2007a. "Immigrants Don't Like Port City, Report Says."
    12 December, A7.
*Telegraph Journal*. 2007b. "Gas Tax Money Flows." 25 June, C1.
Trueman, Mac. 2001. "Selling City's Fresh Image is to be 'All Aboard Effort.'"
    *Evening Times Globe*, 21 October, A1.
– 2003. "Plan in Works to Make Port City a Magnet for Residents and
    Wealth." *Telegraph Journal*, 15 May, A6.
– 2003b. "Industrial City No More." *Telegraph Journal*, 25 October, A1.

– 2005. "Regional Development Commissions Working to Bring Centre for Immigration to City." *Telegraph Journal*, 18 February, C1.

Urban Strategies Inc. 2003. *Saint John Inner Harbour Land Use Plan and Implementation Study*. Saint John. November.

Urquhart, Mia. 2003. "New Logo Blends Heritage With Future." *Evening Times Globe*, 25 October, A1.

White, Alan. 2002. "Funding to Cities Isn't Enough, Says Official," *Telegraph Journal*, 19 February, A8.

Williams, Christopher. 2005. "Saint John Port Authority, ILA Defends Land Use." *Canadian Sailings*, 7 March, 19.

Young, David. 2004. "Smoke Got in Our Eyes." *Evening Times Globe*, 1 January, C4.

Zed, Paul. 2005. "Team Saint John Returns from Ottawa." 9 November. http://www.paulzed.parl.gc.ca/.

– 2007. "Paul Zed Welcomes Announcement by Premier." 1 August. http://www.paulzed.parl.gc.ca/.

# 7

# Policy Making in Saskatoon in a Multilevel Context: The Link Between Good Governance and Good Public Policy

JOSEPH GARCEA AND DONALD C. STORY

In Saskatoon, as in other cities, the content and quality of public policy is a function of the interplay of an array of factors within the context of multilevel governance. The central objective in this chapter is to provide an analysis of the quality of public policies produced just prior to and during the first decade of the twenty-first century and the factors that have affected their quality in four of Saskatoon's policy sectors – immigration, emergency planning, federal property, and infrastructure. For immigration and emergency planning, the focus is on several interrelated policy initiatives. The focus in each of the other two policy sectors is on a single policy initiative – in federal property, the initiative is the transfer of the international airport from a federal agency to a local special purpose agency; and, in infrastructure, the initiative is a large downtown riverfront redevelopment project.

In analyzing the quality of those policies, we examine whether they have achieved the policy goals pursued by the key governmental stakeholders for the purpose of advancing the public interest or common good in the community. In analyzing the factors that affected the quality of the policies, we examine various aspects of multilevel governance and management. Special attention is devoted to governance dynamics and governance and management capacity. Governance dynamics refers to policy making involving key governmental and non-governmental actors within the policy community in each policy sector. Governance and management capacity refers to the ability to perform key functions based on the availability of jurisdictional authority and resources to governmental actors in a particular policy field. The chapter concludes that factors related to good governance have important implications for the quality of public policy.

## SASKATOON'S DEMOGRAPHY AND POLITICAL ECONOMY

A full appreciation of public policies in Saskatoon requires an understanding of the city's demography, political economy, and the policy-making roles within city hall. Saskatoon's population has grown rapidly during the past decade. Whereas in 2001 it was 196,845 and in 2006 it was 202,340 (Canada 2006), in 2009 it was 218,900 (Saskatoon 2009a). This growth made Saskatoon Saskatchewan's largest city and Canada's twenty-third largest city (Canada 2006). The fact that Saskatoon has approximately 25 percent of the provincial population gives it both prominence and power within the multilevel governance context at both the program and political level. At the program level, the city can make claims on provincial and federal funding that are commensurate with the size of its population. At the political level, its relatively large electoral base within the province renders it very important in provincial elections and of some importance in federal elections. Its political importance has tended to increase when potential or actual minority government situations arise.

In recent years, the Aboriginal and immigrant populations in Saskatoon have become increasingly important factors in the formulation and implementation of public policies. In the multilevel context, governments have had to reconcile the needs of the Aboriginal population with those of the existing and incoming immigrant population. In 2006, Aboriginals constituted approximately 10 percent of Saskatoon's population, which placed it just behind Winnipeg among large cities for having the highest proportion of Aboriginals. Immigrants constituted 8.4 percent of the population in 2006, and new immigrants (i.e., arriving within the previous five years) constituted 1.6 percent of the population. Visible minorities made up only 7.3 percent of the population (Canada, 2006).

For many decades Saskatoon has been branded a "hub city" not only because it is centrally located in the province, but also because it has been, and remains, a major industrial, commercial, transportation, and service centre for the entire province. These factors have contributed to the size of the city's property tax base, which is the largest among cities in the province (Saskatchewan Assessment Management Agency 2007). In recent decades, it has had a relatively strong and stable economy, but since the turn of the century it has experienced an unexpected economic boom that has given it both a national and international profile through coverage in prominent publications such as the *Globe and Mail* and the *Economist*, as well as on major television networks such as CNN (Beauchesne 2007). The boom had many benefits, but one of the adverse effects was a dramatic increase in real estate prices that reduced its ranking as one of the most affordable Canadian cities in which to live (Ralko 2007). Still, it continued to rank highly as an attractive Prairie city that provides a very good quality of life for most of its residents, including children (Waytiuk and Brearton 2001). This high quality of life is largely attributable to the resources that have been devoted over time to developing and maintaining both infrastructure and community services. Saskatoon has had a reputation as one of the best run cities in Canada (Coyne 2009). That reputation has been based in part on its prudent financial management, which has given it a high bond rating (Patel and Ogilvie 2009). Saskatoon also has had a reputation as a city that is a cost-effective location for businesses. During the past decade KPMG reports on business locations have ranked Saskatoon as either first or second among cities in western Canada and the American mid-west, and sixth or seventh among Canadian cities (KPMG 2008; KPMG 2009).

An important aspect of policy making in city hall during the past decade has been a reliance on a strong council system rather than a strong mayor system. Mayors have not had either extraordinary *de jure* power or the political clout to dominate council. Most decisions have been a function of evolving issue-based coalitions within council and its committees. Three important committees have been: the Budget Committee, composed of the entire council, which prepares the operating and capital budgets that are debated and voted on at regular council meetings; the Planning and Operations Committee, composed of five members, which provides policy advice and oversight for all land use, infrastructure services, and leisure services; and the Administration and Finance Committee, composed of five council members, which oversees human, financial, and capital resources as well as protective and utility services.

At the administrative level, the most important body has been the Management Committee, which consists of the city manager and all departmental general managers. This committee is responsible for coordinating all citywide management and operational matters (Saskatoon 2009a). Collectively and individually, members of this committee and the mayor have been responsible for dealing with intergovernmental relations. In dealing with such relations, the mayor and the management committee have been assisted by the city manager and the manager of intergovernmental relations. The city's protocol on intergovernmental relations has been based on the model that the mayor interacts with elected provincial and federal officials, while the city's senior administrators interact with their appointed provincial and federal counterparts (Interview 5 and 6).

The City of Saskatoon has generally taken a pragmatic approach rather than a partisan one in its relations with the provincial and federal governments. As well, it has been collaborative rather than confrontational. Reliance on these two approaches has stemmed from a belief among mayors and councillors that this is the more prudent way to advance the city's interest within the context of multilevel governance over the long term (Interviews 2, 5, and 6). The result is that intergovernmental relations have generally taken on a hue of low-profile politics rather than high-profile politics.

## IMMIGRATION

In Saskatoon the overarching goals of immigration policy have been to meet city's needs for immigrants and the needs of immigrants in the city (Saskatoon 2004a; Saskatoon 2004b; Saskatoon 2006a; Saskatoon 2007a; Saskatoon 2008a). In meeting the city's needs, the objectives have been to attract and retain immigrants who can provide the local economy with needed human and financial resources and to increase the size of the city's population. In meeting the needs of immigrants, the objective has been to provide them with services to facilitate their successful settlement and economic and social integration (Pontikes and Garcea 2006; Garcea and Garg 2008).

Recently, improvements in federal, provincial, and municipal policies and programs have contributed to advancing all of those goals. Improvements have occurred in the recruitment and selection of immigrants and in the settlement and integration services provided to many of them. The principal factors behind those improvements have been the initiatives undertaken and the resources provided, either individually or jointly, by key governmental and non-governmental stakeholders within the immigration sector (Interviews 13, 14, 18, and 19).

The recruitment and selection of immigrants has involved primarily the federal and provincial governments. Whereas the federal government has continued to recruit and select immigrants through the national immigration and refugee programs, the provincial government has become actively involved in recruiting and selecting immigrants through the Saskatchewan Immigrant Nominee Program (SINP). Under the SINP, which was established through the Canada-Saskatchewan Immigration Agreement originally signed in 1998, the provincial government has been recruiting and selecting immigrants who fall within certain designated categories of nominees (Canada 2005). The federal and provincial governments have collaborated extensively to improve the SINP, and toward that end the provincial government has steadily increased the amount of funding devoted to the recruitment and selection of provincial nominees.

In recent years, the recruitment efforts of the federal and provincial governments have been supplemented by a few municipal initiatives. There is a web page devoted to immigration, and the mayor promotes immigration while travelling abroad on official business on his own or as part of provincial trade and immigration recruitment missions. Stakeholder groups have also been active in immigrant recruitment. These include private-sector companies seeking immigrant workers, immigration consultants, ethnocultural organizations aiming to recruit immigrants from particular countries or language groups, and organizations involved in refugee sponsorship.

Between 1998–99 and 2008–09, the number of immigrants arriving in Saskatoon increased as a result of special recruitment efforts and the exceptional economic boom. As a result of those two factors, the total number of immigrants arriving in Saskatoon through both the national and provincial programs has increased from approximately 760 in 1998–99 to 4,250 in 2008–09 (Saskatoon 2009a).

Particularly instrumental in that increase have been the provincial government's recruitment efforts through the SINP. Whereas in 1998–99 almost all immigrants arrived in Saskatoon through the national program, by 2008–09 approximately 75 percent arrived through the SINP program, and only approximately 25 percent arrived through the federal immigration program. The provincial government's immigration strategy, released in June 2009, indicated that by 2010, 3,400 principal applicants would be admitted, which, when combined with their spouses and children, would result in more than 10,000 immigrants arriving to Saskatchewan for that year (Saskatchewan 2009b). The special recruitment efforts under the SINP and the booming economy made it possible for the provincial government to achieve the target immigration flows stipulated in its immigration strategy.

The increased volume of immigration to Saskatoon has not generated any major public debates. It has been widely supported within both the governmental and non-governmental sectors because it is perceived to advance the economic and demographic goals and objectives of the city and the province as a whole. Still, there has been some criticism of the policy. It has been argued that greater reliance should be placed on training Aboriginals and non-Aboriginals in this province to meet the human resource needs of the economy, rather than seeking immigrants (Pontikes and Garcea 2006). This view is articulated by those who are opposed to immigration and by many who support it. Among this opposition are some labour leaders in the city who have been concerned about the effect that increased immigration would have both for Aboriginal and non-Aboriginal unionized workers and for their unions if a substantial number of immigrants are recruited to work in a non-unionized context (Pontikes and Garcea 2006). Federal, provincial, and city officials have been very sensitive to this criticism, and they have made special efforts to ensure that training and hiring programs targeted for Aboriginals and non-Aboriginals are expanded and publicized. Another criticism has been that insufficient regulations are in place to ensure that consultants who deal with immigrants are qualified and use ethical procedures. This is a problem that continues to be neglected by federal and provincial policies and by the national and provincial professional associations established by consultants (Interview 13).

During the past decade settlement and integration policy has improved. Indicators of such improvement include an increase in the number of settlement service agencies and a wider range of services provided to immigrants and refugees within the first few years of their arrival in Saskatoon. The improvements have resulted primarily from increased federal and provincial funding for the settlement and integration services provided by community-based organizations. Federal funding has been provided primarily by Citizenship and Immigration Canada's major programs. Some additional funding has been provided by other federal agencies, particularly Service Canada for programs that are designed to facilitate the economic integration of immigrants. In 2008–09, the federal contributions for settlement and integration programs in Saskatchewan was just over $6 million (Canada 2008a). A substantial amount was devoted to settlement and integration in Saskatoon. The province has also been increasing its funding for settlement and integration. Programs include information and orientation services, language training, assessments and referral services, employment training and bridging programs, and foreign credential recognition. In 2008–09, the provincial government devoted $5.4 million for such services (Saskatchewan 2009a).

In Saskatoon, settlement and integration policy has been strengthened as a result of two important initiatives. Both involve collaboration among governmental and non-governmental stakeholders. The first of these initiatives was the creation of the Saskatoon Immigration Coordinating Committee (SICC) to facilitate collaboration among its members in the provision of settlement and integration services. The SICC consists of the executive directors of the four major settlement service agencies (Saskatoon Open Door Society, Saskatchewan Intercultural Association, Global Gathering Place, and International Women of Saskatoon), officials from the federal and provincial governments, and the city's Immigration Community Resource Coordinator (ICRC). The SICC's composition has been debated since it was established. At issue has been the question of whether to retain the current membership or to include some ethnocultural organizations that have been active in delivering some settlement services (e.g., Assemblée Fransaskoise and Ukrainian Canadian Congress of Saskatoon), advocacy groups (e.g., the Refugee Coalition), and a representative of newcomers (Interviews 16 and 21).

Despite the continuing debates regarding its membership, the prevailing view is that within a short time the SICC has been very beneficial for information sharing, planning, and even programming. One of the most significant accomplishments occurred in 2009 when SICC agreed to establish the Newcomer Information Centre (NIC), a central location where newcomers can get information, application forms, and referrals to other agencies (Vellacott 2009). The NIC operates under the auspices of its own coordinating committee, which consists of representatives of the four major settlement service agencies, the City of Saskatoon, and the Health Region. Here too, the city is represented by the Immigration Community Resource Coordinator.

Funding for the initial year of operation of the NIC was provided by Citizenship and Immigration Canada and Saskatchewan's Ministry of Advanced Education, Employment and Immigration and the Saskatoon Health Region. In subsequent years, however, only the federal and provincial ministries continued to provide funding. Although the Health Region wanted to ensure that immigrants receive information about health services that they may need, it decided that it could not make a long term funding commitment. The governmental and non-governmental partners have all been monitoring the project since it was launched to see how well it works before making a longer-term commitment (Interviews 15, 16, 20, and 21). To date the consensus among the partners has been that the NIC has been quite successful in performing its key functions and that they should continue to operate it.

Still, problems persist both for community-based organizations that provide services and for newcomers. Although community-based organizations that provide settlement and integration services welcome increased federal and provincial funding, they continue to say that the funding is still not sufficient for them to do all that they do, let alone what they should be doing to meet the needs of newcomers. They also say that the continued heavy reliance on single-year governmental funding arrangements, rather than multi-year commitments, presents challenges for effectiveness and efficiency in planning and delivering settlement and integration services (Pontikes and Garcea 2006; Interview 12).

It is recognized that many immigrants face problems related to economic and social integration, particularly during their first few years in the city. Many are unemployed, underemployed, or underpaid, and therefore face challenges in securing basic needs such as housing, clothing, food, and transportation (FCM 2009). The booming economy in Saskatoon has helped to alleviate these problems for some newcomers, but not for all. Similarly, in terms of social integration, challenges posed either by discrimination or other factors persist for many immigrants (Interview 12).

In an effort to deal with these and other problems, a tri-level partnership has been established between the federal, provincial, and municipal governments. Proposed by the city, this partnership was based on a recommendation by its Cultural Diversity and Race Relations Committee that the city seek funding from the federal and provincial governments to produce a report on Saskatoon's need for immigrants and the needs of immigrants in Saskatoon (Garcea and Garg 2009). The partnership commenced in 2005 when the federal, provincial, and municipal governments agreed to co-fund a report on issues and options related to immigration and integration in Saskatoon. It was agreed that the federal and provincial governments would assume the costs of producing the report and the city would make a comparable in-kind contribution of managerial and administrative support. It was also agreed that general oversight of the project would be done by a three-member steering committee consisting of representatives of the three governments. The funding and oversight arrangements would be retained for all subsequent initiatives undertaken within the scope of the partnership.

The partners conducted a series of public consultations and produced several reports that identified key issues and options related to immigration and integration in order to facilitate better place-based policy in the immigration field. The first report, *Making Saskatoon a Global City: A Framework for an Action Plan* (Pontikes and Garcea 2006), was based on extensive consultations with approximately 200 members of non-governmental organizations, newcomers, and the general public. One of the recommendations was that the three levels of government should take the lead in establishing an organizational framework, involving governments and non-governmental stakeholders, to develop and implement an immigration action plan in order to achieve greater policy coherence and organizational capacity within the immigration sector.

That recommendation led to an agreement between the three levels of government in the spring of 2008 to continue the partnership through the Saskatoon Immigration Project (SIP). In a joint press release, the federal and provincial ministers responsible for immigration and Saskatoon's mayor announced that the SIP was to "promote and co-ordinate early settlement and integration support for immigrants and refugees ... fostering a welcoming environment for newcomers, developing a governance model for the immigration plan, developing sector specific strategies, and increasing residents' awareness of the positive contributions of immigrants to Saskatoon" (Saskatchewan 2008). The press release also noted that the city had hired an Immigration Community Resource Coordinator (ICRC). Both the ICRC position and the initiatives undertaken within the scope of the SIP were to be co-funded by the three governments using the same formula adopted to produce the initial report. Elected and appointed city officials adopted the position that had been articulated by the Big City Mayors' Caucus (BCMC 2006) and the Federation of Canadian Municipalities (FCM 2009). The basic principle of that position was that while the city should perform some key roles and also collaborate with the provincial and federal governments in recruiting and retaining immigrants, the two senior orders of government should provide the bulk of funding (Saskatoon 2007a).

In keeping with the overarching goal of the SIP, the principal focus of the ICRC was the organization of eight forums and the production of the resulting reports (Insightrix 2008; Saskatoon 2009c). The forums engaged approximately 800 participants, many of whom were representatives from key stakeholder organizations, as well as newcomers and informed members of the community. The prevailing view was that the forums were useful not only in highlighting the key issues related to immigration, but also in building an appreciation of the need for collaboration among the many governmental and non-governmental agencies and in facilitating networking and partnerships between them. The last forum was particularly valuable because it included a workshop on models of inter-organizational networking and partnerships and the means by which partnerships could be established and maintained.

Although there is widespread agreement that the tri-level partnership has been valuable, different views exist among the three partners and other stakeholders regarding the extent to which it has been valuable. Moreover, as the current iteration of the partnership comes to an end, the three partners are faced with the same questions that have emerged at the end of each iteration – whether the partnership would continue, what would be its principal purpose, and how would it be resourced. This is another instance within this sector, as in others, of challenges in reconciling short-term agreements with longer-term planning and programming.

The consensus is that there have been major improvements in immigration and settlement policy for Saskatoon during the past decade, largely as a result of the increased commitment and collaboration among governmental and non-governmental organizations involved in this policy sector. However, it is generally recognized that additional improvements are needed not only through the efforts of these organizations, but also by many others performing functions that impinge on immigration and integration.

## EMERGENCY PLANNING

During the past decade, the City of Saskatoon has been proactive and successful in improving its emergency measures policy and system. Our objective in this section is to identify and assess both the key strategies and initiatives that it has undertaken within the context of multilevel governance to achieve that improvement and the factors that have facilitated or hindered those strategies and initiatives. It is useful to begin with an overview of the key roles and responsibilities in the emergency measures system in Saskatoon.

The Saskatchewan Emergency Planning Act (Saskatchewan 1989) mandates the City of Saskatoon to create and sustain an emergency planning system. In keeping with this, the city has established an Emergency Measures Organization (EMO), an Emergency Measures Organization Coordinator (EMOC), an Emergency Operations Centre (EOC), and an Emergency Planning Committee (EPC). The city is responsible for the bulk of the costs of the emergency measures system, but it receives some funding from the federal and provincial governments, largely through cost-shared programs (Saskatoon 2007d).

The alignment of roles and responsibilities between the city, provincial, and federal governments has been and remains asymmetrical. Pursuant to the provincial statutory requirement, the city has the primary responsibility for emergency measures for the entire community within its boundaries. This includes the Indian urban reserves within its boundaries, for which emergency services are covered under bilateral bylaw compatibility agreements, and the University of Saskatchewan, with which the city has a special bilateral agreement on emergency measures. For their part, the provincial and federal governments have complementary or supplementary roles in planning for catastrophic emergencies and in assisting the city to deal with them. They also perform valuable roles in providing specialized training for some of the city officials who have key roles in the emergency measures system (Saskatoon 2006c, 18; Interviews 3 and 17).

Since the terrorist attacks of 11 September 2001 in the United States, the provincial and federal governments have proposed greater collaboration with the city in implementing preventative measures against terrorist activities, but have not imposed any additional mandatory responsibilities on the city. Instead, they have invited the city to collaborate in improving the existing systems and in training officials and volunteers (Saskatoon 2006c, 34; Interview 3).

During the first decade of the twenty-first century, the bulk of intergovernmental collaboration related to emergency measures has involved a small number of officials – the city's manager for Fire and Protective Services and its emergency measures coordinator; the province's federal programs coordinator located within Saskatchewan's Emergency Management Organization (SaskEMO), a provincial agency that maintains the provincial emergency plan and is to coordinate the activities of provincial, federal and municipal agencies during an emergency (Saskatchewan 2009c); and two federal officials from the Canada Public Safety office in Regina, namely the senior emergency manager and the senior program manager for National Security and Critical Infrastructure (Canada 2009a; Canada 2009b). The positions occupied by federal and provincial officials were created during the latter part of the first decade of the twenty-first century in order to improve intergovernmental coordination in the emergency sector (Interview 19). The consensus among officials from all three levels of government is that adding these positions improved intergovernmental communication, coordination, and collaboration in the development and maintenance of physical infrastructure, the acquisition of technology and equipment, and personnel training (Interviews 3, 17, 18, and 19).

Intergovernmental collaboration has been spawned by two interrelated factors. One is the decision by all governments to improve emergency preparedness systems in the wake of the terrorist acts of 9/11 and of a number of major natural disasters in Canada involving floods and storms, including a snowstorm in Saskatoon (Interviews 3 and 18). The other factor is the effective operation of the federal government's Joint Emergency Preparedness Program (JEPP) in providing small amounts of funding to municipalities each year on a cost-shared basis for planning, training and education, purchasing emergency response equipment, and developing emergency infrastructure (Canada 2009a; Interviews 3, 17, and 18).

The process for reviewing and approving JEPP applications involves Public Safety Canada and SaskEMO. The city's proposals for JEPP funding are first reviewed and prioritized by a SaskEMO committee, which forwards them to Public Safety Canada's regional office in Regina, which, in turn, transmits them to the national JEPP office in Ottawa (Saskatchewan 2004a). Although the SaskEMO participates in the proposal review process, the province does not contribute any funding for JEPP. Moreover, the province does not have a separate funding program devoted exclusively to the emergency sector. Any funding that it provides for emergency planning comes from general funding programs for communities (Interview 17).

During the past decade, Saskatoon has been successful in leveraging some of its own funds to access money for equipment and training through JEPP. Much support has come from the special projects portion of JEPP that is devoted to particular national priorities, rather than from the standard funding portion of the program. Special projects funding has included $135,000 for planning and training from the chemical, biological, radioactive, and nuclear response program (Saskatoon 2003a); 75 percent of the cost for equipping and training the Urban Search and Rescue Team (Saskatoon 2004c); $49,000 to purchase a Haz-Mat SensID system to identify unknown materials at emergency scenes (Saskatoon 2006b, 10); and $100,000 to help pay for situational activity software and technology required in the new EOC (Saskatoon 2009d). In addition to this JEPP funding, the city has been able to access some funding from the provincial government for equipment and training required by the regionally-based mutual aid organizations to which it belongs and for emergency evacuations from northern communities (Saskatoon 2008, 7).

The benefits gained from JEPP have been constrained because the program has restrictive funding criteria. For example, proposals must meet national and provincial priorities, and funds may not be used "to finance events or equipment purchases of departments or agencies for activities considered to be part of their normal responsibilities" (Canada 2009a). As well, accessing grants from JEPP or other programs usually means that the city must provide matching funding. Such requirements create uncertainties, as do two other features of the JEPP arrangements. First, given the relatively small amount of money that is available for the entire country (i.e., $5 million), there is no guarantee that a funding proposal will be approved. Second, project funding is normally approved for a limited amount of time with no guarantee that it will be renewed or that the funds will remain the same the following year (Canada 2009b). The city would clearly prefer to have funding mechanisms that provide fewer constraints, more certainty, and more money, because the funding that it has been able to access through JEPP and other sources covers only a small fraction of the emergency system budget (Interview 3).

A major goal of the city has been to build organizational capacity and to improve management in the emergency measures sector (Interviews 3 and 10). Part of the city's strategy has been to create multilateral or bilateral committees to enhance consultation and collaboration between governmental and non-governmental agencies within and beyond Saskatoon. The city has established four committees. The three multilateral committees are the Emergency Planning Committee (EPC), the Emergency Social Services Committee (ESSC), and the Saskatoon Industrial Mutual Aid Committee (SIMAC). The EPC has two subcommittees. One of these is the interdepartmental operations subcommittee, which consists of the EMOC and the general managers of four city departments (Fire and Protective Services, Infrastructure Services, Community Services, and Utility Services). It is mandated to assist the EPC in updating emergency plans and procedures. The second subcommittee consists of the same five senior city officials plus approximately two dozen representatives from community-based organizations, all of whom are organized into project-based working groups. The groups, and the subcommittee as a whole, work to improve the emergency measures system. This subcommittee replaced a similar one that had been proven to be ineffective and unproductive (Interviews 3 and 10). Responsibility for appointment of the members of both subcommittees rests with the general manager of Fire and Protective Services (Saskatoon 2007c).

The ESSC works in conjunction with the city's EMO in assisting evacuees who come to Saskatoon because of emergencies in other communities. The ESSC has played a key role during evacuations of people from northern Saskatchewan to Saskatoon as a result of floods and forest fires (Interview 3). The ESSC consists of the general manager of the Department of Community Services, who serves as its chair, and representatives from the University of Saskatchewan, the Saskatchewan Institute of Applied Sciences and Technology, the Saskatoon Health Region, Saskatchewan Health, the Salvation Army, the Red Cross, St John Ambulance, MD Ambulance, the Prince Albert Grand Council, and the federal Department of Indian and Northern Affairs.

SIMAC is mandated to increase expertise and resources for responding to major emergencies created by hazardous materials. This committee consists of the representatives of the city's Department of Fire and Protective Services, employees of various industrial plants that use or produce materials that could create emergencies, and some community-based emergency response organizations.

The fourth committee established by Saskatoon involves the city and the University of Saskatchewan. The university has always had its own organizational framework for emergency measures for the campus, one that mirrored the city's framework (University of Saskatchewan 2009). The bilateral committee was successful in producing a new agreement between the city and the university regarding emergency measures (Interviews 3 and 11). This new agreement replaces the one signed in the late 1950s and reaffirms that the university falls within the purview of the city's emergency system, subject to one important condition. The city cannot take any action that could affect any research project without the university's permission. The new agreement also clarifies the relationship between the city and university on various emergency measures, including the sharing of resources and facilities. The relationship between the city and the university has been a constructive one largely because of the agreements and the positive rapport between their officials (Interviews 3 and 11). The city hopes that this agreement will serve as a model for establishing comparable relationships with other large institutions (Saskatoon 2007b).

To increase its capacity to deal with emergencies, the city has undertaken two initiatives to increase the amount of human resources and equipment that it could use in an emergency. The first was to establish a partnership with a 4x4 vehicles club in the city. The club members agreed to make themselves and their vehicles available during an emergency to provide transportation in areas where the terrain is treacherous; in exchange, the city agreed to allow the club to hold events on vacant city land (Interview 3). The second initiative has been the development of a Volunteer Group Activation Plan, which generated a pool of at least eighty volunteers ready for deployment in the case of an emergency (Saskatoon 2008b, 6).

The city's emergency planning officials have also worked to improve intermunicipal collaboration within and beyond the Saskatoon city-region. They were instrumental in establishing the North Saskatoon Mutual Aid Committee (NSMAC), an intermunicipal "mutual aid area" that includes the city and fifteen municipalities located within 100 kilometres of the northern reaches of Saskatoon. NSMAC initiatives include establishing a shared mobile operations centre for the region and assisting the smaller communities in preparing their emergency planning bylaws and lists of resources (Saskatoon 2008b, 8). In 2004, similar considerations about collaboration led the city to sign the Major Urban Disaster Mutual Aid Agreement with eight cities in the province that had professional fire departments (Saskatoon 2005a, 10).

The prevailing view among informed observers is that capacity within the emergency system has been improved substantially in the recent past but that additional improvements are needed (Interviews 3, 17, and 19). The most notable proposed improvements would be to have the city's EOC fully implement innovative emergency measures systems, such as the "incident command system" and the "three levels of activation system," to purchase some additional emergency equipment, and to better train all persons who perform key roles in developing and implementing emergency measures. Other improvements include eliminating some of the financial constraints and uncertainties that the city faces in intergovernmental funding arrangements. Some of the improvements suggested in the evaluation of the administration of JEPP would also be beneficial for intergovernmental relations and the emergency measures system in Saskatchewan (Canada 2009c). There could also be more formal written agreements between the city and various governmental and non-governmental organizations concerning roles and responsibilities within the emergency sector (Interview 3). Another important suggestion is to institutionalize a tri-level committee involving representatives of the city and the federal and provincial governments (Interviews 3 and 17).

A barrier to this is that the federal and provincial governments would have to establish trilateral committees with a large number of municipalities.

The improvements in the emergency measures system are largely due to the proactive approach taken by the city in this sector. It has improved organizational capacity in three ways. First, it has devoted more of its own financial and human resources to the system (though some suggest that more should be done and that officials in the system should press for more resources). Second, it has successfully accessed funding for emergency measures from the federal and provincial governments. Third, it has established a multicentric inter-organizational network of committees, within and beyond the city, consisting of representatives from governmental and non-governmental agencies that have key roles or interests in the emergency sector.

The patterns of intergovernmental and inter-organizational relations in this sector can described as collaborative and constructive. The collaboration has involved all three levels of government, including the neighbouring municipalities and large cities, as well as public authorities and community-based organizations. There is no evidence of any major controversies among key stakeholders or among members of the general public regarding any particular aspect of the emergency system.

There are at least three possible reasons for the substantial collaboration and the absence of controversies. First, there have not been any major competing views advanced about any aspect of the emergency policy or system. Second, officials from the three orders of governments have shared goals and a sense of a shared responsibility that have led them to perform their respective functions in a collaborative manner. Third, there have not been any devastating disasters that would produce debates about problems with the system and accusations of failure on the part of some governmental or non-governmental agency. This last point suggests that the cordial working relationships in the emergency planning system may exist not only because of good governance and good will, but also because of good luck.

## FEDERAL PROPERTY: THE INTERNATIONAL AIRPORT

In the 1990s the City of Saskatoon decided that authority over the John G. Diefenbaker International Airport, which is located in the northwest part of the city, would be transferred from Transport Canada to the Saskatoon Airport Authority (SAA). A sixty-year lease started on 1 January 1999, with the possibility of a renewal for an additional twenty years

(SAA 2002). Our objective in this section is to provide an overview of the intergovernmental relations and societal forces that impinged on the creation of the SAA, its leasing arrangements with Transport Canada, and its property tax arrangements with the City of Saskatoon. As well, we provide a brief assessment of the effect that the SAA has had on the policy goals of improving the airport infrastructure, the services at the airport, and the air transportation service.

The decision to transfer responsibility for managing the airport from Transport Canada to the SAA stemmed from the National Airports Policy (NAP) enacted by Prime Minister Brian Mulroney's Conservative government (Canada 1999). Under the NAP, the federal government was to retain ownership of its international airports that were part of the National Airports System but would devolve responsibility for their management to local community-based, not-for-profit authorities incorporated under the Canada Corporations Act (Canada 2008b; Padova 2005).

So, in 1994, Transport Canada proposed the creation of a local airport authority in Saskatoon, comparable to those that had been created in Vancouver, Calgary, and Toronto, to manage the John G. Diefenbaker International Airport. The plan was subject to approval by the city, the provincial government, and the rural municipality (RM) of Corman Park, which surrounds both Saskatoon and the airport. Initially, all three governments were reluctant to approve the creation of the SAA because they feared becoming financially and politically responsible for a troubled operation (Interviews 1, 17, and 18). Despite those concerns, in 1995 the three governments agreed to support it for two reasons. First, they hoped that the SAA would create improvements to the airport infrastructure, the airport services, and the air transportation service. Second, they did not want to be unsupportive of a policy initiative that was favoured strongly by non-governmental stakeholders in the airport sector (that is, the major business associations, the small airline companies based in the province, and private aircraft owners). Many stakeholders were members of the Airport Services Group (ASG). The ASG was an advocacy group that lobbied Transport Canada for improvements to the airport and pressed the large airline companies for improvements to the number, scheduling, and routing of flights (Interview 22). Some prominent members of the ASG performed key roles in advocating the SAA's creation, and, after it was formed, they joined the SAA board.

The SAA is an intergovernmental limited partnership that exists for the purpose of leasing and managing an airport facility that is owned by an agency of one of the four governmental partners (i.e., the Government of

Canada). The partners created the SAA and continue to approve the appointment of members of the board of directors, all of whom must be drawn from the community because the federal government's NAP policy prohibits the appointment of government officials. During the negotiations, it was agreed that each of the four governmental stakeholders would approve the appointment of a percentage of the directors. More specifically, they would be responsible for approving the slates of nominees presented to them by the nominations committee of the SAA's board of directors. The initial board of fifteen directors was reduced after three years to twelve in order to make it operationally and financially more efficient; of these, six are approved by the city, two by the Government of Canada, one by the Government of Saskatchewan, one by the RM of Corman Park, and two by the SAA itself (SAA 2008). The SAA is also responsible for appointing interested community members from the Saskatoon city-region and northern Saskatchewan to sit on the SAA's Community Consultative Committee (CCC) (SAA 2008). This method of appointing members to the board of directors and the CCC, along with the approach taken by the four governments not to become directly involved in airport management issues, has provided the SAA with extensive autonomy in managing the airport. The SAA also enjoys considerable autonomy from the community because the CCC and its three working groups have tended to perform a limited consultative function, rather than a substantial advisory or planning function (Interviews 22 and 23).

Since it was established in 1995, the SAA has negotiated some important agreements with Transport Canada on the leasing arrangements and with the city on the property tax arrangements. During those negotiations the SAA won some important concessions that have been beneficial for its financial sustainability while it develops and operates the airport. Its negotiators were skilled, and Transport Canada and the city sought to ensure that the SAA would have the requisite financial resources to perform its airport management functions effectively (Interviews 1, 22, and 23). They, along with the provincial government and the RM of Corman Park, had a shared interest in the success of the SAA, and this led Transport Canada and the city to adopt what might be described as a flexible and supportive stance in the negotiations on financial matters. The city and the provincial government also helped the SAA during its negotiations on the leasing arrangements with Transport Canada, the city by providing some legal expertise, and the province by delegating environmental experts to help the SAA produce the environmental impact assessment required in the transfer of management of the airport to the SAA (Interviews 1, 5, 22, and 23).

In its negotiations with Transport Canada the SAA received important benefits. It would receive close to $20 million to cover the costs for improvements to the airport, and it would not pay any rent during the first five years of the lease. Later the SAA negotiated a relatively reasonable rental rate after the five-year exemption expired. In the meantime, the SAA joined with other airport authorities across Canada in an effort to convince the federal ministers of transport and finance of both the Liberal and Conservative governments not to implement a rental fee for smaller airports, but this failed. Still, it was able to negotiate a rent that was approximately one-third of that initially proposed by Transport Canada. Thus, as of 1 January 2006, the SAA started paying rent calculated on a formula based on adjusted annual gross revenues, which excludes from the calculation both any financial contribution by the government and the first $5 million of revenues. The SAA has to pay a rent of one percent of adjusted gross revenues in excess of $5 million and five percent of adjusted gross revenues in excess of $10 million. The rent was approximately $144,276 for 2006, $258,274 for 2007, and $345,739 for 2008 (Saskatoon Airport Authority 2006, 2007a, 2008).

Negotiating about property tax in 1999, the city granted the SAA a tax exemption on some airport components – runways, taxi-ways, and aprons – for the first five years of operation. The SAA had argued that without the exemption it would have had to pay $1.5 million more in the first year alone than what Transport Canada had been paying in the form of grants-in-lieu of taxes. Consequently, it could not operate the airport on a financially sustainable basis and it would likely revert back to Transport Canada (Saskatoon 1999). In making this concession the city had to be creative and flexible because the existing provincial regulations did not authorize it to grant any new tax exemptions. However, the regulations did authorize the city to continue to honour existing ones, and so it treated the property tax exemption for parts of the airport as a continuation of an exemption that had existed for Transport Canada as a federal Crown agency (ibid.). In 2003, the SAA and the city extended this arrangement for another year to give both of them more time to develop a new taxation regime (SAA 2003a).

In 2005, the city agreed to levy property taxes based on a special assessment regime that would link the amount of taxes to the level of business activity (SAA 2004, SAA 2005). The argument provided that the SAA would assess property tax based on the passenger traffic rather than the conventional formula of market value of the property multiplied by the mill rate. Furthermore, the level of taxes collected in any given year would be no less than the equivalent of the taxation level in 1989 plus all subsequent mill rate increases. Lastly, the runways would continue to be exempt from any taxation. This regime had the effect of limiting the fluctuation of rents from year to year. The variation over the 2003–08 period was only about $70,000 from a low of $567,763 in 2003 to a high of $641,301 in 2008 (SAA 2003b, SAA 2008). To make it possible for the city to switch from a conventional property taxation formula to one based on passenger traffic, the SAA had to join forces with the Regina Airport Authority to convince the provincial government to change the existing regulations, which prohibited cities from using the proposed formula (Saskatoon 2005b).

The consensus among representative governmental and non-governmental stakeholders and informed observers is that creating the SAA and devolving responsibility to it for managing the airport was a good policy (Interviews 1, 5, 22, and 23). The prevailing view is that this contributed substantially to the achievement of three key policy goals. First, the airport infrastructure improved. Since the SAA started managing the airport it has renewed most components of its infrastructure – the buildings, runways, roadways, and parking lots. Second, the air transportation service has improved in terms of the number, scheduling, and routing of flights. This has contributed to a steady increase in the number of passengers using the airport. Passengers numbered one million by 2007 (SAA 2007b). While some growth can be attributed to the SAA, some of it is attributable to the boom experienced by the local and provincial economy. Finally, the new management has improved several services provided at the airport.

Two minor service problems have persisted, in part because the SAA cannot deal with them on its own. Security screening is problematic because long line-ups develop in the early morning when several flights are scheduled to depart within a relatively short time. The SAA has not been able to solve this problem because responsibility for the passenger security screening function rests with the Canadian Air Transport Security Authority (CATSA), a federal government agency. For many years, CATSA was not responsive to requests from SAA to resolve this issue (Interview 1). However, in the fall of 2009, CATSA agreed to add a fourth screening lane with the requisite equipment (*StarPhoenix* 2009). A second problem is the relatively long time that people sometimes have to wait for a taxi at the airport (Coolican 2009). This issue arises from a complex set of competing interests and perspectives involving the SAA, the city, and the taxi companies (Interview 14). In 2009, the SAA signed a ten-year contract with one taxi company to provide pick-up service at the airport. As well, there is now an open stand for limousine service and a taxi service coordinator to help people who need taxi service. Indications are that these changes have resulted in some improvements to the system, but some of the past problems still emerge from time to time (SAA 2009a).

In explaining the creation of the SAA and its success in managing the airport, observers commonly highlight several factors (Interviews 1, 5, 22, and 23). One is the collaborative nature of intergovernmental relations, especially after the governments involved agreed to proceed with the initiative. Of particular importance after the SAA was created were the concessions made by Transport Canada and the City of Saskatoon to ensure that the SAA had the requisite financial resources to succeed during the initial phase of managing the airport. Also important, however, was the role played by some prominent and capable members of the ASG both in advocating and facilitating the creation of the SAA, and then in providing positive leadership in its negotiations with Transport Canada and the City of Saskatoon. The success is also attributed to the existence of good governance and management regimes.

INFRASTRUCTURE: THE RIVER LANDING PROJECT

Saskatoon's River Landing Project (RLP) is a downtown riverfront redevelopment initiative for which the development plan was approved in 2004. It includes two large tracts of land on the east and west sides of the Senator Sid Buckwold Bridge that for planning purposes are designated as Phase 1 and Phase 2 respectively. The RLP is a phoenix that rose out of the ashes of several conceptual and development plans produced between 1978 and 1998 that aimed to develop various parcels of land in the south downtown, including two major anchor development projects that were aborted during the 1990s (McLoughlin 2005, 58–74).

The RLP is being developed as a mixed-use area that combines open public spaces for recreational and cultural purposes, an indoor-outdoor farmer's market, a theatre and art gallery, high density housing units, a large hotel complex, restaurants, and boutiques (Saskatoon 2009e). Between 1999 and 2009 some notable progress was made with the RLP: the development plan was produced and approved; the site preparation work was completed; some of the outdoor features were constructed; an existing city-owned building was renovated; and a local theatre group constructed a theatre. However, most of the major facilities envisioned in the development plan still have not been built, including a large hotel complex and a large arts and culture centre on the Phase 1 site and several residential complexes on the Phase 2 site. Thus, as of 2011, the RLP is an incomplete project, or, it could be said, a work in progress, without certainty about its final configuration or when it will be completed.

The progress made since 1999 is attributable to three interrelated factors. The first is the widespread support among key governmental and non-governmental stakeholders and the general public, as revealed in a public consultation process, for the overarching policy goals of the RLP and for the concept plan of 2004 (Saskatoon 2004d). One goal was to revitalize the downtown and the adjacent commercial and residential parts of the Riversdale neighbourhood. The RLP development would increase economic, cultural, social, and recreational activities in that part of the city. Another objective was the remediation of a contaminated "brownfield" and a couple of other contaminated parcels of land on the Phase 2 site, which was particularly important to NDP Premier Lorne Calvert because the Phase 2 parcels were in his constituency (Saskatchewan 2003a; *Saskatoon Sun* 2003). It also became important for the federal Liberal governments led by Jean Chrétien and Paul Martin because it was consistent with their environmental protection and urban development agendas (Interviews 4 and 5).

The second key factor is the collaborative relationship between the city and the Meewasin Valley Authority (MVA), the agency responsible for protecting the environmental integrity of the river valley. This relationship led to the 2004 RLP development plan being formulated and approved in less than one year. Such efficiency was possible because many of the issues and options had been broached during previous iterations of planning processes for that area, especially the one that had earlier produced a development plan for Phase 2 of the RLP (Saskatoon 2001). The 2001 plan was simply incorporated into the 2004 plan without any notable modifications. As well, the 2004 plan was consistent with the special Direct Control District regulations that the city and the MVA had already established jointly for any projects in that area.

The third key factor is the collaborative relationship between the city, the MVA, and the federal and provincial governments. This collaboration produced most of the funding needed for planning and preparation of the site as well as for the few real estate developments that were undertaken over the 2003–09 period. Substantial funding for the project started to flow in the fall of 2003 when, just before calling the provincial election, Premier Calvert announced that his government was contributing $4 million to the development of a strip of land close to the river. That development included a riverbank promenade between two major parks in that area, a water play area for children with a relief map of the South Saskatchewan River, two small outdoor amphitheatres for special performances, and a docking area for boats (McLoughlin 2005, 89–90). The city and the provincial government hoped that the redevelopment of that strip of land would serve as a catalyst for the development of the rest of the lands between the riverbank and the downtown (Interviews 6, 24, and 25). One year later, the provincial government contributed another $5 million, the federal government contributed $13.7 million, and the City of Saskatoon contributed $10.6 million, for a total of $29.3 million (Saskatchewan 2004b).

A financial report produced by city officials indicated that as of August 2009 the estimated cost for preparing the entire RLP site was approximately $82.1 million (Saskatoon 2009f). The city provided about $35 million through a combination of its existing funds and borrowed funds. The provincial government contributed $9 million through its general municipal projects development fund and $0.15 million through its Provincial Community Share Fund. The federal government contributed $13.7 million through the Federal Strategic Infrastructure program and $3.0 million through Western Economic Diversification. The MVA contributed approximately $3 million from its own capital funds and funds it generated through fundraising and sponsorships. Other sources of funding included $0.616 million from the tripartite Urban Development Agreement fund (to which the federal government contributed 50 percent and the provincial and city governments each contributed 25 percent), $12.667 million from land sales, and $0.6 million from sponsorships.

Most of the allocations by the provincial and federal governments were made by the provincial NDP government and the federal Liberal government. The governments that replaced them honoured the financial commitments of their predecessors; further, in the fall of 2009, Prime Minister Stephen Harper and Premier Brad Wall signed an agreement in principle with the city to provide funding for the proposed $51 million Destination Centre. The provincial and federal governments agreed to contribute $13.02 million each for a total of $26.4 million or approximately 50 percent, and the city and its partners were to provide the remainder (Saskatchewan 2009d). The federal government's share of funding, to be provided from the Major Infrastructure Component of the Building Canada Fund, was conditional on a positive project review, the completion of any environmental assessment requirements, securing the balance of the costs, and signing contribution agreements for the projects.

According to city officials, the changes in partisan complexion of the provincial and federal governments, as the Conservatives replaced the Liberals at the federal level, and the Saskatchewan Party replaced the NDP at the provincial level, involved a "seamless transition" in dealing with RLP funding (Interview 6). Even the intense and sometimes acrimonious disagreements between the federal and provincial governments on other financial issues such as equalization and farm subsidies did not adversely affect negotiations on the RLP. In addition to the fact that the governments shared the policy goals mentioned above, all governments were highly interested in funding major infrastructure projects during this period. As well, there were political incentives for governments to collaborate on such projects because they were in competitive electoral contexts that included coalition, minority, and slim majority government situations. Despite their willingness to collaborate on funding matters, there were still the usual challenges of establishing efficacious consultative processes, setting clear project priorities, and making funding commitments in a timely manner, not only in this sector but also in the other sectors examined in this chapter (Interviews 4, 5, 6, 7, 8, and 9).

Although the provincial and federal governments were willing to provide financial support for the RLP, they were not interested in planning or managing the project through a Community Development Corporation (CDC). An invitation to join such an entity was issued by city council in 2003, in response to the demands of community and business leaders who attended a special meeting to consider refurbishing or demolishing the old Gathercole building (Saskatoon 2003b). Creating a CDC had been advocated before – both by the Mayor's Task Force thirteen years earlier (Saskatoon 1990) and by a task force of the business community in 2003 (Saskatoon and District Chamber of Commerce 2003). Whereas the federal government declined the invitation to participate in a CDC, ostensibly because it believed that local planning and development decisions should be left to local stakeholders (Canada 2003), the provincial government indicated that it was prudent to discuss the proposal at a future date, in conjunction with the emerging trilateral Urban Development Agreement (Saskatchewan 2003b). Evidently, however, the letter from the provincial government was simply a stalling tactic: a provincial government fax sent accidentally to a proponent of the CDC revealed that it had no intention of becoming involved in creating, operating, or funding such an agency (Interviews 24 and 25). These governments were not willing to get involved in the highly charged political atmosphere related to decisions about the Gathercole building, an atmosphere that was likely to continue given the competing visions and views about the development of the rest of the site. A few months later, the newly elected city council rescinded the motion to explore a possible partnership with the provincial and federal governments. The proponents of the CDC were very disappointed and upset with this outcome, and some continue to believe that the decision not to create the CDC during the early stages of the planning and development processes was one of the major factors contributing to delays and the limited success of the RLP (Interviews 24 and 25). This continues to be a debated point.

Although the city did not establish a Community Development Corporation for the RLP in 2004, just four years later it approved the creation of "a civic-owned non-profit corporation" (Saskatoon 2008c) headed by an executive director and a board of directors similar to the one that managed the main arts and convention centre in Saskatoon, TCU Place (Interviews 24 and 25). It was envisioned that the board would consist of two city councillors, the city manager, and four or five board members selected from applicants who lived in the city. The fundamental difference between this civic-owned non-profit corporation and the CDC proposed in 2003 is that the federal and provincial governments would not be represented on the board of directors and, therefore, would have no legal, financial, or political responsibility for its action. Interestingly, the recommendation approved by city council indicated that the corporation's mandate would involve "maintenance, operations, and governance" related to the RLP, but it would not make decisions about "the current capital construction plan" (Saskatoon 2008c). Clearly, city council and its administration were not prepared to give up control of the current construction plan and the corresponding financial assets. Such concerns may well explain why as of 2011, the proposed corporation has still not been established.

Between 1999 and 2009, two factors limited progress in planning and developing the RLP. First, there were protracted negotiations and debates about a parcel of land and a building that the city purchased from the Public School Board. The negotiations, which at times were intense and acrimonious, lasted for more than two years. Eventually, the city, with the strong support of influential business leaders, was able to persuade the Public School Board to sell the land and the building. Then an intense debate began about the historic Gathercole building and its future (Nickel 2002). The debate, from 2001–04, focused on whether the building should be demolished or renovated. The city council that was in power from 2000 to 2003 was more or less evenly divided on the issue. The business community generally supported demolition, though there were some opposing entrepreneurs who were interested in acquiring the entire building or space within it. Community groups became involved in the debate either to oppose demolition outright or to defer it until an appropriate decision-making process was established to determine the best option. Demolition opponents within and beyond city hall delayed demolition of the Gathercole building but did not stop it. In the 2003 municipal election, most of the city councillors who opposed the demolition either did not run or were defeated. The new city council, which had a stronger pro-development bent than its predecessor, commissioned a consultant to make recommendations about the building (Nickel 2003). In 2004, council voted to accept the consultant's recommendation that the Gathercole building be demolished. Its decision was eased because the current RLP development plan provided for the relocation of the farmers' market to a city-owned building to be renovated on the Phase 2 site of the RLP.

A more important impediment to progress on the RLP was the lack of finding private-sector developers capable of building the larger real-estate projects on both city-owned and privately-owned land. Four major projects did not materialize from 1999 to 2009. One of these was the 1999 proposal by Princeton Developments to build a large commercial and theatre complex as the first step in developing the entire site. When one of its prospective anchor tenants – Cineplex Odeon – filed for bankruptcy that year, Princeton Developments was unable to find another tenant or to raise more capital. A second project was proposed by Remai Ventures Inc. a few years later. Remai proposed to build a large complex consisting of a hotel, a mineral spa, banquet halls, a restaurant, and underground parking. The developer backed away from this project because of rapidly escalating construction costs, growing pressures in the financial markets, and some constraints in the regulatory framework established by the city and the MVA for real estate developments near the riverfront (*StarPhoenix* 2007). Then there was the massive $200 million hotel-condominium-office complex proposed by Lake Placid River Landing Incorporated. This proposal failed because, even with an extension by the city, the developer could not access the investment capital it needed given the global financial crisis (Hutton 2009a).

The crisis also created problems for a $25 million residential and retail complex proposed by Prairie Ecovillage Development Corp. (PEDCO). In 2009, city council set a deadline for PEDCO to pay the city $1.5 million by 31 May 2010, to get all approvals by 31 March 2011, and for excavation to be completed by the fall of 2012 (Hutton 2009b).

Although Saskatoon's economy remained strong, the persistence of global financial difficulties dampened the optimism about some of the largest real estate projects envisioned for Phase 1 and Phase 2 of the RLP. Some critics of the RLP policy maintain the policy goals were not achieved because of an unduly heavy reliance on large-scale real estate development projects that were to be funded and undertaken by the private sector. In their view, a mix of publicly and privately owned projects, more limited in scale, would have resulted in greater success (Interviews 14, 24, and 25). This remains a talking point in Saskatoon as the discussion continues about how to facilitate more real estate development on both Phase 1 and 2 of the RLP.

In summary, the progress that was made on the RLP is attributable to the widespread consensus on the overarching goal and the collaborative relationships between the city and the MVA and between the city and the provincial and federal governments. Progress was limited both by difficulties in acquiring the Gathercole building and the debate about what to do with it. Most significant were the challenges faced by private developers and cooperatives in accessing the funds they needed to build large facilities.

## CONCLUSIONS

Our central objective here has been to assess the quality and determinants of policies in four policy sectors in Saskatoon. In this concluding section we provide a brief overview and analysis of the findings.

The prevailing view among governmental and non-governmental stakeholders and observers is that the quality of policy in the four policy sectors was good in that it generally achieved the policy goals and goals of the key governmental stakeholders. But the policy was by no means optimal. In the case of emergency services, the suboptimality lay in the limited capacity of the system to deal with larger scale disasters. In the case of immigration, it lay in the capacity to meet the needs of both newcomers and the agencies that served them. In the case of the airport, suboptimality lay in the problems with security screening and taxi service. And in the case of the RLP, it lay in aiming for large real estate developments on the site. Suboptimality in policy was most evident in the emergency measures and immigration fields because there were more significant problems, actual or potential, for individuals and the community as a whole.

The four cases studies suggest that in Saskatoon the quality of policy outputs was a function of the quality of governance and management. More specifically, the quality of policy outputs was a function of three elements of governance and management: (a) the leadership and the degree of commitment of governmental and non-governmental stakeholders to achieving policy goals and objectives; (b) the degree of collaboration among key governmental and non-governmental stakeholders in working towards the achievement of the policy goals and objectives; and (c) the amount of resources devoted to achieving the policy goals and objectives. These factors affected the quality of policy positively when they were present to an appropriate degree and at the appropriate time, and negatively when they were not.

In all four cases, the leadership and level of commitment in governments were generally high. But the leadership role varied. In the emergency measures and RLP cases, the leadership and strongest commitment came from the city. By contrast, in the airport case, the leadership role and strongest commitment came initially from a federal government agency – Transport Canada – and subsequently from the Saskatoon Airport Authority. In the immigration case, there was leadership and commitment by all three levels of government, but it was the unprecedented commitment of the provincial government to improve immigration policy, and its willingness to assume key responsibilities, that made the most significant contribution. In effect, in all four cases there was at least one champion committed to advancing the policy goals and objectives.

In explaining the causes of some suboptimality in policy or in making recommendations for addressing it, several of the interviewees spoke of insufficient leadership and commitment in the past on the part of governmental and non-governmental stakeholders (Interviews 4, 9, 17, 24, and 25). They also spoke of the need for a broader set of stakeholders to accept responsibility for improving public policies in each policy sector.

The quality of policy in all four cases was also positively affected by the relatively high degree of collaboration among governmental and non-governmental stakeholders. This included collaboration not only between the municipal, provincial, and federal governments, but also between these governments and other municipal governments, local public authorities, and community-based organizations that had key roles or responsibilities. In each case, collaboration was undertaken to enhance policy coherence or governance capacity. Toward that end, governmental stakeholders established joint committees and joint funding arrangements for various programs and projects. The creation of joint committees was particularly noteworthy in the emergency measures and immigration fields. Joint funding involving at least two of the three levels of government was particularly significant in the immigration case where it was undertaken on a bilateral federal-provincial basis and in the RLP case where it was undertaken on trilateral federal-provincial-municipal basis.

The high degree of collaboration among the governmental and non-governmental stakeholders was influenced by the degree of consensus among them on the policy objectives and on the means by which to pursue them. Second, it was affected by the degree of compatibility between their respective policy agendas or priorities. The most notable example of this was the compatibility between the policy agendas of the municipal, provincial, and federal governments in the case of the RLP. As well, good interpersonal relations among key governmental and non-governmental actors facilitated collaboration. Finally, collaboration among the governmental stakeholders was also affected by their respective political imperatives for electoral success. However, neither partisan political allegiances nor differing ideological orientations among members of the municipal, provincial, and federal governments diminished the level of collaboration among them. Overall, the prevailing view of many of the interviewees was that for the quality of policy to improve, governmental and non-governmental stakeholders must continue to work at achieving greater collaboration.

Finally, the quality of policy in all four cases was also positively affected by the amount of financial and human resources that governmental and non-governmental stakeholders were willing to devote to achieving the policy objectives. The prevailing view in all four cases was that, although substantial resources were devoted to the various policies, more resources will be required for their further advancement. Some of the case studies suggest that additional required resources were expected to come not only from the public sector but also from the private sector. This was clearly evident in the RLP case where the major real estate developments stalled consistently because of challenges faced by private sector developers in seeking to access the required financial resources.

In summary, the quality of public policy in Saskatoon has been affected both positively and negatively by the quality of governance and management in the context of multilevel governance. More specifically, the quality of public policy was affected by the quality of three facets of governance and management – leadership and commitment to achieving policy goals, collaboration among key stakeholders, and the amount of resources devoted to achieving the policy objectives. This suggests that efforts to improve the quality of policy in the future must devote attention to these three facets of governance and management in a coherent and consistent manner.

## LIST OF INTERVIEWS

1 Saskatoon, 3 December 2007.
2 Saskatoon, 13 December 2007.
3 Saskatoon, 7 January 2008.
4 Saskatoon, 22 September 2008.
5 Saskatoon, 30 September 2008.
6 Saskatoon, 5 October 2008.
7 Saskatoon, 30 September 2008.
8 Saskatoon, 30 September 2008.
9 Saskatoon, 15 October 2008.
10 Saskatoon, 13 March 2009.
11 Saskatoon, 13 March 2009.
12 Saskatoon, 23 April 2009.
13 Saskatoon, 8 May 2009.
14 Saskatoon, 8 October 2009.
15 Saskatoon, 15 October 2009.
16 Saskatoon, 13 November 2009.
17 Saskatoon, 25 November 2009.
18 Saskatoon, 27 November 2009.
19 Saskatoon, 27 November 2009.
20 Saskatoon, 14 December 2009.
21 Saskatoon, 14 December 2009.
22 Saskatoon, 15 December 2009.
23 Saskatoon, 21 December 2009.
24 Saskatoon, 27 February 2010.
25 Saskatoon, 27 February 2010.

## REFERENCES

Beauchesne, Eric. 2007. "Saskatoon Economy Among Canada's Best." *StarPhoenix*, 4 December.
Big City Mayors' Caucus (BCMC). 2006. *Our Cities, Our Future: Addressing the Fiscal Imbalance in Canadian Cities Today.* http://www.canadascities.ca/pdf/2006_BCMC_Our_Cities_Our_Future.pdf.
Canada. 1999. Transport Canada. "Control of John G. Diefenbaker-Saskatoon Airport Transferred to the Saskatoon Airport Authority. National Airport Policy." Press Release, 14 January. http://www.tc.gc.ca/eng/mediaroom/releases-nat-1999-99_h005e-3447.htm.
– 2003. Minister of State for Western Economic Diversification to Mayor of Saskatoon, 17 September. City Clerk's Office, Saskatoon.
– 2005. Citizenship and Immigration Canada. *Canada-Saskatchewan Immigration Agreement.* http://www.cic.gc.ca/english/department/laws-policy/agreements/sask/sask-agree-2005.asp.
– 2006. Statistics Canada. "Selected Trend Data for Saskatoon (CY) 2006, 2001 and 1996 Censuses." http://111.12/statcan.gc.ca/census-recensement/2006/dp-pd/92-596/P2-1.cfm?Lang=eng&T=PR.
– 2008a. Citizenship and Immigration Canada. "Backgrounder–Settlement Funding Allocations for 2009–10." http://www.cic.gc.ca/english/department/media/backgrounders/2008/2008-12-22.asp.
– 2008b. Transport Canada. *The National Airport Policy.* http://www.tc.gc.ca/eng/programs/airports-policy-nap-72.htm.
– 2009a. Public Safety Canada. *Joint Emergency Preparedness Program (JEPP).* http://www.publicsafety.gc.ca/prg/em/jepp/index-eng.aspx.
– 2009b. Public Safety Canada. *Joint Emergency Preparedness Program (JEPP).* "Annex A: Terms and Conditions." http://www.publicsafety.gc.ca/prg/em/jepp/index-eng.aspx.
– 2009c. Public Safety Canada. *2008–2009 Summative Evaluation of the Joint Emergency Preparedness Program (JEPP).* http://www.publicsafety.gc.ca/abt/dpr/eval/jepp-pcpc-eng.aspx.
Coolican, Lori. 2006. "City Drops Post Office Building Bid." *StarPhoenix*, 24 August. http://www.canada.com/story_print.html?id=a8109336-746a-44d1-bfd6-71c9d5c3a22d&sponsor.
– 2009. "Airport Taxi Awaits a 'Crisis' Criticisms from Councillors Unfounded: Cab, Airport officials," *StarPhoenix*, 19 August. http://www2.canada.com/saskatoonstarphoenix/news/story.html?id=fe5c5390-b92a-4822-835f-86c6b1e18b78.

Coyne, Andrew. 2009. "Canada's Best and Worst Run Cities." *Maclean's*, 16 July. http://www2.macleans.ca/2009/07/16/canadas-best-and-worst/run-cities/.

Federation of Canadian Municipalities (FCM). 2009. *Quality of Life in Canadian Communities: Immigration and Diversity in Canadian Cities and Communities*. http://www.fcm.ca//CMFiles/QofL%20Report%205%20 En1JPA-3192009-2422.pdf.

Garcea, Joseph, and Smita Garg. 2009. "Cultural Diversity, Race Relations, Immigration, and Integration in Saskatoon: The Processes of Developing Institutional Arrangements." *Our Diverse Cities*, 6 (Spring):150–5.

Hutton, David. 2009a. "Lake Placid development at River Landing Seemingly a Dead Deal." *StarPhoenix*, 31 October.

– 2009b. "Payment Deadline Set for Prairie Ecovillage at River Landing." *StarPhoenix*, 15 December. http://communities.canada.com/saskatoonstarphoenix/blogs/cityhall/archive/2009/12/15/payment-deadline-set-for-prairie-ecovillage-at-river-landing.aspx.

Insightrix. 2008a. *Immigration Action Plan Gap Analysis*. Report prepared for the City of Saskatoon, 22 May. http://www.saskatoon.ca/DEPARTMENTS/Community%20Services/Communitydevelopment/Documents/gap_analysis_report.pdf.

– 2008b. *Checklist for Immigration Action Plan*. May. Document prepared for the City of Saskatoon. http://www.saskatoon.ca/DEPARTMENTS/Community%20Services/Communitydevelopmenet/Documents/checklist.pdf

KPMG. 2008. "Saskatoon and Winnipeg Edge Out US Mid-West Cities As Most Cost-Effective Business Locations." News Release, 27 March. http://www.kpmg.ca/en/news/pr20080327f.html.

– 2009. *Competitive Alternatives – Downloads: KPMG's Guide to International Business Location (2002, 2004, 2006, 2008)*. http://www.competitivealternatives.com/download/archive.aspx.

McLoughlin, Megan. 2005. "South Downtown Revitalization in Saskatoon, Saskatchewan, Canada: A Review and Reconsideration." MA Thesis, Department of Geography, University of Saskatchewan.

Nickel, R. 2002. "Gathercole a Money Pit." *StarPhoenix*, 19 October, A1.

– 2003. "Council to Decide Fate of the Gathercole," *StarPhoenix*, 25 November, A3, A5.

Padova, Allison. 2005. *Federal Commercialization in Canada*. http://www2.parl.gc.ca/Content/LOP/ResearchPublications/prb0545-e.html.

Patel, Bhavini, and Stephen Ogilvie. 2009. *Report Card: Canadian Municipalities Manage to Stay the Course Despite the Recession*. (Standard & Poors Report 2009). 25 July. http://www.york.ca/NR/rdonlyres/

rc6usmkdeuq6j5e3ujrbgkic3hvoc3ytfe2rjfs33yruohhlxxjk6xm5d4fr2be5dttt
nz2a754t2i3uvadeivfjee/2009+StandardandPoor's+Credit+Rating.pdf.

Pontikes, Ken, and Joseph Garcea. 2006. *Building Saskatoon to Become a Global City: A Framework for an Immigration Action Plan.* Report prepared for the City of Saskatoon. http://www.saskatoon.ca/DEPARTMENTS/ Community%20Services/Communitydevelopment/Documents/immigration_study_executive_summary.pdf.

Ralko, Joe. 2007. "Celebrating in Saskatoon." *Western Investor*, April. http:// www.westerninvestor.com/regional/saskatoonapril07.pdf.

Saskatchewan. 1989. *The Emergency Planning Act.* http://www.qp.gov.sk.ca/ documents/English/Statutes/Statutes/E8-1.pdf.

– 2003a. "Saskatoon Receives Funding for Riverfront Improvements." News Release, 6 October. http://www.gov.sk.ca/news?newsId= b550d406-f1cd-41d3-85e1-e402e8a896e5.

– 2003b. Minister of Government Relations to Mayor of Saskatoon, 30 July. City Clerk's Office, Saskatoon.

– 2004a. Corrections and Public Safety. *Joint Emergency Preparedness Program (JEPP): Guidelines.* http://www.cpsp.gov.sk.ca/adx/aspx/adx GetMedia.aspx?DocID=713,712,94,88,Documents&MediaID=252& Filename=Guidelinesfortheweb.pdf&l=English.

– 2004b. "Saskatoon's River Landing Project to Receive 29.3 Million." News Release, 10 December. http://www.gov.sk.ca/news?newsId= 0816b873-f4e0-4dca-9b7a-0483c63a0f0c.

– 2008. "Saskatoon Announces Immigration Project Designed to Support Settlement and Retention of Newcomers." News Release, 28 March. http:// www.gov.sk.ca/news?newsId=e9a32bc3-9db1-40ee-b111-f284cf4bec98.

– 2009a. Advanced Education, Employment and Labour. *Annual Report.* http://www.aeel.gov.sk.ca/2008-09-annual-report.

– 2009b. "Province Unveils New Immigration Policy." News Release, 19 June. http://www.gov.sk.ca/news?newsId=cff28780-f5c1-4fd5-ab91-c848d027efa8.

– 2009c. Corrections, Public Safety and Policing. Saskatchewan Emergency Management Organization (SaskEMO). "Provincial Preparedness." http:// www.cpsp.gov.sk.ca/SaskEMO/Provincial-Preparedness.

– 2009d. "Canada and Saskatchewan Invest in Saskatoon." News Release, 23 September. http://www.gov.sk.ca/news?newsId=8e94105f-9c1b-484d-a9df-c3842a8f9d2c.

Saskatchewan Assessment Management Agency. 2007. *Roll Confirmation Reports: Confirmed Municipal Assessment Totals,* "Table 7: 2007 Total Assessment." Accessed 24 Sept. 2011. http://sama.sk.ca/sama/ sama/33_display_assess_report.asp?year=2007&munic=C&report=Total.

Saskatoon. 1990. South-*Downtown Development: Report of the Mayor's Task Force.* http://www.riverlanding.ca/reports_public_input/reports/mayors_task_force/mayors_task_force.pdf.

– 1999. *Minutes of the Regular Meeting of City Council.* 20 September. http://www.saskatoon.ca/CITY%20COUNCIL/Pages/MinutesandAgendas.aspx.

– 2001. *Southeast Riversdale Development Plan.* http://www.riverlanding.ca/reports_public_input/reports/south_east_riversdale/south_east_riversdale.pdf.

– 2003a. *City of Saskatoon, Annual Report 2002.* http://www.saskatoon.ca/DEPARTMENTS/City Managers Office/Documents/annual_report_2002.pdf.

– 2003b. *Minutes of the Special Meeting of City Council.* 16 June.

– 2004a. "Proposal for Development of a City of Saskatoon Immigration and Refugee Resettlement Plan." Report No. 18-2004 of the Planning and Operations Committee, in *Minutes of Regular Meeting of City Council,* November 29. http://www.saskatoon.ca/CITY%20COUNCIL/Documents/m2004/m_council_291104.pdf.

– 2004b. *Corporate Business Plan 2004–2006.* http://www.saskatoon.ca/DEPARTMENTS/City%20Managers%20Office/Documents/corporate_business_plan_2004–2006.pdf.

– 2004c. *City of Saskatoon Annual Report 2003.* http://www.saskatoon.ca/DEPARTMENTS/City Managers Office/Documents/annual_report_2003.pdf.

– 2004d. *South Downtown Concept Plan; Public Input Summary.* http://www.riverlanding.ca/reports_public_input/reports/summary_of_public_input/public_input_summary.pdf.

– 2005a. *City of Saskatoon Annual Report 2004.* http://www.saskatoon.ca/DEPARTMENTS/City Managers Office/Documents/annual_report_2004.pdf

– 2005b. *Minutes of the Regular Meeting of City Council.* 4 April. http://www.saskatoon.ca/CITY%20COUNCIL/Pages/MinutesandAgendas.aspx.

– 2006a. *Corporate Business Plan 2006–2008.* http://www.saskatoon.ca/DEPARTMENTS/City%20Managers%20Office/Documents/corporate_business_plan_2006-2008.pdf.

– 2006b. *City of Saskatoon Annual Report 2005.* http://www.saskatoon.ca/DEPARTMENTS/City Managers Office/Documents/annual_report_2005.pdf.

– 2006c. *City of Saskatoon Annual Report 2005: Centennial Edition.* http://www.saskatoon.ca/DEPARTMENTS/City%20Managers%20Office/Documents/centennial_report_2005.pdf.

– 2007a. *Report to City Clerk and Executive Community from General Manager, Community Services Department.* (File number RR 115–2 and LS 220–48.) 23 March. http://www.saskatoon.ca/DEPARTMENTS/Community%20Services/Communitydevelopment/Documents/city_council_mar_07_immigration_report.pdf.
– 2007b. *City of Saskatoon Annual Report 2006.* http://www.saskatoon.ca/DEPARTMENTS/City Managers Office/Documents/annual_report_2006.pdf.
– 2007c. *The Emergency Planning Bylaw (Bylaw No. 7269).* http://www.saskatoon.ca/DEPARTMENTS/City Clerks Office/Documents/bylaws/7269.pdf.
– 2007d. *2008 Capital Budget/2009-2012 Capital Plan.* http://www.saskatoon.ca/DEPARTMENTS/Corporate%20Services/Office%20of%20the%20City%20Comptroller/Pages/FinancialReports.aspx.
– 2008a. *Corporate Business Plan, 2008-2010.* http://www.saskatoon.ca/DEPARTMENTS/City%20Managers%20Office/Documents/corporate_business_plan_2008-2010.pdf.
– 2008b. *2007 Productivity Improvements, Presented to City Council – 17 March.* http://www.saskatoon.ca/DEPARTMENTS/City Managers Office/Documents/2007_productivity_improvements_report.pdf.
– 2008c. *Minutes of the Regular Meeting of Council.* 17 March. Administrative Report, No. 5-2000, Section F – City Manager (Sub-section F1: River Landing Management Structure and Operations). http://www.saskatoon.ca/CITY%20COUNCIL/Pages/MinutesandAgendas.aspx.
– 2009a. *Committee List.* http://www.saskatoon.ca/DEPARTMENTS/City%20Clerks%20Office/Boards%20and%20Committees/City%20Boards%20and%20Committees/Pages/default.aspx.
– 2009b. *Quick Facts.* http://www.saskatoon.ca/QUICK%20FACTS/Pages/Quick%20Facts.aspx.
– 2009c. *Welcome Home Immigration Action Plan.* http://www.saskatoon.ca/DEPARTMENTS/Community%20Services/Communitydevelopment/Documents/ImmigrationActionPlan.pdf.
– 2009d. *2008 Productivity Improvements, Presented to City Council – 16 March.* http://www.saskatoon.ca/DEPARTMENTS/City Managers Office/Documents/2008_productivity_improvements_report.pdf.
– 2009e. "About the Landing." http://www.riverlanding.ca/about/index.html.
– 2009f. *Minutes of the Regular Meeting of City Council.* 14 September. River Landing Project Funding Update (Section B: Corporate Services, Administrative Report 18 – 2009). http://www.saskatoon.ca/CITY%20COUNCIL/Pages/MinutesandAgendas.aspx.

Saskatoon Airport Authority (SAA). 2002. *Annual Report*. http://www.yxe.ca/about/pdf/annual_report_2002.pdf.

– 2003a. *Bylaw No. 1: A Bylaw relating generally to the transaction of the business and affairs of Saskatoon Airport Authority*. http://www.yxe.ca/about/pdf/Bylaws.pdf.

– 2003b. *Annual Report*. http://www.yxe.ca/about/pdf/annual_report_2003.pdf.

– 2004. *Annual Report*. http://www.yxe.ca/about/pdf/annual_report_2004.pdf.

– 2005. *Annual Report*. http://www.yxe.ca/about/documents/SAA_ARfinal_000.pdf.

– 2006. *Annual Report*. http://www.yxe.ca/about/documents/06sAAAR_mar27_000.pdf.

– 2007a. *Annual Report*. http://www.yxe.ca/about/documents/AnnualReport2007.pdf.

– 2007b. "John G. Diefenbaker Welcomes 1 Millionth Passenger of 2007." 18 December. http://www.yxe.ca/documents/MillionthPassenger.pdf.

– 2008. *Annual Report*. http://www.yxe.ca/about/documents/SAA_2008_AR.pdf.

– 2009a. *Role of Saskatoon Airport Authority*. http://www.yxe.ca/about/role.php#ccc.

– 2009b. "Saskatoon Airport Authority Awards Taxi Service." Press Release. http://www.yxe.ca/pressreleases.php.

Saskatoon and District Chamber of Commerce. 2003. *Report of Saskatoon and District Chamber of Commerce South Downtown Taskforce*. http://www.saskatoonchamber.com/file/Newsroom/Research_Papers/2003/RP-South_Downtown.pdf.

*Saskatoon Sun*. 2003. "Riverbank Development Receives Funding," 12 October.

*StarPhoenix*. 2007. "Remai Backs Out: The Only Private-sector Investor Involved with Saskatoon's River Landing is Pulling out of the Project." 8 March.

– 2008. "Saskatoon Airport Hits Million Passenger Mark." 28 November.

– 2009. "Extra Time Advised for Airport Screening." 24 October.

Vellacott, Maurice. 2009. "MP Vellacott Makes Funding Announcement at Newcomer Information Centre of Saskatoon." 8 May. http://www.mauricevellicott.ca/maurice.html.

Waytiuk, Judy, and Steve Brearton. 2001. "The 5 Best Cities for Families." *Today's Parent*, April. http://www.todaysparent.com/lifeasparent/article.jsp?content=3304.

# 8

# St John's, A City Apart:
# An Essay in Urban Exceptionalism

CHRISTOPHER DUNN AND CECILY PANTIN

St John's, the capital of Newfoundland and Labrador, is a city apart. It is apart from the rest of the province, and indeed from the rest of the country, in its history, its pattern of municipal development, its jurisdiction, and in the policy areas that are the focus of this project – that is, in infrastructure, immigration, image building, and urban Aboriginal policy. Every city is of course unique, but St John's has taken a path different from the general pattern of city government and programming in almost every case. To study it is an exercise in urban exceptionalism.

First, the history. No other city in the continent has had to battle a motherland that did not want it, or any settlement on the Island, to exist. Historically, St John's was the nexus of a fishing trade that was not meant to promote settlement. This marked the province as apart from the rest of the continent, which had to be explored and exploited on the expectation that settlement would follow. The only resource like the fishing trade was perhaps the fur trade, which discouraged settlement from the agricultural sector, but this is an imperfect analogue.

The net effects of this forced estrangement were, in retrospect, predictable. There was delayed development of the institutions of governance. Judicial forms of a permanent nature came to the colony before the legislative or executive. Despite centuries of habitation, judicial forms had been rudimentary, consisting of "fishing admirals" (the first captain to reach a bay) or later, officers of the Royal Navy. Continuous judicial administration came only in 1791 and colonial status came only in 1825. Representative government came in 1832, two centuries after it was inaugurated in the Thirteen Colonies. Nova Scotia had had it since 1758, PEI since 1773, New Brunswick since 1786, and the Province of Canada since 1791 (Hogg 1999). Representative government in Newfoundland was given up from 1934–49, replaced by a Commission of Government appointed by Britain.

What experience eighteenth- and nineteenth-century Newfoundlanders had of government was generally negative. Yet, they were able to escape government, and taxation, by residing in scattered outports far from the reach of His Majesty's Navy. The tradeoff for less taxation was that there was little municipal infrastructure and more mutual aid.

Municipal government was unpopular in Newfoundland and Labrador because the people feared the property taxes that would follow. The right to own property was not won until 1824, and the people were afraid that under local government they would lose the property they valued so much. After several attempts to provide legislation for municipalities failed, the Commission of Government (1934–49) decided it would pass a special act for each area as it became incorporated, which would allow each area to specify the form of taxation it preferred. By 1948, twenty municipalities had been formed under special acts. This method of incorporation was replaced in 1949 by the Local Government Act, which included all municipalities outside St John's.

Geographic distance helped engender estrangement from the capital. St John's was where the colonial government resided, and where most (though not all) of the principal merchants lived. The merchants held many outports in their thrall by virtue of the "truck" system, through which credit was extended to fishers to allow them to subsist over the winter, but at the cost of semi-permanent financial obligations to the merchants. This historic hostility to St John's remains in vestigial form to this day and colours much of the politics of provincial and local government. St John's was always, and will remain, a city apart from the rest of the province.

The fact that the most important merchants were located in St John's lent a business tenor to the city that remains to this day. At first, the merchants directly serviced the outports themselves. In the nineteenth century, the merchants' relationship to the outports changed, and they effectively became wholesalers for smaller merchants in the larger outports. There then followed a period of diversification wherein the merchants combined their normal trading with manufacturing activity or other economic activities.

In the twentieth century, the merchants' importance in the economic firmament first waned as the Commission of Government acted to shore up political support by opposing merchant power. Then, Confederation in 1949 resulted in a common market with Canada and dominance by both Canadian and foreign corporations (Adams 2001; Cadigan 2009; Neary 1988; Wheaton 2002). What did remain, however, was the preoccupation of St John's with business. In Confederation, St John's politics has always been about positioning itself in the corporate sector. This emphasis on business colours infrastructure planning, image building, immigration, and other matters.

St John's lacked municipal government until the late nineteenth century. The most prominent explanatory factor for the lack of municipal government was fear of taxation, as mentioned above. There were other factors, like the effect of absentee landlords on urban development. Another was political culture. Still another factor involved class considerations. (For more on these factors, see Baker 1974, 1976, and 1984.) The legislature finally gave St John's self-government in 1888. At this point, St John's was a latecomer. Municipal self-government had come to St John's many years later than in other centres in the North Atlantic region. Saint John, New Brunswick, received it in 1785, Halifax in 1841, and Charlottetown in 1855.

### THE PATTERN OF MUNICIPAL DEVELOPMENT

With all these factors conspiring against it, St John's self-government was not only hard-won and late to arrive; it was also intermittent. St John's lost its municipal government from 1898–1902 and 1914–16 because it could not manage the burden of its financial obligations. It was well into the twentieth century that the city came to experience urban government with a degree of security analogous to that of most of North America. So, again, it was unlike the rest of the capital cities in the then Dominion of Canada, as is shown by a history of the acts governing the capital (Smallwood 1991, 645–60). As well, self-government was not entirely meaningful; until Confederation, the finances of the city were largely controlled by upper levels of government.

Beginning during the Second World War, the autonomy and powers of the capital city began to increase, along with its powers to plan, develop infrastructure, and tax. This development is unique because St John's now has more powers than the municipalities outside the capital. The level of self-direction is substantially beyond that of the other municipalities in the province.

The city has sole control of property assessment, public transit, solid waste collection, solid waste disposal, and animal control. If the city wishes, it may assume responsibility for public health and parks and recreation. Like all municipalities, St John's is enabled to conduct economic development activities, but the level of activity conducted in the capital far surpasses that in other jurisdictions. The city even has its own economic development department.

St John's is generally protected from the economic downturns that affect the rest of the province, and it benefits disproportionately from the upturns. Historically, St John's has always been the economic, political, and cultural hub of Newfoundland, and little has changed over the years. One political economist says that, while St John's was, and continues to be, the commercial hub of the province, rural Newfoundland represents a hinterland to be exploited (Summers 2001, 24–5).

Population decline has been asymmetrical. Though Newfoundland's population decreased 1.2 percent from 1991 to 2001, the decrease in the Northeast Avalon – where St John's is located – was small compared to rural areas of the island. The west coast of the island, for example, lost 17.5 percent of its population from 1991 to 2001 (Newfoundland and Labrador 2002, 39). Loss of population had severe consequences for rural communities. Limited resources and small communities created challenges in caring for an aging population and providing other services. Further, the skilled workers required to develop communities were lost.

Small communities in Newfoundland struggle to survive as they face out-migration, reduced economic activity and employment, and rapidly aging populations. Labour force statistics show that in 2009 the unemployment in the Avalon economic region was significantly less than it was in the rural ones (21.9 percent in the Burin Peninsula/South Coast, 18.7 percent in West Coast – Northern Peninsula – Labrador, and 21.9 percent in Notre Dame – Central – Bonavista Bay). From 1989 to 2009, total employment decreased in the Burin Peninsula/South Coast region (down from 18,000 to 12,500), the West Coast – Northern Peninsula – Labrador region (from 45,300 to 41,000) and the Notre Dame – Central – Bonavista Bay region (from 53,900 to 50,800) while it increased from 99,200 to 121,700 in the Avalon economic region (Newfoundland and Labrador 1987–2009, 39).

## INFRASTRUCTURAL SPECIFICITY

A tax base declining largely because of out-migration further exacerbates a community's inability to maintain infrastructure. During the period 1998–2004, the rural municipalities spent an average of 47.34 percent of

their revenue on debt servicing, whereas the nineteen urban municipalities spent an average of 24.54 percent (Newfoundland and Labrador
2003, 379). The figure for St John's has historically been around 10 percent. This imbalance could mean that rural Newfoundland has less
opportunity to develop infrastructure and attract new people than the
more urban areas such as St John's. The capital city would be better
placed to take advantage of federal and provincial offers to leverage its
preferred projects.

So it was good news that the first decade of the twenty-first century
was to be a decade of multilevel cooperation for municipal infrastructure. All prime ministers ultimately came on board, through a combination of factors, such as necessity, electoral strategy, and interest group
pressure. The decade started slowly, but the tempo of infrastructural
programming and financial commitments increased significantly. Part of
the reason for the tempo of development in St John's was that the province's finances began to improve considerably later in the decade at the
same time that federal financing became more generous. The maturing
of resource royalty regimes and the rise in the price of oil were good
news for the development lobby. It was a fine time to be in government
provincially and locally.

Not only did the level of infrastructure funding increase in that decade,
but St John's did relatively well in the race for federal and provincial
infrastructure dollars. As each iteration of federal and provincial money
came about, St John's made sure it was in line for multilevel participation in big-ticket projects.

Early in the decade, it accessed funds under the Canada-Newfoundland
Infrastructure Program (CNIP), which was the agreement established
under the Infrastructure Canada Program and managed provincially by
the province's Department of Municipal and Provincial Affairs. The
province chose to concentrate its CNIP money on such infrastructure as
disinfection assistance, and water and sewer projects, while it handled
costs of paving and road reconstruction, solid waste management,
recreation and firefighting equipment out of provincial and municipal
money. Each level played a role in CNIP projects. St John's, like other
municipalities, proposed most CNIP projects, although up to a fifth of
the value of approved projects could be federally and provincially
nominated. Fully 60 percent of approved projects had to be for green
municipal infrastructure.

The Canada Strategic Infrastructure Fund (CSIF), announced in the
December 2001 federal budget, was to prove of significant importance

for St John's. CSIF focused on large-scale infrastructure projects such major urban transportation projects and sewage treatment systems too large to be funded under the Infrastructure Canada Program. The story of the harbour cleanup had been one of growing consensus among the three levels of government. The city had pushed for secondary sewage treatment in the city's famously filthy harbour since the 1970s. However, there was inaction due to the significant cost and to the fact that the province and the federal government lacked comprehensive strategies for such matters. Things changed early in the new millennium. St John's and the other two municipalities involved lobbied the province to support a harbour cleanup project, and the province committed finances to the project officially in 2000. Now the pressure was on the federal government. The province had asked for the federal government participation in a cleanup effort since 1997. St John's Mayor Andy Wells also put friendly pressure on the federal Finance Minister Paul Martin, with whom he was on good terms. The federal government finally decided on the CSIF mechanism for the St John's cleanup and for other analogous projects.

In November 2002, the federal government announced it would sign a formal agreement on the harbour cleanup. It was indeed to be a tri-level agreement involving the federal, provincial, and municipal governments (the cities of St John's and Mount Pearl, and the Town of Paradise). It would also be an even three-way split in financing, with each level committing $31 million to build a world-class centralized treatment facility on the south side of St John's Harbour, together with infrastructure for sewage collection and disposal of treated effluent (Canada 2002). The provincial and federal governments spent over $11 million in preparatory engineering work.

The federal government originally thought that the committee managing the contribution agreement should only feature federal and provincial officials, but the province, amenable to St John's involvement, successfully prevailed upon Ottawa to make it a tripartite management committee, with three co-chairs (federal, provincial, and St John's). When it was finished, the facility would be controlled by an oversight committee made up of councillors from all three affected municipalities. By September 2009, the treatment plant was operative. At first, sewage from a restricted area – west of Waldegrave Street in St John's, and the City of Mount Pearl and the town of Paradise – was treated. Along the way, the project had encountered sizable cost overruns because of rising labour and construction costs, said city spokesmen (CBC News 2009b).

Costs rose more than 50 percent over the initial budget of $93 million in 1999 to reach $144 million by November 2008. The municipalities involved had to pick up all the extra costs. What was generally not known, however, is that city officials had only two days in 2002 to react to information that federal financial support was forthcoming and a figure ($93 million) had to be established almost immediately with no chance to do detailed project design work due to federal pressure. In retrospect, a higher cost for the cleanup was probably inevitable.

2004–06 was a period of relative quiescence for federal and provincial funding. The expenditures from several programs like the CSIF, the Border Infrastructure Fund, the Municipal Rural Infrastructure Fund (MRIF), and the Public Transit Capital Trust were "sunsetted," meaning that they had a limited life span. CSIF, which covered highway and railway expenditure, local transportation infrastructure, urban development, water and sewage, and broadband, was fully used up, with only limited funding remaining in Ontario, Yukon, and Newfoundland and Labrador. By June of 2007, the MRIF money of $1 billion (used for smaller scale municipal infrastructure like water and wastewater treatment and recreation projects) was largely committed and then topped-up, but only to $200,000. The Public Transit Fund was supplemented by the Public Transit Capital Trust, which was at first to be just a one-time only payment; and then it was renewed briefly in 2008. And although the 2005 Budget had forecast over $9 billion from the Gas Tax Fund and the GST/HST rebate would be flowing to the provinces between 2004–05 and 2009–10, it was early days for these funds.

There was, however, a sympathetic ear at the senior levels. Coming into office in 2003, the new premier, Danny Williams, took the city's priorities as his own. For a few years, infrastructure projects were funded in the traditional way through the Municipal Capital Works Program and the Multi-Year Capital Works Program. The first program covered a wide range of municipal infrastructure, like water and waste water treatment, roads, and recreational facilities. The 2005–08 Multi-year Capital Works Program invested a total of $85 million for municipal infrastructure, of which $42.5 million was provincial money. Then, in 2007 the new Harper government decided to make the infrastructure file one of the mainstays of its policy arsenal. It devoted $33 billion to the Building Canada Plan and further augmented this plan in 2009 as part of its response to the economic crisis gripping the world. Under "Canada's Economic Action Plan" (EAP), the federal government established a $4 billion Infrastructure Stimulus Fund that provided funding to construction-ready infrastructure projects, focusing on short-term fund-ing (two years, to March 2011) for economic stimulus. This brought total national infrastructure funding to $37 billion. The immediate advantage for St John's and the provincial government was that what once had been provincial-municipal cost-sharing could now become tri-partite federal-provincial-municipal spending. Instead of having to pay half the costs, the city now could get by with about a third. As finances improved due to oil royalties and other factors, the province even assumed 10 percent of the municipal share of the cost of projects.

The four funds, which formed the bulk of funding for the city in the period 2008–11, were the Building Canada Fund (BCF), the Infrastructure Stimulus Fund, the Gas Tax Fund, and the GST/HST rebate. The GST/HST rebate had been discussed for several years. It was to increase the rebate of sales tax paid by municipal governments to 100 percent. In the 2004 federal budget, under the sympathetic eye of Paul Martin, it became a reality. At the time, the GST/HST rebate was estimated to be worth $7 million over ten years. The Gas Tax Fund, also the result of years of discussion and municipal advocacy, was announced in the 2005 federal budget. Advocates for the gas tax reasoned that some money collected from the gas pump for automobile transport – which imposes heavy costs on municipal governments – should be returned to municipalities. Originally, funds were to be used for urban public transit, but uses were quickly expanded to include local roads and bridges and infrastructure for drinking water, waste water, community energy, and solid waste management. Budget 2008 announced that the Gas Tax Fund would become a permanent measure beyond 2013–14, when it was originally supposed to end, and be set at $2 billion per year. The Building Canada Fund (not to be confused with the Building Canada Plan, which was the umbrella name of the whole package of infrastructure plans) was itself a collection of programs. The important one for St John's was the Major Infrastructure Component (MIC). BCF-MIC targeted large strategic projects of national or regional importance. Two-thirds of the funding was for priorities such as core national highways, drinking water, wastewater, public transit, and green energy, and other environmental projects like solid waste management. Public infrastructure owned by provincial, ter-ritorial, and municipal governments, and sometimes private firms, was eligible for MIC funding. Decision making for funding was through federal-provincial committees, with the funds allocated based on population.

There were four big-ticket items that received funding through the tri-level process, the Robin Hood Bay Recycling Facility, the Bay Bulls Big

Pond Water Treatment Plant, the Petty Harbour-Long Pond Water Treatment Plant, and the Municipal Depot renovations.

Municipalities in the eastern region of Newfoundland, and indeed the provincial government itself, have attempted for more than a decade to come up with an integrated approach to waste management. In 2010, their efforts came to a head in the establishment of an integrated regional waste management facility at Robin Hood Bay, which had previously served only the City of St John's, Mount Pearl, Paradise, Portugal Cove-St Phillips, and the other smaller municipalities north of St John's. The total cost of re-engineering Robin Hood Bay to become an integrated waste management facility was $53.2 million. In this project, the federal level did the heavy lifting, with $40.2 million coming from the federal Gas Tax Fund, $6.5 million from the province, and $6.5 million from the City of St John's (Canada 2010c).

The St John's Region gets its drinking water from several sources. Two of the major sources are Bay Bulls Big Pond and Petty Harbour Long Pond. Facilities at both sources have benefitted from cash provided under the Infrastructure Stimulus Fund, together with the province and the city. In May 2009, the three levels announced new funding of $35 million to improve water quality at the Bay Bulls Big Pond Water treatment plant. The Government of Canada contributed up to a maximum of $11.7 million under the Infrastructure Stimulus Fund, the province $12.8 million and the City of St John's provided $10.5 million (Canada 2010b). The proportional spending was similar for the Petty Harbour Long Pond Water treatment facility: of the $37 million total cost, the contributions were $12,333,333 federal, $13,556,667 provincial, and $11,100,000 St John's.

St John's also accesses other funds. The Public Transit Capital Trust was used to help build the new Metrobus Depot, which cost an estimated $34,205,586. Once again, the federal government was doing the heavy lifting. St John's was to contribute $8.2 million toward construction, whereas $26 million was to come from the federal Public Transit Capital Trust (CBC News 2009a). The Recreational Infrastructure Canada Program has also been used, but other programs were either under-utilized or withheld. The Private-Public Partnership (P3) Fund is not utilized in St John's, or, for that matter, in the province, although the province was seeking it for the Newfoundland-Nova Scotia underground energy cable. Atlantic Gateway Fund money was sought by the province, but unsuccessfully. The Knowledge Infrastructure Program (KIP) has yielded little money for post-secondary education in the capital: of $24 million for KIP projects in the province, a little more than $2 million went to the College of the North Atlantic for a roof upgrade (Canada 2009).

The situation may be different in other parts of the province, but in St John's the infrastructure process has been surprisingly apolitical and technocratic. Unlike some other cities covered in this collection, there is no business lobby in St John's for the types of major infrastructure projects that have been funded in the last decade or so. Most of the projects have been to meet needs that have been recognized for decades, like sewer and water treatment. They are based on recommendations from the city's engineering department, buttressed by input from the other departments like building and property management, and public works and parks, in consultation with the city manager (the most senior public servant). The list is only then brought to city council, which usually does not make major changes.

If normal municipal capital works expenditures are involved, the list of preferred infrastructure projects is sent to an assistant deputy minister in the province's Municipal Affairs Department. If major Building Canada Plan infrastructure is involved, the proposal would go to the BCP-MIC Management Committee, but even here the city's priorities were not generally questioned.

It is worth noting that almost all of this infrastructure activity generally goes unnoticed by the average citizen of the province. The funding categories are of Byzantine complexity, and few outside government understand them. Signage placed around the city is small, sparse, vague, and credits the Economic Action Plan only, not the intergovernmental aspects of the expenditure, unlike past generations of infrastructure project announcements. EAP infrastructure in the province may be exploited as election fodder in a federal election, but until then the federal government's role is as a banker while the other two levels are the decision makers, joint management bodies notwithstanding. This is how open federalism worked on the ground, at least with bricks and mortar, in a province that had no Conservative MPs (due to the Danny Williams "Anyone But Conservatives" [ABC] strategy) and a provincial government that was unfriendly to its federal counterpart. Williams, upset by federal treatment of Newfoundland resource revenue in the new equalization formula introduced by the Conservative Harper government, had orchestrated an anti-federal-Conservative-candidate strategy in the 2007 election.

IMMIGRANT SETTLEMENT

Immigration has always played an important part in the demographic growth of Canada. Currently, almost one in five of Canada's population is foreign-born. Based on the 2001 census statistics, there are 6,186,950 foreign-born members of Canada's population (Statistics Canada 2001). Immigrants tend to be attracted primarily to the major urban centres of Canada, such as Toronto, Montreal, and Vancouver. Cities like these have more diverse cultures and more economic opportunity than smaller cities. In 2005, Atlantic Canada represented 7.6 percent of Canada's population yet attracted only 1.2 percent of all immigrants to the country. Of the four Atlantic Canadian provinces – Newfoundland and Labrador, Nova Scotia, New Brunswick, and Prince Edward Island – Nova Scotia attracts the majority of the region's immigrants (Newfoundland and Labrador 2005a). Because Atlantic Canada has too few jobs and too few immigrants, new immigrants tend to shy away from it (Ibbitson 2004). However, immigration is increasingly the lifeblood of the Canadian economy.

Even by the weak rates of immigration to Atlantic Canada, the number of immigrants to Newfoundland and Labrador has been and continues to be very low. The province, which has 1.6 percent of Canada's population, attracted less than 0.3 percent of Canada's immigrants between 2001 and 2006. These numbers, coupled with an equally low retention rate of 36 percent, leave much room for improvement in both attracting and retaining immigrants (Newfoundland and Labrador 2007b, 2). The 2006 census indicates the foreign-born population of Newfoundland was 8,385, as compared to the Canadian-born population of 490,855 (Statistics Canada 2007a). The foreign-born represent just 1.7 percent of the total population.

Furthermore, the demographic challenges the province faces are staggering. Since the 1970s, Newfoundland and Labrador has gone from having one of the highest birth rates in Canada to the lowest. During the period from 1991 to 2001, the population of the province declined approximately 10 percent, and this trend continued (Newfoundland and Labrador 2005a, 14). In 2007, the Progressive Conservative party platform of Premier Danny Williams indicated a plan to develop and implement a "Progressive Family Growth Policy" to promote higher birth rates and population expansion by providing money for each new child born (Progressive Conservative Party 2007, 6). Low birth rates, coupled with ever-increasing out-migration and an aging population, have negative effects on the provincial economy and only help accentuate the potential benefits of increased immigration.

The overall unemployment rate in the province has been steadily declining in recent years, but is still relatively high for Canada. Nevertheless, with big economic projects underway, such as the development of the Hebron-Ben Nevis oil field and extensions of other fields, it is likely that employment levels will increase and there will be skills shortages in various sectors. Immigration can be an important tool for addressing such problems.

For many years the government of Newfoundland and Labrador did not have a significant role in immigration policy. It simply complied with federal government policy and programs and administered the Provincial Nominee Program. General assistance has also been provided to the Association for New Canadians (ANC), which also receives funding from several federal departments and the United Way. However, the Government provincial government has begun to look more closely at increasing the number of immigrants in the province. The government saw immigration as a way to enhance economic growth in the province, attract more international students, help address economic challenges, and alleviate skills shortages. The province believes that it has much to offer new immigrants.

On 21 March 2007, the provincial government launched the province's first immigration strategy. It was labeled *Diversity – "Opportunity and Growth:" An Immigration Strategy for Newfoundland and Labrador.* The primary goal of the strategy was to increase the attraction and retention of immigrants to the province. The government committed $6 million over three years to implement the strategy (Newfoundland and Labrador 2007b.) The most significant initiative within *Diversity* was the establishment of the Office of Immigration and Multiculturalism in the Department of Human Resources, Labour and Employment. The province had previously lacked an office to coordinate and address immigration issues.

The strategy involved a series of goals – eighteen in total – for the province to meet over the next number of years with relation to attracting, retaining, and providing services to immigrants. The government saw the immigration strategy as a key support for other provincial policy initiatives such as the Provincial Innovation Strategy, the Regional Diversification Strategy, the Cultural Industries Strategy, and the Tourism Development Strategy.

Compared to the relative lack of initiative historically in matters of immigration, the Williams government's actions arising from the strategy were significant (Newfoundland and Labrador 2007b). The bulk of the new funding went to promote Newfoundland and Labrador as a destination of choice for immigrants. Other money was allocated for immigration initiatives in education, community services, and women's policy.

More recently the government supplemented the immigration strategy with a multiculturalism policy. It supported both these initiatives by investments for more access to settlement services, an internship program for immigrants, and help for international graduates facing labour market challenges. It is working with federal and other provincial governments to extend the reach of the Foreign Credential Recognition system. It has created and made available an Employer's Guide to Hiring Immigrants. It made immigration initiatives a specific part of its high-profile youth retention strategy. The province's universities are increasing the numbers of foreign students on their campuses. The level of provincial concern with immigration and settlement has apparently ramped up.

Although immigration is a policy area only recently given more attention by the provincial government, it is a field with the potential and need for interaction between all three levels of government. The municipal government of St John's is missing in action. Although the most significant immigrant population is located within St John's and the surrounding area, the city has not developed a significant immigrant settlement strategy to address immigrant issues. The task of dealing with immigration tends to fall mainly on the federal government, the provincial government (though only in the past few years), and the Association for New Canadians (ANC), a non-profit organization. It is however anticipated by the province that municipalities, and St John's in particular, will play a greater role in immigration in the years to come.

Newcomers generally arrive in Canada as either immigrants or refugees. An immigrant wishing to settle in St John's or any other city in Newfoundland and Labrador has to go through the same federal government process as immigrants settling in other areas of the country. The City of St John's has little involvement with the immigration process, from the perspective of bringing new people into the province. The city has some interaction with non-profit groups involved in settlement, but that is predominantly the extent of its participation. Immigrants may enter Newfoundland as skilled workers and professionals; investors, entrepreneurs and self-employed persons, or relatives sponsored by a family member. As well, immigrants may be nominated by a provincial government. In 1999, the government of Newfoundland and Labrador signed an agreement with Citizenship and Immigration Canada (CIC) to establish the Newfoundland and Labrador Provincial Nominee Program. Through this, the province seeks to recruit immigrants who have specialized occupational or entrepreneurial skills. The provincial government may nominate those who they believe will contribute in a beneficial way to the province's economy. Foreign nationals accepted under the program can apply for permanent resident status. The Provincial Nominee Program is a key tool that will be instrumental in increasing the number of immigrants to the province.

CIC has numerous settlement programs to assist newcomers with the transition to Canada. Through immigrant settlement and adaptation programs, the federal government funds organizations to provide services such as reception, orientation, interpretation, language training, counseling, and help with job search for immigrants. The levels of funding are determined by applying a formula based on a rolling three-year average of the numbers of immigrants annually. CIC funds service-providing agencies through a competitive bidding process. In Newfoundland and Labrador, the Association for New Canadians (ANC) has been the successful bidder, and CIC has a contribution agreement with them to deliver services to newcomers (Newfoundland and Labrador 2007b, 8). The services of the ANC are generally limited to St John's. The provincial design is that further municipalities will come under the association's umbrella of services as the immigration strategy progresses.

The Coordinating Committee on Newcomer Integration (CCNI) was established by the ANC and is a collaborative partnership with key immigration stakeholders. Such stakeholders include the ANC, the Newfoundland and Labrador Federation of Municipalities, CIC, Canadian Heritage, Service Canada, the City of St John's, the Atlantic Canada Opportunities Agency, the Leslie Harris Centre (affiliated with Memorial University), and others. The mandate of the committee is to support immigrant inclusion, integration, and retention through targeted projects and research (Newfoundland and Labrador 2005a, 8). This committee has provided a mechanism through which the various levels of government, as well as other stakeholders, have been able to come together to discuss policy. As well, the CCNI provides an avenue for the ANC to give advice to senior government officials regarding immigration policy for Newfoundland and Labrador. The ANC played a pivotal role in the development of the provincial government immigration strategy, along with many other organizations.

The ANC has influence locally due to relations the association has built with federal and provincial officials. The ANC has always been most

closely linked to the federal government; however, it is obvious that ties
with the provincial government are being strengthened through the creation and release of the immigration strategy. Interaction with the
municipal level is also increasing. Given the emphasis placed on immigration by cities during the Atlantic Mayors Congress in 2005, it is likely
that interaction between the ANC and the City of St John's will increase
(Newfoundland and Labrador 2007b, 8). With the advent of the immigration strategy, the City of St John's should have more influence in this
policy field beyond the provision of basic services, such as housing, that
are available to all but that can be tailored to new immigrants.

### APART FROM THE COUNTRY WITH A DISTINCT IMAGE

St John's is a city apart in terms of its image nationally and provincially.
Image-building initiatives are undertaken predominantly by the City of
St John's itself. However, the provincial government tourism initiatives
for the province obviously have the aim of attracting people to all corners
of Newfoundland and Labrador; St John's as the capital city and transportation hub for the province, is an obvious stop. As Paul O'Neill writes

> St John's has been sneered at and held in deep affection. It engenders
> hostility and love. Few who ever became involved in the life of
> the place remain indifferent. It has brazen charm that overflows the
> boundless hospitality for which it has become world famous. The
> city does not hide the scars of its centuries of neglect and hostility
> any more than it hides its haphazard streets quietly poked from the
> rush and roar of a commercialized world. It has survived centuries of
> handicaps that have challenged its existence. Often naïve, frequently
> cheeky, it is among the few interesting cities on this North American
> continent. (O'Neill 2003, 36)

Such is the character of St John's. The image of St John's is one where
tourism and business compete for the attention of policy makers; but
given the history of the place, it is business that gets pride of place.

The oil industry tends to recreate certain cities in its image. Texas oil-
fields have Dallas, the Alberta tarsands have Calgary, and the North Sea
has Stavanger and Aberdeen. The Atlantic offshore has St John's. In the
last quarter century, Newfoundland and Labrador became a petroleum
province, and St John's a petroleum capital, another characteristic that
sets it off from the rest of the province. Offshore petroleum activity had

been ongoing since the 1960s, with the first exploration well drilled as early as 1966. Exploration activity led to the discovery of the Hibernia field in 1979, Hebron in 1981, and the Terra Nova and White Rose fields in 1984. After several unsuccessful attempts, both political and constitutional, to establish provincial control over offshore development, Newfoundland and Labrador was able to establish a more workable regime with the Mulroney government that was elected in 1984. The Atlantic Accord of 1985 allowed for the establishment of a single regulatory framework for the exploration and management of offshore oil and gas and allowed for provincial taxation of the resource, just as though it were on land.

The development of Hibernia began in 1990, with its first oil in 1997. Terra Nova, produced its first oil in 2002, and White Rose, came into production in 2005. Significant new reserves were discovered nearby later in the decade, and new frontiers such as the Orphan and Laurentian Subbasin were slated for exploration and development.

A review of the contributions of petroleum development to the province between 2005 and 2007 noted that petroleum and its related activities are "almost certain to be a cornerstone of the province's economy and society for decades to come" (Stantec 2009, 20). Indeed, by 2007, the industry accounted for nearly 30 percent of the provincial GDP.

The preoccupation with oil is reflected in the mission the city has assumed, and the way it goes about achieving it. All of this takes place in a context of a city that has long held a concern to foster close contacts with outside capital. The city has branded itself on its website according to its new interests. In addition, as if to drive home the fact, the city gives the most space to its Petroleum Information Centre in its Economic Development headquarters.

The leader in business-related image building for the province is the City of St John's Economic Development Division. This division is the dynamic, imaginative centre of business thinking in the city government and has been responsible for most of the new branding exercises of the past decade. The division works with partners in industry, government, and education to develop business expansion strategies, streamline business-related policies, programs, and regulations for the city. The Economic Development Division operates the St John's Business Information Centre, a partner of the Canada-Newfoundland and Labrador Business Service Network.

The city takes its energy mission very seriously. St John's became a member of the World Energy Cities Partnerships in 2002, which allows it to partner with other energy capitals. The city is also a partner with the Centre for Energy, which is a lobby for the Canadian energy sector. It is a member of the Energy Council, a continental energy industry body specializing in trade strategy. The idea of image building is critically important to the department and, by relation, the city in general. The department focuses primarily on marketing the city from a business and technology perspective.

The core thrust here for the city is helping to profile, develop and nurture the ocean and marine technology field to package St John's as a "Centre of Ocean Excellence." A lot of that work is motivated by the energy sector, but it also links to natural advantages the city has related to technology coming out of the fishery, navigation, and shipping industries. Newfoundland and Labrador's close relationship with the sea has allowed its people to amass considerable knowledge and expertise. This expertise has been applied to ocean technology and is now being recognized internationally. The ocean technology sector of the province consists of fifty-two companies and eleven public sector organizations. Annual sales of these ocean technology companies in 2005 totalled $230 million (City of St John's 2007a). In support of this sector, the provincial government is implementing an Ocean Technology Sector Strategy to position Newfoundland and Labrador as a centre of excellence. The City of St John's is therefore undertaking initiatives to develop a marketing strategy for this sector. The city has begun to market itself as a "Centre of Ocean Excellence" and a "Port of Potential."

The city includes a number of items under its rubric of centre of ocean excellence, including offshore energy, ocean technology, fishery and marine biotechnology, marine tourism, education and training, research and development, infrastructure, and arts, culture, and lifestyle. Of these, ocean technology and offshore energy are plainly the strategic priorities for the city's image making, and ones to which there is significant attention paid.

Whereas energy marketing is handled in-house by the city administration, tourism marketing is primarily the role of the arms-length Destination St John's, an industry-driven destination marketing organization that works with local and regional businesses to promote and develop the tourism industry in Eastern Newfoundland, predominantly St John's. The mission of the company is to increase economic development in the region through tourism while maintaining a sustainable ecological environment. Destination St John's is a not-for-profit organization (Destination St John's 2005, 24).

That organization is more closely linked with the provincial government's Department of Tourism, since it pertains to a wider area than just St John's. Tourism marketing is a very time-consuming, resource-intensive activity, and so the City of St John's does not get overly involved. Most of the city's activities vis-à-vis tourism have more to do with local facilitation (Interview 5). Destination St John's helps build an image that is a mix of urban and rural, combined with a unique culture, rich history, and renowned hospitality.

On the tourism front, the Newfoundland and Labrador Tourism Marketing Council, created in 2002, is the major (collective) actor. The council is an industry-government team committed to ensuring that tourism continues to grow in Newfoundland and Labrador. The council is responsible for advising the Minister of Tourism, Culture and Recreation in establishing, implementing, managing, and evaluating the Newfoundland and Labrador tourism marketing strategy. Each year the council puts out a publication on marketing activities and partnership opportunities, which highlights marketing initiatives for tourism operators. The directory lists the different ways in which operators can promote the province of Newfoundland as a tourist destination as well as their own business (Newfoundland and Labrador Tourism Marketing Council 2007).

In 2006, the province also developed a strategic cultural plan, which focused on enhancing cultural awareness in the province, with consideration given to increasing cultural tourism as well. Such an initiative is a good image-building opportunity for St John's, as it is one of the cultural centres of the province. St John's of course markets itself as a city apart from a cultural standpoint, in a province that is far from the beaten track. It feeds into the province's unique advertisements that are aimed to have people across the country talking about the distinctive attributes of the place. As one of the ads goes, "It's about as far from Disneyland as you can possibly get."

In 2002, the government of Canada introduced Cultural Capitals of Canada, a national program to recognize and support Canadian municipalities for special activities that draw on the many benefits of arts and culture in community life. Each year cities compete to be granted this distinction. Designation as a cultural capital enables the community to invest more in arts and culture, increase and improve cultural services, and strengthen connections with other communities through shared cultural experiences and attributes. Obtaining this recognition also helps to profile the municipality across the country, which is beneficial for building its image. In 2006, St John's competed for and won the title of Canadian Cultural Capital and was awarded $500,000 towards an array of celebrations. The program and grant was meant to allow the city to invest in new or enhanced cultural initiatives, whether that was to profile what was already in the city or to increase access to the local population and tourists. The city has a regular summer lunchtime concert series; based on the funding foreseen in 2006, the organizers were able to do more with it. The city buys art for visiting dignitaries; in 2006, they were able to buy more. There was also a very big marketing effort called "St John's Time," which brought together four festivals in eleven days over the summer. This was a huge initiative that came out of the capital year. It was continued in successive years.

While it serves mostly a facilitative role with small-scale tourism business, the city is heavily invested with the cruise industry because of the nature and scale of the industry. It markets to cruise lines and services them when they arrive. Other functions are the purview of the private group Destination St John's, but the city provides back-up support as necessary. The Cruise Association of Newfoundland and Labrador (CANAL) is a body that lobbies directly with cruise lines to have Newfoundland's various thirty-six ports-of-call included on their itineraries. CANAL plans, manages, promotes, and leads the development of a substantial cruise ship industry in Newfoundland. They work to elevate the cruise ship industry to a new level, to meet the demands of the global market, and to position Newfoundland and Labrador as a destination for cruises. As the province's primary port-of-call, such promotion of the Newfoundland cruise ship industry is promotion for St John's. In Atlantic Canada, ports see visits by Carnival, Holland America, Norwegian, Princess, and Royal Caribbean (Klein 2003, 5). In 2009 and 2010, the visits planned to St John's were by cruiser lines Carnival, Holland America, Norwegian, Princess Cruises, P&O Cruises, Fred Olsen Cruises, AIDA Cruises, and Silversea Cruises (St John's Port Authority n.d.).

The cruise ship industry is growing around the world, but it has been subject to a variety of criticisms. One is that the method of registering the nationality of the ships – with countries that have looser environmental, labour, and security standards – allows for companies to bypass the stricter standards common in most Western countries. The city has not released studies relating to these matters, if they exist. There is arguably a need for more public discussion on these matters.

Criticism leveled at the industry is the tendency to play ports off against one another, and in particular to yield returns to the ports visited that are disproportionate to the costs involved in attracting the industry in the first place. Here also there is no publicly published material about the cost-benefit question; the only publicly available documentation is that provided by the Downtown Development Corporation (2006), a body founded by downtown businesses to fend off challenges by suburban malls. It reveals that the cost of renovations to the Port, which admittedly serves other than cruise purposes, was over $10.5 million from 2000–05. The economic benefit of the cruise industry to the city was consistently in the $1.2–1.6 million range from 2000–03. By contrast, in its role as an active fishing port, St John's saw the value of landings in the port of St John's at $27,777,167 over 2000–05 (Downtown Development Commission 2006). In any event, the number of cruise ships announcing plans to visit seems to have plateaued and to be in decline. In 2000, there were twenty cruise ships carrying a total of 12,001 visitors (passengers and crew); in 2001, twenty-one, with 16,401; in 2002, eighteen, with 18,268; in 2003, sixteen with 12,890; in 2004, sixteen, with 7,953. For 2009, the Port Authority forecast sixteen ships, and for 2010, just thirteen.

Image building affects, and is often directed toward, not only potential investors and tourists who are based elsewhere, but also the citizens of the municipality. Here the historic image of the city has been in conflict with development pressures. A great number of St John's residents feel an attachment to the built heritage of the city. For them, the image of the city has already been "built," and it is a matter of protecting it. However, given the historic preoccupation of the city with business, the heritage lobby has not been successful in any of the major showdowns since the mid-seventies. On historic waterfront Water Street, Atlantic Place was constructed in 1975 (built on the site of the main Ayres store, which was built by a merchant). TD Place was approved in 1981; Scotia Plaza was completed in 1985; and supermarkets were built in Shamrock Field and the old Memorial Stadium. There were other, more minor, heritage lobby defeats as well. All of these had had significant public opposition based on heritage grounds, but were approved by city council anyway.

The Rooms development showed the weakness of the local heritage forces. This was not, strictly speaking, a development that fit in with the preceding examples, since it involved provincial, not municipal, decision making. However, it became woven into the fabric of heritage losses that the city had experienced. Fort Townshend, a late-eighteenth-century fort overlooking St John's harbour, played a central role in Britain's control of the Newfoundland fishery. Of all of the heritage sites in the area, it was the most ignored. From 1870, when the last garrison left, until 2000, it experienced progressive decay. Fort Townshend is now about 235 years old, about half as old as St John's itself. It was central to the empire until the War of 1812. Newfoundland's first resident governor, Admiral Pickmore, lived there. In 1800, it housed 400 Irish soldiers and was the site of the failed United Irish Uprising, the only uprising of Irish nationalists outside Ireland itself. Shanawdithit, one of the last of the Beothuks, met the governor of the day there. But it had fallen into disuse in the late nineteenth and early twentieth centuries, and its above-ground facilities had been torn down in the 1940s.

The fort was, however, rediscovered in the public imagination during the building of The Rooms, the $40 million provincial cultural centre and home of the Newfoundland Museum, the Provincial Archives of Newfoundland and Labrador, and the Art Gallery of Newfoundland and Labrador. Defenders of the fort were met with promises from the provincial government that there would be a "comprehensive interpretive program ... to tell the story of Fort Townshend. Longer term concepts for the archaeology level of the new facility are now being developed" (Newfoundland and Labrador 2000). However, no such interpretive program has been started, despite the fact that The Rooms has now been in existence since 2005. One observer noted how the fort's case fit into the general narrative on heritage matters. He noted that "for many of those residents who wrote letters to newspapers or posted emails, then, Fort Townshend was just the most recent demonstration of government's ineffectiveness in protecting heritage resources" (Latta 2005, 23–4).

## APART FROM THE COUNTRY IN ABORIGINAL PRESENCE

Somewhat analogous to immigration, St John's is apart from the rest of the province, and indeed from most urban mainland centres, in its virtual lack of an Aboriginal presence and an Aboriginal plan. Urban Aboriginal policy has never been a significant area of attention for either the City of St John's or, for that matter, until recently, the Government of Newfoundland and Labrador. It continues to be a minimally highlighted and underfunded policy area; in fact, there is no policy that deals specifically with the Aboriginals in major urban areas like St John's. The general Aboriginal population in Newfoundland and Labrador is low compared to many bigger provinces and territories and those in the west and the north. Statistics Canada information from the 2001 Census gives the Aboriginal population for the province as 18,775 and for the

St John's CMA as 1,195 (Statistics Canada 2003b). The 2006 census statistics revealed a very significant rise in the urban Aboriginal population. The 2006 census shows the Aboriginal population for the province as 23,455 and for the St John's CMA as 2,015 (Statistics Canada 2008).

The majority of the Aboriginal population of the province resides in Labrador. Those who currently reside in St John's and other urban areas, of which there are few, generally come from the rural areas of Labrador. There are four major Aboriginal groups living in the province that the Department of Labrador and Aboriginal Affairs addresses: the Miawpukek First Nation (also known as the Mi'kmaq of Conne River), the Innu and Inuit of Labrador, and the Labrador Métis Nation. The majority of these Aboriginal groups reside in towns outside of the Avalon peninsula and predominantly in Labrador, including Cartwright, Charlottetown, Happy Valley-Goose Bay, Hopedale, Makkovik, Mary's Harbour, Miawpukek, Natuashish, Nain, Port Hope Simpson, Postville, Rigolet, St Lewis, and Sheshatshiu. None of the levels of government plays a very significant policy role in the lives of urban Aboriginal people in St John's. Aboriginal policy is overall a mandate of the federal government of Canada. The Department of Canadian Heritage takes a lead role in improving the quality of life of urban Aboriginal people and increasing their full participation in Canada's civic and cultural life. The department gives particular attention to the National Association of Friendship Centres, which in turn helps fund the various centres around the country. The department has multiple initiatives, particularly in the area of assisting urban Aboriginal youth. The Department of Indian and Northern Affairs also takes responsibility for larger Aboriginal policy, such as those relating to land claims and self-government. In 1998, the department introduced the Urban Aboriginal Strategy (UAS) to address the serious socioeconomic needs of urban Aboriginals and to improve policy development and program coordination at the federal level with other levels of government. The UAS was allocated $50 million for a four-year period to serve existing partnerships and fund pilot partnerships. In 2007, funding was ramped up and extended to a five-year horizon at the level of $68.5 million nationally to reflect a long-term commitment on Aboriginal issues in urban centres.

While the province agrees that Aboriginal policy is a federal responsibility, it involves itself only in areas of its own choosing. Labrador and Aboriginal Affairs is responsible primarily for the tripartite negotiation and implementation between the province, Canada, and Aboriginal groups and governments of land claims agreements, self-government, and related agreements. The work of the department also involves taking a lead on agreements with other departments, creation and expansion of reserves, provision of programs and services for the Aboriginal communities, providing advice on consultation with Aboriginal groups, and generally working with other departments on government's overall approach to Aboriginal issues. The department is not a program delivery type of entity. It does deliver Aboriginal programs in a general sense, but provides small grants towards the creation and delivery of programs by other groups, such as the St John's Native Friendship Centre.

Most programs targeted at urban Aboriginal people are federal programs. The provincial government has little to no contact with municipal government with relation to Aboriginal affairs. The community it deals with primarily is Happy Valley-Goose Bay, though it is not a city. Depending on how loosely "urban" Aboriginal is defined, Goose Bay has the highest population of Aboriginals of any community in the province. These urban Aboriginals are not eligible for the federal programs made available for First Nations people on reserve, but Goose Bay does have a Friendship Centre. Indian Affairs and Health Canada have offices there, and the Innu nation has corporate presence there as well (Interview 1).

Like all other residents of the province and the city of St John's, urban Aboriginal people can access provincial programs. They would not be discriminated against or ineligible based on their status. They may also be able to access certain federal programs that are not available to the rest of the population. The small population of urban Aboriginals yields small costs for most levels of government. The greatest expenditures are in post-secondary education and health care. Many urban Aboriginals complain that there is little access to Aboriginal-specific programs in the city and in particular to anything related to language and culture. The St John's Native Friendship Centre has taken the lead in urban Aboriginal issues such as these, but they do not have the resources to be as effective as they would like.

St John's Native Friendship Centre Association (SJNFCA) has taken the lead with respect to urban Aboriginals in the capital city. The Centre provides a wide range of services to Aboriginal people residing in or visiting the St John's area. The Aboriginal population served by SJNFCA includes all status and non-status Indians. In addition, there are a number of other Aboriginals from various areas of Canada who access the services offered by the SJNFCA. The association supports Aboriginal people through such services as a homeless shelter/hostel, a youth drop-in centre, cultural programs, after-school programs, an employment counselor, a women's group, and other social, legal, and educational services. The Centre has little involvement in the way of policy making in this field. They may be consulted on certain issues pertaining to Aboriginals, but there is little policy to begin with.

Funding is varied. The federal government's Department of Canadian Heritage is the primary source of funding for the Centre. When the City of St John's took part in the Cultural Capital Year in 2006, part of the funding was to be used to promote Aboriginals in the city. The Centre held a youth arts exhibition, as well as multiple arts workshops. The federal government paid 75 percent of the costs, and the province picked up the other 25 percent. The project was very successful, but such events are rare. Occasionally, funding will come from other departments. Health Canada, for example, has contributed $27,454 for Health Benefits under the First Nations/Inuit/Aboriginal Health Services Delivery program (Canada n.d.). The province may provide short-term grants for certain projects, such as violence prevention. In 2005, the provincial government granted $80,000 to help prevent violence against women and children of Aboriginal ancestry and to provide services to victims of violence in their communities (Newfoundland and Labrador 2005b). However, they provide no long-term funding that the Centre can rely on annually. The Royal Bank of Canada has provided some money to run an after-school program as well.

Despite financial help from the different levels of government and other contributors, the Centre is unable to provide the services necessary for the growing urban Aboriginal population in St John's. As the primary provider of Aboriginal services, the Centre is understaffed and tremendously underfunded. They would like to have a social worker, addictions counselor, cultural worker program, shelter coordinator, and a settlement worker, but they do not have the funds to obtain these necessary services. The SJNFCA's shelter is the only one in the city not to receive provincial funding. There is no provincial money for operations because Aboriginal issues are seen by the province as a federal responsibility. There is a very clear gap in urban Aboriginal strategy in the province. Any funding and assistance tends to be given to Labrador communities and little attention is paid to urban Aboriginals, particularly the growing population in St John's. Urban Aboriginal policy is neglected in the province: this is a situation that needs to change.

Memorial University, the province's only university, has come late to the Aboriginal file. Since the university recently started asking for voluntary self-identification of Aboriginal students, 291 were identified

in September 2009, an increase from 223 in September 2008. Of
the 291, 271 were undergraduates and 20 were graduate students.
St John's campus had 180, the Corner Brook campus 59, the Marine
Institute 1, Distance Education 32, Western Regional School of Nursing
9, the Centre for Nursing Studies 9, and one was unidentified (Memorial
University 2009).

At Memorial University, the *Report of the Presidential Task Force on
Aboriginal Initiatives* reported in November 2009 that the university
was not providing adequate service and recommended a variety of educational and institutional supports. The Aboriginal Studies Minor was
plainly not sufficient. Its offerings were sporadic and interstitial and did
not have enough Aboriginal content. It recommended a bachelor's program in Aboriginal Studies, supported by three additional faculty positions, enough to establish a rigorous program of studies. It also suggested
encouragement of the moves by the then Canada Research Chair to
establish an Aboriginal master's program by considering this idea in
the future hiring of academic staff. It recommended the establishment of
an Aboriginal network within the university, composed of two already
existing institutes, the Leslie Harris Centre of Regional Policy and Development and the Labrador Institute, the major Memorial centre for service
to the northern part of the province, including the 10,000 Aboriginal
residents of Labrador. Supplementing this would be a new Special Advisor to the president for Aboriginal affairs, and a grants facilitation
officer to promote Aboriginal initiatives with federal, provincial, and
private enterprise sources. On the outreach front, the Native Liaison
Officer would become a permanent officer and be funded by the university directly, rather than externally (Memorial University 2009). The
university has experienced significant flux in its senior leadership since
2009 due to issues with the provincial government, and action on this
file took some time. New initiatives at Memorial University would further heighten the profile of the city's Aboriginal people, and more action
at the provincial and even the municipal level might follow.

CONCLUSION

So, we have a city apart. It is apart from the rest of the province and,
indeed, from the rest of the country. It is a city that is historically most
unusual. It struggled to exist in the first place; its pattern of municipal
development was a troubled one; and it often endured outright antagon-
ism from higher levels of government, which made it bear the brunt of

their financial mismanagement. Its jurisdiction is greater than that of the province's other municipalities. It is also apart in its concentration of the business drivers of the day: first merchant families, then the representatives of Canadian and multinational corporations, and, in the last quarter century, the petroleum industry. It is the fastest-growing cultural growth area in the Atlantic region and in the country (Hill Strategies 2006, 7). It has few immigrants, unlike most other areas of the country, but is becoming engaged in ways to make those who arrive feel welcome, and it supports provincial efforts to increase immigration levels. It is similarly lacking in a significant Aboriginal presence, despite its status as a centre of higher education. As the provincial capital and population centre, its infrastructure needs tend to take up a large percentage of the available federal and provincial funds. The city's image-making exercises trade on, and indeed depend on, its status as a city apart. It is at one and the same time a petroleum capital, a centre of ocean excellence, a cultural capital of Canada, a cruise destination, and a heritage location – a variety that not many, if any, other capitals in the country can match. In an era that is marked by a drift towards convergence in urban lifestyles and policies, St John's continues to travel a unique path.

## LIST OF INTERVIEWS

1 Confidential, 8 December 2006.
2 Confidential, 21 December 2006.
3 Confidential, 22 December 2006.
4 Megan Morris (Program Development Coordinator for ANC), email interview by author, 22 December 2006.
5 Confidential, 5 April 2007.
6 Confidential, 27 September 2007.

## REFERENCES

Adams, Gordon. 2001. "The Complexity of the Merchant-Fisher Relationship: Revising the Merchant Domination Thesis." MMS Thesis, Memorial University.
Antle, Rob. 2010. "Return to Spender." *Telegram*, 3 April.
Baker, Melvin. 1974. "The Origins of the St John's Municipal Council: 1880–1888." Mimeograph. St John's: Memorial University of Newfoundland. December.

– 1976. "The Politics of Municipal Reform in St John's Newfoundland, 1888–1892." *Urban History Review* 2 (76):12–29.
– 1984. "Absentee Landlordism and Municipal Government in Nineteenth Century St John's." Paper presented to the Canadian Historical Association. Guelph, ON. June.
Cadigan, Sean T. 2009. *Newfoundland and Labrador: A History.* Toronto: University of Toronto Press.
Canada. Health Canada. n.d. *Grants and Contributions Disclosure, Accountability.* Accessed 20 July 2007. http://www.gcdisclosuredivulgationsc.hcsc. gc.ca/dpfad/gcdisc.nsf/WEBbydetails/B18FCE6321D1098D8525748D0067 E42E?OpenDocument&lang=eng&.
– Statistics Canada. 2001. "Immigrant Status By Period Of Immigration, 2001 Counts, for Canada, Provinces and Territories." Ottawa: Government of Canada. Accessed 1 August 2007. http://www12.statcan.ca/english/ census01/home/index.cfm.
– 2003a. *Population By Immigrant Status By Period Of Immigration, 2001 Counts, for Canada, Province, Territories, Census Metropolitan Areas and Census Agglomerations – 20% Sample Data* (table). Immigration and Citizenship Highlight Tables. 2001 Census. Ottawa. 21 January. http:// www12.statcan.ca/english/census01/products/highlight/Immigration/Page. cfm?Lang=E&Geo=CMA&Code=10&View=2&Table=1&StartRec=1&Sor t=2&B1=Counts.
– 2003b. *Aboriginal Identity Population, 2001 counts, for Canada, Provinces, Territories, Census Metropolitan Areas and Census Agglomerations – 20% Sample Data* (table). Aboriginal Peoples Highlight Tables. 2001 Census. Ottawa. 21 January. http://www12.statcan.ca/english/census01/products/ highlight/Aboriginal/Page.cfm?Lang=E&Geo=CMA&View=2a&Code= 10&Table=1&StartRec=1&Sort=2&B1=Counts01&B2=Total.
– 2003c. *Immigrant Status By Period Of Immigration, 2001 Counts, for Canada, Provinces And Territories.* Ottawa. http://www12.statcan.ca/ english/census01/home/index.cfm.
– 2007a. *Population By Immigrant Status And Period Of Immigration, 2006 Counts, for Canada, Provinces and Territories, and Census Metropolitan Areas and Census Agglomerations – 20% Sample Data* (table). *Immigration and Citizenship Highlight Tables.* 2006 Census. Statistics Canada. Catalogue no. 97-557-XWE2006002. Ottawa. 4 December. http://www12.statcan.ca/ english/census06/data/highlights/Immigration/Table403.cfm?Lang=E&T= 403&GH=6&SC=1&S=0&O=A.
– 2007b. *Culture, Tourism and the Centre for Education Statistics, Post-secondary Enrolment Trends to 2031: Three Scenarios Research Paper.*

Catalogue no. 81-595-MIE – No. 058. http://www.statcan.gc.ca/pub/81-595-m/81-595-m2007058-eng.pdf.

– 2008. *Aboriginal identity population by age groups, median age and sex, 2006 counts, for Canada, provinces and territories, and census metropolitan areas and census agglomerations – 20% sample data* (table). *Aboriginal Peoples Highlight Tables.* 2006 Census. Statistics Canada Catalogue no. 97-558-XWE2006002. Ottawa. 15 January. http://www12.statcan.ca/english/census06/data/highlights/aboriginal/index.cfm?Lang=E.

– 2010. "Study: Projections of the Diversity of the Canadian Population." *The Daily.* 9 March. http://www.statcan.gc.ca/daily-quotidien/100309/dq100309a-eng.htm.

Canada and Newfoundland. 2009. "Canada and Newfoundland and Labrador Create Jobs Through Investments in Rural Infrastructure – Backgrounder, St John's, Newfoundland and Labrador, May 14, 2009." http://www.buildingcanada-chantierscanada.gc.ca/media/news-nouvelles/2009/20090514stjohns-eng.html.

City of St John's. Department of Economic Development, Tourism and Culture. 2004a. *Executive Summary: Local Economic Impact Study of the Offshore Oil and Gas Industry.* St John's, 1–4.

– 2004b. Department of Economic Development, Tourism and Culture. *Local Economic Impact Study of the Offshore Oil and Gas Industry.* Fall.

– 2007a. Economic Development Division, with the provincial Department of Finance. *Economic Outlook 2007: St John's Metropolitan Area.* 6 June.

– 2007b. "City Wins National Marketing Award." News Release, 24 September. http://www.stjohns.ca/csj/NewsDetails?id=62.

– n.d. "St John's: Energy Capital." Accessed 15 January 2010. http://www.stjohns.ca/business/energycapital.jsp.

City of St John's Centre for Ocean Excellence. n.d. *Delivering Innovative Ocean Technologies.* St John's: Department of Economic Development and Culture.

Destination St John's. 2005. *2005 Annual Report.* St John's.

Downtown Development Commission. 2006. "Quick Facts." March. http://www.downtownstjohns.com/quick-facts.html.

Hill Strategies Research Inc. 2006. Research for the Arts. *Statistical Insights on the Arts.* Report Funded by the Canada Council for the Arts, the Department of Canadian Heritage and the Ontario Arts Council. March, vol. 4, no. 4.

Hogg, Peter W. 1999. *Constitutional Law of Canada, 1999 student edition.* Toronto: Carswell.

Ibbitson, John. 2004. "Why Atlantic Canada Remains White and Poor." *Globe and Mail,* 20 August, A4.

Klein, Ross A. 2003. *Cruising – Out of Control: The Cruise Industry, the Environment, Workers, and the Maritimes*. Halifax: Canadian Centre for Policy Alternatives – Nova Scotia.

– 2005. *Playing off the Ports: BC and the Cruise Tourism Industry*. Canadian Centre for Policy Alternatives. Vancouver: CCPA BC Office.

– 2009. *Cruising Without a Bruising: Cruise Tourism and the Maritimes*. Halifax: Canadian Centre for Policy Alternatives – Nova Scotia.

Latta, Peter. 2005. "Contested Space: A Place on the Way to Collaborative Government." *Ethnologies* 27 (2): 17–42.

Locke, Wade, and Scott Lynch. 2003. "What Does Newfoundland and Labrador Need to Know about the Knowledge-Based Economy to Strengthen Its Place in Canada? A research and analysis paper prepared for the Royal Commission on Renewing and Strengthening Our Place in Canada." Research Paper. March. St John's: The Commission.

Memorial University. 2009. President's Office. *A Special Obligation: Report of the Presidential Task Force on Aboriginal Initiatives*. St John's. November.

Neary, Peter. 1988. *Newfoundland in the North Atlantic World, 1929–1949*. Montreal and Kingston: McGill-Queen's University Press.

Newfoundland and Labrador. 2001. Statistics Agency. "St John's: Profile of Immigrant Population by Gender: Census 2006 & 2001." *Community Accounts*. St John's. http://www.communityaccounts.ca/communityaccounts/onlinedata/display_table.asp?whichtabl=table_censusprofile_immigration_gender&comval=com492.

– 2002. Department of Finance. Economics and Statistics Branch. *Demographic Change: Newfoundland and Labrador Issues and Implications*.

– 2003. Office of the Auditor General. *Report of the Auditor General to the House of Assembly on Reviews of Departments and Crown Agencies*. St John's: Government of Newfoundland and Labrador.

– 2005a. Human Resources, Labour and Employment. Immigration Policy and Planning. June. "Diversity – Opportunity and Growth – An Immigration Strategy for Newfoundland and Labrador." Discussion Paper.

– 2005b. "Funding for Violence Prevention Projects For Aboriginal Women and Children." News Release, 8 December.

– 2007a. Department of Finance. *Budget 2007*. http://www.budget.gov.nl.ca/budget2007/.

– 2007b. Human Resources, Labour and Employment. "Government Launches Provincial Immigration Stategy." News Release, 21 March. http://www.releases.gov.nl.ca/releases/2007/hrle/0321n03.htm.

– 2007c. Tourism and Marketing Council. "Marketing Activities and Partnership Opportunities." http://www.tcr.gov.nl.ca/tcr/publications/2007/2007 MarketingPlan_Text.pdf.
– 2008. Human Resources, Labour and Employment. "Provincial Employment Level at Highest Level in 30 Years." News Release, 17 January. http://www. releases.gov.nl.ca/releases/2008/hrle/0117no1.htm.
– 2009. Department of Finance. Newfoundland and Labrador Statistics Agency. "Labour Force Characteristics, Economic Regions of Newfoundland and Labrador, 1987 to 2009, Annual Averages." http://www.stats.gov.nl.ca/ Statistics/Labour/PDF/LFC_EconomicRegions.pdf.
– 2010. "YRAS: Youth Retention and Attraction Strategy." Accessed 1 March 2010. http://www.lmiworks.nl.ca/yras/about.html.
– 2010b. "Strengthening the Economy for a Prosperous Future: $1 Billion Slated for Infrastructure Spending in Budget 2010." 29 March. http://www. releases.gov.nl.ca/releases/2010/tw/0329no6.htm.
Newfoundland Book Publishers. 1981a. "Local Government." *Encyclopedia of Newfoundland*. Vol. 3, 645-60. St John's.
– 1981b. "Cities," *Encyclopedia of Newfoundland*. Vol. 1, 444–5. St John's.
O'Neill, Paul. 2003. *The Oldest City: The Story of St John's, Newfoundland*. Portugal Cove-St Phillips: Boulder Publications Ltd.
Progressive Conservative Party of Newfoundland. 2007. *Proud, Strong Determined: The Future is Ours*. St John's: PC Party.
St John's Port Authority. n.d. *2009–2010 Cruise Ship Schedule*. Accessed 22 April 2009. http://www.sjpa.com/en/tourism/index.htm.
Stantec, Jacques Whitford Consultants. 2009. *Economic Benefits from Petroleum Industry Activity in Newfoundland and Labrador, 2005–2007*. Petroleum Research Atlantic Canada. 13 February.
Summers, Valerie. 2001. "Between a Rock and a Hard Place: Regime Change in Newfoundland." In *The Provincial State in Canada: Politics in the Provinces and Territories*, edited by Keith Brownsey and Michael Howlett, 23–48. Toronto: Broadview Press.
Wheaton, Carla J. 2002. "'As Modern as Some of the Fine New Departmental Stores ... Can Make It': A Social History of the Large Water Street Stores, St John's, Newfoundland, 1892–1949." PhD diss, History Department, Memorial University.

# 9

# Multilevel Governance in Toronto: Success and Failure in Canada's Largest City[1]

MARTIN HORAK

## INTRODUCTION

With 2.6 million residents, Toronto is by far the largest municipality in Canada. Situated at the centre of an urban area of nearly six million people, it is Canada's financial and media capital, and it is home to more than a quarter of all new immigrants to the country. Toronto is also a city that faces many serious urban policy challenges, ranging from managing Canada's largest public transit system to addressing social deprivation and violence in some of the country's poorest neighborhoods. It is no surprise, then, that municipal government in Toronto has tremendously dense and complex interactions with other levels of government and with local societal groups. Multilevel governance in one form or another is omnipresent in Toronto.

Drawing on empirical data from the late 1990s through to 2009, this chapter analyzes five cases of multilevel policy initiatives in Toronto, spread across four policy fields: federal infrastructure funding, the management of federal property, municipal image building, and emergency management. Given the time period under investigation, the chapter primarily focuses on multilevel governance during the mayoralties of Mel Lastman (1998–2003) and David Miller (2003–10). By and large, it does not discuss developments since the 2010 election of Rob Ford as mayor. The insights developed through the case studies can nonetheless help us to understand how recent changes in the landscape of Toronto politics are likely to affect patterns of multilevel policy making.

The text proceeds as follows: the next section defines key concepts, reviews case selection and research methods, and lays some theoretical groundwork. The section after that outlines the local governmental and societal context in Toronto. The next five sections each discuss one of the five case studies: securing multilevel funding for Toronto's public transit, redeveloping the federally-owned Downsview lands in Toronto's north end, implementing the city's Tourism Action Plan, coordinating emergency management, and revitalizing Toronto's long-derelict central waterfront. Finally, the last section reviews data from the case studies and identifies some factors that account for the varied quality of policy outputs across these five multilevel policy initiatives. These factors include the complexity of the multilevel coordination that agents must undertake in order to meet their policy goals, the degree of administrative capacity and cohesion in the relevant policy field, the consistency of political leadership on the initiative in question, and the ability of agents to exploit windows of policy opportunity.

## CONCEPTS, METHODS, AND ANALYTICAL FOUNDATIONS

The concept of multilevel governance (MLG) is subject to multiple definitions. However, most scholars now agree on two key points. First, MLG occurs when power is fragmented among autonomous agents who nonetheless must engage with each other in order to achieve policy goals. Early work in this field usually focused on the fragmentation of power among multiple levels of government (Marks 1993), but recent definitions also draw attention to the fragmentation of power across the public-private divide (Peters and Pierre 2004, 82). Second, MLG itself is a set of coordinating activities that respond to this condition; in other words, it involves "mechanisms and strategies of coordination adopted in the face of complex reciprocal interdependence among operationally autonomous actors" (Jessop 2004, 52). As we will see, the Toronto case studies reaffirm the usefulness of this definition of MLG, but they also underline an important caveat: coordinating the policy power and agendas of various agents[2] is often a very complex undertaking, and it does not always succeed. Much of the large European literature on MLG treats coordination as a given. The Toronto data, by contrast, suggest that coordination is a key challenge for agents who pursue multilevel policy initiatives and that focusing on the nature of the coordination problem, and how agents address it, can help us to explain variation in the quality of policy outputs across cases.

The five cases examined in this chapter are spread across four policy fields that were pre-assigned to the study: federal infrastructure funding, the management of federal property, municipal image building, and emergency management. Each case involves an instance where a government agent undertook a policy initiative that required coordination with other state and societal agents operating at various scales, ranging from the local to the federal. Given the focus of this volume, priority was given to cases of municipally-initiated policy action, where these existed.

Since the four policy fields vary in scope, and some presented more potential case studies than others, the degree to which each case covers a particular policy field varies. In the infrastructure funding field, the case focus is on the city's efforts to secure multilevel capital funding for the Toronto Transit Commission (TTC). In the federal property field, the focus is on federally-led efforts to redevelop the former Downsview Air Force Base, in Toronto's north end, into an urban park. Municipal image building potentially encompasses activities ranging from cultural policy to investment marketing; the case focus here is the implementation of the city's 2003 Tourism Action Plan. In the field of emergency management, where no single policy initiative stood out, the case study reviews a bundle of recent city initiatives that aim to improve coordination among state and societal agents. Finally, the chapter reviews a prominent case that touches on multiple policy fields – the long-planned revitalization of Toronto's central waterfront.

In order to evaluate the quality of policy outputs in these cases, this chapter adopts a simplified set of standards based on two questions. First, to what extent does the policy output fulfill the goal(s) of the lead agent – that is, the government agent that initiated the policy process? The chapter answers this question by comparing initial goals, as stated in relevant policy documents, with outputs as reported through documents and related by interview respondents. Second, to what extent are local stakeholders satisfied with the policy output? The chapter answers this question using data from interviews with stakeholder representatives. The emphasis on local stakeholders – that is, local government agents and local societal agents with an interest in a given policy case – does *not* take into account the views of provincial and/or federal government agents. This localist perspective is deliberate and follows from this volume's focus on localized policy in Canadian municipalities. In this chapter, then, "good quality" policy outputs are those that fulfill the basic goals of lead agents in a way that satisfies all (or virtually all) local stakeholders; "bad quality" policy outputs do neither of these things. As might be expected, outputs in most of the five cases fall between these two extremes.

Specific factors that account for variation in policy quality across the cases will be discussed in the second to last section of the chapter. However, let us now briefly set the stage for that analysis. As noted earlier, a key challenge for proponents of a multilevel policy initiative is achieving sufficient coordination among multiple autonomous state and societal agents. There are two basic things that require coordinating: policy power and policy agendas. Policy power, for the purposes of this chapter, consists of decision-making authority and material resources. At the outset of a multilevel policy initiative, the relevant decision-making authority and resources are fragmented among a multiplicity of agents, necessitating a sustained coordination effort on the part of the lead agent. Since the agents that hold relevant resources and authority are autonomous of each other, they typically also have a variety of distinct, and sometimes incompatible, policy agendas.[3] In order for a multilevel policy initiative to succeed, these agendas must also be coordinated. Agendas need not become identical, but they must become compatible – that is, agents must be able to find common policy ground. As we will see, the varying complexity of these coordination challenges helps to explain variation in the quality of policy outputs across the five cases.

A word on data collection is in order. Given the complexity of the subject and the scarcity of relevant literature, the research approach was largely inductive, and data from multiple sources were triangulated. In addition to reviews of newspaper coverage and extensive documentary work, the research involved forty-six tape-recorded interviews with key informants who represented a broad variety of governmental and non-governmental organizations (see List of Interviews). Initial informants were selected based on written documentation, and further ones were identified by referral. In the interest of obtaining accurate data on sensitive topics, interviews were conducted anonymously.

THE TORONTO CONTEXT

Like other Canadian municipalities, Toronto is in legal terms a creature of the province, its powers and resources subject to provincial control. That said, in practice the city has in recent years had substantial intergovernmental policy clout. A key reason for this is Toronto's size. In its current form, the city is the product of a municipal amalgamation imposed by the provincial government in 1998 (Horak 1998; Boudreau 2000). It is a giant on the Canadian municipal stage. As of 2006, Toronto had 2.5 million residents, as compared to 1.6 million in the next largest

Canadian municipality, Montreal. The city had a 2006 operating budget of $7.6 billion and employed 45,000 people (City of Toronto 2007), making it by spending the sixth largest unit of government in Canada, irrespective of level of government.

Toronto's exceptional size enhances its intergovernmental clout in several ways. First, the city possesses a large administrative apparatus with considerable technical expertise. Second, the scale and the variety of public policy problems in Toronto ensure that the city is often "on the radar" at other levels of government (Interview 14) and that city administrators have a dense network of interactions with their provincial and federal counterparts. Third, the city's huge population base can give Toronto's political leadership the weight of substantial popular legitimacy on the intergovernmental stage. Finally, the city's large population also means that the wishes of Toronto residents often figure prominently in the electoral calculations of other levels of government.[4]

Although size enhances the municipality's multilevel policy power, it also contributes to internal power fragmentation. The city is governed by a forty-four-member, non-partisan city council, with councillors elected on a ward basis. The mayor is elected at large, but has few significant governing powers of his own.[5] While recent reforms (2006) granted the mayor the power to appoint heads of standing committees, in most respects the city retains a council-committee system of government. The net result of these institutional arrangements is a fragmentation of political power that tends to weaken strategic leadership. In addition, Toronto's council often faces decision overload (Bellamy 2005), leaving strategic questions of policy direction to be resolved in the administrative realm. Yet, in some policy fields, political fragmentation is mirrored on the administrative side by bureaucratic segmentation and internal competition for influence and resources. There are instances in which the city has successfully overcome internal fragmentation and has functioned as a single policy agent. On the whole, however, internal fragmentation adds significantly to the complexity of the coordination challenges that municipal policy makers face in multilevel policy processes.

Another defining feature of Toronto politics since amalgamation is the ongoing sense of fiscal crisis in the city. This is the combined product of several factors (Slack 2005; Horak 2008). Two key factors bear brief mention. First, in 1998 the provincial government realigned provincial and local service responsibilities in a way that loaded nearly $300 million in annual new costs onto the city (City of Toronto 2002). Second, the city has long had much higher rates of business property taxes than the rapidly growing outer suburbs that surround it. This places the city at a competitive disadvantage in regional context and generates pressure to contain costs.

The sense of fiscal crisis in Toronto has led municipal leaders to focus heavily on questions of finance in their interactions with other levels of government. As early as the year 2000, council called for a "new relationship with Ontario and Canada," one that would include access to enhanced fiscal resources and new provincial legislation that would expand the city's policy authority and revenue raising powers (City of Toronto 2000). Upon coming into office in 2003, Mayor David Miller picked up on this call and made the city's campaign for a "New Deal" with other levels of government a centerpiece of his governing platform. By far the most effort went into the fiscal component of the campaign (Horak 2008). The results of this were mixed, but at least on one front – intergovernmental funding for the Toronto Transit Commission – the city had remarkable success. However, in other policy areas, fiscal concerns have often constrained the city's policy agenda and have weakened the position of municipal officials vis-à-vis other agents. In 2003, policy agendas at city hall shifted to the left, following a municipal election that brought David Miller and fourteen new councillors into office. This shift enhanced political attention to a number of issues such as neighbourhood poverty, environmental quality, and public transit. However, fiscal constraints continued to significantly limit the City's options on these issues, and ultimately contributed to the swing back to a focus on fiscal conservatism that came with the 2010 election of Rob Ford as mayor.

Toronto's constellation of local societal actors also influences the landscape of policy-making power and agendas in the city. Toronto houses the head offices of five of Canada's six major banks and is home to 40 percent of the Canadian companies on the *Fortune* Global 500 list (City of Toronto 2008, 10–11). The City's business elite thus has tremendous potential influence in multilevel policy processes, which it has increasingly chosen to use in recent years. For example, the Toronto Board of Trade provided powerful support to the city's demands for a "New Deal" with other levels of government, but has also been an influential critic of some of the City's own fiscal policies. The Toronto City Summit Alliance (TCSA), a policy advocacy group led by societal actors from both the corporate and non-profit sectors, has become another major player in Toronto politics, throwing its support behind selected city initiatives and spearheading its own initiatives in fields ranging from culture to immigrant settlement.[6]

Toronto is also the media capital of English Canada. It is the home of several of Canada's television broadcasters, including the public-sector CBC, and has three major daily newspapers, including both of Canada's nationwide papers (the *Globe and Mail* and the *National Post*), and the country's largest-circulation daily (the *Toronto Star*). This ensures that Toronto political and policy issues are subject to an extraordinary degree of media scrutiny. Even though they do not participate formally in policy processes, the media thus have a major influence on multilevel policy making in Toronto.

A final feature of Toronto's societal landscape that deserves mention is its multicultural character. The Greater Toronto Area (GTA) receives about 40 percent of all new immigrants that come to Canada each year, and the majority of these settle within the City of Toronto. The result is extraordinary ethnocultural diversity – some 50 percent of Toronto's residents were born outside Canada, and the city has large concentrations of many ethnocultural groups. That said, groups representing ethnocultural interests were almost entirely absent from the policy processes examined in this chapter. In part, this is a function of the policy fields examined here, as diversity concerns have in fact been prominent in some fields in Toronto in recent years. However, the striking absence of ethnocultural concerns also suggests that recent immigrants tend to remain outsiders to politics in a city where the voices of established resident groups dominate the "community" agenda (Interview 13).

### SECURING MULTILEVEL FUNDING
### FOR THE TORONTO TRANSIT COMMISSION (TTC)

Toronto has by far the largest public transit system of any city in Canada. Until 2002, the federal government did not fund the TTC in any way. By contrast, until 1998 the provincial government contributed 25 percent of operating costs and 75 percent of capital costs to the TTC each year. In 1998, all provincial funding was withdrawn, which sent the TTC into a fiscal crisis. The commission's capital investment program was severely curtailed, and service expansion plans were put on hold. It was not long before city politicians began lobbying for a restoration of intergovernmental transit funding. At the provincial level, the immediate prospects for this appeared poor; so, in 2001, city officials began to build alliances with other urban municipalities across Canada to lobby the federal government to directly fund municipal infrastructure needs. Because not all of these municipalities had the same infrastructure needs, however, the focus shifted from public transit in particular to securing general-purpose infrastructure funds.

Between 2001 and 2003, Toronto lobbied for federal infrastructure funding through two alliances of urban municipalities: the five-member "C5" caucus of urban mayors, and the Federation of Canadian Municipalities' twenty-two-member Big City Mayors' Caucus. Toronto played a leading role in these organizations thanks in part to support from its newly created six-person corporate office of intergovernmental relations (IGR), which reports to the city manager (Interviews 11 and 31). While the lobbying effort failed to persuade the federal government of Jean Chrétien to set aside new infrastructure funds that would flow money directly to municipalities, in 2002 the government did beef up its existing tri-level infrastructure funding programs, supplementing the $2 billion Infrastructure Canada Program (ICP) with a new, $4 billion Canada Strategic Infrastructure Fund (CSIF).[7] Furthermore, the lobbying convinced aspiring Liberal leader Paul Martin to endorse the principle of direct federal funding for municipal infrastructure (Kuitenbrouwer 2005). Martin succeeded Chrétien as prime minister in November 2003, promising a "New Deal" for Canada's cities; in the spring of 2005, his government followed through, dedicating two cents of the federal gas tax (rising to five cents by 2009) to municipal infrastructure needs.

By taking a leading position in pan-Canadian lobbying efforts, the City of Toronto thus helped to secure enhanced federal funding for municipal infrastructure. The question remained how much of this funding would flow to Toronto, and to the TTC in particular. At first, the city lacked a focused strategy to maximize the inflow of federal infrastructure funds. In 2001, it applied for ICP funding for a variety of infrastructure projects. The results were disappointing. Although the city did secure the first-ever federal funding for the TTC, a one-time contribution of $76 million, most ICP money in Toronto went to private cultural institutions. City officials realized that if they were to secure a larger slice of the infrastructure funding pie, they "needed to have a consistent and concerted messaging to the federal and provincial governments about what our need was" (Interview 15). Encouraged by the IGR office and by the TTC itself, city council decided in late 2002 to focus all future demands for federal infrastructure funding on transit capital needs (Moloney 2002; Interview 15). At the same time, council began to include the provincial government as a target of transit funding requests and adopted a longer-term policy goal of getting to the point where the federal, provincial, and municipal governments would each fund one-third of the TTC's capital budget (Interview 15).

Several factors enhanced Toronto's power vis-à-vis other levels of government as it pursued these goals. First, local administrative and political agents agreed on both goals and strategy, with the IGR office, the TTC, and key councillors consistently working together (Interviews 20 and 30). Second, the relevant administrative bodies – the IGR office and the TTC – brought strong intergovernmental and technical expertise to bear on interactions with their provincial and federal counterparts (Interviews 11, 13, and 17). Third, Toronto's powerful business community – through organizations such as the Board of Trade – added its voice to the chorus calling for more TTC capital funding (Lu 2003). Fourth, in early 2003, Toronto officials helped to coordinate broader societal support for the campaign by catalyzing the formation of the Toronto City Summit Alliance, a private-sector urban policy advocacy group that provided strong support for the city's drive to secure enhanced TTC funding. Finally, as soon as he was elected in November 2003, Mayor David Miller made the push for multilevel TTC funding a central plank of the city's "New Deal" campaign for more powers and resources. In short, the campaign for multilevel TTC capital funding was bolstered by the internal cohesion and capacity of the administration, by broad agenda support from local societal agents, and by strong mayoral leadership, especially after 2003.

The city's first major success on transit funding came in February 2004. The city signed a five-year tri-level CSIF agreement, committing each level of government to providing $350 million towards the TTC's capital program (Infrastructure Canada 2004). Changes in provincial and federal government soon brought more opportunities to access intergovernmental funding for the TTC. At the provincial level, a new Liberal government moved to implement a 2003 election promise of gas tax funding for municipal transit. Negotiations over the allocation formula took place in the fall of 2004. Shortly beforehand, Toronto had withdrawn from the Association of Municipalities of Ontario (AMO), which gave the city a separate voice in the negotiations. This, in turn, helped to ensure that the gas tax funds were allocated to municipalities based largely on transit ridership, an outcome that brought the TTC some $163 million per year (Interview 20; James 2004).

Meanwhile, at the federal level, the Martin government introduced its own gas tax funding scheme in 2005. Having withdrawn from AMO, Toronto secured its own seat at the federal allocation formula negotiating table, a position achieved by no other Canadian municipality. Here,

Table 1
Intergovernmental funding for TTC, 2000–07 ($ million)

|             | 2000 | 2001 | 2002 | 2003 | 2004 | 2005 | 2006 | 2007 |
|-------------|------|------|------|------|------|------|------|------|
| Provincial  | 0    | 0    | 63   | 141  | 141  | 159  | 271  | 329  |
| Federal     | 0    | 0    | 62   | 14   | 12   | 163  | 166  | 112  |
| Total       | 0    | 0    | 125  | 155  | 153  | 322  | 437  | 441  |

Note: All of the federal funding listed is for capital purposes. Provincial figures include operating
subsidies, which started at $70 million in 2003 and increased to about $90 million in 2005 and
thereafter.
Source: Toronto Transit Commission Annual Reports 2002–07

however, the city did not achieve its goals. Unlike the provincial gas tax,
the federal gas tax was earmarked for all municipal transportation
needs, not just transit. Facing political pressure from smaller municipalities, Martin's Liberal government decided in June 2005 to allocate
this gas tax on a per capita basis across the country (Gillespie 2005).
However, the Martin government was a minority government, and
Toronto political leaders were able to use their connections to Jack
Layton, a former Toronto councillor who led the federal New Democratic
Party, to secure a budget promise of one extra cent per litre dedicated
specifically to public transit (Interviews 31 and 35).

Between 2002 and 2006, the City of Toronto thus had remarkable
success in its campaign to coordinate the resources of various levels of
government to fund the TTC's capital needs. Total amounts of federal
and provincial funding disbursed to the TTC between 2002 and 2007 are
summarized in Table 1. Interviews conducted for this project revealed a
broad-based consensus among local stakeholders – politicians, administrators, and representatives of societal groups – that the city's campaign
with respect to transit capital funding was largely successful (Interviews 5,
10, 11, 15, 17, 19, 20, and 36).

That said, it is also clear that the willingness of provincial and federal
governments to share resources with the city for the purpose of TTC
funding is in part a product of higher-level political dynamics that the
city has had limited ability to influence. The change in federal government in 2006 has highlighted the city's vulnerability to such dynamics.
February 2006 saw the election of a Conservative federal government
with no political representation from the city of Toronto. While the
Ontario provincial government remained receptive to new transit funding demands from the city, and in 2008 committed major funds to a
fifteen-year TTC project to expand light rail across the city, the federal

government under Stephen Harper rejected most new city demands for TTC funding (Mihevc 2008). Yet, even the federal Conservatives retained the previous Liberal government's transit funding initiatives, suggesting that in this field, the City of Toronto's campaign had successfully established a new multilevel policy reality.

## DEVELOPING DOWNSVIEW PARK

The 231-hectare former Downsview air force base in Toronto's north end is by far the largest of the 155 federal government properties in Toronto (Treasury Board of Canada 2008). After the base closed in the early 1990s, the minister of defence, David Collenette, who represented the Toronto constituency that housed the base, proposed to the federal cabinet that the government redevelop the site as a park (Interview 26). The Downsview Park project was announced by the Liberals in their 1994 budget, which said that the "Downsview site will be held in perpetuity and in trust primarily as a unique urban recreational green space for the enjoyment of future generations," and referred to the grand ambition of creating "Canada's first national urban park" (cited in Office of the Auditor General 2000). In 1995, the government specified that the project would be self-financing; a minimum of 50 percent of the total land would be redeveloped as a park, and the rest would be redeveloped for residential and commercial use to provide funding for park development (Office of the Auditor General 2000).

The initiative was slow to get off the ground. Redeveloping a large parcel of urban land for public use was not something the federal government was used to doing, and it did not have relevant administrative structures or expertise in place (Interview 22). Furthermore, the Downsview lands were still owned by the Department of National Defence (DND), which was reluctant to transfer them to another agency for less than market value. As one federal administrator noted, "having decided to [create Downsview Park] without, shall we say, the support or initiation of the bureaucracy, [federal politicians] then weren't quite sure how to do it" (Interview 25).

In 1997, the government directed the Canada Lands Company (CLC) – a government corporation that sells surplus federal property – to establish a subsidiary to redevelop the Downsview lands. The subsidiary, Parc Downsview Park Inc. (PDP), began operating in February 1999 with a board of directors appointed by the minister of infrastructure. However, PDP did not have the power to fulfill its mandate. The Downsview lands were still owned by the DND, so PDP could not engage in large-scale development activity. Furthermore, since it had no land to sell or lease, PDP had no start-up capital. Finally, PDP encountered an agenda conflict with its parent company, CLC. CLC's mandate is to sell surplus federal lands at market value, not to redevelop lands for public use on a cost-recovery basis. CLC officials thus resented the creation of PDP and sought to shut it down and manage the land directly (Interview 25).

In an effort to bolster the public profile of the project, PDP held an international design competition for the park portion of the Downsview land in 1999. Given the large scope of the project, the competition attracted leading names in urban design. The winning concept was "Tree City," designed by Toronto's Bruce Mau in association with Dutch architect Rem Koolhaas. Envisioned as a broad conceptual document, "Tree City" was maddeningly vague to many observers (Hume 2002). Nonetheless, the plan raised expectations among area residents that a major park would be forthcoming in the near future. Yet, PDP did not have the necessary authority and resources to turn plans into reality, and over the next eight years, it struggled at length to secure these.

In order to resolve the agenda conflict with CLC, PDP officials lobbied federal politicians to incorporate PDP as an autonomous corporation. Here again David Collenette played a key role. In 2003, he convinced Prime Minister Jean Chrétien of PDP's case. In September, Collenette and Chrétien made a widely-publicized appearance at Downsview, where they unveiled detailed plans for a $40 million park and said that construction would start the following spring (Kuitenbrouwer 2003). However, PDP still lacked control over the land. To force the DND to transfer title, PDP needed to "persuade Treasury Board, Finance, Privy Council Office, three key central agencies, that what started off as a political idea that they were resisting is actually good public policy" (Interview 22). According to one PDP official interviewed for this project, many federal officials thought that PDP's park plans were far too ambitious: "People in Ottawa [were] saying 'What the hell are you doing? You are supposed to create some green space. Just put some benches out and create a couple of baseball diamonds'" (Interview 22).

Armed with a detailed twenty-five-year business plan, PDP officials managed to get a critical mass of federal politicians and officials onside by late 2003. The government seemed set to enact the land transfer, as well as to grant PDP substantial borrowing authority. However, the November 2003 election brought a new set of politicians to the fore, many of whom opposed the Downsview Park project, and the initiatives stalled. After two more years of PDP lobbying, when it once again appeared that the land transfer and borrowing authority were imminent, the government fell again and was replaced by a minority Conservative government under Stephen Harper. To the surprise of PDP officials, it did not take long to convince the new government of the need to strengthen PDP. In July 2006, the DND's title to the Downsview Lands was transferred to PDP for a nominal sum, and $100 million in borrowing authority followed suit (Interview 25).

At the beginning of 2007, PDP thus finally had the power necessary to begin fulfilling its mandate. However, having been preoccupied for years by its struggle for authority and resources, PDP had not paid much attention to the interests of local governmental and societal agents, and relations with these had deteriorated. City of Toronto officials resented the fact that PDP, invoking its "paramountcy" as a federal body, had begun to plan development of the site on its own instead of going through the municipal planning process (Interview 27). In March 2007, city council passed a resolution declaring that the city would not engage with PDP on concrete planning issues until the agency agreed to go through the municipal planning process (Lorinc 2007). Meanwhile, local area residents had from the outset been opposed to major new residential and commercial development in the area (Interviews 27 and 29). The emphasis in PDP's public announcements on park development fed a widespread misconception among residents that *all* of the Downsview land would be used for park purposes (Parc Downsview Park 2007). As a result, in 2006 when PDP unveiled a draft plan that included large-scale residential and commercial development, there was much local consternation (Downsview Lands Community Voice Association 2007).

In 2007, the new Conservative federal government moved to address the conflict between PDP and local agents. It replaced most of the members of the PDP board of directors and appointed as Chair David Soknacki, who had served as the City of Toronto's budget chief from 2003 to 2006. The new board moved to improve relations with the city and with local area residents by agreeing that PDP would submit to municipal planning authority after all. While this shift was cautiously welcomed by municipal officials, local resident groups remained skeptical (Interviews 27 and 29). Furthermore, the municipal planning process that PDP and the City were engaged in threatened to delay the planned residential and commercial development, leaving PDP with fewer park construction funds in the short term (Parc Downsview Park 2008, 7). In view of this fact, in 2007 the new PDP board extended the proposed construction timeline for the park, whose price tag had grown to $75 million, in the name of fiscal prudence (Parc Downsview Park 2007b, 5; Parc Downsview Park 2006, 26–7). As of fall 2009, initial park construction was underway, financed by borrowing, but residential and commercial development remained at the planning stages, which in turn raised doubts about the longer-term financial viability of park construction (Parc Downsview Park 2009). In short, nearly fifteen years after "Canada's first national urban park" was first proposed, its future remained very much an open question.

### IMPLEMENTING THE TOURISM ACTION PLAN

Toronto is one of Canada's leading tourist destinations, attracting almost 20 million visitors in 2006 (Tourism Toronto 2007, 4), but over the last ten years it has not shared in the global tourism boom. By 2002, the combined effects of aggressive tourism marketing by many other North American cities and the post-9/11 travel downturn convinced city officials that they needed to market more effectively to visitors. For many years, tourism marketing in Toronto had been dominated by Tourism Toronto, a public-private partnership that was partly funded by the city, but whose membership and agenda were dominated by hotel and convention interests. In the initial years after amalgamation, the City of Toronto itself did not have an explicit tourism policy and did not devote substantial resources to the file. The only administrative body in the city specifically devoted to tourism-related concerns was the Toronto Special Events Unit, which helped to run city-sponsored festivals and holiday celebrations (Interview 4).

In 2002, council moved to strengthen the city's administrative capacity in the tourism field by creating a Tourism Division under the aegis of the Economic Development, Culture and Tourism Department. In the same year, it commissioned a consulting firm to produce a strategic tourism policy document for 2003–08. The Tourism Action Plan (TAP) was approved by council in the spring of 2003. Among the policy goals enshrined in the TAP, three were particularly prominent. The first was to institutionalize coordination among agents. The TAP pointed out that Toronto's tourism marketing suffered from a lack of coherent leadership and strategic direction, and proposed the creation of a "high-level Tourism Advisory Committee" with representation from the city and Tourism Toronto. Second, the TAP recommended that resources for tourism promotion be increased by transforming Tourism Toronto into a financially independent organization funded by a self-imposed 3 percent "destination marketing fee" (DMF) on local hotel stays. Finally, it recommended that the Tourism Advisory Committee develop a strategic tourism plan that specified timelines and funding for specific initiatives, and that the city itself set up "Toronto International," a new administrative unit that would specialize in attracting major one-time events (City of Toronto 2003, 22–4).

In the spring of 2003, Toronto was hit by the Severe Acute Respiratory Syndrome (SARS) epidemic, which killed forty-three people and led to a steep drop in tourism. In the wake of SARS, Toronto-area hotels quickly instituted the 3 percent DMF recommended by the TAP; over the following three years, this tax tripled Tourism Toronto's revenues (Tourism Toronto 2007, 16). Meanwhile, the city moved quickly to set up the Toronto International special events unit. However, responses to SARS also highlighted a lack of multilevel coordination. All three levels of government partnered with different societal agents and simultaneously launched major but uncoordinated tourism recovery initiatives. As one city official put it, "When SARS hit, everybody just panicked ... everybody just created their own thing. It became this one-upmanship thing and it was ridiculous" (Interview 8).

The TAP had recommended that the city and Tourism Toronto address the issue of coordination at the local level by setting up a public-private tourism advisory committee. This never happened. Instead, between 2003 and 2005 the relationship between Tourism Toronto and the city was marked by severe conflict. One city councillor described the relationship as "horrible," while a tourism industry official stated bluntly that "the relationship with the mayor sucked" (Interviews 37 and 43). The conflict stemmed from an effort by Toronto's political leaders to gain control of Tourism Toronto's new destination marketing fee – in contravention of their own TAP policy. Many local politicians, including Mayor David Miller, felt that Tourism Toronto's agenda remained too focused on hotel and convention interests, and sought control of the DMF in order to place the city at the helm of tourism promotion. In 2004, city politicians began lobbying the provincial government for authority to impose a hotel tax that would replace the destination marketing fee.

Conflict over this issue came to a head in 2005, when Tourism Toronto unveiled the results of a $4 million branding initiative. The product – featuring the slogan "Toronto Unlimited" and an associated ad campaign – was widely panned as ineffective and even embarrassing

(DiManno 2005). Following the launch, David Miller and other city politicians publicly criticized the product, even though council had already approved it. Miller suggested that the incident demonstrated the need for municipal control over tourism marketing in Toronto and reiterated the city's demand that it be allowed to levy a hotel tax (Barber 2005). This effort ultimately failed, but the damage to the working relationship between the city and Tourism Toronto was lasting. When in 2006 the city launched a province-sponsored review of tourism policy, the "Premier Ranked Tourism Destination Project" (PRTD), Tourism Toronto was only marginally involved (City of Toronto 2008b). The main recommendation of the PRTD review, published in 2008, was that "a cross-sectoral industry leadership group should create and implement a formal destination development plan for Toronto" (City of Toronto 2008b, 14). In other words, the review identified the same coordination and planning goals that had been prioritized in the TAP five years earlier, but not acted on since then.

As of fall 2009, the city had also failed to develop the tourism events strategy recommended by the TAP. This failure is mainly due to conflict within the city's Economic Development, Culture and Tourism Department (EDCTD). Since 2003, the EDCTD has housed two administrative units that deal directly with tourism concerns. One is the Tourism Division, which includes Toronto International. The other is the older Special Events Unit, whose mandate is to provide administrative support for hundreds of annual events in Toronto, ranging from neighborhood festivals to Gay Pride Week. The division of responsibilities between the units is not clear. When combined with endemic budget constraints, this lack of clarity has produced ongoing conflict over priorities and resources and an inability to develop an events strategy, despite years of effort. "Honestly, I could chew off my right arm because it is so frustrating to do this," said one administrator involved in the process (Interview 42).

Without an events strategy, council authorizes funding for any one event on an ad hoc basis. The resulting funding insecurity has made it more difficult for administrators to secure private events sponsorship. As one administrator noted, reports of possible funding cuts to city-sponsored events are routinely "bashed around in the media for three months and the sponsors read this and go – 'you know, you have to wonder if this is a viable product'" (Interview 42). The absence of a longer-term strategy has made it more difficult to secure events support from other levels of government. As one respondent put it: "Municipalities that are well organized and have strategies and policies in place are in a better position ... That way you can clearly communicate where you want to go and what you want to do and how you want to achieve it" (Interview 39).

Toronto's events administrators have achieved some concrete successes despite these difficulties. Since 2006, the Special Events Unit has run a highly acclaimed "Nuit Blanche" contemporary arts event. Toronto International, for its part, has helped private-sector organizing bodies in Toronto to attract major one-time events such as the International Dragon Boat Racing Championships (2006) and the FIFA Under-20 World Cup of Soccer (2007). Overall, however, as of 2009, dissatisfaction with the functioning of the events promotion system was widespread among stakeholders and mirrored a broader dissatisfaction with the state of tourism promotion in the city (Interviews 4, 8, 37, 39, 40, 42, and 43). In most respects the city had not met the policy goals outlined in the 2003 Tourism Action Plan. Indeed, one city administrator referred to it as "the 'Tourism Inaction Plan' because it really hasn't done much" (Interview 42). The TAP initiative notwithstanding, the sector retained serious problems of power and agenda fragmentation, both between the public and private sectors, and within local government itself.

## COORDINATING EMERGENCY MANAGEMENT

In Canada, most of the services typically required in an emergency situation, such as firefighting, ambulances and policing, are municipally run. Accordingly, municipalities have the "first responder" role when a large-scale emergency occurs. If a municipality's emergency response resources are overwhelmed, it can call on the provincial government for help, and the provincial government can in turn call for federal assistance if required. Coordination is at the very heart of the practice of emergency management. In order to respond effectively, municipalities must be able coordinate resources and response protocols both horizontally (among key municipal departments and other relevant local actors) and vertically (with other levels of government).

Toronto has long had a strong internal capacity to respond to emergencies. Its three core emergency services – the Toronto Police Service, Emergency Medical Services, and Fire Services – are the largest municipal emergency services in Canada, with a combined 2007 budget of nearly $1.2 billion (City of Toronto 2008). The city also has a long-standing corporate Emergency Plan, which was first developed in the 1970s by the Municipality of Metropolitan Toronto.

In 1999, in the wake of municipal amalgamation, city council moved to strengthen the citywide integration of emergency services by creating the Office of Emergency Management (OEM) as an independent corporate-level coordinating body. As of 2007, the OEM had a full-time staff of eight and a budget of just over $2 million (Interview 1). It is responsible for a number of activities, including ensuring that the emergency plans of various city divisions are harmonized with the corporate Emergency Plan, developing specialized "Emergency Operating Procedures" for different kinds of emergencies, and running training exercises that bring together emergency response leaders from various city and private organizations. In 2001, the OEM opened the Emergency Operations Centre (EOC). Equipped with sophisticated communications technology, the EOC is where the city's emergency decision makers meet to coordinate the response to a major emergency. Since its inception, the EOC has been activated five times in actual emergency situations; however, it functions much more frequently than this as a training facility for simulation exercises (Interview 1).

In developing citywide emergency management capacity, the OEM has faced some tension between the need to have a small, efficient core group of emergency decision makers and the need to engage with dozens of relevant stakeholders, ranging from chemical companies and utility firms to major sports venues and hospitals (Interview 33). The city's current emergency plan goes part way towards addressing this issue. Citywide emergency management policies are the responsibility of a large program committee with almost forty members, including city administrators, politicians, and representatives of a variety of societal stakeholder groups. However, in an actual emergency a smaller control group composed only of city officials takes charge and liaises with those societal agents who are seen as key in that particular case (City of Toronto 2005b, 7–8).

According to most local stakeholders, emergency management in Toronto is dominated by consensual relations among agents who share the same overall agenda (Interviews 1, 24, 28, 33, and 34). OEM officials have actively built relationships and conducted training exercises with a wide variety of societal organizations – including a recently-formed emergency planning group for large downtown Toronto facilities such as the CN Tower and the Air Canada Centre (Interview 33). Representatives of societal stakeholder groups interviewed for this project were happy with the OEM's efforts to include them (Interviews 24 and 34).

The city's ability to respond to emergencies was tested twice in 2003, first with SARS in the spring, and then with a blackout that plunged the entire city (as well as much of the rest of Ontario) into darkness for about a day in August. The two events were very different kinds of emergencies. The blackout was a short-term event without fatalities. According to officials interviewed for this project, the city coordinated the corporate emergency response through the EOC without much difficulty and did not need to call on other levels of government for resources (Interview 28; Gillespie 2003).[8] The SARS epidemic, by contrast, involved significant loss of life and lasted some three months. Although the EOC was operational throughout the crisis, it was Toronto Public Health (TPH) – a health unit funded in part by the provincial government – that led the municipal response (Toronto Public Health 2004, 1). Most respondents interviewed for this project evaluated the TPH response to SARS very well (Interviews 7, 28, 33, and 44). Sheela Basrur, the city's chief medical officer of health at the time, won widespread public acclaim for her leadership during the crisis. However, the provincial government was also involved in coordinating the SARS response, as it has primary responsibility for health care in Ontario. Its activities were heavily criticized after the fact, in part because three provincial agents – the chief medical officer of health, the provincial emergency management office, and the office of the premier – all attempted to lead the response and did not fully coordinate their strategies (Campbell 2006).

The SARS crisis had a significant effect on emergency management policy in Toronto. The experience of this "focusing event" (Henstra 2003) increased city council's attention to the problem of infectious disease emergencies. As a result, Toronto Public Health received more local funding and political support for its ongoing pandemic influenza planning process, and in 2005 it produced a comprehensive *Toronto Public Health Plan for an Influenza Pandemic* (revised in 2007 – see Toronto Public Health 2007). The provincial government increased its share of funding for municipal public health from 50 percent to 75 percent,[9] developed its own pandemic flu plan, and made efforts to clarify its emergency response structure for public health incidents (Interview 44).

A public health emergency is just one of many emergency risks in the city, however, and the overall emergency management system in Toronto has not enjoyed such political attention. As Dan Henstra (2003) notes, absent a "focusing event" (such as SARS) that makes the threat of a particular kind of emergency seem real, political leaders have little incentive to devote resources and energy to planning for events whose occurrence is uncertain and unpredictable. While Mayor Miller was praised by emergency management officials for consistently taking an interest in their work, the OEM saw no budget increase in the wake of SARS and the blackout (Interview 33). At the provincial and federal levels, the willingness of politicians to pay attention to Toronto's particular emergency management priorities has been even weaker.

Given the weak political focus on emergency management federally and provincially city officials have had little success at improving vertical coordination, despite persistent lobbying. At the provincial level, for example, in 2003 Ontario passed new provincial emergency management legislation. The city was not consulted about the legislation. The legislation mandates that municipalities meet a number of basic standards of emergency preparedness, such as having an emergency plan and conducting emergency training exercises, but, as one city administrator noted, the legislation is tailored towards smaller municipalities, and "Toronto exceeded the requirements of the legislation long ago" (Interview 28). The net effect of the legislation on the city has simply been to increase paperwork, as the city has to report regularly on its compliance (Interview 28).

At the federal level, the lead agency, Public Safety Canada, has little interaction with Toronto's emergency management officials. "We are simply not on their radar screen," said one Toronto official (Interview 28). This perpetuates a number of coordination problems. For example, the federal government has a multilevel funding program called the Joint Emergency Preparedness Program (JEPP), which operates on a cost-shared basis. However, Toronto has had difficulty in using funding from the program because the federal and municipal budget cycles are not synchronized, so by the time the federal government approves a JEPP funding request, the window of time available for emergency management officials to spend the budgeted municipal contribution is almost over (Interview 28). Likewise, the federal government runs the Disaster Financial Assistance Arrangements (DFAA), a disaster relief funding program. However, the program is aimed only at "natural disasters" (Public Safety Canada 2008), so many of the emergencies that Toronto is at above-average risk for – terrorist attacks, infrastructure collapse, infectious disease outbreaks – are ineligible for DFAA funding (Interview 28). In short, efforts to improve the coordination of emergency management in Toronto in recent years have had significant success at the municipal level, and local agents appear satisfied with them, but improved intergovernmental coordination remains elusive.[10]

## REVITALIZING THE CENTRAL WATERFRONT

Toronto's central waterfront represents an extraordinary revitalization opportunity. Located immediately next to the city's central business district, it was once the home of a major shipping operation and numerous industries, but these gradually declined between the 1950s and the 1970s. Today, the majority of the central waterfront consists of vacant land – close to 800 hectares worth – of which 86 percent is owned by various levels of government and their associated agencies (Lewington 2004). However, years of conflict between federal and municipal interests on the waterfront have produced a difficult environment for coordinated revitalization efforts.

For decades, the bulk of central waterfront land was owned by the Toronto Harbour Commission (THC), an agency run by a board consisting of three municipal and two federal appointees (Tassé 2006, 8). The THC's primary purpose was to manage the Toronto port, but it also managed extensive adjacent industrial landholdings, and operated a small island airport on one of the islands that ring the harbour (Tassé 2006, 10). After the 1950s, the volume of shipping in the port entered a steady, long-term decline, and associated industries abandoned the adjacent area, leaving most of the port lands derelict. Taking advantage of its control of the THC board, in the early 1990s, the City of Toronto transferred 250 hectares of derelict land to the municipally controlled Toronto Economic Development Corporation (TEDCO), in return for only nominal compensation to the THC (Tassé 2006, 1–2). The transfer was made over strenuous objections from THC management and some Toronto-area federal politicians (Interviews 24 and 26).

In 1996, the federal government introduced legislation that would divest it of the vast majority of its ports across Canada and introduce federally controlled port authorities to run a handful of major commercially viable ports. Toronto's port was initially slated for divestment, but a number of influential Toronto members of Parliament, led by Dennis Mills, lobbied successfully for the transformation of the THC into a federally controlled Toronto Port Authority (TPA) (Tassé 2006, 19–24; Interview 26). Created in 1999, the TPA soon launched a lawsuit against the City of Toronto for return of the TEDCO lands. The lawsuit was settled in 2003. The TPA did not regain the lands, but it did receive a multi-year, $69 million compensation package from the city, to be paid in part by TEDCO, as well a city council commitment to approve construction of a bridge to the Island Airport to improve the airport's viability (Tassé 2006, 39).

City council duly approved an airport bridge, but the Island Airport was not popular among Toronto residents. In the fall 2003 municipal election, David Miller's pledge to withdraw approval for the bridge played a major role in his victory in the mayoral campaign. After the election city council withdrew its approval, sparking threats of further lawsuits from the TPA and associated construction companies and airlines. In 2005, Martin's federal government, which was trying hard to build a positive relationship with Toronto, settled the dispute by paying the TPA and other affected parties $35 million in compensation (Safieddine and James 2005), but animosity between city politicians and the TPA remains strong (Interviews 24 and 37).

The long dispute between the THC/TPA and the city received exhaustive media coverage and suggested to many observers that multilevel coordination on waterfront revitalization was a lost cause. However, after 1999, such coordination nonetheless began to emerge. Even as the TPA/city conflict mounted, a major effort to kick-start waterfront revitalization was launched by the City of Toronto at the end of the 1990s. Having secured control over extensive port lands through the TEDCO transfer, city officials saw an unparalleled opportunity to secure multilevel funding for waterfront revitalization in 1999, when the city launched a bid for the 2008 summer Olympics. The bid enjoyed strong support from senior governments, and the vast and empty waterfront lands provided a natural site for Olympic venues.

In November 1999, the three levels of government created a Waterfront Revitalization Task Force (WRTF), with a mandate to produce a plan for waterfront revitalization that would also prepare the site for the Olympics. The WRTF reported back with a massive revitalization plan that called for $5 billion in government investment and for the creation of a Toronto Waterfront Revitalization Corporation (TWRC) to manage implementation on a fifteen-year timeline. The TWRC was to be run by a board with appointees from all three levels of government and was to have the power to sell and lease land and borrow money (Waterfront Revitalization Task Force 2000). In short, the WRTF report proposed institutionalized multilevel governing arrangements to respond to the fiscal and organizational challenge of waterfront revitalization.

Given the strong incentives to collaborate on the high-profile Olympic bid, the three levels of government approved the TWRC in principle, and in November 2000 they pledged $1.5 billion in public money – $500 million each – to fund its activity. In July 2001, Toronto lost the Olympic bid to Beijing, and the strong incentives to collaborate vanished. However, the TWRC was nonetheless created in late 2001. In October 2002, it released its first major document, a long-range revitalization plan. The plan reduced total proposed government investment in the waterfront to $2.8 billion and extended the implementation timeline to thirty years (MacKay 2002), but it remained an ambitious scheme. For a number of reasons, prospects for its realization initially appeared dim.

First, all three levels of government were having second thoughts about creating a strong waterfront revitalization entity that no one level could control. As a result, the TWRC did not receive final provincial enabling legislation until April 2003; even then, it was granted neither borrowing power, nor the power to sell or lease land (City of Toronto 2005, 3). Second, absent the time pressure and unifying goal of preparing a site for the 2008 Olympics, no level of government was eager to release much of the previously pledged $1.5 billion. Given Toronto's financial difficulties, city council was especially reluctant, and proposed that the city make the bulk of its contribution in kind, in the form of the above mentioned TEDCO lands (Monsebraaten and Moloney 2002). Third, the TWRC had no land of its own. The bulk of vacant waterfront land was held by TEDCO and by the provincially-controlled Ontario Realty Corporation.[11] Finally, the TWRC had no legal planning authority, and thus had to rely on city planning approval.

For the first three years of its existence, the TWRC got little done. Several expensive infrastructure projects that were originally slated for early implementation – most notably, the burying of the elevated Gardiner Expressway along the waterfront – foundered as city council balked at their costs. In 2003, as the TWRC struggled to implement anything and the conflict over the Island Airport hit its peak, a consensus began to emerge that the waterfront revitalization effort would fail. However, no level of government felt like it could afford the political fallout of actually pulling the plug on the TWRC, and this gave the agency the time to develop a strategy to bolster its legitimacy (Interviews 7 and 32).

The TWRC's strategy was essentially two-fold. First, it shifted its short-term focus away from expensive infrastructure projects and towards designing detailed "precinct plans" for two waterfront areas: The West Don Lands, a thirty-hectare area adjacent to existing neighborhoods that was to be developed for residential purposes, and the East Bayfront, twenty-two-hectare site along the water's edge that was to be developed as a mixed residential and commercial area. Second, in developing the precinct plans and other proposals, TWRC actively sought the involvement of resident associations representing adjacent neighborhoods, a variety of community interest groups, and the broader public. As one TWRC official put it, the strategy was that "we get public support, then we get press support, then we get political support" (Interview 32).

As societal agents and the local media began to support the TWRC's planning activities, political support for the agency also began to solidify. In 2005, the TWRC received tri-level government approval for a ten-year business plan that included specific yearly financial commitments by each level of government. As of 2007, about $600 million had been delivered to the TWRC by the governments (Interview 32). In 2005, city council approved both the West Don Lands and the East Bayfront precinct plans. However, the TWRC still needed control over the land to proceed with development. In 2005, it signed a memorandum of understanding (MOU) with the Ontario Realty Corporation (which owns the West Don Lands) that gave TWRC full development authority in the area.

The East Bayfront case proved more problematic. The majority of the land here was owned by TEDCO, which also owns much other waterfront land. In part because it used revenue from land leases to pay compensation to the TPA under the terms of the 2003 lawsuit settlement, TEDCO was unwilling to cede control of these lands. In 2006, city council forced TEDCO to sign an MOU that stipulates the phased transfer of most lands on the waterfront to the TWRC over the next fifteen years (City of Toronto 2006). In September 2008, the city moved to further consolidate land control on the waterfront in the hands of the TWRC. It announced that TEDCO would be replaced by a new economic development corporation, Build Toronto, but that most of TEDCO's waterfront lands would be separated out from Build Toronto's portfolio and managed directly by city administrators until TWRC was ready to redevelop them (City of Toronto 2008c, 11–12).

In the wake of these developments, TWRC – which in 2008 re-named itself Waterfront Toronto – forged ahead with brownfields remediation and infrastructure construction in the West Don Lands and East Bayfront, with the aim of creating 14,000 new residential units and 8,000 employment spaces by 2020 (Waterfront Toronto 2008). As of fall 2009, construction was underway on – among other things – a new 3,500-student waterfront campus for George Brown College, and developers were advertising pre-sales for the first 850 units of West Don Lands housing

(Waterfront Toronto 2009). Waterfront Toronto had completed several small parks and open space projects and was planning larger ones. While most of the central waterfront remained derelict, significant revitalization was thus underway. With the notable exception of representatives of TEDCO, most local stakeholders interviewed for this project expressed satisfaction with the functioning of Waterfront Toronto and were quite optimistic about the future of revitalization (Interviews 7, 24, 26, 32, 37, 38, 39, and 45).[12]

### ANALYZING THE CASES: WHAT SHAPES THE QUALITY OF PUBLIC POLICY OUTPUTS?

In the second section of this chapter, we introduced two basic measures of the quality of policy outputs in multilevel initiatives: achieving the policy goals of the lead agent (the one that spearheads the initiative), and satisfying local stakeholders. Clearly, there is a great deal of variation on these measures across the five cases. What explains this variation? While the limited scope of the Toronto research precludes definitive answers, some fascinating insights nonetheless emerge from the case histories presented here.

First, there is a significant correlation between the complexity of coordination challenges and the quality of policy outputs. In the second section, we noted that multilevel policy initiatives typically require their proponents to coordinate policy-making power (that is, decision-making authority plus material resources) and policy agendas (that is, preferences regarding policy goals and instruments), both of which are initially fragmented among multiple state and societal agents. As is clear from the case histories related above, the degree of initial power and agenda fragmentation, and therefore the complexity of the coordination challenges, varies widely from case to case.

Table 2 lists the Toronto cases from most to least successful in terms of policy outputs and juxtaposes this against the degree of power and agenda fragmentation present at the outset. When we look at the cases as a group, there is a clear correlation between the overall complexity of the initial coordination challenges and the quality of policy outputs. In general, the more fragmented power and agendas initially were, the poorer the eventual policy outputs of a given policy initiative were.

A brief contrast between initial conditions in the best and worst output cases can illustrate these correlations. The clearest policy success was in the municipal campaign for intergovernmental TTC funding. In this

Table 2
Quality of policy outputs as related to initial coordination challenges

| Case | Goals achieved? | Local stakeholders satisfied? | Initial power fragmentation | Initial agenda fragmentation |
|---|---|---|---|---|
| Securing multilevel TTC funding | yes | yes | quite low | quite low |
| Revitalizing the central waterfront | in part | mostly | high | high |
| Coordinating emergency management | in part | in part | quite high | quite low |
| Implementing the Tourism Action Plan | mostly not | no | high | quite high |
| Developing Downsview Park | no | mostly not | high | high |

case, the initial coordination challenge was, relatively speaking, not that complex: the city had full decision-making authority regarding public transit, so all it needed was money; and most governmental and societal agents agreed about the desirability of more transit funding. The key question was who would provide this funding and how. The poorest policy output was in the Downsview case. Here, the initial coordination challenge was very difficult. The Downsview Park initiative was born in the absence of any public-sector body that had the authority to realize it, and it lacked any initial source of funding. Furthermore, once the Parc Downsview Park corporation was created, it had to deal with a number of other federal agencies that were skeptical about, and in some cases entirely hostile to, the park initiative.

There are a number of reasons why this correlation between the complexity of coordination and the quality of policy outputs exists. Full treatment of these is beyond the scope of this chapter, but they bear brief mention. First, overcoming highly complex coordination challenges requires lead agents to expend much of their energy and resources on aligning resources and agendas. The more difficult the initial coordination challenge was, the more lead agents had to focus on lobbying, persuading, bargaining with, threatening, or cajoling other agents instead of on realizing policy goals directly. Second, since complex coordination challenges take time and effort to address, the likelihood that political leaders will lose interest in a policy initiative increases with the complexity of coordination. Cases such as the Downsview Park initiative and the TAP clearly illustrate this. Third, the more fragmented policy agendas are, the more lead agents may face tradeoffs between securing their policy goals and securing the support of other agents. A final observation concerns the relationship between the complexity of coordination and the inclusiveness of policy processes. Evidence from the Downsview, TAP, and (prior to the establishment of TWRC) waterfront cases suggests that, when faced with very complex coordination challenges, lead agents sometimes use exclusionary and coercive tactics in order to amass power and dominate the agenda, and this may alienate the some of the very agents whose support they ultimately need.

All that said, it is also clear from Table 2 that the correlation between coordination challenges and policy outputs is by no means perfect. In other words, in some cases lead agents were more successful in overcoming a given set of coordination challenges and producing good public policy outputs than in others. The most striking case in this regard is that of the waterfront, where major and broadly supported revitalization initiatives are now underway against the historical backdrop of vicious conflict among government agencies. A review of the cases reveals three factors that, when present, increased the likelihood of such positive outcomes.

First, the cases illustrate the importance of a technically competent and internally cohesive set of administrative bodies that can help to drive and sustain the policy initiative at the lead level of government. In three of the five cases – transit funding, waterfront revitalization, and emergency management – a competent, cohesive group of administrators existed at the local level. They helped to forge policy goals and coordinating strategies and to sustain policy activity if and when political interest at city hall waned. Conversely, in two cases – Downsview and the TAP – relevant administrative bodies were either internally fragmented, or lacked appropriate competence, or both. As a result, pursuing sustained multilevel coordination became much more difficult, and the quality of policy outputs ultimately suffered.

Second, the cases suggest that consistent political leadership is also a key asset to a multilevel policy initiative. The consistency of political leadership varied widely across the five cases. At one end of the spectrum is TTC funding, where Mayor Miller and Toronto City Council consistently and forcefully made the case for intergovernmental capital funding assistance over a period of several years. At the other end of the spectrum are the cases of Downsview Park and the TAP; in both of these, political leaders launched an initiative and then either lost interest in it, or altered their priorities. When present, consistent political leadership enhances the profile of an initiative, provides public legitimacy, generates opportunities for aligning political agendas across levels of government and with societal agents, and supports the detailed coordination and policy-making work carried out by administrators. An absence of consistent political leadership deprives a multilevel initiative of these important assets.

Finally, since the agendas of other agents may shift due to factors beyond a lead agent's control, successful multilevel policy coordination often turns on the capacity of lead agents to identify and exploit windows of policy opportunity as they emerge. This capacity was most clearly demonstrated in the transit funding and waterfront revitalization cases. In the former case, lead agents took advantage of changes in government at other levels in order to coordinate financial resources for the TTC. In the latter case, Toronto's political leaders exploited a key opportunity to secure intergovernmental funding, build societal support and institutionalize implementation arrangements for waterfront revitalization in conjunction with the city's Olympic bid.

## CONCLUSION

This chapter has reviewed five recent cases of multilevel policy initiatives in the City of Toronto. Given the tremendous scope and variety of urban governance in Toronto, the chapter has not addressed a number of key contemporary issues in the city, including housing and homelessness, economic growth, poverty, and immigrant integration. However, the cross-section of policy initiatives surveyed here paints a vivid picture of the complexities and challenges associated with policy making in Toronto. As the largest municipality in Canada, and the central municipality in Canada's largest urban area, Toronto experiences multilevel political dynamics that are no doubt different from those experienced in other Canadian cities. As a result, the insights developed in this chapter cannot be assumed to transfer unproblematically to other settings. Nonetheless, the analysis has a number of implications for the broader study of multilevel governance.

First, the chapter suggests that if we are to advance our understanding of the prospects for successful multilevel policy making we must not assume that coordination exists, but we must instead place coordination challenges and the way in which they are (or are not) overcome at the centre of the analysis. Doing so may lead us to re-think the common proposition that multilevel policy making is superior to the exercise of authority by discrete levels of government (see Hooghe and Marks 2003, 233). On the one hand, some policy fields (such as immigrant settlement, environmental policy, or housing) present problems that are likely to require multilevel coordination. On the other hand, it appears that the higher the power and agenda fragmentation in a particular policy field, the higher too is the risk of "governance failure" (Jessop 1998).

The chapter also produces a number of propositions whose relevance could be explored in other empirical settings. First, the more difficult the initial multilevel coordination challenge is in relation to a particular policy initiative, the less likely it is that good public policy outputs will eventually emerge. Second, strong and cohesive administrative expertise at the lead level of government is important to success in multilevel policy initiatives. Third, sustained political leadership over time at the lead level of government is likewise very important. Finally, in order to align power and agendas in an environment that they cannot control, multilevel policy makers must identify and exploit unexpected windows of policy opportunity as they emerge.

## NOTES

1 The author would like to acknowledge the valuable assistance of many people who contributed to the research and writing of this chapter. These include, but are not limited to: Ajay Sharma, who provided research assistance; John Elvidge, who opened many doors at the City of Toronto; Carol Brookbanks, who meticulously transcribed dozens of hours of taped interviews; Andy Sancton, Kelly McCarthy, Chris Leo, Anthony Perl, and Susan Clarke, who all provided valuable feedback on early versions of the written product; and Bob Young, who has given his guidance, support, and feedback throughout the development of the work. The author also gratefully acknowledges the financial assistance of the Social Sciences and Humanities Research Council of Canada (SSHRC).

2 In this chapter, an "agent" is defined as an entity that behaves in a unitary manner in a given policy case. Agents, in this sense, can be individuals (such as political leaders), organizations (state or societal), or entire levels of government; their defining feature is internal cohesion in relation to a policy initiative.

3 An "agenda," as the term is used here, refers to a set of goals and associated policy instruments advocated by a particular agent.

4 The implications of this are mixed. While the city's strategic electoral importance sometimes presents a window of opportunity for municipal concerns,
at other times it leads provincial and federal officials to focus on short-term
spending initiatives and announcements that maximize electoral appeal. The
case studies to follow provide evidence of both phenomena at work.

5 Post-amalgamation Toronto has had three mayors: Mel Lastman, who served
two terms (1998–2000 and 2000–03); and David Miller, who also served two
terms (2003–06 and 2006–10), and Rob Ford (2010–).

6 See www.torontoalliance.ca for an overview of the TCSA's activities.

7 The ICP and the CSIF worked on a matching funding basis. They provided
one-third of the funding for infrastructure projects proposed by municipalities
or private-sector agents; matching contributions for each project were required
from the provincial government and from the project proponent.

8 The provincial government did declare a state of emergency, but it directed its
assistance to smaller municipalities that did not have Toronto's strong emergency response capacity.

9 A cash-strapped city council reallocated some of the resulting municipal wind-
fall to other programs.

10 Although detailed evidence on emergency management in Toronto was not
gathered past 2009, more recent (2011) informal conversations with informants suggest little has changed recently in this policy field.

11 The TPA no longer owned a great deal of land on the waterfront – about forty
hectares of remaining port land, a small marina, and the Island Airport.

12 Recent events have illustrated both the continuing challenges of governing
waterfront redevelopment in Toronto and the success that Waterfront
Toronto has had in building public support for its vision of redevelopment.
In 2009, the City established the Toronto Port Lands Company as a municipal corporation tasked with managing the lands that had belonged to the
Toronto Economic Development Corporation until such time as Waterfront
Toronto was ready to develop them. In the summer of 2011, Toronto's new
mayor, Rob Ford, endorsed a radically revised vision of waterfront redevelopment proposed by his brother, City Councillor Doug Ford. This vision
abandoned Waterfront Toronto's emerging mixed-use plans for the port
lands, proposing instead that development center on the construction of a
suburban-style shopping mall and a giant Ferris wheel. To facilitate this, the
Fords also proposed giving the Toronto Port Lands Company full control
over development of City-owned part lands. These proposals, which went to
city council in September 2011, aroused strong public and professional opposition and were rejected by council in favour of the existing strategy led by
Waterfront Toronto.

## LIST OF INTERVIEWS

1  Municipal emergency management official, Toronto, 17 May 2006.
2  Municipal finance official, Toronto, 17 May 2006.
3  Municipal economic development official, Toronto, 17 May 2006.
4  Municipal economic development official, Toronto, 17 May, 2006.
5  Transit activist, Toronto, 18 May 2006.
6  Municipal property development official, Toronto, 18 May 2006.
7  Municipal public health official, Toronto, 18 May 2006.
8  Municipal tourism official, Toronto, 19 May 2006.
9  Municipal culture promotion official, Toronto, 19 May 2006.
10  Municipal intergovernmental relations official, Toronto, 20 June 2006.
11  Municipal intergovernmental relations official, Toronto, 20 June, 2006.
12  Municipal corporate affairs official, Toronto, 7 July 2006.
13  Academic urban policy analyst, Toronto, 13 July 2006.
14  Former Toronto political aide, Toronto, 13 July 2006.
15  Municipal intergovernmental relations official, Toronto, 14 July 2006.
16  Provincial Ministry of Municipal Affairs official, Toronto, 14 July 2006.
17  Provincial Ministry of Municipal Affairs official, Toronto, 26 July 2006.
18  Municipal intergovernmental relations official, Toronto, 21 August 2006.
19  Toronto City Summit Alliance official, Toronto, 21 August 2006.
20  Municipal intergovernmental relations official, Toronto, 4 August 2006.
21  Former provincial official, Toronto, 4 August 2006.
22  Parc Downsview Park official, Toronto, 6 July 2007.
23  Private sector policy lobbyist, Toronto, 9 July 2007.
24  Toronto Port Authority official, Toronto, 9 July 2007.
25  Federal official, Toronto, 30 July 2007.
26  Former member of Parliament for Toronto, Toronto, 17 September, 2007.
27  Aide to Toronto city councillor, Toronto, 21 September 2007.
28  Municipal emergency management official, Toronto, 27 September 2007.
29  Downsview Park activist, Toronto, 28 September 2007.
30  Toronto city councillor, Toronto, 24 September 2007.
31  Toronto city councillor, Toronto, 3 October 2007.
32  Waterfront Toronto official, Toronto, 3 October 2007.
33  Municipal emergency management official, Toronto, 5 October 2007.
34  Private sector emergency manager, Toronto, 25 October 2007.
35  Municipal intergovernmental relations official, Toronto, 5 November 2007.
36  Toronto Transit Commission official, Toronto, 7 November 2007.
37  Toronto city councillor, Toronto, 7 November 2007.
38  TEDCO official, Toronto, 9 November 2007.

39 Municipal finance official, Toronto, 12 November 2007.
40 Municipal tourism official, Toronto, 13 November 2007.
41 Academic urban policy analyst, Toronto, 13 November 2007.
42 Municipal tourism official, Toronto, 13 November 2007.
43 Former tourism industry official, Toronto, 16 November 2007.
44 Toronto Public Health official, Toronto, 16 November 2007.
45 Waterfront activist, Toronto, 23 November 2007.
46 Municipal emergency management official, Toronto, 14 March 2008.

## REFERENCES

Barber, John. 2005. "There's No Limit to Nasty Turf War Over Toronto Unlimited Slogan." *Globe and Mail*, 29 July.

Bellamy, Denise E. 2005. *Toronto Computer Leasing Inquiry/ Toronto External Contract Inquiry Report*. Toronto: City of Toronto.

Boudreau, Julie-Anne. 2000. *The MegaCity Saga: Democracy and Citizenship in the Global Age*. Montreal: Black Rose Books.

Campbell, Archie. 2006. *Spring of Fear: The SARS Commission Final Report*. Accessed 5 October 2008. http://www.sarscommission.ca/report/index.html.

City of Toronto. 2000. *Towards a New Relationship with Ontario and Canada*. Report prepared by the Chief Administrative Officer, 6 June.

– 2002. "Provincial Auditor Confirms Downloading is Not Revenue Neutral." Press release, 3 January.

– 2003. *Five Year Tourism Action Plan*. http://www.toronto.ca/divisions/pdf/edct/edct_tourism_consultant_report_May3003.PDF.

– 2005a. "Implementation of a New Governance Structure for Toronto Waterfront Renewal." Consolidated clause in *Policy and Finance Committee Report 8*.

– 2005b. *The City of Toronto Emergency Plan*. http://www.toronto.ca/wes/techservices/oem/pdf/emergency_plan.pdf.

– 2006. "Toronto Waterfront Revitalization: Memorandum of Understanding between the City of Toronto, City of Toronto Economic Development Corporation and Toronto Waterfront Revitalization Corporation." Consolidated Clause in *Policy and Finance Committee Report 1*.

– 2007. "Government Structure." *City of Toronto*. http://www.toronto.ca/toronto_facts/government.htm.

– 2008. *City of Toronto 2008 Recommended Operating Budget*. http://www.toronto.ca/budget2008/pdf/2008_operating_intro_bc_jan28_pres.pdf.

– 2008b. *Toronto's Premier Ranked Tourism Destination Project Results – Making Toronto the Best it Can Be*. http://www.toronto.ca/tourismstudy/pdf/prtd_staffreport_april2008.pdf.

– 2008c. *New Model to Enhance Toronto's Economic Competitiveness*. http://
www.toronto.ca/legdocs/mmis/2008/ex/bgrd/backgroundfile-15926.pdf.

DiManno, Rosie. 2005. "Toronto Unlimited or Just Unimaginative?" *Toronto
Star*, 29 June.

Downsview Lands Community Voice Association. 2007. Newsletter, 1, no. 1.
Accessed 15 October 2008. http://www.savedownsviewpark.com/Sept07.JPG.

Gillespie, Kerry. 2003. "Command Centre Keeps City Running." *Toronto Star*,
16 August.

– 2005. "Gas-tax Formula a Blow to TTC." *Toronto Star*, 16 June.

Henstra, Dan. 2003. "Federal Emergency Management in Canada and the
United States after 11 September 2001." *Canadian Public Administration*
46 (1):103–16.

Hooghe, Liesbet, and Gary Marks. 2003. "Unraveling the Central State, but
How? Types of Multilevel governance." *American Political Science Review*
97 (2):233–43.

Horak, Martin. 1998. "The Power of Local Identity: C4LD and the Anti-
Amalgamation Mobilization in Toronto." Research paper 195, Toronto:
Centre for Urban and Community Studies.

– 2008. "Governance Reform from Below: Multilevel Politics and Toronto's
'New Deal' Campaign." Global Dialogue paper series 4, Nairobi:
UN-Habitat.

Hume, Christopher. 2002. "Forgotten Lands a Canvas for Ideas." *Toronto Star*,
31 July.

James, Royson. 2004. "Transit Grant Not All it May Seem." *Toronto Star*,
22 October.

Jessop, Bob. 1998. "The Rise of Governance and the Risks of Failure: The
Case of Economic Development." *International Social Science Journal* 50
(155):29–45.

– 2004. "Multilevel Governance and Multi-level Metagovernance." In *Multilevel Governance*, edited by Ian Bache and Matthew Flinders, 49–74.
Oxford: Oxford University Press.

Kuitenbrouwer, Peter. 2003. "Chrétien Gives Blessing to Downsview Park
Remodeling." *National Post*, 30 September.

– 2005. "No Deal for Cities?" *National Post*, 2 May.

Lewington, Jennifer. 2004. "On the Waterfront." *Globe and Mail*, 21 February.

Lorinc, John. 2007. "Green Acres? Not Really." *Globe and Mail*, 17 March.

Lu, Vanessa. 2003. "It's Time to Build 'The Toronto of Tomorrow.'" *Toronto
Star*, 23 January.

MacKay, Brad. 2002. "Redeveloping the Waterfront: The Blueprint." *National
Post*, 18 October.

Marks, Gary. 1993. "Structural Policy and Multilevel Governance in the EC." In *The state of the European Community: The Maastricht Debates and Beyond*, edited by A. Carfuny and G. Rosenthal, 391–410. Boulder, CO: Lynne Rienner.

Mihevc, Joe. 2008. "Green Light for Transit After Years of Stagnation." *Toronto Star*, 17 January.

Moloney, Paul. 2002. "Building the TTC, $100M at a time." *Toronto Star*, 6 December.

Monsebraaten, Laurie, and Paul Moloney. 2002. "Funding Partners See Roadblocks to Fung Plan." *Toronto Star*, 19 October.

Office of the Auditor General of Canada. 2000. *October 2000 Report*. http://www.oag-bvg.gc.ca/domino/reports.nsf/html/oomenu_e.html#october.

Parc Downsview Park. 2006. *Summary of the Corporate Plan 2007–2008 to 2011–2012*. Toronto, November.

– 2007a. "2nd Annual Public Meeting." Webcast. Originally posted 11 September 2007. http://www.pdp.ca/en/corporate/meeting2.cfm.

– 2007b. *Minutes of the Meeting of the Board of Directors*. November. http://www.pdp.ca/media/Minutes_BOD_Meeting_Nov7-07-finaldraft_website.pdf.

– 2008. *Building the Downsview Park Sustainable Community: Corporate Plan Summary*. http://www.pdp.ca/media/PDPCorpPlanSummary.FinalApril21.pdf.

– 2009. "Parc Downsview Park's 4th Annual Public Meeting." Webcast. 4 June. http://www.downsviewpark.ca/eng/apm4.shtml.

Peters, B. Guy, and Jon Pierre. 2004. "Multilevel Governance and Democracy: A Faustian Bargain?" In *Multilevel Governance*, edited by Ian Bache and Matthew Flinders, 75–92. Oxford: Oxford University Press.

Safieddine, Hicham, and Royson James. 2005. "Bridge Battle Finally Over." *Toronto Star*, 5 May.

Slack, Enid. 2005. "Easing the Fiscal Restraints: New Revenue Tools in the City of Toronto Act." International Tax Program Paper 0507, Toronto: Institute for International Business.

Tassé, Marcel. 2006. *Review of Toronto Port Authority*. Report commissioned by Canadian federal government.

Toronto Public Health. 2004. *Learning from SARS: Recommendations for Emergency Preparedness, Response and Recovery*. http://www.toronto.ca/legdocs/2004/agendas/committees/hl/hl041018/itoo3.pdf.

– 2007. *Toronto Public Health Plan for an Influenza Pandemic*. http://www.toronto.ca/health/pandemicflu/pandemicflu_plan.htm.

Tourism Toronto. 2007. *Tourism Toronto Annual Report 2006: Drawing Inspiration*. http://www.torontotourism.com/web.cms/pdf/AnnualReport2006.pdf.

Treasury Board of Canada. 2008. "Directory of Federal Real Property." http://
www.tbs-sct.gc.ca/dfrp-rbif/home-accueil.asp?Language=EN.

Waterfront Revitalization Task Force. 2000. *Our Toronto Waterfront, Final
Report*. March.

Waterfront Toronto. 2009. *September 2009 Newsletter*. http://www.
waterfrontoronto.ca/newsletter/viewnewsletter.php?id=4ac2415f459b2&
template=5.

# Multilevel Governance and Urban Development: A Vancouver Case Study

THOMAS A. HUTTON

## INTRODUCTION: MULTILEVEL GOVERNANCE AND POLICY INNOVATION IN CANADA

The constitutionally enshrined subordination of local government in Canada is a product of political and economic conditions that prevailed in nineteenth-century Canada. The very different conditions of the early twenty-first century present challenges that have increasingly stretched the capacity of local authorities. These challenges include industrial restructuring, the destabilizing pressures of globalization, international immigration and associated issues of settlement and integration, gaps in the financing of infrastructure, and new commitments to sustainable development. At the same time, local governments in Canada have had to adapt to changes in federal-provincial relations ensuing from the practice of "asymmetrical federalism," linked to the perceived need to accommodate Quebec's political aspirations, and to the implications of Aboriginal treaty claims and prospective settlements of land and other resources, which will increasingly affect (and in important ways constrain) the ambit of local government. Cities and towns in Canada have thus been thrust forcefully into arenas of globalization and the pursuit of competitive advantage, while simultaneously contending with new pressures derived from domestic sources.

The pressures (and uncertainties) of change have stimulated the search for policy innovation throughout the Canadian urban system, including the possibilities of collaboration with senior governments, as well as new forms of engagement with social forces. Federal and provincial actors have likewise experimented in new forms of inter-level and multi-level governance across a spectrum of policy fields, while social forces have participated in innovative policy formulation, development, imple-mentation, and monitoring. These experiments in collaborative policy making can be examined under the rubric of multilevel governance.

The purpose of this chapter is to examine the practice of multilevel governance in Vancouver, Canada's third largest city. The externalities associated with sustained high growth rates in Vancouver, as well as the region's growing importance within national arenas, have stimulated the search for new forms of governance and innovation in policy and pro-grams. Both the scope of Vancouver's development potential, as well as the depth and complexity of governance problems, have generated new forms of governance. In some cases, the City of Vancouver has taken the lead in eliciting the participation of the federal government and social actors, while in others, senior governments have provided the initial stimulus for collaboration.

The chapter focuses on Vancouver's experiences in two policy fields: infrastructure and image building.[1] In each of these policy fields, the significance of the patterns uncovered will be discussed and lessons for public policy will be highlighted. Reference will be made to other policy fields associated with each, demonstrating facets of connectivity and interdependency between policy domains. Each policy field case will comprise both an overview of the field as a whole and a profile of a pro-gram that demonstrates some exemplary features of multilevel gover-nance through the Vancouver experience. The Canada Line rapid transit project will be examined under the policy field of infrastructure; and the 2010 Olympics will serve as the case study for image building.

The broader metropolitan context ("Metro Vancouver," formerly the Greater Vancouver Regional District, whose 2006 population was 2.524 million) will be brought in where appropriate, but the focus will be on the City of Vancouver, whose 2006 population was 578,000). There are conceptual and analytical limitations posed by this spatial framework, as the city now accounts for only about one-quarter of the metropolitan population and approximately one-third of employment, and is one of twenty-two constituent municipalities and electoral dis-tricts in Metro Vancouver. That said, the City of Vancouver continues to represent the most intense staging ground for processes of transfor-mative urban change within the metropolitan region, for policy innova-tion, and for case studies in multilevel governance across a spectrum of policy fields.

Regarding data, primary sources include a comprehensive interview process undertaken in 2007 and 2008 with twenty key decision makers (both elected and senior staff officials) drawn from each level of government and from business and non-governmental agencies engaged in processes of multilevel governance in Vancouver. The list of informants and dates of interviews are included at the end of the chapter.

The rest of this chapter begins with an overview of Vancouver's economic development trajectory, emphasizing the strategic interdependencies between development and policy innovation. Next, the chapter offers a description and analysis of multilevel governance structures and processes in the two policy fields of infrastructure and image building. Finally, the concluding section acknowledges the signal achievements of multilevel governance in contributing to Vancouver's progressive development since the 1960s, while not shrinking from recognition of the more discordant voices emanating from marginalized and oppositional constituencies.

## RECONFIGURATIONS OF VANCOUVER'S DEVELOPMENT TRAJECTORY

Over the last quarter century, Vancouver has transitioned from its post-war vocation as an urban core within a provincial staples (that is, resource-based) economy, encompassing specialized management, production, and transportation functions associated with industries such as forestry and mining, to that of a transnational metropolis, shaped by international immigration, foreign direct investment (FDI), and networks of global connectivity. The 1980s represented a decisive decade of transformation, marked by coincident processes of globalization within labour, housing and property markets, and a decline in Vancouver's traditional relationships with the resource periphery of British Columbia.[2]

The present does not mark a complete break with the past, of course. Vancouver maintains its position as principal point of export for BC's resource commodities, while service industries in the city (management consulting, legal and accounting services, engineering) still cater in part to resource sector firms. Major utilities and Crown corporations derive their primary inputs from natural resource stocks (oil, gas, minerals, water) and are still largely concentrated within Vancouver. But steady contraction in the former centrepieces of the resource economy based in Vancouver, notably those of finance, head offices and corporate control, as well as processing and production, constitutes a defining marker of change. The resource sector is no longer the principal driver of Vancouver's development, but rather just one of multiple economic plat-forms (Brownsey and Howlett 2007).

Since the deep recession of the early 1980s, the most serious down-turn since the Great Depression of the 1930s, Vancouver has consis-tently ranked among the growth leaders within the Canadian urban system.[3] This sustained high growth, accommodated within the most geographically constricted land base of all Canada's major city-regions, has generated increasingly stringent growth management policies that have created recurrent conflicts and tensions between the regional planning authority (Metro Vancouver) and the municipalities, which possess the strongest legal powers of land management. The city consistently ranks highly on international indices of quality of life and "livability" (Punter 2003, Sandercock 2005) and projects an imagery of affluence derived from the quality (and price) of housing and other markers of wealth and consumption.[4] But a closer interrogation of conditions discloses problematic externalities that include a chronic housing affordability crisis, pockets of poverty and the formation of an urban underclass, increasing development pressures on the city-region's high-value ecological stocks, and an incidence of serious crime that significantly diminishes civil order.[5]

In place of the structures of production and distribution that marked Vancouver's role as the nodal point of the provincial staples system, we find now a more diverse economy of service sector industries, firms, and labour. Belying Vancouver's notional status as a medium-size metropolis, the city-region as a whole boasts few propulsive-scale industries, cor-porate head offices, or locally-based multinationals. A well-established syndrome of foreign buyouts and takeovers of principal firms in key sec-tors (forestry, media, and advanced-technology industries), described by Richard Smith of Simon Fraser University as a "build to sell" model of enterprise, serves to attenuate the region's indigenous economic strength. As a prime example, MacMillan Bloedel, BC's largest forestry company in the postwar period, and arguably Vancouver's most important head office firm, was taken over by Noranda in 1981 and then sold to Weyerhaeuser of Seattle in 1999 (Barnes and Hutton 2009). Vancouver lost 30 percent of its head office jobs between 1999 and 2005 (Census Canada 2006).

Vancouver projects only modest power within the hierarchy of global-izing cities, but constitutes an almost classic exemplar of the entrepre-neurial small- and medium-sized economy (SME) economy, with key

Table 1

Employment by industry for Greater Vancouver, 1996, 2001, 2006

Annual averages (thousands of employees)

| | 1996 | 2001 | 2006 |
|---|---|---|---|
| TOTAL EMPLOYED, ALL INDUSTRIES | 946.5 | 1,039.1 | 1,187.1 |
| Goods producing sector | 182.2 | 176.2 | 211.9 |
| Agriculture | 5.9 | 6.6 | 10.0 |
| Forestry, fishing, mining, oil and gas | 10.0 | 5.6 | 8.1 |
| Utilities | 5.3 | 5.5 | 3.7 |
| Construction | 59.4 | 53.5 | 85.3 |
| Manufacturing | 101.6 | 104.9 | 104.7 |
| Services producing sector | 764.3 | 862.9 | 975.2 |
| Trade | 152.0 | 165.7 | 191.8 |
| Transportation and warehousing | 58.1 | 66.8 | 67.6 |
| Finance, insurance and real estate | 78.2 | 77.8 | 88.0 |
| Professional, scientific, & technical | 74.1 | 95.8 | 112.0 |
| Business, building, & support services | 37.6 | 42.7 | 54.5 |
| Educational services | 55.8 | 72.5 | 92.4 |
| Health case and social assistance | 88.6 | 96.1 | 115.8 |
| Information, culture and recreation | 50.4 | 66.3 | 70.3 |
| Accommodation and food services | 74.6 | 84.9 | 86.9 |
| Other services | 45.3 | 52.8 | 52.7 |
| Public administration | 49.5 | 41.4 | 43.3 |

Source: Statistics Canada

specializations (intermediate services, higher education, film, video and new media, and other "new economy" industries) providing a base for resiliency (Coe 2001). That said, average earnings from salaries and wages are only moderately high in the Canadian urban context (Spencer and Vinodrai 2007), so a substantial portion of the money economy of the city is derived not from the production sector, nor from wages and salaries, but from property transactions, foreign investments and other international capital flows, consumption, intergenerational transfers, and the proceeds of crime.

Vancouver's post-staples development has a defining socioeconomic correlate, expressed in emergent ethnocultural, demographic, and class reconstructions. While the professional and managerial cohorts of the "new middle class" (Ley 1996; Hamnett 2003) have been established as the dominant social aggregate since the 1970s (Table 1), new actors and groups have recently increased Vancouver's social diversity and complexity. These actors include international immigrants, particularly entrepreneurial and trading cohorts from the Asia-Pacific region; members of the "transnational elite," who possess very large incomes and

Table 2
Population group by geographical distribution and degree of concentration,
1996 and 2001, Vancouver CMA.

| | 1996 | | | 2001 | | |
|---|---|---|---|---|---|---|
| | Population | Percent in City | Index of Segre-gation | Population | Percent in City | Index of Segre-gation |
| Total – all group | 1,813,935 | 28.1 | | 1,967,520 | 27.5 | |
| Total visible minority pop. | 564,595 | 40.3 | 39.5 | 725,700 | 36.5 | 41.1 |
| Chinese | 279,040 | 50.2 | 49.3 | 342,620 | 47.0 | 50.0 |
| South Asian | 120,140 | 21.7 | 48.9 | 164,320 | 18.7 | 52.8 |
| Black | 16,400 | 30.2 | 31.0 | 18,460 | 25.9 | 32.8 |
| Filipino | 40,715 | 40.7 | 33.2 | 57,045 | 38.7 | 37.8 |
| Latin American | 13,830 | 40.5 | 36.6 | 18,765 | 34.6 | 36.4 |
| Southeast Asian | 20,370 | 61.2 | 52.0 | 28,550 | 51.5 | 48.4 |
| Arab/West Asian | 18,155 | 20.6 | 41.6 | 27,270 | 17.0 | 47.0 |
| Korean | 17,080 | 24.0 | 42.2 | 28,880 | 21.3 | 44.5 |
| Japanese | 21,880 | 36.9 | 30.4 | 24,025 | 34.4 | 32.7 |
| Visible minority, n.i.e. | 6,775 | 31.6 | 48.6 | 3,290 | 35.1 | 56.3 |
| Multiple visible minority | 10,215 | 35.7 | 35.9 | 12,450 | 36.5 | 36.3 |
| All others | 1,249,340 | 22.5 | 39.5 | 1,241,815 | 22.2 | 41.1 |
| Average, weighted | | | 41.5 | | | 43.5 |

Source: Statistics Canada, 1996 Census and 2001 Census (in Hiebert 2005)

exercise high purchasing power in the region's housing and other consumer markets; and less privileged migrants, including a small but significant refugee population who confront barriers to entry in Vancouver's
labour and housing markets. The rising number of international immigrants has reconfigured the socio-ethnic profile both of the City of
Vancouver and, increasingly, the region as a whole (Table 2), including
the emergent "ethnoburbs" situated in Richmond, Surrey, and other
suburban municipalities (Li 2006). Estimates indicate that by 2020 over
one-half of the city's population will consist of visible minorities, with
particularly dense connections to the societies, cities, and markets of
Asia. During the 1980s, Vancouver was perhaps prematurely described
as an Asia-Pacific city by politicians and others, but that descriptor now
seems in many ways apposite.[6]

Table 3
Vancouver workforce employed as professional and low-level service workers:
1971 and 2001

| Area | Professionals | | | Low-level Service Workers | | |
|------|------|------|--------|------|------|--------|
|  | 1971 | 2001 | Change | 1971 | 2001 | Change |
| Inner City | 4,895 | 23,680 | 18,785 | 4,395 | 8,010 | 3,615 |
|  | [0.168] | [0.440] | [0.272] | [0.159] | [0.159] | [–] |
| City of Vancouver | 27,060 | 86,985 | 59,925 | 24,770 | 35,860 | 11,090 |
|  | [0.164] | [0.369] | [0.205] | [0.162] | [0.162] | [–] |
| Vancouver CMA | 81,190 | 320,695 | 239,505 | 57,845 | 156,190 | 98,345 |
|  | [0.170] | [0.305] | [0.135] | [0.131] | [0.145] | [0.014] |

Notes: Number of workers, shown as a proportion of total workforce in [brackets].
Occupational definitions based on Alan Walks's (University of Toronto: 2001) groupings of census variables.
Source: Markus Moos, Department of Geography, University of British Columbia
[Calculations using Statistics Canada census tract data (1971, 2001)]

Despite the city's apparent affluence, many (including the lower ranks of the service workforce enumerated in Table 3 above, as well as the growing ranks of the homeless and unemployed) have found it difficult to establish security of tenure in Canada's most expensive housing market, which underscores residential supply and affordability as first-order policy issues in the city and Metro Vancouver Region. The deep deprivation of many Aboriginals resident in Vancouver presents perhaps the most entrenched of socioeconomic problems in a city typified by coincident processes of professionalization and polarization.

NEW FORMS OF GOVERNANCE AND POLICY RESPONSES

The structure of governance in the Vancouver region ("Metro Vancouver") includes twenty-two municipalities, whose primary responsibilities include land use regulation and local service provision. In addition, Metro Vancouver, a federation of municipalities administered by an appointed board made up of elected municipal officials, conducts regional planning and carries responsibilities for sewage and wastes, regional parks, and a modest housing program. Finally, TransLink is a separate agency primarily responsible for public transit investments and operations. The City of Vancouver operates under its own charter, which confers upon the city somewhat broader policy and taxing powers that other British Columbia municipalities have, reflecting its size and importance. Notwithstanding, just as for other units of local government in BC, the Canadian Constitution accords the Province of British Columbia jurisdiction over all of the regional and municipal authorities within Metro Vancouver, including the (rarely-invoked) power to fire municipal councils and boards, as well as financial and policy oversight powers.

Given its distance from the national capital – the locus of the federal political executive and administrative departments and policy agencies – and given also the dominance of right-of-centre provincial governments for most of the postwar era, it might be thought that Vancouver's development has been shaped largely by markets and the interests of capital. To be sure, the private sector has wielded a preponderance of influence in the city's growth. But in the postwar period, the development of Vancouver – and BC as a whole – has been increasingly supported by the state and its agencies by means of investments, development programs, and fiscal measures.

In the earlier postwar period, the central commitment of the Social Credit provincial government was to "opening up" the vast resource economy of the interior and the north. But in the 1980s, the provincial government assumed a more assertive role in the development of Vancouver and its region, marked by major initiatives in Vancouver and the Lower Mainland. This period also marked a new era in multilevel government action in support of Vancouver's development, notably investments made jointly by the federal and provincial governments in transportation (including the fixed rail transit system linking Vancouver to the inner suburbs) and in Expo '86, a "hallmark event" that signaled the city's reorientation from provincial to international arenas (Olds 2001). Changes in political representation at the local level were also influential, notably in the mayoralty of Michael Harcourt (1980–86), who pursued both a more activist economic program, and a form of international network development and outreach Patrick Smith has termed "para-diplomacy" (P. Smith 1992). Harcourt's successor, Gordon Campbell, was discernibly less interested in promoting this Asia-Pacific connection during his mayoralty, but assiduously followed Harcourt's commitment toward a larger national presence for Vancouver in the forums of policy debate and advocacy. Harcourt and Campbell each went on to become premier of British Columbia (1991–96 and 2001–11, respectively), demonstrating the larger possibilities of the Vancouver mayoralty, as well as the growing political power of the city in a province hitherto dominated by interior political figures.

## MULTILEVEL GOVERNANCE AND URBAN INFRASTRUCTURE

The provision of municipal infrastructure represents a fundamental domain of local government in Canada. Given the capital-intensive nature of most forms of urban infrastructure (roads, bridges, schools, sewerage) and the problem of infrastructure renewal generated by a natural aging process, the financial capacity of many local governments is increasingly stretched, requiring higher levels of borrowing. In the City of Vancouver, council's guiding policy is for a level of expenditures that supports the comprehensive replacement of the city's infrastructure over a 100-year period. This program evidently enjoys popular support, as no capital spending referendum has been defeated in the modern era.[7]

As the city's budgets become increasingly constrained, and as municipal taxes continue to rise at levels exceeding the rate of inflation, infrastructure priorities and choices seem likely to grow in importance as policy issues. These pressures are felt both in capital planning and on the program side of expenditures, as local governments are prohibited from running deficits on operating budgets. Vancouver's mayor and members of council are active in the national urban bodies, such as the Federation of Canadian Municipalities (FCM) and the Big Cities Mayors' Caucus, which advocate for more federal spending on municipal/urban infrastructure.

While infrastructure provision occupies a prominent position within the policy agendas of most Canadian cities, Vancouver has particularly acute infrastructure needs in housing (which is dominated by affordability issues in Canada's most expensive housing market), and in relation to the region's strategic gateway roles and functions. Both housing and gateway infrastructure in Vancouver have been the subject of multilevel governance initiatives in recent years. This chapter will focus on strategic transportation infrastructure that supports Vancouver's role as a gateway both to western Canada's interior and to the Asia-Pacific region.

Given its long-standing position as a nodal point for both internal and transnational flows of goods and people, Vancouver concentrates significant gateway infrastructure. Key features include the port, by far the largest in Canada, and Vancouver International Airport (YVR), the most important in western Canada, as well as the complex of highways, roads and rail lines, which comprise essential supporting infrastructural elements. Enhancements are financed both through capital and operating budget allocations, often involving the participation of senior governments and accompanied by memoranda of understanding (MOU) that set out development objectives, roles, and responsibilities for each level of government.

In support of Vancouver's critical gateway roles, all levels of government since the 1980s have participated in a succession of policy dialogues conducted within the rubric of the Asia-Pacific Initiative, an important expression of multilevel governance and policy discourse in the infrastructural domain.[8] Consistent with the development of other advanced international gateway centres, such as Rotterdam, Los Angeles-Long Beach, and Singapore, expenditures are increasingly required within the services (or human capital) component of gateway installations; these include management, marketing, engineering, logistics, IT, and other technical support services essential to efficiency, productivity, and competitiveness.[9] These inter-level and multilevel governance programs and policies are crucial in augmenting Vancouver's development capacity, but major infrastructure for cities, both for municipal needs as well as for gateway functions, remains a "lumpy" portfolio of spending, requiring huge one-time borrowing transactions as well as long term repayment horizons.[10]

Multilevel governance arrangements for the development of Vancouver's strategic transportation and trading functions arise in the context of complex divisions of federal, provincial, and local (regional and municipal) jurisdictions, responsibilities and powers in these spheres; the strategic importance of Metro Vancouver's transportation systems for each level of government; and the heavy cost implications of major infrastructure provision. Transportation infrastructure planning has a significant regional dimension and includes major installations located in suburban municipalities, notably the Vancouver International Airport in Richmond and the Roberts Bank Superport in Delta. At this broader regional level, Metro Vancouver has broad responsibilities for regional structure planning, land use, the environment, secondary waste treatment, and a limited economic development role. A separate regional body, TransLink, is responsible for strategic transportation and transit planning. The administrative division of land use and transportation planning responsibilities in the Vancouver region was contentious from the start, and, in the view of many, leads inevitably to inter-agency conflict, lack of congruence in investments and programming, and suboptimal results in terms of furthering the goals of creating "compact and complete" communities within Metro Vancouver.[11]

There is, at the same time, a rich record of infrastructure provision in the City of Vancouver, Metro Vancouver's central municipality, typified by formalized and ad hoc multilevel governance involvement. The city, after all, owes its establishment in 1886 both to the extension of the national rail system (Canadian Pacific Railroad) to the west coast of Canada and to the development of a major deep-water port on what is now the central waterfront, which entails large corporate and government investments. As a further point of interest, since the 1980s, Vancouver has seen the vigorous insertion of social forces into the infrastructure of its planning processes, including, in many cases, business interests, NGOs, and community-based organizations (CBOs), although their interests (and degree of influence) have not always been congruent.

An early example of the engagement of social forces in infrastructure planning was Project 200 in the 1970s, which was to involve the construction of a major freeway through the northern part of the city, to be cut through Strathcona and the Downtown Eastside, then run along the central waterfront, culminating in a major new waterfront commercial office district. Project 200 was enthusiastically backed by the private sector, including business organizations such as the Vancouver Board of Trade, as well as by Mayor William Rathie, himself a prominent businessman. An increasingly assertive and confident public opposition to this plan and its projected externalities (including, foremost, dislocations in Strathcona, a low-income community in the Downtown Eastside) contributed to the abandonment of most elements of Project 200.[12] In many ways, the increasingly sophisticated opposition to the freeway project represents a seminal experience in the evolution of social movements in Vancouver, inserting both emergent social cohorts and fresh narratives into the city's development pathway.[13]

The current Gateway Program, involving all levels of government as well as a diverse representation of social agents and actors, has likewise involved both multiple levels of government and local social forces in a complex and contentious policy process. The Gateway Program was officially launched in 2005 by the British Columbia Ministry of Transportation. Its goals include: (1) addressing congestion; (2) improving the movement of people and goods in and through the region; (3) improving access to key economic gateways through improved links between industrial areas, railways, the airport, and border crossings; (4) improving quality of life in communities by keeping regional traffic on regional instead of local streets; (5) reducing vehicle emissions by reducing congestion-related idling; (6) facilitating better connections to buses and SkyTrain, cycling, and pedestrian networks; and (7) reducing travel times along and across the Fraser River during peak periods.[14]

The multilevel Gateway Program entails capital planning for major highway expansion, including the North Fraser and South Fraser Perimeter Road projects, and a new crossing of the Fraser River (Port Mann Bridge), as well as other system upgrades, with a projected budget of $3 billion. But this ambitious infrastructure project has also disclosed a number of conflicts and tensions. These are reflected in the contrasting policy discourses enunciated by the different levels of government. The federal government, for its part, underscores the broad strategic purpose of the Gateway Program in serving the national interest, notably in facilitating the movement of goods and commodities from western provinces for export trade; while the provincial government has naturally played up the benefits for the population of British Columbia, downplaying the costs and dislocative aspects of the planned Gateway investments. The latter impacts include the opportunity costs of major capital investments in new highway, road, and bridge construction, seen by transit activists as displacing more sustainable possibilities of improving the regional public transit infrastructure.[15]

### Case Study: The Canada Line

The recently completed Canada Line (formerly Richmond-Airport-Vancouver or RAV line) rapid transit infrastructure project is a major multilevel project that also demonstrates the tensions that can emerge among actors in relation to a complex multilevel infrastructure initiative. The Canada Line entailed significant capital investments by several orders of government and governance organizations, including Vancouver International Airport, as well as the federal and provincial governments and local/regional bodies. The provincial government was the lead agency both for project funding and for advocacy, while the federal government's role was limited to that of "contributor," rather than "partner," carrying on an eighty-five-year policy tradition of Transport Canada and its federal forbears (Interview 10). The distinctive features of the Canada Line experience – including both mechanics of capital provision as well as more ideological issues – shed light on the evolution of multilevel governance in major infrastructure projects in Canada.

The management of the Canada Line project took the form of a Crown corporation of sorts (Canada Line Rapid Transit Inc.), although one Vancouver councillor preferred to see the agency as a "cobbled together" partnership that masked important differences in ideology and priorities

(Interview 12). The corporation's governance structure includes the federal and provincial governments, the regional authority (TransLink), the cities of Vancouver and Richmond, and Vancouver International Airport, which is situated on leased federal lands but operates as a non-profit private sector organization. The Canada Line Rapid Transit corporation operated as a largely cohesive body once financial commitments had been secured; but funding arrangements for the project's capital costs had to be undertaken separately, which contributed to the complexity of final approval processes. The federal monies required both ministerial commitment and approval from the treasury board, and a similar process was followed by the provincial government. In the words of a senior Transport Canada official, the federal government's role in the project entailed "no responsibility and limited risk" (Interview 10); that said, the federal government's financial support is reflected in the renaming of the RAV line to the Canada Line.

With regard to local government involvement, the City of Vancouver viewed itself as the opportunistic beneficiary of a major federal investment in transit: the monies were "on the table" for this specific project and were not available for other, competing project alternatives (Interviews 14 and 16). The City of Richmond was an enthusiastic partner, as the Canada Line represented a strategic-level development project that offered greatly enhanced transit connections between Richmond and downtown Vancouver, the business hub of the region and province as a whole. The project also allowed the proponents of the Vancouver-Airport-Richmond line to (as some saw it) "jump the queue" of established regional priorities for capital investments in fixed-rail transit. As in the case of the earlier SkyTrain project in the 1980s, federal support represented a kind of sublimated regional/industrial policy, in that the conditions of support included contracts for central Canadian suppliers (e.g., Bombardier, SNC-Lavalin, and certain Ontario firms). The Canada Line project's champions included, notably, provincial Minister of Transportation Kevin Falcon, and at the regional level, TransLink Chair (and long-time Vancouver City Councillor) George Puil. Puil in particular had been impressed by the speed and efficiency of the rail connections from Heathrow Airport in west London to the central city of the capital, including both the long-established Piccadilly Line Underground service, as well as the private sector Heathrow Express service to Paddington Station, and this experience fed into his enthusiasm for the Canada Line enterprise.[16]

The regional board approval process was far more problematic, owing to disagreements concerning the place of the Canada Line among the region's transit priorities, as well as to the internal politics within the board. The Canada Line experience included a significant escalation of inter-agency conflict as well as collaboration. As a first-level conflict, decision making for the Canada Line included a serious cleavage of values and preferences expressed at the provincial, regional, and more intensely localised scales.

The TransLink board, comprised of elected officials appointed to the board by constituent Greater Vancouver municipalities, twice rejected the (then) RAV Line (7 May and 18 June 2004). In the words of one local official, the RAV project "died" twice at the regional board level, which cited as an objection the implied subversion of established regional transit priorities.[17] Under unremitting pressure (and intense lobbying) from provincial Transportation Minister Kevin Falcon and his officials, the board approved the Canada Line on a third vote, held 30 June 2004.

The decision making for the Canada Line might be interpreted as exhibiting features of a multilevel model, but an alternative viewpoint might position it rather as a case study in more traditional power politics, derived from the asymmetries between provincial agencies and the local authorities who are subject to the far-reaching policy, regulatory and fiscal powers of the province. As Matti Siemiatycki sees it (2005), the approval of the RAV/Canada Line reflects a long-established provincial obsession with megaprojects over more incremental investments in, for example, public transit and bicycle routes, derived at least in part from British Columbia's history of resource-based industries, and from the heavy capital requirements of infrastructure provision in such a vast and mountainous territory.

### Private-Public Partnerships as Innovation in Multilevel Governance

Chief among the innovations in multilevel governance for the Canada Line was the government of British Columbia's commitment to private-public partnerships (or P3s) as both a funding model and management approach. This provincial commitment extended to the formation of a special-purpose agency, Partnership BC, a body tasked to promote P3s throughout the province. In British Columbia, P3s could be established as a means both of enlarging the sources of project capital in an era of fiscal restraint and of spreading risk across a more diverse set of actors. From the provincial government's perspective, a P3 model in the transportation domain also imparts a larger private sector (or market) dynamic to decision making, to route selection, and to operational considerations

(Interview 9). In contrast, the federal government's participation in the project through Transport Canada represented its first experience in private-public partnerships for infrastructure development, so this federal involvement constituted something of an experiment (Interview 10).[18]

The most controversial feature of the project for local social forces and for the political opposition in BC concerned the ideological underpinnings of private-public partnerships. A number of public officials interviewed for this study acknowledged the politically divisive nature of the P3 approach (Interview 16), although others saw it pragmatically as a means of achieving policy goals not otherwise feasible (Interview 19). At least some analysts asserted that, in the case of the Canada Line project, the public sector partners (and specifically the government of British Columbia and local authorities) carried a disproportionate share of the risk, driven by optimistic forecasts of likely ridership and revenue projections. Objections were also raised concerning the confidentiality of deal making, which violated principles of transparency in the allocation of public resources (Siemiatycki 2007). As for other multilevel capital projects, including the Gateway project described earlier, conflicts were most intense at the local level, where the balance of benefits and costs – and winners and losers – was most clearly evident. These conflicts included the contentious policy processes surrounding the Canada Line project, with the provincial government as the lead advocate, with regional and local governments and agencies expressing more mixed postures, and with social forces exhibiting polarized views bifurcated between business and community groups. Opposition to the Canada Line included (in addition to dissenting municipalities and TransLink board members) alternative transportation NGOs such as BEST (Better Environmentally Sustainable Transportation, www.best.bc.ca) and individual businesses along the cut-and-cover Canada Line route down Cambie Street. Many of the latter have joined a class action suit filed against the government of British Columbia, claiming costs and damages associated with the disruption to business brought about by tunnel construction.

Further cleavages among interests were disclosed at a more intensely localized level, prior to and following the implementation stage of the Canada Line project. City support for the Canada Line, shaped by a largely pro-business and pro-development council, was based in part on the plan for construction involving a bored tunnel through the city's neighbourhoods along Cambie Street, a prominent north-south thoroughfare that takes in middle-class neighbourhoods as well as substantial retail activity. Just prior to construction, however, the project management announced that rising costs (e.g., for labour and energy) necessitated a switch to a cut-and-cover method, entailing far greater disruption of neighbourhoods and local businesses. This decision was seen as a betrayal of a pact between the project sponsors and local interests, and it stimulated civic protests in Vancouver as many businesses suffered losses in sales and revenues and, in a number of cases, were obliged to relocate or to close outright.

City council evinced sympathy with the plight of those negatively affected by the cut-and-cover construction over two years, but the provincial government maintained an aloof posture, citing long-term benefits that would offset short-term costs. In 2007, Carole Taylor, the provincial minister of finance, whose riding occupies part of the area directly affected by the construction of the Canada Line, expressed a willingness to consider compensation for those bearing the largest proportion of externality costs, but the premier elected to effectively ignore the issue, beyond issuing token expressions of sympathy. In this case, at least, it might be argued that the blended policy cultures of "big government" and the private sector engaged in megaproject planning that failed to account for the interests of an important local constituency (see also Leo 2009).

## MULTILEVEL GOVERNANCE
## AND MUNICIPAL IMAGE MAKING

Governments have been interested in the potential of major projects and events to convey imageries of progress since the advent of the great international exhibitions of the nineteenth century. While the provenance of image building as conscious policy thus dates back at least a century and a half, the pressures of globalization and the relentless search for competitive advantage now lend exigency to this enterprise. Major development sites, hallmark events, and iconic buildings are projected as expressions of new development vistas. Image-building programs are often directed toward cities, regions, and urban communities, reflecting the prominence of cities in the pursuit of international competitive advantage. Cities are key basing points of globalization, both as sites and agents of change (Scott 1997). The emergence of the "new cultural economy" of the city has inserted a new instrument of image building into the repertoire of the state and presents possibilities of socioeconomic regeneration (Evans 2001). In addition, a shift in local policy models and practice from managerial to entrepreneurial governance (Harvey

1989) reflects broader civic commitments to building competitive advantage through attracting investment and human capital, induced by programs that frequently entail the production of new imaginaries.

All of these factors have prompted multiple levels of government to get increasingly involved in urban image-building exercises, both in Canada and beyond. This section of the chapter develops a profile of multilevel governance in the iterative (and recurrently contested) image-building exercises for Vancouver, which involve a rich mixture of social forces, policies, and programs. Special attention will be paid to an initiative that has recently dominated Vancouver's image-building efforts: the hallmark event of the 2010 Winter Olympic Games.

### Rebranding Vancouver: From Ecotopian Village to Transnational Metropolis

The classic imagery (or mythology) of Vancouver is as outpost of wilderness. Here referencing concepts include the depiction of Vancouver's origins as a village in the western rainforest (Oke, North, and Slaymaker 1992; Ley, Hiebert, and Pratt 1992); Vancouver as an urban centre within the "Ecotopia" region (Garreau 1981); and, latterly a repositioning of Vancouver as a "sustainable city" within "Cascadia" (Brunet-Jailly and Smith 2008), an ecological zone roughly coterminous with the Pacific North-West. The imagery presented here is one of a city that has developed almost organically from the regional biosphere and its abundant natural assets, drawing on this ecological bounty for material and spiritual sustenance.

This conceit may still hold a measure of resonance for some. But the environmentalist identity of the city has been under increasing pressure since the 1980s from a number of sources, including the decline of the staples economy and recent immigration inflows. To the extent that the natural environment comprises part of the consciousness of many Vancouver residents at all, it is likely to take the form of episodic recreation, or a fuzzy concept of BC's early history framed by boreal landscapes, mountains, and valleys.

The conscious image-building tactics of federal, provincial, and local governments are also reshaping Vancouver's foundational identity. Here we can identify a master narrative vigorously articulated by each level of government since the 1980s that repositions Vancouver as an Asia-Pacific city, or, perhaps less ambitiously, as Canada's Pacific gateway metropolis. There is, to be sure, a powerful logic to this master narrative of Vancouver as an Asia-Pacific city, expressed in volumes of trade, in the dense network of transpacific travel and communications, and in the transformative sociocultural processes shaped by immigration. These dynamics collectively produce a powerful development pathway of embedded urban transnationalism (M. Smith 2001).

As we shall see below, while governmental and other institutional resources are deployed on a large scale to construct and convey this master narrative, the increasing pluralism and fragmentation of social groups in Vancouver generates a spectrum of different voices. The City of Vancouver as a key institutional actor actively supports this increasing pluralism, proclaiming the city as a bastion of progressive multiculturalism, while at the same time projecting a localised inflection of the larger Asia-Pacific imagery. But the struggle for identity in the city concerns not only symbolic values but also conflict over resources, including funding, since imageries are powerful tools for mobilizing social forces and for making claims upon collective resources.

These conflicts are manifested in a darker imagery of contemporary Vancouver, generated by the deep deprivation and social disorder within the Downtown Eastside, with its pervasive poverty, squalor, and crime. Here we find a harsh counterpart to the glittering contemporary urbanism of the "new inner city." As the high-impact new inner city construct of condos, new economy firms and spectacle is inserted forcefully within the low-income districts of the "old inner city," insistent rebranding exercises have been launched by developers, which implicitly treat the long-standing residents of the area as mere residuals (Hutton 2008).

## Hallmark Events and Image Building in Vancouver

Since the 1980s, multilevel governance processes have performed important roles in building the central narrative of Vancouver as an Asia-Pacific city, with its defining trajectories of globalization and transnationalism. Federal and provincial investments and initiatives served to bolster Vancouver's image as an Asia-Pacific city, expressed most forcefully in the hallmark event of the 1986 international exposition, Expo '86. The reconstruction of the obsolescent industrial landscape of North False Creek converted the physical space and imagery from one of dereliction to one of globalized spectacle and consumption – an essential stimulus to the larger reconfiguration of the city's identity which followed.

Aside from the building program on-site, which produced the most tangible legacies of the era, there was also substantial expenditure on marketing Vancouver as Expo '86 host city. A budget in the range of $100 million was committed by the federal and provincial governments for international marketing, including particularly assertive programs in Asia and in California (API 1988). An important multilevel governance innovation also arose in the form of the Asia-Pacific Initiative, an agency comprising representatives of each level of government as well as private sector members and aimed at devising programs for extending Vancouver's presence in the Asia-Pacific. This multilevel governance innovation has had a lasting presence; a contemporary Asia-Pacific Initiative task force is extending the work of its 1980s predecessor, involving many of the same agencies and indeed some of the same individuals who were enlisted in the first enterprise.

By most measures Expo '86 was a success, both in material terms (the numbers of visits exceeded 13 million) and also in the production of new imageries. This was especially the case in the sphere of infrastructure, where the legacies included a new waterfront convention centre, built as the federal government pavilion for Expo '86; new international class hotels that continue to underpin Vancouver's tourism and convention functions; and the construction of SkyTrain, Vancouver's first fixed-rail rapid transit system, linking the downtown with the inner suburbs.

As with the earlier, largely abortive Project 200 plan, the city's business interests were enthusiastic about Expo '86 and its potential for stimulating new development opportunities. But the exposition also disclosed discordant community voices, as well as a measure of ambivalence among the mayor and city council. In fact, a year or so before the decision point for Expo '86 Mayor Michael Harcourt sent a letter on behalf of council to the Bureau of International Exhibitions opposing the bid, citing projected community impacts and the lack of general public benefits. There were also concerted community protests concerning the eviction of about 1,000 low-income residents from rooming houses converted to tourist hotels for Expo '86, a refrain that was heard again in the run-up to the 2010 Olympics.

### Case Study: The 2010 Olympics as an Image-Building Project

The 2010 Vancouver Olympics represent a new benchmark in the role of multilevel governance in the image-building process for Vancouver. While Expo '86 may be seen as a kind of "coming out party" for this nascent globalizing city, the Olympics provides a far more exigent force for municipal re-imaging than the class B fair – despite the sixteeen-day tenure of the Games, compared to the six months duration of the Exposition.

Indeed, the Olympic Games is widely seen as the pinnacle of the municipal image-building enterprise, the grandest of *grands projets* in the lexicon of international hallmark events. The potential risks and benefits of hosting the Olympics are commensurately great. Risks include huge cost overruns and drawn-out debt repayment, exemplified in the Montreal 1976 and Athens 2004 Olympics; benefits include the potential for financial success (as in the Los Angeles Games of 1984) and the showcasing of athletic achievements and cultural aesthetics, perhaps best exemplified in the 1992 Barcelona Olympics.

*Winning the Bid: Leading Actors and Agencies in a Multilevel Setting.* Qualities of place (environment, infrastructure, facilities, and identity) are clearly central to forming compelling bids for international hallmark events. Leadership is also critical to fronting competitive bids. But success in the ultracompetitive arena of Olympic bidding is also highly contingent on commitment to a cohesive multilevel governance approach, including social forces as well as all levels of government. The successful integration of all stakeholders in a multilevel governance structure is essential not just for assembling the enormous capital resources required to stage the Olympics, but also for mobilizing the full range of inputs (political, human, intellectual, social, cultural) associated with the staging of the modern Games; for giving voice to diverse partners and interests; and for adding weight to the bid team's dialogue with International Olympic Commission officials, including the complex backroom deal-making negotiations among delegates in advance of the final vote.

The Canadian bid for the 2010 Olympic Games benefitted greatly from the intrinsic qualities of the two principal sites, notably Vancouver, with its international cachet both as tourist destination and as a highly desirable place to live, work, and recreate; and Whistler, one of the world's premier winter sports resorts.[19] Vancouver's candidacy for the 2010 Olympics was initiated by senior political and business leaders, notably, Glen Clark, NDP premier of British Columbia (1996–99), and Arthur Griffith, scion of a well-known family of sporting investors and entrepreneurs. Interviews conducted among members of VANOC disclosed that Clark, leader of a centre-left government following the resignation of Michael Harcourt, was seen as an "early driver" of Vancouver's Olympic bid (Interview 17). And for Arthur Griffiths, the Olympics was seen as the most effective and dramatic vehicle for "showcasing" Vancouver within the international arena (Interview 16), playing upon a civic identity of outdoor lifestyles, elite athletic endeavor, and commitment to environmental values. At the municipal level, the mayor of Vancouver (Philip Owen) traveled to Lausanne to receive a briefing on bid approaches and protocols from IOC Chair Juan Antonio Samaranch and to register the city's interest in a formal bid (Interview 6). At the national level, and following a two-year site selection process, Vancouver won out over two other candidate cities, Calgary, which hosted the 1988 Olympic Winter Games, and Quebec City. Once Vancouver was selected as the Canadian candidate city for the international competition, the resources of the federal government were brought fully into play.

Elections at the provincial and municipal levels inserted new actors and issues into the Vancouver Olympic bid. The provincial election of 2001 resulted in a crushing victory for Gordon Campbell's Liberal Party, reducing the NDP to only two seats. But while the election implied both a significant ideological turn and a new policy agenda, high-level political support for Vancouver's Olympic bid represented an important continuity. It is generally acknowledged that the most influential individual in Vancouver's successful bid was not the mayor of Vancouver or other local leaders, but rather Premier Gordon Campbell, a perception supported by former mayors Philip Owen and Larry Campbell, by councillors, and by city staff interviewed for this study. One interviewee observed that "the political champion was Gordon Campbell ... [his] character is all over it: methodical, thought out" (Interview 16). Campbell's leadership on the Olympics presents a departure from his tight focus on managerial (as opposed to entrepreneurial) practices as mayor of Vancouver, a conversion of sorts, or possibly a belief that the premiership is the more appropriate platform for extravagant gestures on the scale of the Olympics.

A year after the Liberal victory in the provincial election, municipal elections in Vancouver produced an opposite shift, from centre-right to a progressive slate headed by Larry Campbell (no relation to the premier), a former city policeman and coroner. Campbell had gained election as the standard-bearer of Vision Vancouver, a newly-formed centre-left municipal party that operated in coalition with the long-established (and more radical) Committee of Progressive Electors (COPE). Campbell personally supported Vancouver's Olympic bid, but as part of the brokering of left of centre factions to defeat the right of centre Non-Partisan Association, he agreed to a special municipal referendum to gauge the extent of public support. Campbell was widely criticized for jeopardizing the bid by convening the referendum, given that no such exercise had ever yielded a favourable result in a prospective candidate city and in the almost certain knowledge that a negative response would doom the bid. But the referendum in February 2002 produced 65 percent approval for the bid, enough to strengthen Campbell's hand in going forward with the city's endorsement of the Olympic bid and to favourably impress the IOC's Jacques Rogge with the depth of public support (Interview 16). In July 2003, following a vigorous contest, the Vancouver bid emerged as the winner, with a margin of 56–53 over the South Korean bid (PyeongChang) on the final ballot.

*Multilevel Governance and the Vancouver Organizing Committee (VANOC).* The governance structure for the 2010 Olympics included as senior partners the federal and provincial governments, supported by senior staff officials. Given the scale of entailed costs, it was imperative that senior governments earn political credit for these investments of public funds. Senior government "ownership" of the Games was expressed in signage, the ubiquitous presence of logos, and, of course, in the relentless production of press releases and elaborate websites.

The Vancouver Organizing Committee (VANOC), which comprised representatives of the respective supporting governments, the private sector, and Canadian Olympic Committee members, was the primary organ of multilevel governance, with John Furlong as CEO. By and large, the board membership comprised appointees who had management experience in at least one domain (business, government, large public associations), rather than individuals drawn from the broader community (see Appendix A for list of VANOC directors). This body was responsible for strategic direction and oversight, with reporting responsibilities to the political executive. Tasks included ensuring that conditions governing the award of the Games to Vancouver were adhered to and that the chief pre-Olympics benchmarks (site development, scheduling, budgets) were achieved. The 2010 Olympics' operating budget was set at $1.76 billion, with a contingency of $77 million, and with a venue construction budget of $580 million.[20]

Aside from the day-to-day cooperation between and among agencies of the three levels of government on operations management for the 2010 Olympics, there was also collaboration on a wider range of related issues. A senior member of the federal secretariat described a multiparty mission to Beijing associated with the Olympics this way: "We had a combination of provincial officials, federal officials, city officials, BC Tourism representatives, First Nations representatives and communications consultation contractors. We all went to Beijing on a specific mission around the BC Canada Place which is a joint project between the feds and province to make the links between Beijing 2008 and Vancouver 2010 ... [this is] one of the strongest relationships I have ever seen within my career in government" (Interview 1). The structure of multilevel governance for the Vancouver 2010 Olympics therefore included both a program of site development and operations, managed by the VANOC staff, as well as extracurricular projects that brought together the resources of all parties to realize a larger portfolio of opportunities.

The City of Vancouver might be seen as the junior government partner, but as host city it stood to reap a large share of the benefits, as well as assuming a significant element of risk. Indeed, city staff identified no fewer than twenty-seven policy fields directly or indirectly impacted by the 2010 Olympics, including civic properties, housing, transportation and traffic, land use, culture, social and economic development, and policing (Interview 7). The workings of multilevel governance from the city's perspective were described by a senior official in the following terms: "We meet with VANOC formally once every two weeks to ... advance government positions ... we meet ad hoc around specific topics, dealing with live sites, dealing with issues of coordinated action between the governments and also have a direct relationship with the federal government on a number of projects, particularly the live sites where the federal government is providing direct funding to the City of Vancouver"(Interview 7).

While the multilevel governance structure for the 2010 Olympics ensured a predictable flow of senior government funds for the multiple sites and for operational expenses, a number of the City of Vancouver officials interviewed – including both elected and senior staff representatives – acknowledged the potential risks for the city of cost overruns, citing municipal limits on taxes and borrowing (Interviews 6, 7, 16, and 17). Here the spectre of the financial debt burden of the 1976 Montreal Olympics, only recently retired, was invoked as a worst-case scenario.

Apart from the regular VANOC meetings that brought together senior representatives of each level of government and appointees from the social forces constituencies, the governance model for the 2010 Olympics allowed for direct municipal-federal dialogue. Federal financial allocations to municipal government included $20 million for public venues in the downtown, and $10 million for operational costs incurred during the staging of the Games in the city (Interview 14).[21] As a senior city representative observed, the city enjoyed a relationship with the federal government that operated in some ways "to the exclusion of the provincial government and to the exclusion of other municipalities ... it's a direct relationship between ourselves and the federal government" (Interview 7). Multilevel governance in this case thus encompassed different forms of government-to-government linkages, reflecting specific responsibilities, policy capacity, and particular funding arrangements for certain spending areas.

The City of Vancouver as lead local government agency and principal host city brought important strengths to the governance structure for the 2010 Olympics. The city has a highly professional senior staff, many of whom have extensive experience in planning for major projects and events. As a senior member of the city planning department noted, "From a city perspective, the City of Vancouver has for twenty years managed large events, whether they were Olympics, Expos, G8 conferences or large development projects and that sort of thing ... It is a very efficient government ... very well organized to do what it has to do" (Interview 15). Evincing perhaps just a touch of municipal hubris, this senior official suggested that "In many ways, for the Olympics, for the City of Vancouver it was just business as usual" (Interview 15).

As in other image-building efforts on this scale, the role of social forces was important in many ways and again presented features of complementarity and conflict. Preparations for the Vancouver Olympics included, more or less formally, legions of social actors incorporated within rubrics of the "inclusive Games," as well as those who represented putative ideals of the Olympics (leaders among the arts and culture, community leaders, members of the elite athletic community, influential media professionals, and others). At the same time, there were also numerous oppositional social forces, either those excluded from the benefits of the Games, those threatened with physical displacement, and still others reflexively opposed to the concept of the Games, its costs, and its grandiose image making.

As a former mayor observed, the scale of the Olympics as a public enterprise ensures that "all social forces are in play ... We have people that are involved with poverty, mental illness, drugs, urban Aboriginals" (Interview 16). That said, a number of interviewees suggested that many if not most of the social forces could be situated within the rubrics of the "green agenda" and public housing advocacy. In the words of a former Vancouver city manager, "The housing agenda was here before the

Olympics and it will be here after the Olympics, but the Olympics is a very convenient issue, because it will create some pressure on housing in the first place. But it's also a nice opportunity to say, 'well, do you really want the world coming to Vancouver with all these people on the street?'" (Interview 17). The formation of social forces around the issues of sustainability and housing comprised a coalition of environmental and social activists committed to shaping both the substantive outcomes and symbolic markers of the 2010 Vancouver Olympics.

*Branding and Image Building for the 2010 Olympics.* Image building represents a crucial element of the Vancouver 2010 Olympics in two ways: first, in the deployment of key features of identity (environment, historical legacies, culture, amenities) in the service of constructing a competitive bid (i.e., the "process"); and, secondly, in articulating a successful Olympic bid as a strategic instrument for the development of Vancouver and Whistler (the "product"). For both phases, *sustainable development* (or sustainability) was deployed as the foundational concept in the narrative. This imbued the bid with a clear ecological emphasis, but also embodied socioeconomic and cultural content keyed to the IOC audience as well as to local constituencies beyond the elite athletic cohort.

As one actor observed, the link between sports and sustainability was central to a successful bid (Interview 2). A former federal Liberal cabinet minister with responsibilities for the Games asserted that the intention of the bid committee was that the Vancouver Olympics "was going to be the most sustainable Olympics ever" (Interview 5). Another interviewee noted that "we sort of went with the beautiful BC theme, sort of Bryan Adams tugging at our hearts with songs ... something like that" (Interview 16). Beyond this articulation of overarching principles, other interviewees suggested a grandiose agenda of local, provincial, and national benefits and outcomes from a successful Olympics: "we want Vancouver, Whistler, British Columbia, Canada to be a better place [*sic*] because of the Games" (Interview 2).

The sustainability message thus incorporated an ambitious social program: at the local level, the Olympics were to be "an agent to assist the revitalization of the Downtown Eastside, with no displacement ... There would be social housing, assistance for the homeless, for people with drug addiction who make up a good proportion of the homeless" (Interview 5). Apart from the good intentions inherent in such a declaration, Olympic officials were concerned that ignoring the Downtown Eastside would compromise the positive image-building program.

As might be expected in a jurisdiction with a long history of social activism, social forces included community-based organizations opposed to the 2010 Vancouver Winter Olympic Games, as well as the national Bread Not Circuses coalition.[22] These local groups included the No Games! group, a coalition that promoted a petition against the convening of the Games in Vancouver on the grounds of financial costs and the displacement of social spending priorities, as well as the First Nations group No 2010 Olympics on Stolen Native Land (Resist the 2010 Corporate Circus).[23] The British Columbia Teachers' Federation complained recurrently about the costs of the 2010 Olympics, contending that provincial resources could have been better allocated to public education programs. Vocal opposition was also mounted by more localized social forces concerned about community or neighbourhood-scale impacts, exemplified by West Vancouver residents opposed to the widening of the Sea-to-Sky Vancouver-Whistler Highway (a major capital project associated with the 2010 Games).

That said, opposition to the 2010 Vancouver Winter Olympics was less vociferous than might be expected, certainly in political terms. Here we can cite the Vancouver referendum that generated a two-thirds approval rating, which conferred a measure of broader public acceptance of the Vancouver 2010 bid. Mayor Larry Campbell's personal endorsement of the 2010 Olympic bid also served to mute opposition from centre-left factions with the City of Vancouver, although the more radical Committee of Progressive Electors (COPE) municipal party has sustained objections to the Games. And the early support for a Vancouver Olympic bid enunciated by former New Democratic Party Premier Glen Clark also likely weakened the NDP's potential for effectively opposing the Vancouver bid.

*Image Building in Situ: South East False Creek and the Olympic Village.* Like other Olympics, the Vancouver 2010 Games encompassed multiple sites, both within the metropolitan area and also in Whistler, 120 km north of the city. Each site carried its own narrative of place making, re-making and re-imaging. Here we will discuss South East False Creek, site of the 2010 Olympic Village, which represents a vivid case study in multilevel governance and image building.

South East False Creek had its origins as an element of the industrial economy of Vancouver's urban core, specializing in resource processing, warehousing, and distribution. These functions were in decline by the 1960s. In the early 1970s the municipal government led the conversion of the adjacent False Creek South area from obsolescent industry to medium-density, mixed-income housing, marking the ascendancy of post-industrialism as political marker (Hutton 2004).

Although an important civic enterprise, the redevelopment of False Creek South also represented an important exemplar of multilevel governance. The city owned a large proportion of the land base for the new housing, which was funded in part by the federal Canada Mortgage and Housing Corporation (CMHC), near the high point of the federal commitment to urban housing. Further, the redevelopment of Granville Island reinforced the role of multilevel governance in this crucial terrain of the city, as the federal government owned the site, and CMHC acted as landlord. Certainly the mix of retail, restaurants, cultural activities, and public realm improvements represented a salient complement to the new housing, evoking the "convivial city" as a key feature of image building in Vancouver.

The redevelopment of False Creek South was followed by the dramatic reconstruction and re-imaging of False Creek North, initially with the clearing of vestigial industries for the 1986 Exposition, and then the comprehensive remaking of this district on the edge of the downtown in the form of the Concord Pacific Place megaproject. South East False Creek was thus the last district of False Creek to be redeveloped, and has accordingly been the subject of intense planning visions, community debates, and political discourses. Early discussions on the future of South East False Creek, shaped perhaps in part by a reaction to the forest of point towers on the north and eastern shores of the creek, identified sustainability as a key value reference. Schematics produced by city staff, consultants, NGOs, and CBOs indicated the possibilities of a true exemplar of sustainable development for the site, with a balanced land use strategy incorporating spaces for living, working, and recreating, and including encouragement for innovation in sustainable practices and technologies.

The awarding of the 2010 Olympics to Vancouver in 2002 generated a forceful new dynamic for the redevelopment of South East False Creek, in part endorsing the sustainability motif or brand, but imparting as well a new global inflection to the future trajectory of the site. According to the vision articulated by senior government and the city, the deployment of South East False Creek as Olympic Village would offer a spectacular setting for the elite participants over the course of the competition, while producing a progressive legacy of a sustainable community. As a senior city official observed, "we wanted to make a world class model of a sustainable inner city community of 15,000 people" (Interview 15). Benefits in the form of a generous allocation of social housing and public amenities for the city would include a significant "value-added"

element in the larger demonstration of sustainable development practices for a global audience.

While the senior governments representatives had an interest in the
planning for the Olympic Village (including the $30 million allocated
to the city to develop the site for the Village), planning and development included a diverse set of local stakeholders. These included sustainability and social housing advocates, who saw the potential of
leveraging Olympic funding to generate wider community benefits, as
well as prominent members of Vancouver's real estate and property
development sector. The city was eager to solicit the views of this
business constituency to determine a feasible mix of market and non-
market housing and amenity provision. When the initial plan for the
Village was unveiled, near the peak of the long Vancouver real estate
boom, the site plan included a generous allocation of social housing
and co-ops, based on the likelihood of commanding high prices for the
market housing.

Yet the global economic downturn of 2008–09, and more particularly
the financial situation for the Olympic Village in South East False Creek,
ultimately compromised some of the expectations concerning public
benefits. The parlous financial position of the lead developer and capital
provider, combined with the temporary attrition in property values in
the City of Vancouver, generated a crisis for the city. The province of
British Columbia, as key partner in the multilevel governance structure
for the Olympics, declined to provide additional capital for the project,
beyond the $30 million already allocated, although the province allowed
a special borrowing initiative on the part of the city to finance the completion of the Village. As a cost-cutting measure, the proportion of public housing units in the project was appreciably reduced, while rising
costs dictated that the level of subsidies of each public unit approached
the high end of the scale. This recent experience demonstrated again the
unique exposure (both in terms of international profile and exposure to
risk) for local governments acting as host cities for the Olympics, as well
as the contradictions associated with the distended agendas and heightened expectations generated in the construction of imageries for international hallmark events.

CONCLUSION: MULTILEVEL GOVERNANCE –
OBSERVATIONS FROM THE VANCOUVER CASE

This chapter has demonstrated some instructive features of multilevel
governance innovation in the Vancouver case, drawing on evidence from

two key policy fields: infrastructure and image building. The discussion included a description of general practices of multilevel governance in each policy field, as well as case studies for each: the Canada Line rapid transit project and the 2010 Olympics. As we have seen, the broader context for the multilevel governance innovations in these two policy fields was set by a series of industrial restructuring experiences that have materially shaped the comprehensive transformation of Vancouver since the 1960s. But while market forces have been potent agencies of change, it is clear that both *government* (elected officials and the formal mechanisms of the state at all three levels) and *governance* (in the form of partnerships and coalitions encompassing social forces) have been influential and, at times, decisive instruments of Vancouver's development.

While senior levels of government maintain core functions in Vancouver, including the program delivery responsibilities of departments and ministries, and while the city undertakes local services provision and land use management policies as central administrative functions, there is clear evidence of a tendency toward multilevel governance since the 1980s. The adoption of multilevel governance practices in a general sense adds to the quantum of resources to be brought to bear on an issue, including the multiple fiscal, regulatory, and intellectual capacities of the different levels of government. Multilevel governance is more inclusive of the increasingly diverse and plural constituencies characteristic of the multicultural state and society. And it provides more opportunity for flexibility and innovation. There are also inherent problems, which can include higher start-up and transactional costs, the potential blurring of objectives as more players are added to the mix of agencies and actors, and the likelihood of an uneven distribution of benefits and ensuing discord, as observed both in the Canada Line and 2010 Olympics case studies.

At one level, the capital resources committed by the senior governments speak at least implicitly to the growing importance of Vancouver City and region at national and provincial levels. Vancouver has enjoyed high levels of investments from senior governments over the past quarter century, despite a continuing discourse (in some circles, notably among business organizations) of the region's marginality within the national polity. The City of Vancouver in particular was acknowledged by several of the informants as a major player within intergovernmental circles, characterized by influential mayors interacting with federal and provincial ministers, supported by a mature, "highly professional" bureaucracy. Former Prime Minister Jean Chrétien's appointment of Larry Campbell to the Senate offers a confirmation of the productive relationships between political executives in a multilevel governance setting. At the same time, successive federal governments have recognized the growing economic, sociocultural, and electoral influence of Vancouver and its region and have actively sought partners across a range of policy fields, as this chapter has demonstrated. As a senior, long-serving official with the provincial government observed, Vancouver enjoys considerable political power within the councils of senior government, a status that clearly works to its developmental advantage (Interview 20).

In the Vancouver example, the practice of multilevel governance across a range of policy fields has now been well established, although the exceptionalism of the city may limit the replicability of the experiences documented herein. It is also the case that multilevel governance is often deployed either for major capital projects (e.g., transit systems) or hallmark events, such as international expositions and the Olympics, projects that generate their own peculiarities of organization, funding, and management. Yet, the practice of multilevel governance in one domain may generate benefits that carry over into others. Numerous individuals and departments in the City of Vancouver have now been involved in two or more multilevel governance processes, so there is the probability of learning about best (or at least better) practice, including goal formation, implementation, and monitoring. Indeed, a senior city official with a long record of policy experience remarked that the extended staff participation in the tri-level Vancouver Agreement for the Downtown Eastside generated valuable expertise, both in goal formation and in day-to-day management practices of dealing effectively with senior government, which has served the city well in successive multilevel governance enterprises (Interview 3).

That said, Vancouver's multilevel governance experiences are in some respects *sui generis*, involving one-time coalitions for a specific purpose. It is also the case that, as we have seen, leadership and even personality are critical factors in the formation of multilevel governance, perhaps limiting the possibility of producing multilevel governance "templates"; although, perhaps generating "typologies" might be feasible, given a sufficiently broad range of experiences.

Multilevel governance implies not an equal representation of players, but rather a model of policy and program development that reflects the unequal division of powers set out in the constitution, as well as asymmetries of power within participating social forces. In the private-public partnership model deployed for the Canada Line some novel features were observed, including the federal government's initial experience in P3s, and blending of public and private sector cultures. But the deployment of P3s is clearly contingent on market conditions. For example, as we have seen, changing economic conditions drove a shift in construction techniques for the Canada Line tunnel from a bored method to a far more disruptive cut-and-cover method, with no compensation for affected parties along the right of way. And in the case of the athletes' village (Olympic Village) described in our second case study, deteriorating economic conditions and the project's financial situation dictated improvisation in the development phase, suggesting post-Olympics legacies that seem likely to diminish the social benefits of public investments and increase the city's exposure to fiscal risk. The master narrative of image building for Vancouver as a globalizing city, shaped in no small part by multilevel governance initiatives, carries its own momentum, but at a finer level of resolution the ongoing reconstruction of Vancouver's physical realities and images exhibits less ebullient, and more discordant, storylines.

## APPENDIX A: VANOC BOARD OF DIRECTORS

| Board of Directors | Nominated by |
|---|---|
| Jack Poole | Vancouver 2010 Board |
| Peter Brown | Government of Canada |
| Michael Chambers | Canadian Olympic Committee |
| Charmaine Crooks | Canadian Olympic Committee |
| Ken Dobell | Province of British Columbia |
| Barrett Fisher | Resort Municipality of Windsor |
| Jaques Gauthier | Government of Canada |
| Jim Godfrey | Resort Municipality of Whistler |
| Rusty Goepel | Province of British Columbia |
| Gibby Jacob | Squamish and Lil'Wait First Nations |
| Patrick Jarvis | Paralympic Committee |
| Jeff Mooney | City of Vancouver |
| Michael Phelps | Canadian Olympic Committee |
| Richard Pound | Canadian Olympic Committee |
| Penny Ballem | City of Vancouver |
| Chris Rudge | Canadian Olympic Committee |
| Beckie Scott | Canadian Olympic Committee |
| Walter Siever | Canadian Olympic Committee |
| Carol Stephenson | Government of Canada |
| Richard Turner | Province of British Columbia |

## NOTES

1 Analysis of four policy fields was originally planned; however, changes in the personnel associated with the Major Collaborative Research Initiatives (MCRI) project in Vancouver precluded completion of a study of four policy fields in this case.

2 For an analysis of defining continuities and disjuncture in Vancouver's provincial roles, see T.A. Hutton, "The Innisian Core-Periphery Revisited: Vancouver's Changing Relationships with British Columbia's Staple Economy," *BC Studies* 113 (Spring 1997): 69–100.

3 The severity of the early 1980s recession in Vancouver, in which unemployment approached 14 percent, was precipitated by a global commodity price shock, the effects of which were transmitted to Vancouver from BC's resource-producing regions, and potentiated by the tight linkages between the core and periphery in a classic staples economy. Conversely, the recession of the early 1990s principally afflicted manufacturing economies in Canada, concentrated in Toronto and Montreal, and was only minimally experienced in Vancouver. Canada has largely escaped the worst ravages of the 2008 (and continuing) financial crisis, owing in part to its tighter regulatory regime governing banks and financial institutions; and, in any case, Vancouver is more closely integrated with Asia-Pacific capital circuits, which are seen to be less vulnerable to the crisis than the US and numerous European jurisdictions.

4 In their *Globe Investor* story, "Vancouver Ranks First for Net Worth," Heather Scoffield and David Ebner reported that "Vancouver has stolen Calgary's crown as the city with the highest net worth," based on real estate and other "household assets." In this calculation, Vancouver's net worth per household averages $575,826, compared to $569,926 for Calgary. The same article suggested that the principal drivers for Canada's wealthiest cities included finance (Toronto), oil and gas (Calgary), and "creativity" (Vancouver). The *Globe and Mail's Globe Investor*, 19 July 2009, http://www.theglobeandmail.com/globe-investor.

5 Although "reported crime" has experienced a decline in some categories, Vancouver suffers from one of the highest property crime rates in Canada (and indeed North America) and from ongoing gang-related violence. The city is seen by at least one scholar (Glenny 2008) as a major node of international criminal networks and activity.

6 See, for example, Barnes et al. (1992) and Hutton (1998) for accounts of Vancouver's integration within the markets and societies of the Asia Pacific and the implications for development (economic, social, cultural, spatial and physical).

7  As an example of the strength of citizen support for maintaining the quality of infrastructure in Vancouver, we can cite the case of the public approval of funding for the new Connaught (Cambie Street) Bridge across False Creek, built during the deep recessionary conditions of the early 1980s.

8  The tri-level Asia-Pacific Initiative was established in the wake of Expo '86 as a vehicle for capitalizing on Vancouver's emergent Asia-Pacific trajectory, driven notably by immigration and investment, and comprising a secretariat of senior federal, provincial, and local officials and representatives.

9  See *Building a Gateway Economy: The Role of Three Service Sectors in Western Canada*. Vancouver, The Asia-Pacific Foundation of Canada, 4 June 2008.

10 The City of Vancouver has long enjoyed the benefits of a AAA credit rating among the bond rating agencies of New York, a status buoyed by a municipal reserve of cash and land (the Property Endowment Fund) with a value of over $2 billion, but the 2008 financial crisis (and continuing recession), reduced property values, and significantly increased debt obligations incurred from the 2010 Olympics has led to a downgrade and credit watch.

11 The establishment of TransLink has presented new issues for regional governance, as Metro Vancouver is increasingly squeezed by the constituent municipalities, which enjoy primary legal powers over land use and zoning; by TransLink, which has a significant budgetary capacity that can be deployed to influence its preferences; and by the province, which has overall constitutional authority and jurisdiction over local governments.

12 A single office building at the foot of Granville Street and the Georgia Viaduct represent the only infrastructural legacies of Project 200.

13 Michael Harcourt, later mayor of Vancouver, and then premier of BC, was an early organizer of the opposition to the freeway proposal in his capacity as storefront lawyer.

14 For details, see Gateway Program description at http://www.th.gov.bc.ca/gateway/1_program.htm.

15 Local social forces opposed to the Gateway initiative include the Western Wilderness Committee, the Gateway to What group (http://gatewaytowhat.org), APE (Against Port expansion) (http://www.againstportexpansion.org), and Gateway Sucks (http://www.gatewaysucks.org).

16 One interviewee (Interview 19), a former city councillor now in the academy, described this enthusiasm as "BLT" – "boys like trains." The same interviewee observed that senior decision makers more generally "get" (the attraction of) trains, but don't "get" buses.

17 The regional (Metro Vancouver) board had ranked the RAV line as a third priority for investment in fixed rail transit, behind a line to the fast-growing

north-east corridor of the Greater Vancouver and an extension of the rapid transit system to the University of British Columbia (Interview 11).

18 Interviewee 10, a senior Transport Canada executive, also noted that since the P3 experience in the Canada Line, the federal government has participated in five new such ventures.

19 But note that only Vancouver was named as the designated candidate city, as only one is allowed for each competition.

20 See http://www.vancouver 2010.com.en/news-releases/.

21 While the federal government provided substantial funding for the construction of the Canada Line described in the previous section, this project was not directly related to the 2010 Vancouver Olympics. That said, it is widely assumed that the Olympics represented a stimulus to the construction of the Canada Line, much as Expo '86 is seen as a factor in the decision to develop the initial SkyTrain fixed-rail transit system from Vancouver to the inner suburbs of the metropolitan region.

22 Bread Not Circuses, accessed 10 September 2010, http://www.breadnotcircuses. org.

23 Resist the Corporate Circus, accessed 10 September 2010, www.no2010.com. node/207.

## LIST OF INTERVIEWS

1 Representative of federal government secretariat, VANOC, 1 November 2007.
2 Senior executive, VANOC Construction, 22 November 2007.
3 Senior planning official, City of Vancouver, 22 October 2007.
4 Senior VANOC official, Whistler, 21 October 2007.
5 Federal minister responsible for 2010 Olympics, 21 November 2007.
6 Former mayor of Vancouver (1), 26 November 2007.
7 Senior manager for 2010 Olympics, City of Vancouver, 22 October 2007.
8 Assistant deputy minister, government of British Columbia, 6 November 2007.
9 Senior manager, RAV/Canada Line project, 1 November 2007.
10 Senior manager, Transport Canada, 20 November 2007.
11 Senior planning department manager, City of Vancouver, 8 November 2007.
12 Former councillor (1), City of Vancouver, 29 October 2007.
13 Former councillor (2), City of Vancouver/TransLink director, 1 November 2007.
14 Former city manager (1), City of Vancouver, 28 November 2007.
15 Former co-director, City of Vancouver Planning, 16 October 2007.
16 Former mayor of Vancouver (2) and senator, 26 October 2007.
17 Former city manager (2)/City of Vancouver consultant, 30 October 2007.
18 Senior official, Vancouver Board of Trade, 16 October 2007.

19 Former councillor (3), City of Vancouver, 18 October 2007.
20 Senior director, Government of British Columbia, Ministry of Community
   Services, 14 October 2007.

## REFERENCES

Barnes, Trevor J., and Thomas A. Hutton. 2009. "Situating the New Economy:
   Contingencies of Regeneration and Dislocation in Vancouver's Inner City."
   *Urban Studies* 46:1247–69.

Brownsey, Michael, and Keith Howlett. 2007. *Canada's Resource Economy
   in Transition: The Past, Present and Future of Canadian Staple Industries.*
   Toronto: Emond Montgomery.

Brunet-Jailly, Emmanuel, and Patrick J. Smith. 2008. "Constructing a Cross
   Border Cascadia Region." *Canadian Political Science Review* 2:1–5.

Coe, Neil. 2001. "A 'Hybrid' Agglomeration? The Development of a Satellite-
   Marshallian Industrial District in Vancouver's Film Industry." *Urban Studies*
   38:1753–75.

Evans, Graeme. 2001. *Cultural Planning: An Urban Renaissance?* London:
   Routledge.

Garreau, Joel. 1981. *The Nine Nations of North America.* Boston: Houghton
   Mifflin.

Glenny, Misha. 2008. *McMafia: A Journey Through the Criminal Underworld.*
   New York: Knopf Books.

Hamnett, Chris. 2003. *Unequal City: London in the Global Arena.* London:
   Routledge.

Harvey, David. 1989. "From Managerialism to Entrepreneurialism: Transformation in Urban Governance in Late Capitalism." *Geografiska Annaler
   Series B – Human Geography* 88B:145–58.

Hutton, Thomas. 1997. "The Innisian Core-Periphery Revisited: Vancouver's
   Changing Relationships with British Columbia's Staple Economy." BC *Studies*
   113 (Spring):60–100.

– 1998. *The Transformation of Canada's Pacific Metropolis: a Study of Vancouver.* Montreal: Institute for Research on Public Policy.

– 2004. "Post-industrialism, Post-modernism, and the Reproduction of Vancouver's Central Area: Retheorising the 21st Century City." *Urban Studies*
   41:1953–82.

– 2008. *The New Economy of the Inner City: Restructuring, Regeneration and
   Dislocation in the Twenty-First-Century Metropolis.* London: Routledge.

Ley, David. 1996. *The New Middle Class and the Remaking of the Central
   City.* Oxford: Oxford University Press.

Ley, David, Daniel Hiebert, and Gerry Pratt. 1992. "Time to Grow Up? From Urban Village to World City, 1966–91." In *Vancouver and its Region*, edited by Timothy Oke and Graeme Wynn, 234–66. Vancouver: University of British Columbia Press.

Li, Wei, ed. 2006. *From Urban Enclave to Ethnic Suburb: New Asian Communities in Pacific Rim Countries*. Honolulu: University of Hawai'i Press.

Oke, Timothy, Margaret North, and Olav Slaymaker. 1992. "Primordial to Prim Order: A Century of Environmental Change." In: T. Oke and G. Wynn, *Vancouver and its Region*, 149–170. Vancouver: University of British Columbia Press.

Olds, Kris. 2001. *Globalization and Urban Change: Capital, Culture, and Pacific Rim Megaprojects*. Oxford: Oxford University Press.

Punter, John. 2003. *The Vancouver Achievement: Urban Planning and Design*. Vancouver: University of British Columbia Press.

Sandercock, Leonie. 2005. "An Activist Civic Agenda in Vancouver." *Harvard Design Magazine* 22 (March):36–43.

Scott, Allen John. 1997. "The Cultural Economy of the City." *International Journal of Urban and Regional Studies* 21:323–39.

Siemiatycki, Matti. 2005. "The Making of a Mega Project in the Neoliberal City: The Case of Mass Rapid Transit in Vancouver." *City* 9:67–83.

– 2007. "What's the Secret? The Application of Confidentiality in the Planning of Infrastructure Using Private-Public Partnerships." *Journal of the American Planning Association* 73:388–403.

Smith, Michael Peter. 2001. *Transnational Urbanism: Locating Globalization*. Oxford: Blackwell.

Smith, Patrick J. 1992. "The Making of a Global City: Fifty Years of Constituent Diplomacy: The Case of Vancouver." *Canadian Journal of Urban Research* 1:90–112.

Spencer, Gregory, and Tara Vinodrai. 2007. "Statistical Overview for Annual Meeting of the Innovation Systems Research Network." University of Toronto.

Statistics Canada. 2006. *Census of Canada*. Ottawa: The Queen's Printers.

# Multilevel Governance
# without Municipal Government:
# Minimalist Government in Winnipeg[1]

CHRISTOPHER LEO WITH MARTINE AUGUST, MIKE PYL,

AND MATTHEW D. ROGERS

## INTRODUCTION

The recent, burgeoning interest in multilevel governance (Young and Leuprecht 2004; Bradford 2005) is no mere intellectual fashion. It is grounded in an as yet incomplete attempt to come to grips with a world caught up in fundamental changes in the way we govern ourselves, or are governed by others. A common theme of the multilevel governance literature is that a growing recognition of the importance of respecting community difference in national policy (Leo 2006) is and will be a central feature of twenty-first-century governance.

## THE CONTEXT

To make matters more complex, and interesting, the changes that push us in this direction come at a time when municipal government is caught up in two profoundly contradictory trends. One of them, represented by such coinages as "federal urban agenda," "city charter movement," and "new deal for cities" starts from the premise that city governments are being squeezed in a vice consisting of growing challenges on one side and inadequate resources on the other. Another strand of this argument, following Jane Jacobs (1969, 1984), asserts that cities are the real source of economic growth and government revenues, but that senior levels of government are creaming off the fruits of their productivity.

In their most extreme manifestation, these ideas take the form of the Toronto City Charter Movement's demand that the city be declared "an autonomous and accountable order of government," (Big City Mayors' Caucus 2002, 3) reflected in the everyday political arena by statements such as Toronto City Councillor Joe Mihevc's urging that municipal government should expand the scope of its activities, that it should "just do [whatever it decides is important] because there's a legislative vacuum at the provincial level" (Good 2006, 105). More practically, these ideas find expression in the now widespread demand that cities be given access to more sources of revenue; in former Prime Minister Paul Martin's offer to "cities and communities" of a "seat at the table" of federal-provincial consultation; and in such municipal activism as Toronto's and Vancouver's policy initiatives in the former federal-government preserve of immigration and settlement (Good 2006).

The other, contradictory trend, backed by a century and a quarter of municipal tradition, but renewed with a fresh infusion of ideas from the American public choice movement (Bish 1971), argues for an increasingly minimalist vision of municipal government. In its earlier version, the position is that local governments are primarily administrative, not political, and that their focus should be "services to property," with "services to people" being left to senior governments – the view famously parodied by former Winnipeg Mayor Glen Murray when he asked rhetorically whether municipal government should only be about "police, pipes, and pavement" (Andrew 2004).

In its modern version, the minimalist view, best represented by David Osborne and Ted Gaebler's (1992) *Reinventing Government*, holds that, in a variety of functions formerly performed by government, the introduction of market principles will lead to improved outcomes. Proponents of this view of municipal government are fond of arguing that local authorities should "get out of jobs they have no business doing," by not only eschewing as many "services to people" as possible, but also contracting out, privatizing, or simply divesting their administrations of as many regulatory activities and "services to property" as possible.

The minimalist view of the municipal role and functioning finds its strongest support in local business communities, and the degree to which it holds sway generally reflects the degree of business dominance in local politics. In Winnipeg, the social forces that most vocally and influentially advocate for the business community are the Winnipeg Chamber of Commerce, the Manitoba Home Builders' Association, and such major local developers as Qualico Developments, Ladco Company Ltd., and Genstar Development Company.[2]

## THE STUDY

The findings of this study are best understood in the context of changing intergovernmental relations, shaking out into local ideological conflict over expansive vs. minimalist local governance. The study looks at federal-municipal interactions in Winnipeg across four policy areas: Aboriginal policy, federal property, immigration settlement, and emergency planning.

The objective is to look at the structure of intergovernmental relations in those policy areas and the relevant social forces that influence, or fail to influence, the policy process; to compare and contrast policy making in the four areas; to determine what is distinct about how these policies are formulated and implemented in Winnipeg; and to draw out the lessons that can be learned.

In the process, the research tries to learn what is involved in the achievement of good policy. In order to do that, we assessed the outcome of each policy process in two ways. In the first place, inherent in any policy is a set of objectives, and our first order of business was to identify those objectives and assess whether they had been met. However, since the investigation deals with instances of multilevel governance, we also had to address the question of why this mode of administration was chosen in favour of centralized rule. A number of reasons have been offered for multilevel governance (Leo and Pyl 2007, 1–3), but a bedrock rationale is that it is deemed necessary to ensure that the policy in question be adjusted to the specific circumstances of each community, that it reflect local expertise, and that it benefit from local resources rather than being implemented in a uniform manner across the country.

In judging the appropriateness of our policies to the specific circumstances in Winnipeg, we kept two considerations in mind. First, we considered the effectiveness with which the reasonable interests and concerns of constituents were being addressed. Secondly, we proceeded on the understanding that good policy is most likely to grow out of knowledge of the impacts upon those affected by it. That understanding, in turn, requires effective communication with constituents, and sometimes cooperative action. In other words, I deemed a good policy to be one that was effectively implemented while appropriately respecting community difference. I have referred to this elsewhere as deep federalism (Leo 2006).

This study is particularly interesting because Winnipeg, which has always been a literal crossroads for Canadians travelling east to west and back, is figuratively at the crossroads of the ideological conflict over expansive vs. minimalist municipal government. Former Mayor Glen Murray briefly held centre-stage in the campaign of five major Canadian cities for a greater role in national political deliberations and more tax revenues. Under Murray's successor Sam Katz, Winnipeg has become a poster child for minimalism, a reality that is reflected in this study in the form of initiatives begun under Murray and, at this writing, lying fallow. Under both mayors, the business community was highly influential in shaping local policy, but under Murray this influence was balanced somewhat by attention to other social forces, such as the various elements of the local Aboriginal community, and advocates for causes like affordable housing and poverty amelioration. Under Katz, the balance has shifted noticeably in favour of business dominance.

The policy outcomes reviewed in these pages present a mixed picture, some notable successes, especially in the areas of immigration settlement and federal property, together with other cases in which successes are absent, less evident, or slow in coming. Mixed results such as these are to be expected. The most arresting finding, however, is that, whether deep federalism was achieved or not, the municipal government was largely absent from the policy process. Throughout the study, the city functioned, for the most part, neither as a representative of local interests in decision making, nor as a petitioner on behalf of the locality or particular local groups. At most, it served as an administrative agent for another level of government.

There was only one conspicuous success, a case in which good policy was achieved in a manner that was clearly responsive to the social forces that advocated both for immigration and for effective settlement policies. But it was the provincial government, working directly with community groups, that tapped into the knowledge and skills of the local community, while the City of Winnipeg stood aside. In this case it could be argued that the province was doing such a good job that the city's participation was unnecessary.

In three case studies of policy regarding federal property, the government of Winnipeg also stood aside, even where its participation might have been helpful in representing the interests of local social forces. In those three cases, the city could and did argue that the absence of municipal government from the policy field freed managers to do their jobs without interference. In the formulation and implementation of Aboriginal policy, the actions, or rather, for the most part, inaction, of city government is more suggestive of lack of interest. It is in the case of emergency planning that city officials served effectively as agents of the other two levels of government. But here too it could be argued that opportunities were missed for involving the public in the process of policy making and implementation, as a means of improving both implementation and representation of a variety of social forces.

I begin with a look at Aboriginal policy, proceed by summarizing briefly the findings of three case studies regarding federal property, and then turn to immigration settlement and emergency planning. I conclude with a discussion of the significance of the findings for our understanding of multilevel governance.

## ABORIGINAL POLICY

Winnipeg is the urban Aboriginal capital of Canada. That is one of those rare statements that can be made without any qualification at all. With persons identifying themselves as Aboriginal constituting 8.4 percent of the population and numbering almost 56,000, Winnipeg has the largest number of urban Aboriginals in the country. Population projections foresee Aboriginal people constituting one in four of those eligible for the workforce in 2020 (City of Winnipeg 2001b).

Winnipeg's Aboriginal community is a study in contrasts. Aboriginal people are well-represented in the community by such leaders as Wayne Helgason, executive director of the Social Planning Council of Winnipeg, and Dan Vandal, a long-serving, influential member of Winnipeg City Council.

At the same time, Aboriginal Winnipeggers face some of the city's most serious social problems. Relatively low education and employment rates contribute to inadequate housing, poor social conditions, and poverty (Canada-Manitoba-Winnipeg 2004). In 2000, Aboriginal people in the Winnipeg census metropolitan area were nearly three times as likely to be classified as low-income as the general population. While 16.2 percent of Winnipeg residents were low-income, down from 17.5 percent two decades earlier, the 8 percent of the population who identified themselves as Aboriginal had a poverty rate of 46.2 percent. Aboriginal people constituted 23.8 percent of Winnipeg's low-income population (Statistics Canada 2001, 2004, 2005).

Table 1

| Aboriginal Identity Population: Selected Metropolitan Areas | |
| --- | --- |
| Winnipeg | 68,385 |
| Edmonton | 52,105 |
| Vancouver | 40,310 |
| Calgary | 26,575 |
| Toronto | 26,575 |
| Saskatoon | 21,535 |
| Regina | 17,105 |
| Montreal | 17,865 |

Source: Statistics Canada, 2006

## Municipal Aboriginal Pathways

Former Mayors Susan Thompson and Glen Murray accepted the growing prominence of the Aboriginal community as an opportunity for the municipal government to address the problems associated with urban Aboriginals and build relationships. As a result, a number of municipal policy documents spoke to the importance of Winnipeg's Aboriginal community, including CentrePlan (Winnipeg CentrePlan Committee 1994), the Mayor's Task Force on Diversity (City of Winnipeg 2001b), and A Homegrown Economic Strategy for Winnipeg (City of Winnipeg 2001a). As well, Plan Winnipeg 2020 Vision (City of Winnipeg 2001c) identifies the goal of promoting "self-reliant Aboriginal communities" (20) and recommends a comprehensive policy addressing Aboriginal concerns.

During Murray's mayoralty, a committee was assembled to examine the issues surrounding the Aboriginal experience in Winnipeg and develop a policy framework. James Allum, a consultant, wrote the policy, entitled First Steps: Municipal Aboriginal Pathways (MAP) (City of Winnipeg 2003). MAP calls on the city to integrate Aboriginal people into the city workforce, enhance recreational opportunities in primarily Aboriginal neighbourhoods, encourage the establishment of urban reserves, and cultivate dialogue between the Aboriginal community, the city administration, and the rest of the community.

In 2004, shortly after Murray's resignation of the mayoralty to run for the House of Commons, Winnipeg City Council decided to make up to $1.4 million available for the improvement of educational and employment opportunities for Aboriginal youth in Winnipeg. That decision was not acted upon during the next three years. In 2007, Councillor Dan

Vandal presented a motion to council's Executive Policy Committee calling for the money finally to be appropriated. The committee decided to postpone a decision for another year (City of Winnipeg 2004, 2007a). In short, after a promising start, the city had, by 2007, refrained from taking action on any of the proposed Aboriginal initiatives.

## Federal Programs in Winnipeg

In order to understand the federal government role in Aboriginal policy in Winnipeg, we must consider two programs: the Winnipeg Partnership Agreement (WPA), and the Urban Aboriginal Strategy (UAS). The WPA is a tri-level agreement that took effect in 2004 and ended 2009; it was the most recent in a series of such agreements beginning in 1981 with the Core Area Initiative, intended to promote the physical, economic, and social renewal of Winnipeg's struggling inner city.

The WPA consists of four components, only the first of which, Aboriginal participation, is relevant for our purposes (Canada-Manitoba-Winnipeg 2004, 16–21). It comprises three elements: economic development; training, education and employment; and health, wellness, quality of life, and social development. The agreement promises that Winnipeg's Aboriginal community "will play a lead role in ... development and implementation" (Canada-Manitoba-Winnipeg 2004, 17). Each level of government is obligated to contribute $25 million over the period covered by the agreement.

The Urban Aboriginal Strategy, a $25 million program that was to last three years, was funded in 2003. The purpose was to undertake pilot projects in eight cities, Winnipeg included, with the ultimate objective of finding ways of narrowing the "gap in life chances" between urban Aboriginal people and the rest of the population. In 2004, funding was doubled, four cities were added, and the program was extended for an extra year, ending in March 2007 (Western Economic Diversification Canada 2007; Alderson-Gill and Associates Consulting Inc. 2005).

According to both the UAS website and the consultants' evaluation, the initial infusion of funds was intended to underwrite the testing of innovative policy ideas. During this period, a number of objectives were to be achieved. The first was to build "organizational capacity within urban Aboriginal organizations ... to enhance community leadership" (Alderson-Gill and Associates 2005, 4). At the same time, efforts would be made to develop partnerships and coordinate resources, both across government departments and within the local communities.

At first blush, these programs look very positive: $75 million in WPA funds from three levels of government distributed across four major program components and five years; $50 million from the UAS to be shared by twelve cities over four years; encouragement of innovative policy ideas to address deep-seated and persistent problems. However, there are problems.

The first is the idea of using a federal government program to build "organizational capacity [and] ... enhance community leadership." Winnipeg's Aboriginal leaders do not require the assistance of federal public servants to build their leadership skills. As noted at the beginning of this section, the community has strong leaders within provincial or local organizations involved in Aboriginal governance, as well as in other local organizations. Among the Aboriginal organizations at the provincial level are the Aboriginal Council of Manitoba, Assembly of Manitoba Chiefs, Manitoba Métis Federation, and Mothers of Red Nations. Three of these provincial organizations maintain municipal branches in Winnipeg, including the Aboriginal Council of Winnipeg, the Manitoba Métis Federation, and Mothers of Red Nations.

There are very real conflicts of interest amongst these groups – conflicts, it is fair to add, that are at least in part a product of distinctions that originate in federal legislation and are exacerbated by administration of those laws. But organizational divisions, however artificial to begin with, become real as they become freighted with economic and political interests. The challenge of achieving a unified urban Aboriginal voice is not that of building leadership capacity, but of finding ways of bridging these very real differences. It is conceivable that the federal government could provide incentives that might help motivate leaders and their followers to seek accommodations, but lessons in leadership are not what is needed.

In light of those reflections, it is not surprising to note that one of the conclusions of the consultants who evaluated the program was that "some Aboriginal political organizations take exception to the UAS model because it does not devolve control of the strategy and the funds to what they see as representative Aboriginal organizations" (Alderson-Gill and Associates 2005, 47).

A second problem is the funding for the WPA and the UAS. Apparently, the actual funds available are a great deal less than they appear. Two Aboriginal leaders interviewed for this study complained about the Aboriginal component of the WPA being a "shell game" or "not new money," in that the wpa funds in question actually consisted of uas funding previously allocated. Two public servants involved in the administration of the program – one with the federal government and one with the province – confirmed this, and a municipal official did not deny it when asked.

The federal official said uas and wpa funds were "largely synonymous" and the provincial administrator volunteered, without being asked, that uas funds had been "re-profiled" for inclusion in wpa – a usage that looks like a good candidate for inclusion in the notes on Newspeak in George Orwell's *1984*. The same is true of the $1.4 million in Winnipeg's Municipal Aboriginal Pathways funds, which were to go toward the city's share of wpa funding (Council of the City of Winnipeg 2007, 206).

Moreover, a comparison of the project profiles posted at the uas and wpa websites revealed eighteen cases in which the same projects were posted on both sites, with eleven of these receiving exactly the same amount of funding (Indian and Northern Affairs Canada 2007; Winnipeg Partnership Agreement 2007). To be sure, if a matching formula were in place, the uas and wpa funding might be identical, and not simply a duplication. However, officials of two organizations that the wpa and uas claimed to have funded identically stated independently that their organizations did not receive the funding twice.

A third problem is the way the funds are disbursed. The procedure is that organizations apply for the funding, usually in relatively modest amounts, as organizational budgeting goes. For example, $61,420 went to Mothers of Red Nations to pay a community development worker; $68,415 was allocated for an initiative for Aboriginal youth to develop leadership skills; $73,528, provided work placements for Aboriginal teacher assistants; $15,000 was paid to the Wii Chii Waa Ka Nak Indigenous Education Centre, and so forth.

It seems reasonable to view this funding strategy in relation to the inter-organizational rivalries within the Aboriginal community, referred to earlier. Instead of providing an incentive for competing Aboriginal organizations to bridge their differences, the federal government's method of funding sets them competing with each other to wage paper wars in pursuit of relatively small amounts of funding the need for which, in most cases, is probably keenly felt. If it were intended as a strategy to exacerbate divisions within the Aboriginal community, while providing an incentive for them to deal politely with government officials, it could hardly have been better designed.

To be sure, interviews with Aboriginal leaders made it clear that the cleavages within the community are deep, bitter, and tenacious, and that there were instances of Aboriginal leaders themselves thwarting government attempts to induce inter-organizational cooperation. However, Aboriginal leaders also took for granted that the government always had an "agenda," and that organizations seeking funding had to find ways of making their plans fit with funding conditions. There was no suggestion at all that the government might be persuaded to take advice from Aboriginal leaders regarding program priorities, even though the quality and depth of Aboriginal leadership in Winnipeg strongly suggests that much good advice could be obtained.

Aboriginal leaders also reported that their attempts to bend their organizations' priorities to fit funding criteria were dogged by shifting priorities and ever-changing organizational arrangements within the government. Respondents cited instances in which projects appeared to have been given the go-ahead, only later to be called off. Because of staffing changes in the administration of the UAS, one official's positive response might be vetoed by his or her successor. As a result, time and money invested in a project would be lost, and more time and money expended on re-orientation, or a new beginning.

*Evaluation*

Since the release of the Municipal Aboriginal Pathways report in 2003, the municipal government has been entirely disengaged from Aboriginal policy. The federal government, for its part, has been very much involved through the Urban Aboriginal Strategy and the Winnipeg Partnership Agreement, a colourful mixture of good and bad policy.

Included in this mixture are funding shell games, lamentably poor communications with Aboriginal leaders, and, at the same time, a significant allocation of money to meet a wide variety of very real community needs. It is reasonable to suppose that the money is enabling funding recipients to accomplish many worthwhile things. Moreover, the funding procedures, whatever their faults, do provide an incentive for community groups to define those needs for themselves, though that self-definition is distorted by government priorities that seem to draw little inspiration from local knowledge and understanding.

Whether or not the UAS and WPA succeed in meeting the UAS's objective of narrowing the socioeconomic gap between Aboriginal people and the rest of the population, therefore, it would not be fair to pronounce

them failures. But they can hardly claim a significant degree of responsiveness to public demands, and in the matter of increasing Aboriginal
peoples' control over their own lives, another objective, they probably
take a step backward.

## FEDERAL PROPERTY

Three Winnipeg case studies of the governance of federal property offer
a rare glimpse into the seriously under-researched subject of policies
regarding federal property. The cases chosen for this study were the
three federal properties in Winnipeg most conspicuously significant for
the governance and the economy of Winnipeg: Kapyong Barracks, a
former Canadian Forces base; the James A. Richardson International
Airport; and The Forks, a downtown park, recreational area, and
commercial development, located at the confluence of the Red and
Assiniboine rivers.

These properties are in varying stages of development. Development
planning of the Barracks began after the base was closed in 2004. The
administration of the airport was reorganized to make it a keen instrument of economic development in 1997 when it came under private
control; this has begun to pay off. The Forks, since its beginnings in the
late 1980s and early 1990s, has been one of the most popular public
spaces in Winnipeg. In these pages we condense a more detailed account
of the multilevel governance of these properties (Leo and Pyl 2007).

In these three cases, it is not only the municipal government, but also
the federal government that is largely excluded from policy making
and implementation. The exclusion is self-imposed. All three federal
government properties are, or will soon be, controlled by a third actor:
Kapyong Barracks by Canada Lands Company, a federal Crown corporation; the airport by the Winnipeg Airports Authority, and The Forks
by The Forks/North Portage Partnership. Before the involvement of
these third actors, each property was stagnant and either under-used or
completely unused. The Kapyong Barracks was, and still is, simply a
largely abandoned military base, waiting to be developed into a neighbourhood; the airport was little more than government-funded utilitar-
ian infrastructure; and The Forks was a set of railway tracks flanked by
abandoned industrial structures.

Our studies suggest the importance of involving a third actor in the
development of federal property. Left solely in the hands of a government department, the economic potential of such property is unlikely to

be fully realized. With management that enjoys a degree of freedom from government control, the property can exploit its economic potential more fully. For example, freed of the constraints that necessarily apply to a government department, management will be able to bypass government pay scales and seniority requirements in order to attract the employees it needs; to maintain the secrecy that is necessary in a commercial environment; and to adjust to changing circumstances without having to obtain a change in cabinet orders or legislation.

However, business management is not the same as policy making and implementation. Good policy in multilevel governance, or deep federalism, involves not only getting a job done, but also doing it in a manner that is responsive to constituents and that incorporates local knowledge. Our investigation of the three cases reinforces a lesson that has been taught many times before, but perhaps not always learned: business-like management is a necessary, but not sufficient, condition of good governance.

All three of the cases studied illustrate these points, each in its own way. With the full study available elsewhere,[3] space constraints limit us to presenting one of the cases. The case, however, effectively illustrates the major findings of the larger study.

### James A. Richardson International Airport

"If a member of the private sector is thriving, stay out of its way." This is the credo of Mayor Sam Katz, according to Alex Robinson, former senior advisor to the Winnipeg mayor and the former vice president of business development at the Winnipeg Airports Authority (WAA) (Interview 1).

Both the quotation and Robinson's previous job are indicative of relations between the city and the WAA, the governing body responsible for the operations of the James A. Richardson International Airport. Following devolution of responsibility from Transport Canada, the WAA operates as a private enterprise, and the city has respected that status, employing a decidedly hands-off approach. The assumption behind both the devolution and the city's stance toward the WAA – that an airport is better managed at an arm's length from government – has gained some support from the WAA's performance.

In 1997, Winnipeg became the seventh city in Canada with a locally managed airport. With the signing of a sixty-year ground lease agreement with Transport Canada, the WAA took over management of the airport (Winnipeg Airports Authority 2006c). Although its board of directors comprises representatives from both the public and private sectors, and it is subject to detailed conditions set out in the ground lease, it is an independent, entity, substantially removed from government oversight.

Both parties benefit from a symbiotic relationship. The city reaps the direct benefits of the federal property's payments in lieu of taxes, as well as taxes from spin-off enterprises the airport's business creates. The WAA, in turn, benefits from its close proximity to downtown, Winnipeg's geographic centrality and planning controls that ensure that development adjacent to the airport will not infringe upon its ability to operate twenty-four hours a day (Interview 1).

In pursuit of its mandate to identify and adapt to local needs, and maximize the potential of the airport, the WAA set out to develop the airport as a 24-hour intermodal transportation hub, to improve service delivery, to contribute to the development of the local economy, and to engage the community (Winnipeg Airports Authority 1997). However, the real priority was the development of the airport as a major cargo hub, a concept that had already been put forward and studied while the airport was still under government control.

The initial attempt to fulfill this mandate involved an ambitious and, as it turned out, unexpectedly expensive attempt to establish regular cargo service between Winnipeg and the Chinese cities of Nanjing and Shenzhen. This venture collapsed in the wake of the Asian economic downturn of the late 1990s (Leo and Pyl 2007, 10). After this high-profile failure, WAA shifted to a more incremental approach, involving gradual improvement of its facilities and vigorous marketing of the advantages it offers, including central location and ready access to three major North American rail lines (Canadian National, Canadian Pacific, and Burlington Northern Santa Fe) as well as the mid-continent truck routes (Crockatt 2006).

Accordingly, in 2003 the WAA built a new $4.2 million cargo apron. Allowing up to five 727 cargo jets to be loaded or unloaded at one time, it has greatly increased volumes of business (Bell 2006). WAA officials claim that Winnipeg International Airport is the twelfth fastest-growing cargo airport in the world, second in North America, and the fastest growing in Canada (Interview 2). In 2004, cargo tonnage increased by 24.7 percent from the previous year. In 2003, the percentage increase was 12.6 percent, and the year before, 2.47 percent (Winnipeg Airports Authority 2006a). As of February 2006, there were eleven all-cargo carriers using the airport, including Purolator, DHL, Cargojet, FedEx, and UPS (Winnipeg Airports Authority 2006e, 10).

The airport's strategic location and its 24-hour operation are essential to the realization of these business opportunities. Company officials claim that nearly every cargo flight between eastern and western Canada comes through Winnipeg. For example, every UPS overnight flight from Montreal to Vancouver, as well as every FedEx overnight flight from Toronto to Edmonton, comes through Winnipeg (Crockatt 2006, 2). These operations produce significant economic results. According to the WAA, over the course of a year, each four-times-weekly flight of a 727 cargo aircraft generates forty-eight jobs, $2.1 million in wages, $3.0 million in GDP, and $7.2 million in economic output (Interview 2). The WAA derives revenue from these cargo operations via a $541 landing fee, a concession fee on fuel, and an $80 apron fee for each flight (Interview 3).

Transport Canada has recognized the growing importance of the Winnipeg airport by designating it as one that air carriers are allowed to use in transit between two points outside the country. For example, a cargo aircraft on its way from the United States to Asia is permitted to stop over in Winnipeg and even store goods there, regardless of whether these rights are granted in Canada's bilateral air transport agreements (Transport Canada 2004).

It is the development of the cargo business that is the jewel in the WAA's crown. The development of land adjacent to the airport has moved forward, but at a less impressive pace. The WAA owns approximately 800 acres of developable land in four business parks, accommodating a wide variety of facilities, including petroleum company facilities, an air charter operation and a Department of National Defence facility. Plans for future development include initiatives such as an intermodal facility, e-commerce distribution centres, and foreign trade zone development (Winnipeg Airports Authority 2006d).

The WAA, therefore, is proving to be an appropriate instrument of economic development. Indeed, the WAA has already proven its mettle by showing, despite some missteps, that it is capable of producing impressive results, and likely to be able to continue to do so. Is it also proving an effective vehicle of responsiveness to the social forces with a stake in the airport? The promise in its mission statement "to provide excellent, commercially viable services and facilities in partnership with the community" (Winnipeg Airports Authority 2000, 1) could be taken to mean that it intends to do so. However, performance appears to be falling short of this aspiration.

The WAA's vehicles for public input into its decisions comprise two committees, the Community Consultative Committee and the Airport Advisory Committee on Environment. The first is an apparent vehicle for elite accommodation and has an air of seriousness about it. The second seeks input from the wider community. Its organizational arrangements are suggestive of lack of seriousness.

According to the WAA's website (Winnipeg Airports Authority 2006b), the twenty-member Community Consultative Committee includes five WAA executives and two members from the WAA's design and environment committees. The other thirteen members are representatives of community bodies that obviously have serious, substantive interests in airport affairs, including the Chamber of Commerce; Western Economic Diversification Canada, a federal government body; Destination Winnipeg, the city's tourism and economic development agency; Manitoba Transportation and Government Services, a provincial department; representatives of the Consumers' Association, a local Canadian Forces Air Command base; and representatives of labour, aviation, and aerospace interest groups. The minutes of meetings were available for download from the website. Two positions – the aerospace interest group and a representative of the City of Winnipeg – were vacant at this writing.

By contrast six positions were vacant on the seventeen-member Airport Advisory Committee on Environment, and the composition of the committee falls short of signaling an avid interest in hearing from citizens or organizations with serious concern for the environment. To be sure, two members of the committee, representatives of Friends of Omand's Creek and Friends of Bruce Park, are concerned with the preservation and development of streams located near the airport, but eleven of the seventeen positions were reserved for appointees of local MPs and MLAs. Four of these positions were vacant, as were those that were to be appointed by the City of Winnipeg and the Chamber of Commerce. The remaining two appointees were non-executive employees of the WAA, and the committee's minutes were not available on the website.

On this evidence, it is reasonable to suggest that the WAA is less than enthusiastic about responsiveness to the concerns of the community at large. Appointees of MPs and MLAs – by far the majority of the environment committee – are unlikely to be the best choice for a critical, well-informed examination of environmental issues. The vacant positions suggest that the bodies and individuals empowered to make appointments do not have a very high opinion of the committee's importance, while the absence of minutes from the website and the fact that the WAA appointees are not executives suggests that the WAA shares that view.

Moreover, the limitation of public input into airport operations to a committee concerned with environmental questions seems too fashionable by half. Although any right-thinking person will agree that the environment represents an important concern, there are likely to be other public issues arising out of airport operations, such as airport noise, impact of airport operations on neighbourhood businesses, or opportunities in the airport for local small businesses. On the available evidence, it appears that the WAA is very concerned with maintaining good lines of communication with the local elite – as any well-run corporation would be – but not greatly concerned with input from the wider public.

For its part, the City of Winnipeg appears to be following Mayor Sam Katz's instruction, quoted a the beginning of this section, to stay out of the private sector's way.

## IMMIGRATION SETTLEMENT

Immigration to Canada, and the settlement of new Canadians, is the subject of a series of federal-provincial agreements that are different for each province, in recognition of the fact that each community presents a very different combination of opportunities and problems. For example, in 2002, the most recent year for which Citizenship and Immigration Canada (CIC) offers a tabulation, Saint John, New Brunswick, received 166 immigrants, or 0.07 percent of the Canadian total; Winnipeg received 3,810 (1.66 percent), and Vancouver received 29,922 (13.06 percent) (Citizenship and Immigration Canada 2003b). As a result, Vancouver was primarily concerned with the challenges of settling the very large number of immigrants that could be counted on to arrive at one of Canada's three primary immigrant destinations (Leo and Enns 2009), while both Saint John and Winnipeg, for reasons particular to each community, were keen to attract more immigrants (Anderson and Leo 2006; Leo and August 2009).

In both Winnipeg and Saint John, therefore, provincial nominee agreements, designed to increase the numbers of immigrants, have played a prominent role in policy making and implementation. In this section, we look at Winnipeg's Provincial Nominee Program and then turn to settlement services, summarizing the findings of a more detailed study that is available elsewhere (Leo and August 2009). It is the government of Manitoba, not municipal government, that implements the immigration settlement program. In order to understand immigration settlement in Winnipeg, therefore, we have to evaluate the provincial program. We conclude the discussion of immigration settlement with an assessment of Winnipeg's role.

### Provincial Nominee Program

Canada's provincial nominee programs (PNPs) are incentive-based strategies to draw immigrants to destinations other than Toronto, Montreal, and Vancouver. Immigrants are selected who will fill specified labour market needs, and who are deemed well suited to integrate into life in their new province. Rather than applying to CIC for permanent resident status through the federal family or independent classes, prospective immigrants apply directly to their province of choice. The province reviews applicants based on its own criteria, rather than using the federal points system, and then "nominates" those who qualify.

Provincial nominees receive priority processing by CIC, bypassing assessment at the federal level. The CIC is still responsible for criminal, security, and medical checks, but in other respects the nominating province takes over assessment of PNP applicants. Applying through the PNP offers the carrot of faster processing times, and in most cases, easier-to-meet assessment criteria. Among the categories of immigrants eligible to apply are the following (Province of Manitoba 2004b):

- *Employer Direct*: Gives top priority by the province to applicants already working full-time in Manitoba, or who have a job offer from a Manitoba employer.
- *Family Support*: Acts as a complement to the federal family class, and is for applicants who can prove that they have strong family support in Manitoba.
- *Community Support*: For applicants who have evidence of support from an ethnocultural community.
- *International Student*: For international students who have graduated from a post-secondary program in Manitoba, received a full-time job offer in their field of studies, and have a post-graduation work permit.

The Manitoba government began pursuing immigration as early as the 1970s, partly because of a consensus, at least among elite groups, that would be considered remarkable in many other jurisdictions. Because both the province and Winnipeg are growing slowly, additional population is much more likely to be seen as an asset than it is in areas that are growing more quickly (Leo and Brown 2000). Thus, the business community wants more immigration to address labour shortages; rural communities want more immigrants to live and work in their communities; ethnocultural communities want immigration to increase their numbers, and the City of Winnipeg wants more immigration to expand its tax base and population, and to revitalize decaying neighbourhoods with new residents. The right wants economic growth and more workers, and the left wants to meet humanitarian goals while building a more diverse society.

Therefore, whether under Tory or NDP governments, the provincial government was prepared to make the necessary infrastructure and resources available. Unlike many provinces, where the immigration, settlement, and language activities are split up into different departments and jammed in with files like education or social services, Manitoba has had a dedicated immigration division since 1990 that coordinates all immigration and settlement activity within one department (Clement 2002, 16).

Nevertheless, it took time and persuasion to get an agreement. In 1996, after "a couple years of serious discussion and a lot of arm-wrestling," the Canada-Manitoba Immigration Agreement (CMIA) was signed. The agreement outlines the province's objectives, direction, and priorities and provides a framework within which to negotiate the PNP and settlement service agreements, which would be developed over the next two years (Clement 2003, 198). In 1996, a successful pilot program to recruit sewing machine operators to fill Manitoba skill shortages opened the door to expansion of the program (Huynh 2004, 5), and, as it happened, the province was looking for changes. The federal selection system favoured the high-tech workers sought in central Canada, but rejected the tradespeople Manitoba urgently needed (Interview 4). In 1998, the federal-provincial negotiations paid off with the Provincial Nominee and Settlement Services Annexes to the CMIA, granting Manitoba responsibility for nominating 200 applicants per year.

The original CMIA was extended for an extra year in 2001, and on 6 June 2003 a new CMIA was signed, preserving the provincial nominee program and settlement services agreement and containing new commitments to focus on regional needs, address the issue of qualifications recognition, focus on foreign and temporary workers and international students, and "consult the Francophone minority community" on immigration issues (Citizenship and Immigration Canada 2003a).

Table 2

| Manitoba Immigration Year | Total Manitoba immigration | Provincial nominees and their families | Provincial nominee allocation per year |
|---|---|---|---|
| 1998 | 2,993 | – | 200 |
| 1999 | 3,702 | 418 | 450 |
| 2000 | 4,606 | 1,088 | 500 |
| 2001 | 4,588 | 972 | 750 |
| 2002 | 4,621 | 1,527 | 1500 |
| 2003 | 6,469 | 3,106 | |
| 2004 | 7,421 | 4,036 | Preset limits removed |
| 2005 | 8,097 | 4,619 | |
| 2006 | 9,990* | 6,641* | |

*Preliminary figures
Sources: Province of Manitoba 2001b, 2002, 2004a; Janzen 2005

The program started modestly in 1998, with an initial allocation from the federal government to nominate 200 immigrants and their families each year for two years. The program grew, according to Assistant Deputy Minister of Labour and Immigration Gerald Clement, "beyond our wildest expectations" (2003, 199). By 2003, the limit on provincial nominees had been removed, with annual figures to be determined each year in consultations between Canada and the province (Canada-Manitoba Immigration Agreement 2003b).

Provincial nominees have directly contributed to record immigration levels and population growth figures for Manitoba (Janzen 2005). In 1998, the number of immigrants was 2,993 – a figure that made the province's goal of bringing in 10,000 newcomers by 2006 seem laughable, but the goal was reached (See table). This growth in immigration levels is directly attributable to provincial nominees and their families, who comprised two thirds of Manitoba immigrants in 2006.

## Settlement Services Agreement

The 1998 agreement that set the PNP in motion also included an agreement giving Manitoba complete responsibility for the design, administration, and delivery of settlement services. Manitoba's settlement program includes orientation and counselling, adult language training, labour market access services, and assistance for other organizations that provide settlement services (Citizenship and Immigration Canada 1998). Under the Settlement Services Agreement, Manitoba receives settlement funding annually from Ottawa and is responsible for the design, delivery, and administration of all settlement service programming in the province. In the first two years of the program, Manitoba received $3.55 million per year. In the 2001–02 fiscal year, this was increased to $5.32 million, due to the growth in Manitoba's immigrant intake (Province of Manitoba 2001a). The province has also committed substantial funding of its own to immigration and settlement. For example, in fiscal 2004–05 the provincial immigration and settlement budget was $11,111,800 (Morrish 2004).

In the rest of the country, with the exception of British Columbia and Quebec, which also have settlement agreements, the federal government is responsible for the delivery and funding of all settlement programs. In doing so, it comes in for a considerable amount of criticism, criticism that is suggestive of the problems that arise in trying to apply uniform national criteria to diverse localities, and therefore illustrative of the importance of deep federalism in this policy domain. For example, in a 2003 report, the House of Commons Standing Committee on Citizenship and Immigration reported complaints that the CIC micromanaged the operations of settlement providers, and that "any variation from the line-by-line authorizations leads to significant administrative difficulties" (Standing Committee on Citizenship and Immigration 2003, 9). CIC has also been criticized for focusing too much on meeting "front-end" settlement needs, at the expense of long-run integration needs (Omidvar and Richmond 2003, 8). In Manitoba, the provincial government's management of settlement, backed by widespread public support, has produced a much more favourable result.

Prominent representatives of the settlement provider community, as well as impartial outside observers, speak highly of the provincial government's programs. Although they generally agree that more funding is needed, they contend that Manitoba's performance stands out nationally. According to Tom Denton, chair of the Manitoba Immigration Council and former executive director of the International Centre of Winnipeg, Manitoba's settlement services are "probably the best in Canada." The province scored the highest on a 2002 interprovincial settlement "report card" prepared by the BC Coalition for Immigrant Integration (BCCII), obtaining a "B." Emily Shane, executive director of Jewish Child and Family Services, which works closely with the provincial government in the selection and settlement of immigrants, said the province has "made a real effort" to alleviate problems surrounding qualifications recognition (Interview 5), and Denton said that "Manitoba has a national lead here" (Interview 6). As well, the Standing Committee on Citizenship and Immigration praised Manitoba for having the only advanced language training program offered free to newcomers in the country (2003, 12).

The provincial government has developed two community-based language training programs that meet the unique needs of immigrant women and seniors. The women's program provides English instruction to mothers who find it hard to attend regular training hours, and who may lack confidence and feel isolated. The program for senior citizens recognizes that they are often isolated and lonely in a new country where they suffer a language barrier. The program teaches English at a learner-centred pace, and is as much about providing immigrant seniors a chance to meet, make friends, and get out of the house as it is about teaching English (Doan and MacFarlane 2003). Manitoba has also created an innovative occupation-specific language program, in which newcomers acquire job-specific language skills during the workday, learning while earning wages.

Such creative and innovative programs would not be possible under the federal program, service providers argue. Denton says, "settlement is a local thing requiring fine tuning to the local scene." When Manitoba took over in 1998, Denton reports that it was "an instant improvement" (Interview 6).

To be sure, more could – and, service providers insist – should be done. For example, the main provider of settlement services in Manitoba, the International Centre, had not, at the time of our research, received a funding increase in the past three years, despite steep increases in the numbers of immigrants, and have "cut their administrative staff to the bare bones." Executive Director Linda Lelande (2005) explained that well-educated people with considerable expertise are being lost to higher-salaried positions in other organizations. Shane (2005) argued that while settlement services were adequate, "huge amounts of money" were required. Shane and Lelande did not blame the province for these shortfalls. Manitoba receives its fair share of the nation's settlement budget, and, as noted, tops it up significantly with provincial funds – but the province can only add so much. In short, service providers argued that Manitoba was doing as well as could be expected, considering the resources available.

### Responsiveness to the Community

One of the most important reasons for the success of Manitoba's immigration and settlement programs – and, at the same time, one of their most important benefits – is the provincial government's early and continuing consultation with community stakeholders. Close relations with the community not only made it possible for the program to meet the requirements of deep federalism, but also laid the basis for community collaboration in achieving effective and economical operation of the program.

The Business Council of Manitoba, anxious to find a way of alleviating labour shortages, was an early supporter of increased immigration. The council's support "gave the politicians cover" by framing immigration as an economic, not political issue (Interview 7). Denton explained that "the Business Council fostered community dialogue, the Premier's Economic Council has taken advice from the community, the provincial government has listened and has acted in both predictable and ingenious ways" (Interview 6).

Consultation has gone well beyond the business community to include immigrant-serving organizations, ethnocultural community groups, rural communities, employers, residents in general, and immigrants themselves. The government made a commitment to involve community stakeholders in the immigration agreements, promising both to "encourage community involvement in identifying local settlement and integration priorities" and to "consult with regional and community representatives" (Canada-Manitoba Immigration Agreement 2003, 3.1 b; 2003b, 4.2 f). Clement (2003) argues that community involvement has played a key role in Manitoba's immigration programming, claiming that "one of the keys to our success has been an openness to partnerships with communities ... be it ethnic or geographic, [they] are an important dimension of the immigrant integration process" (199).

Manitoba's approach to immigration and settlement has been based on cultivating an understanding of those communities and their needs. In the prosperous southern Manitoba cities of Steinbach and Winkler, there is both a need for more workers and a desire on the part of many to build on German Mennonite traditions. In Winnipeg, the declining Jewish community was looking for new members, and in the flourishing Filipino community there was a demand to bring in family and friends. There are also community-specific needs to be addressed once immigrants have arrived. Employers want newcomers to learn occupation-specific language skills, and isolated groups, such as single mothers and seniors, need language training to help them break their isolation. These are examples of the case for deep federalism, program requirements that are unlikely to be met by the central government.

The attention the government pays to individual communities is repaid in kind as community organizations rally to help make programming more effective and economical. This is part of the rationale for the community support stream, designed for applicants who have evidence of support from an ethnocultural community. Ethnocultural or regional community organizations may enter into community support agreements (CSAs) with the province, thereby assuming responsibility to pre-screen potential applicants. Applicants may apply to the community support stream if they have a letter of support from a community group that holds a CSA with the province.

Only one organization, the Jewish Federation of Winnipeg (JFW) is party to a support agreement. Under their agreement, the JFW does all pre-screening, invites applicants with potential for an exploratory visit, assists applicants in filling out the application for provincial nominee status, and delivers the application to the province (Interview 8). The JFW does not receive funding for its services, having agreed to take on the assessment of prospective immigrants because it serves its own interests. In effect, the province is capitalizing on the JFW's desire for more immigrants to discharge some of its own administrative responsibilities at no cost.

Other organizations work to bring immigrants to Manitoba without being party to a support agreement. An example is the *Société franco-manitobaine*, long active in support of French-speaking immigrants (Interview 9). But whether the relations are formal or informal, ongoing community consultations can, under favourable circumstances, help to ensure outcomes that are more reflective of community demands, more efficient, and more effective. Manitoba has done a credible job of producing outcomes that are both responsive and efficacious.

### *Where is Winnipeg?*

Why is the provincial government maintaining close liaison with community groups in furthering the recruitment and settlement of immigrants? Why not the level of government whose spokespersons are fond of characterizing themselves as being "closest to the people"? The case for municipal involvement has been made by a number of commentators. The Standing Committee on Citizenship and Immigration (2002) suggest that cities should "directly recruit people to suit their particular needs" (23). Ratna Omidvar and Ted Richmond have recommended that cities should take the lead in settlement programming and act as "brokers in bringing others to the table, including federal and provincial departments ... NGO service providers, and immigrant refugee communities" (2003, 16). Elizabeth McIsaac agrees, arguing that cities should be "positioned as the designer and driver of settlement planning, while federal and provincial governments [should] take the role of facilitators and supporters of locally determined initiatives" (2003, 63).

Under former Mayor Glen Murray, a municipal activist of national stature, there were some tentative moves in that direction. One was the establishment, in 2002, of the Winnipeg Private Refugee Sponsorship Assurance Program. The city set aside $250,000 to cover refugee support in cases where the private sponsor is no longer able to meet the commitment (Citizenship and Immigration Canada 2002). Once established, this program was handed off to Welcome Place, a settlement services provider, for administration.

According to John Peters, manager of sponsorship services at Welcome Place, the idea for the fund originated when former Mayor Glen Murray turned his forty-third birthday party into a fundraiser for a Yugoslavian refugee family. Welcome Place saw an opportunity and pressed Murray for further involvement. The Assurance Program was the result. At this writing, the funds have not had to be drawn upon.

The other Winnipeg policy with some relevance to immigration is the Citizen Equity Committee. A product of Murray's 2001 Mayor's Task Force on Diversity, it possesses a broad mandate to increase diversity in the city's workplace. A more diverse workplace is likely to be one that accommodates more new Canadians.

Under Murray's successor, Mayor Sam Katz, a believer in small government, there have been no further moves toward involvement in immigration or settlement. Is Katz right not to move forward in the directions that Murray was setting? There seems to be a case for municipal minimalism in this instance. Considering the broad scope of Manitoba's provincial nominee program, with small towns prominently involved, provincial administration makes sense, especially given a provincial government that is committed to close working relationships with community groups.

In Toronto and Vancouver, matters stand differently. For both cities, the primary immigration and settlement concern is accommodating large numbers of immigrants that come of their own accord, rather than trying to attract newcomers, and their problem is not one that they share with other parts of their respective provinces. As a result, it makes sense for each of those cities to manage at least some aspects of settlement, and problems arising from settlement, in their own way. And, in point of fact, both municipalities address settlement issues in a variety of ways, including mediation of inter-ethnic conflict, funding service providers, advocating on behalf of immigrants to other levels of government, and ensuring that municipal services are provided in culturally appropriate ways (Good 2006).

That seems to make as much sense for Toronto and Vancouver as Manitoba's very different approach does for that province. The contrast between the circumstances of Manitoba on one hand, and those of Toronto and Vancouver on the other, in effect makes a compelling case for the flexible governance of deep federalism, and the accommodation of community difference that comes with it. Deep federalism is the appropriate accommodation of federal programs to local circumstances, whatever they may be. By forging an administrative machinery that effectively delivers settlement services, working closely with local communities, and drawing on local knowledge and local resources, the provincial government has earned the right to take the lead in bringing deep federalism to the administration of immigration and settlement.

## EMERGENCY PLANNING

The cases we have considered so far all involve topics of lively, ongoing political debate. Aboriginal policy, land use issues, and immigration are all regular fare in newspaper headlines. In these cases, outcomes, in terms of both effectiveness and responsiveness to constituents, have varied, but they all share one common feature: the municipal government is largely absent from policy making and implementation, either because another level of government takes the policy lead (Aboriginal policy and immigration settlement) or because the function in question has been delegated to a semi-independent public agency (federal lands).

Emergency planning is a different matter on both counts. Emergency management has not been a matter for political debate. Although emergencies are big news, day-to-day emergency planning and management is largely a routine matter and, in Winnipeg at least, such frequent emergencies as recurring floods occupy the minds of residents, but it is the emergencies themselves, and not the management of the responses, that has stimulated public discussion.

Nor has the municipal government stood aside. In emergency planning questions particular to Winnipeg, the federal government is an occasional participant and the provincial government is in control, but actual day-to-day administration is in the hands of a municipal government department. There is no reason, however, to change the analysis. As in the other cases, I will evaluate the effectiveness of policy making and implementation and consider the question of responsiveness to constituents.

Emergency management comprises four elements: prevention and mitigation, preparedness, response, and recovery (Public Safety Canada 2007b). As more Canadians move to urban centres, inclusive and comprehensive emergency preparedness becomes increasingly important. Residents of Winnipeg have been particularly aware that disaster can strike at any time because of the recurrent danger of flooding from the Red River watershed, which flows through flatlands that become giant lakes even with relatively modest rises in water levels. Despite the invaluable protection afforded by the Red River floodway – which, at flood times, diverts high water around the city – spring sandbagging is an almost normal feature of Winnipeg life. The threat is all too real. In 1997 alone, flooding in southern Manitoba, which hit the Winnipeg region particularly hard, cost a total of $817,264,000 (Public Safety Canada 2005).

### Federal Role

The federal government established the Joint Emergency Preparedness Program (JEPP) in 1980 to help ensure all levels of government are equally able to respond to emergency situations. In the last quarter-century, the federal government has contributed $135 million to various provinces and territories. The federal government cost-shares projects with provincial and territorial governments that contribute to the enhancement of emergency preparedness and a "reasonably uniform emergency response to all types of emergencies from coast to coast" (Public Safety Canada 2006b, 2007b).

The JEPP funding process is competitive (Manitoba Emergency Measures Organization n.d.). Federal contributions become payable only after completion of the project, after costs have been paid, and the receipts for those costs have been submitted by provincial or territorial governments. Randy Hull, Winnipeg's emergency preparedness coordinator, reports that this source of funds has not played a significant role in Winnipeg (Interview 10).

A far more important source of funds is the federal government's cost-sharing program for disaster assistance relief. Disaster Financial Assistance Arrangements (DFAA) payments are not made directly to individuals or communities, but are paid out to, and distributed by, the province.

Table 3
Disaster Financial Assistance Arrangements (DFAA)
per capita sharing formula

| Eligible Provincial/ Territorial expenditures | Government of Canada share |
|---|---|
| First $1 per capita | Nil |
| Next $2 per capita | 50% |
| Next $2 per capita | 75% |
| Remainder | 90% |

Source: Public Safety Canada, 2006a

Since its inception in 1970, the federal government, through Public Safety and Emergency Preparedness Canada, recently renamed Public Safety Canada, has paid out more than $1.6 billion in disaster assistance to provinces that have experienced large-scale disasters (Public Safety Canada 2006a). During a large-scale emergency, the province bears the costs up-front and is subsequently reimbursed according to a formula after expenditures have been audited. During the auditing process, should conflicts arise between federal and municipal parties, a dispute resolution service is available. Eligible costs include such things as rescue operations, security measures, communication costs, and restoration of infrastructure, businesses and personal property.

Provinces are eligible for assistance when costs exceed one dollar per capita; for Manitoba, this means costs must exceed $1.3 million. The expenses of individuals and families that are eligible for reimbursement include: transportation, shelter and food for affected livestock, security measures, infrastructure repairs, and repairs to homes (Public Safety Canada 2007a). The table 3 illustrates this funding arrangement.

Manitoba has drawn heavily on these funds. In 1997, flooding in southern Manitoba cost Canadian taxpayers $180 million in disaster assistance payments (Environment Canada 2000).

On a day-to-day basis there is very little interaction between Public Safety Canada and Winnipeg's Emergency Preparedness staff. A local official estimated that contact occurs about six times a year, and found this problematic. Canada lacks uniformity in how provinces respond to disasters, he maintained (Interview 10). Not all provinces follow federal rules regarding disaster management making it difficult to transfer emergency management skills from province to province. For example, Ottawa advocates an approach to emergencies called "site management," which emphasizes avoidance of problems, but five provinces employ "incident command" strategies, which emphasize response to emergencies.

The city official argued that the federal government should facilitate better networking between urban centres of similar sizes and encourage communication to ensure effective and unified emergency response. This networking has developed amongst smaller municipalities who have entered into "mutual aid" agreements when dealing with the development of mandatory emergency preparedness programs. Because Winnipeg is well-equipped to deal with emergency situations, it has not joined partnership agreements with other municipalities.

### Provincial Supervision, Local Administration

Unlike the federal government, which provides funding from a distance, the Manitoba government engages in the kind of detailed supervision that is typical of provincial-municipal relations. The provincial Emergency Measures Organization is responsible for coordinating the province's overall emergency plan (Manitoba Emergency Measures Organization n.d.), and Manitoba municipalities are mandated to develop and uphold emergency preparedness plans (Laws of Manitoba 2007, 8[1]d). Winnipeg, like the majority of Manitoba municipalities, has responded to the task by developing its own emergency preparedness program, which takes in all public and volunteer bodies engaged in emergency planning and response activities in the city (City of Winnipeg 2006a).

Built upon the four priorities of emergency response – mitigation, preparedness, response, and recovery – Winnipeg's plan seeks to minimize the effects of a disaster, to protect and preserve the health and property of individuals, and to maintain essential services in time of need. The plan delegates responsibilities to particular officials and civic departments during an emergency.

Carrying out these activities requires research, training, and risk analysis; networking with appropriate departments on risk mitigation programs; establishing and maintaining communication systems; and developing plans and procedures to improve emergency preparedness (City of Winnipeg 2006a). Response to an emergency involves the activation of the Emergency Operations Centre (EOC) and two committees, the Emergency Control Committee (ECC), and the Emergency Preparedness and Coordination Committee (EPCC).

The EOC is responsible for the initial phases of large-scale disaster relief and is led by Winnipeg's Emergency Preparedness Coordinator. The ECC consists of the mayor, members of the city's executive policy committee, the chief administrative officer, and a number of other city officials. It becomes involved in case of events that require EPC or council decision making.

The EPCC includes the city's chief administrative officer, the emergency preparedness coordinator, representation from a number of city departments, and – at the committee's discretion – outside agencies. This committee coordinates the activities of city departments, outside agencies, the public sector, and volunteer organizations during an emergency. It is responsible for creating an emergency response plan, advising the ECC, preparing information for public release, reviewing and updating the city's emergency plan, and staffing the EOC (City of Winnipeg 2006a).

In the absence of an emergency, municipal emergency preparedness is managed by two people, the emergency preparedness coordinator and the coordinator's assistant. Although they are formally part of the city administration, and are funded from the city budget (to the tune of $348,000 in 2006 [City of Winnipeg 2007b, 17]), it is provincial legislation that sets out the rules by which they operate. As with much else in municipal government, in practice they function as administrative agents of the provincial government.

## Evaluation

The competence and effectiveness with which emergencies are managed in Winnipeg is not a political issue. Major floods in 1979, 1993, and 1997 have contributed to a willingness and ability to respond that extends from grassroots sandbag brigades through city and provincial administrations to the political leadership.

Still, even in Winnipeg, it is those who are most vulnerable to begin with that are also the most vulnerable to the consequences of disasters. In 1997, more than 9,000 city residents were evacuated from 3,000 homes. More than 23,000 individuals received social services including shelter, food, clothing, and personal services. Had it not been for a heroic push to build the so-called Z-dike south of the city, together with a substantial measure of good luck, the numbers of those requiring evacuation could have risen to 125,000 city residents (City of Winnipeg 2006b).

It is with such eventualities in mind that Tom Urbaniak (2006) advocates the incorporation of the voluntary sector into emergency planning, arguing that in such events as Hurricane Katrina's destruction of New

Orleans – not a far-fetched scenario for those who have experienced Winnipeg floods – voluntary organizations that work with vulnerable segments of the population would have been particularly well-placed to provide advice on how to avoid the seemingly heartless abandonment of the poor that took place in New Orleans.

In Manitoba, an organization called Partners in Disaster draws on the cooperation of the Mennonite Disaster Service, Salvation Army, Canadian Red Cross, St John Ambulance, and the Christian Reformed World Relief Committee to create its own disaster relief organization. A booklet published jointly by these organizations, strikes a conciliatory note when it states, "Voluntary agencies work in close cooperation with local government disaster agencies and with Emergency Measures Organization, Manitoba, in disaster preparedness, response and recovery."

If that is true anywhere in Manitoba, it does not appear to be so in Winnipeg, where the Emergency Preparedness Coordination Committee consists of a long list of city officials, with "outside agencies" involved only "at the committee's discretion" (City of Winnipeg 2006a). The composition of the EPCC, in addition to emergency coordination staff, includes the city's chief administrative officer, together with representation from the fire paramedic service, police service, public works, utilities, public information, information technology, financial risk management, human resources, and legal services. It has the look of an administrative insiders' club.

Experience with emergencies in Winnipeg demonstrates that it is a highly competent insiders' club, but decades of experience with centralized governance also demonstrate that even competent and well-intentioned administrators can go badly wrong if they shut out the practical knowledge that comes from experience with daily life on the street and in neighbourhoods (Scott 1998).

Martin Itzkow, acting chairperson of the Voluntary and Non-Profit Sector Organization of Manitoba, has been arguing for some time that emergency management in Winnipeg lacks advice from the volunteer agencies that have the most experience in dealing with vulnerable people. He contends that management of emergencies would improve if the representatives of volunteer agencies were involved in both policy making and implementation, but says his representations have not encountered a receptive response from either municipal or provincial governments (Interview 11).

It would be unwise to rush to judgment on this issue. The fact is that emergency management in Winnipeg has been very effective, and perhaps there is a disinclination to try to fix something that is not broken. However, while the City of Winnipeg has shown very little inclination to be open to public participation, the case of immigration settlement, which we considered in a previous section, suggests that the provincial government sees things differently. In its implementation of immigration settlement it gave evidence of a lively appreciation of the way policy making and implementation can be improved by the active participation of those affected. It might pay the government to take another look at Itzkow's proposals, and reconsider them in light of its experience with immigration settlement.

CONCLUSIONS

In these pages, we have observed the workings of multilevel governance in Winnipeg in four policy areas: Aboriginal affairs, federal lands, immigration and settlement, and emergency preparedness. Throughout, we have been concerned with identifying what is distinct about the way these policies work in Winnipeg; tracking the influence, or lack of influence, of relevant social forces; comparing the workings of multilevel governance across our four policy fields; and drawing whatever lessons can be learned.

As we made our observations, the City of Winnipeg's role was strongly influenced by the fact that Glen Murray, a mayor with a strongly interventionist approach to local governance, had been succeeded by Sam Katz, a firm adherent of principles of minimalist governance. The character of the regime undoubtedly influenced our most interesting finding: that, in all the policy areas we investigated, the city government maintained a distinctly hands-off stance, except in the area of emergency preparedness, where it acted as a very effective, and tightly constrained, administrative agent of the provincial government.

Important as it may be, the question of which level of government is involved in which activities bears on procedure, rather than substance. Our investigation also addresses substantive questions, and our objective, as I note in the introduction, was to assess the outcome of each policy process, in terms of: 1) fulfilment of the objectives set for it; 2) the effectiveness with which the reasonable interests and concerns of constituents were represented; and 3) the degree to which policy formulation and implementation drew on the knowledge and resources of the local community. In other words, we judged the degree to which each policy represented good policy, or deep federalism.

In those terms, the most successful policy we studied was immigration and settlement, whose success was a result of effective policy formulation and implementation, a success that was strongly conditioned by good communication and cooperation with community organizations concerned with immigration, and intelligent adjustment of policy in response to what was learned from the community.

Since the study of multilevel governance is primarily concerned with federal-municipal relations, a particularly interesting feature of our findings regarding immigration and settlement was that neither the federal nor the municipal government were actively involved in policy implementation. Rather, the success of the policy was based on direct interactions between provincial officials and local community groups.

In our other two policy areas, Aboriginal policy and federal lands, we found varying degrees of success in meeting policy objectives, generally unmatched by evidence of responsiveness to community interests and concerns. Aboriginal policy consisted of a series of grants to community organizations, many of which undoubtedly served useful purposes. But the terms of the grants, and the objectives they aimed at were largely uninfluenced by any serious engagement with a number of often very capable, but deeply divided, local Aboriginal leaders.

In the federal lands case study of the James A. Richardson International Airport administration was in the hands of an independent agency, the Winnipeg Airports Authority. The evidence pointed to generally effective administration, and apparently meaningful liaison with local leaders, but a response to the wider community that had all the earmarks of tokenism. To put it more concretely, the Winnipeg Airports Authority seemed to be making sure that they would know about it if, say, the Chamber of Commerce or the Canadian Forces Air Command base had a concern with the airport's operation. It was less clear that they were giving any serious thought to possible concerns of nearby residential neighbours or small businesses.

Overall, our study of the four policy areas suggests that multilevel governance can perform reasonably well in meeting federal government objectives, even without great concern for involvement with and responsiveness to the local community, but that, when such concern is present, much more can be achieved. The international airport and The Forks (Leo and Pyl 2007) are both unquestionably successful, far more so than they would have been under centralized control. The Urban Aboriginal Strategy and the Winnipeg Partnership Agreement are funnelling a good deal of money to a range of community groups.

These are all worthwhile accomplishments without being extraordinary. But anyone predicting, in the mid-1990s, that by the middle of the next decade Manitoba would be admitting 10,000 immigrants a year – many of them to address serious labour shortages – and presiding over a formidable network of settlement services to help in their integration into Canadian life, would have been dismissed as a dreamer. Our findings suggest that multilevel governance, adapted to the specific circumstances of different communities, is in itself a worthwhile venture. Unquestionably, however, our most successful case owed much of its success to careful attention to community concerns and thoughtful integration of community knowledge.

## NOTES

1 The author is grateful to Robert Young and the Social Science and Humanities Research Council of Canada for financial support and for organizing the group deliberations without which this chapter would not have been possible. Thanks also to the University of Winnipeg for its ongoing support for quality research. Any shortcomings remain the responsibility of the author.

2 In the preceding paragraphs, and elsewhere in the chapter, where specific sources are not documented, statements are based on more than thirty years of participant observation of municipal and federal-municipal politics in Canada generally and in Winnipeg in particular.

3 The full study is available on the website of the Canadian Political Science Review, at http://ojs.unbc.ca/index.php/cpsr/issue/view/2/showToc.

## LIST OF INTERVIEWS

1 Alex Robinson (Senior advisor, Executive Policy Committee Secretariat), Winnipeg, 8 June 2006.

2 Christine Alongi (manager, Media and Community Relations, Winnipeg Airports Authority), 30 May 2006.

3 Lynn Bishop (general manager of Prairie Region, Winnipeg Airports Authority), 29 May 2006.

4 Mary Backhouse (immigration and multiculturalism policy analyst, Labour and Immigration Manitoba), 8 February 2005.

5 Emily Shane (executive director, Jewish Child and Family Services), 24 January 2005.

6  Tom Denton (chair, Manitoba Immigration Council), 27 February 2005.
7  Jim Carr (president, Business Council of Manitoba), 9 February 2005.
8  Evelyn Hecht (community integration officer, Jewish Federation of Winnipeg), 24 January 2005.
9  Daniel Boucher, (chief executive officer, Société franco-manitobaine), 8 March 2005.
10  Randy Hull (emergency preparedness coordinator, City of Winnipeg), 23 May 2006.
11  Martin Itzkow (managing director, Leadership Winnipeg), 7 June 2006.

## REFERENCES

Alderson-Gill and Associates Consulting Inc. 2005. *Urban Aboriginal Strategy Pilot Projects Formative Evaluation: Final Report.* Ottawa: Office of the Federal Interlocutor, Indian and Northern Affairs Canada. http://www.wd.gc.ca/ced/urban/agreements/may2004/may2004_e.pdf.

Anderson, Katie, and Christopher Leo. 2006. *Immigration and Settlement in Saint John, New Brunswick: Community Perspectives on a Federal-Provincial Agreement.* Winnipeg: Ecommons Research, University of Winnipeg. http://ecommons.uwinnipeg.ca/.

Andrew, Caroline, ed. 2004. "Interview with Glen Murray, Mayor of Winnipeg." *Our Diverse Cities* 1, Spring. Ottawa: The Metropolis Project.

August, Jim. 2006. Chief Executive Officer, The Forks North Portage Partnership. Personal Communication, June 1.

Bell, Jason. 2006. "When Freight Flies, Winnipeg's At Work." *Winnipeg Free Press*, 29 May.

Big City Mayors' Caucus. 2002. "Model Framework for a City Charter." Toronto: Federation of Canadian Municipalities. Discussion paper. 20 May. http://www.canadascities.ca/background.htm.

Bish, Robert L. 1971. *The Public Economy of Metropolitan Areas.* Chicago: Markham/Rand McNally.

Bradford, Neil. 2005. *Place-based Public Policy: Towards a New Urban and Community Agenda for Canada.* Ottawa: Canadian Policy Research Networks.

Canada Lands Company. 2006. "How Canada Lands Acquires Properties." *Canada Lands Company.* Acccessed 11 July 2007. http://www.clc.ca/en/ob/acquireProperties.php.

Canada-Manitoba Immigration Agreement. 2003a. *Annex B: Immigrant Settlement Services.* Accessed 2 July 2007. http://www.cic.gc.ca/english/about/laws-policy/agreements/manitoba/can-man-2003.asp.

– 2003b. *Annex B: Provincial Nominees.* Accessed 25 July 2007. http://www. cic.gc.ca/english/policy/fed-prov/can-man-2003b.html.

Canada-Manitoba-Winnipeg. 2004. *Agreement for community and economic development.* Ottawa: Government of Canada. http://www.wd.gc.ca/ced/ urban/agreements/may2004/may2004_e.pdf.

Canadian Broadcasting Corporation. 2006. "Talks on Kapyong Barracks Future Could Start Soon." *CBC News.* 18 September. http://www.cbc.ca/ canada/manitoba/story/2006/09/18/kapyong-clc.html.

Chartrand, Lionel, President of the Aboriginal Council of Winnipeg. 2007. Personal Communication, June 29.

Citizenship and Immigration Canada. 1998. "Canada and Manitoba Reach Agreements on Provincial Nominees and Immigrant Settlement Services." Press Release, 29 June.

– 2002. "Innovative Pilot Program to Assist Refugees." Press Release, 13 November.

– 2003a. "Canada and Manitoba Sign New Immigration Agreement." Press Release, 6 June.

– 2003b. "Facts and Figures 2002: Immigration Overview." Ottawa: Government of Canada. http://www.cic.gc.ca/english/pub/facts2002/index. html.

City of Winnipeg. 2001a. *A Homegrown Economic Development Strategy for Winnipeg.* Winnipeg: City of Winnipeg, June.

– 2001b. *Mayor's Task Force on Diversity: Final Report.* Winnipeg: City of Winnipeg.

– 2001c. *Plan Winnipeg 2020 Vision.* Winnipeg: Council of the City of Winnipeg.

– 2003. *First Steps: Municipal Aboriginal Pathways.* Winnipeg: City of Winnipeg.

– 2004. *City Council Minutes, Minute No. 389,* 19 May.

– 2006a. *Emergency Preparedness Program.* Emergency Preparedness Coordinator. *Winnipeg.ca.* http://www.winnipeg.ca/epp/default.stm.

– 2006b. "1997 Flood Facts." City Life. *Winnipeg.ca.* http://www.winnipeg.ca/ Services/CityLife/HistoryOfWinnipeg/flood/flood_facts_1997.stm.

– 2007a. *City Council, Executive Policy Committee Minutes, Minute No. 197,* 18 February.

– 2007b. *Preliminary Operating Budget: Service-based View.* Winnipeg: Office of the Mayor. 22 February.

The Clarion Team. 2006. *Comprehensive Review of Winnipeg Zoning By-Law No. 6400/94.* Winnipeg: City of Winnipeg. 17 January. http://winnipeg.ca/ ppd/zoning_6400review.stm.

Clement, Gerald. 2002. "The Manitoba Advantage: Opportunity and Diversity."
    *Horizons* 5 (2): 16–17. http://policyresearch.gc.ca/page.asp?pagenm=
    v5n2_art_07.
–    2003. "The Manitoba Experience." In *Canadian Immigration Policy for the
    Twenty-first Century*, edited by Charles M. Beach and Jeffery G. Reitz, 197–
    200. Kingston, ON: John Deutsch Institute for the Study of Economic Policy.
Colatruglio, Michael. 2006. Personal Communication, 14 June.
Connor, K. 2000. "Developer Proposes Forks Seniors' Centre." *Winnipeg Sun*,
    7 January.
Council of the City of Winnipeg. 2007. "Minutes of 20 March." Audio online.
    http://www.winnipeg.ca/CLKDMIS/MeetingAudio.asp?CommitteeType=C.
Crockatt, Michael. 2006. "Economic Importance of Air Cargo." Winnipeg:
    Winnipeg Airports Authority. Notes for a presentation to the Manitoba
    Association for Business Economics, May.
Doan, L. and S. MacFarlane. 2003. "Immigrant Seniors: No Longer a Forgot-
    ten Group." Presentation Summary. Paper presented at the National Settle-
    ment Conference 11, Calgary, 2–5 October. http://www.integration-net.ca/
    inet/english/vsi-isb/conference2/session/8a.htm.
Environment Canada. 2000. "Costs of Flooding: Disaster Assistance Payments."
    Ottawa: Environment Canada. http://www.ec.gc.ca/water/en/manage/
    floodgen/e_assist.htm#1.
Ford, Barb, Manager, Heritage Programs and Client Services, The Forks National
    Historic Site. 2006. Personal Communication, June 14.
Forks North Portage Partnership. 2006. *Annual Report 06*. Winnipeg: Forks
    North Portage Partnership. http://www.theforks.com/192.
Garrison Woods. 2006. "Awards." http://www.garrisonwoods.com/en/awards.htm.
Good, Kristin. 2006. "Multicultural Democracy in The City: Explaining
    Municipal Responsiveness to Immigrants and Ethno-Cultural Minorities."
    PhD diss., University of Toronto.
Harvey, Paul, Chief, Brokenhead First Nation. 2006. Personal Communication,
    June 16.
Huynh, Vien. 2004. *Closer to Home: Provincial Immigration Policy in Western
    Canada. Building the New West, report no. 35*. Calgary: Canada West Foun-
    dation. June.
Indian and Northern Affairs Canada. 2005. "Facts on File: Treaty Land Enti-
    tlement (TLE) in Manitoba." 8 August. http://www.ainc-inac.gc.ca/nr/prs/
    m-a2005/02693bk_e.html.
–    2007. *Urban Aboriginal Strategy.* http://www.ainc-inac.gc.ca/interloc/uas/
    stpf_e.html.
Jacobs, Jane. 1969. *The Economy of Cities*. New York: Random House.

– 1984. *Cities and the Wealth of Nations.* New York: Vintage.

Janzen, L. 2005. "Manitoba has Record Growth in Population." *Winnipeg Free Press*, 26 March.

Joshi, Ravi, Director, Real Estate, Manitoba, Canada Lands Company Ltd. 2006. Personal Communication, 17 May.

Laws of Manitoba. 2007. *The Emergency Measures Act (C.C.S.M. c. E80).* Government of Manitoba. April 2. http://web2.gov.mb.ca/laws/statutes/ccsm/e080e.php.

Layne, Judy. 2000. "Marked for Success? The Winnipeg Core Area Initiative's Approach to Urban Regeneration." *Canadian Journal of Regional Science* 23 (2):249–78.

Leo, Christopher. 2006. "Deep Federalism: Respecting Community Difference in National Policy." *Canadian Journal of Political Science* 39 (3):481–506.

Leo, Christopher, and Martine August. 2006. "National Policy And Community Initiative: Mismanaging Homelessness in a Slow Growth City." *Canadian Journal of Urban Research* 15 (1):1–21.

Leo, Christopher, and Jeremy Enns. 2009. "Multi-level Governance and Ideological Rigidity: The Failure of Deep Federalism." *Canadian Journal of Political Science* 42 (1):93–116.

– 2009. "The Multi-Level Governance of Immigration and Settlement: Making Deep Federalism Work." *Canadian Journal of Political Science* 42 (2):491–510.

Leo, Christopher, and Mike Pyl. 2007. "Multilevel Governance: Getting the Job Done and Respecting Community Difference – Three Winnipeg Cases." *Canadian Political Science Review* 1, (2). http://ojs.unbc.ca/index.php/cpsr/issue/view/2/showToc.

Leo, Christopher, and Wilson Brown. 2000. "Slow Growth and Urban Development Policy." *Journal of Urban Affairs* 22 (2):193–213.

Lett, Dan, and R.K. Thampi. 1990. "Forks Group Seeks Piece of Wall." *Winnipeg Free Press*, 26 February.

Manitoba Emergency Measures Organization. n.d. "Joint Emergency Preparedness Program." Winnipeg: Government of Manitoba. Accessed 7 June 2007. http://www.gov.mb.ca/emo/jepp/jeppintro.html.

– n.d. "Emergency Measures Organization." Winnipeg: Government of Manitoba. Accessed 7 June 2007. http://www.gov.mb.ca/emo/.

Marsh, David, Planner, Planning and Land Use Division, Department of Planning, Property and Development, City of Winnipeg. 2006. Personal Communication, 30 May.

McIsaac, E. 2003. "Immigrants in Canadian Cities: Census 2001–What Do the Data Tell Us?" Ottawa: Policy Options. http://www.maytree.com/PDF_Files/ImmigrantsInCdnCities.pdf.

Morrish, Margot. 2004. *Manitoba Immigration and Integration Policies and Programs.* Calgary: Prairie Centre of Excellence on Immigration and Integration, Calgary Node Workshop, 1 November. http://pcerii.metropolis.net/events/events_content/Morrish.pdf.

New Urbanism. 2006. *NewUrbanism.org.* http://www.newurbanism.org.

O'Brien, David. 2000. "Mayor Set to Fight Urban Village Plan Proposed for Forks." *Winnipeg Free Press*, 12 April.

– 2003. "Brokenhead First Nation Stakes Claim on Kapyong." *Winnipeg Free Press*, 16 December.

Omidvar, Ratna and Ted Richmond. 2003. *Immigrant Settlement and Social Inclusion in Canada.* Toronto: The Laidlaw Foundation.

Osborne, David, and Ted Gaebler. 1992. *Reinventing Government: How the Entrepreneurial Spirit is Transforming the Public Sector.* Reading, MA: Addison-Wesley.

Partners in Disaster. n.d. *The Manitoba Partners in Disaster Help Book.* Winnipeg: Manitoba Red Cross. 11 June 2007. www.redcross.ca/cmslib/general/ngo_booklet_october15.pdf.

Patterson, Jim, Manager of Economic Development, Department of Planning, Property, and Development, City of Winnipeg. 2006. Personal Communication, 5 June.

Perswain, Vince, Director, Long Plain First Nation Trust. 2006. Personal Communication, June 19.

Province of Manitoba. 2001a. "Canada and Manitoba Expand Immigration Agreement." News release. 27 November.

– 2001b. *Manitoba Immigration Statistics Summary: 2000 Report.* Winnipeg: Manitoba Labour and Immigration, Immigration and Multiculturalism Division.

– 2002. *Manitoba Immigration Statistics Summary: 2001 Report.* Manitoba Labour and Immigration: Immigration and Multiculturalism Division.

– 2004a. *Manitoba Immigration Facts: 2003 Statistics Report.* Department of Labour and Immigration. http://www.gov.mb.ca/labour/immigrate/asset_library/en/resources/pdf/mif_booklet.pdf.

– 2004b. "Manitoba Provincial Nominee Program for Skilled Workers." http://www.gov.mb.ca/labour/immigrate/pnp/eligible.html.

Public Safety Canada. 2005. "Canadian Disaster Database." Ottawa: Government of Canada. http://www.publicsafety.gc.ca/res/em/cdd/search-en.asp.

– 2006a. "Disaster Financial Assistance Arrangements." Ottawa: Government of Canada. http://publicsafety.gc.ca/prg/em/dfaa/index-en.asp.

– 2006b. "Joint Emergency Preparedness Program." Ottawa: Government of Canada. http://www.publicsafety.gc.ca/prg/em/jepp/index-en.asp.

– 2007a. "Guidelines for Administration of the Disaster Financial Assistance Arrangements." http://www.publicsafety.gc.ca/prg/em/dfaa/dfaa3-eng.aspx.

– 2007b. *JEPP Manual*. Ottawa: Government of Canada. http://www.publicsafety.gc.ca/prg/em/jepp/man-en.asp.

Redekop, B. 1999. "Can Condos Get Forks Out of Red?" *Winnipeg Free Press*, 17 October.

Santin, A. 1998. "Forks agency $2.4M in Red, Entertains New Housing Plan." *Winnipeg Free Press*, 28 November.

– 2002. "Housing Off The Fork's [sic] Agenda." *Winnipeg Free Press*, 5 October.

Scott, James C. 1998. *Seeing Like A State*. New Haven: Yale University Press.

St John, Peter. 2003. *"The Forks Today."* In *A History of the Forks of the Red and Assiniboine Rivers,* edited by Barbara Huck, 147–73. Winnipeg: Heartlands Associates Inc.

Standing Committee on Citizenship and Immigration. 2002. *Competing for Immigrants*. Ottawa: Public Works and Government Services Canada Publishing.

– 2003. *Settlement and Integration: A Sense of Belonging, "Feeling at Home."* Ottawa: Communication Canada Publishing.

Statistics Canada. 2001. "Community Profiles." Ottawa: Statistics Canada. http://www12.statcan.ca/english/profilo1/CP01/Index.cfm?Lang=E.

– 2004. "Trends and Conditions in Census Metropolitan Areas." Ottawa: Statistics Canada. Catalogue No. 89-613-MIE, No. 001. http://www.statcan.ca/english/research/89-613-MIE/2004001/winnipeg.htm.

– 2005. "2001 Census Aboriginal Population Profiles." Ottawa: Statistics Canada. Catalogue no. 94F0043XIE. http://www12.statcan.ca/english/Profilo1/AP01/Index.cfm?Lang=E.

Stephenson, W. 1990. "Wall Angers Natives." *Winnipeg Sun*, 27 February.

Thampi, R.K. 1990a. "Centre Plan for Forks Draws Fire." *Winnipeg Free Press*, 26 February.

– 1990b. "City Rejects Forks Centre." *Winnipeg Free Press*, 26 June.

– 1990c. "Forks Ponders New Home for German Cultural Centre." *Winnipeg Free Press*, 6 April.

Transport Canada. 2004. "New International Air Cargo Transshipment Program for Winnipeg International Airport." Press Release, 27 September. http://www.tc.gc.ca/mediaroom/releases/nat/2004/04-h051e.htm.

Urbaniak, Tom. 2006. "The Third Sector, Neighborhood Capacity, And Emergency Preparedness." Paper presented at the Canadian Political Science Association Annual Conference, Toronto, 1 June.

Western Economic Diversification Canada. 2007. *The Urban Aboriginal Strategy.* Edmonton: Government of Canada. 8 January. http://wed.gc.ca/ced/strategy_e.asp?ts=s.

Williams, R. 2000. "Forks, Condos Don't Mix: Foes." *Winnipeg Sun,* 17 April.

Winnipeg Airports Authority. 1997. "A New Era Takes Off. *Winnipeg Free Press,* 11 January.

– 2000. *Airport Development Plan Summary: Bringing 2020 into Focus.* Winnipeg: Winnipeg Airports Authority, December.

– 2006a. "Air Cargo Statistics." 5 June 2007. http://www.waa.ca/?pid=131.

– 2006b. "Community Consultative Committee." 29 May 2007. http://www.waa.ca/?pid=179&mid=0028#minutes.

– 2006c. "History." 29 May 2007. http://www.waa.ca/?pid=185

– 2006d. "Land Development – Airport Business Parks." 29 May 2007. http://www.waa.ca/?pid=203.

– 2006e. "Leading Transportation Innovation & Growth." Winnipeg: Winnipeg Airports Authority Inc. February.

Winnipeg CentrePlan Committee. 1994. "CentrePlan: Working Together for Winnipeg's Downtown. Vision and Strategies." Winnipeg: CentrePlan Committee.

Winnipeg Partnership Agreement. 2007. "Project Profiles." 13 June 2007. http://www.winnipegpartnership.mb.ca/projects.shtml.

Young, Robert, and Christian Leuprecht, eds. 2004. *Municipal-Federal-Provincial Relations in Canada.* Montreal and Kingston: McGill-Queen's University Press.

12

# Conclusion:
# Understanding Multilevel Governance
# in Canada's Cities

MARTIN HORAK

## CANADA'S BIG CITIES: SITES OF MULTILEVEL GOVERNANCE

The study of urban politics in Canada was for many years focused resolutely on local political dynamics. Yet scholars now increasingly acknowledge that politics in Canada's big cities is fundamentally influenced by non-local forces. Some draw attention to the ways in which urban politics in Canadian cities is shaped by the economic, social, and demographic pressures emerging from an internationalized economy (Boudreau, Keil, and Young 2009). While these pressures are indisputable, they are also strongly mediated by political forces that operate at multiple spatial scales *within* the country. Urban politics is fundamentally influenced by the interaction of multiple domestic scales of governance, and analysts ignore this interaction at their peril (Sellers 2005, 441). This book represents the first multicase initiative to map and analyze the operation of multilevel governance in Canadian cities. Much remains to be learned, but our evidence allows us to begin charting the terrain of multilevel governance in urban Canada.

Academic definitions of multilevel governance often presuppose coordinated action. Yet the degree to which policy action is actually coordinated in multilevel governance varies widely. We will address this issue at the end of this chapter, but for now, in order to not presuppose coordination, let us define multilevel governance as *a mode of policy making that involves complex interactions among multiple levels of government and social forces.* Our case studies clearly show that Canada's cities are key sites of such multilevel governance. In every city examined in this book, we find extensive interaction among multiple levels of government and social forces in a variety of policy fields. Furthermore, a clear relationship exists between the size of a city and multilevel governance: in general, the larger the city, the denser and more intensive the multilevel policy interaction.

Why is multilevel governance such a prominent feature of policy making in Canada's big cities? Our evidence suggests two complementary answers. First, it supports the claim (Bradford 2005) that Canada's cities, especially its large ones, concentrate "complex files." These are policy problems whose resolution is beyond the authority and/or capacity of a single governmental agent and that therefore require the simultaneous deployment of authority and resources by multiple policy agents, often both governmental and societal (Smith and Torjman 2004). In addition, it suggests that such "complex files" spur specifically *multilevel* action because they call for policy responses that are tailored to local conditions (thus necessitating local involvement), yet exceed the capacity and/or jurisdiction of local agents (thus necessitating extra-local involvement).

Before we turn to a more detailed survey of the patterns and insights that emerge from our work, two brief caveats are in order. First, as noted in the introduction to this volume, our work covers six policy fields that were chosen in part because of their expected multilevel character, so we neither intend nor claim to present a comprehensive survey of all big-city policy making in contemporary Canada. Second, we have examined a sub-sample of policy fields in each city, so our evidence about any one policy field draws not on all ten cities, but on five to seven of them. Nonetheless, our investigation draws on a sufficient variety of policy fields and cities that it allows us to do three important things: to catalogue the variety of forms of multilevel governance that exist in different policy fields in Canadian cities; to develop insights into how and why the role of specific agents in multilevel governance varies; and to draw some inferences about factors that influence the quality of multilevel policy outputs. The remainder of this chapter addresses each of these tasks in turn.

## FORMS OF MULTILEVEL GOVERNANCE
## IN CANADA'S BIG CITIES

One of the most striking aspects of multilevel governance in Canada's big cities is the tremendous variety of forms that it takes. This variety is, in itself, analytically telling. It indicates that what we are witnessing in

Canadian urban policy is not a standardized extension to the municipal level of federalist intergovernmental relations grounded in the formal division of responsibilities among nested governmental jurisdictions – what Liesbet Hooghe and Gary Marks (2003) call "Type 1 multi-level governance." Instead, the practices documented by our contributors resemble Hooghe and Marks's "Type II multi-level governance" – fluid, problem-driven, task-specific interaction among a varying set of governmental and non-governmental agents (Hooghe and Marks 2003, 236).

How can we make sense of the huge variety of governance forms that we encounter in our big city cases? One way to do so is to categorize forms of multilevel governance according to the agents involved and the manner in which they are involved. We can divide agents into four broad types: local government agents, provincial government agents, federal government agents, and local social forces. These categories stem from the initial conceptual framework that guides our work. These categories can be subdivided, but for the sake of parsimony we will use the four-fold categorization for now. Each type of agent can in turn be involved in multilevel governance processes in one or more of four ways. First, an agent can engage in *policy advocacy* – lobbying for a particular framing of the problem in a given policy area, and/or advocating for a particular set of solutions to a given problem. Second, an agent may be involved in *resource provision*. We use this term broadly here; "resources" may take various forms, including money, ownership of fixed assets (such as land or infrastructure), and policy-relevant knowledge/expertise. Third, an agent can be involved in *policy development* – the process of deciding on a course of action that responds to a policy problem. As we shall see later on, while formal jurisdictional authority in a policy area certainly influences who is involved in policy development, in cases of multilevel governance it by no means determines who is involved. Finally, an agent may be involved in *policy implementation* – the execution of a chosen policy.

Table 1 is a graphic representation of our categorization schema for forms of multilevel governance. It can be used to plot which agents are involved (and how) in any particular instance of multilevel urban policy making. Even with this simplified set of classificatory categories, the potential for variation in forms of multilevel governance is tremendous, since varying numbers of agents can be involved in a varied number of ways in any one policy case or field. That said, the evidence presented by our authors suggests that each policy field displays some dominant patterns or tendencies. Let us, then, review dominant forms of multilevel governance in our cities in each of the six policy fields.

Table 1
Categorization schema for forms of multilevel governance

|  | Type of Involvement | | | |
|---|---|---|---|---|
| Type of Agent | Policy advocacy | Resource provision | Policy development | Policy implementation |
| Local government agents |  |  |  |  |
| Provincial government agents |  |  |  |  |
| Federal government agents |  |  |  |  |
| Local social forces |  |  |  |  |

## INFRASTRUCTURE

Of the policy fields we have examined in our work, infrastructure is most closely associated with the core municipal functions of governing land and property. It is not surprising, then, that municipal governments are heavily involved in advocacy, resource provision, policy development, *and* implementation in this field. But urban infrastructure is very capital-intensive, and municipal resources are rarely adequate for meeting infrastructure needs in major cities. Therefore, municipal advocacy on infrastructure is often dominated by the search for multilevel funding support. Indeed, cities of all kinds seek multilevel infrastructure funding, despite their very different infrastructure needs. So, for example, Calgary seeks multilevel funding to support the infrastructure needs generated by rapid economic growth, while Saint John seeks infrastructure funding in order to stimulate growth in an economically stagnant city. Given the perceived connections between infrastructure and growth, it is not surprising that dominant business interests, such as Chambers of Commerce, are key players in such multilevel lobbying and often work together with municipal officials on this front.

The search for multilevel infrastructure funding takes two basic forms. On the one hand, municipalities form alliances to lobby provincial and federal governments to set up multilevel infrastructure funding schemes. Perhaps the most prominent example is the pan-Canadian lobbying drive that helped to convince the federal government of Paul Martin to launch its New Deal for Cities and Communities in 2004. On the other hand, individual municipalities, often supported by local business elites, compete vigorously for project support from existing multilevel funding sources.

While provincial governments have long helped to fund municipal infrastructure development, the advent of Martin's New Deal signaled the growth of tri-level infrastructure funding schemes, most of which survived the change to a Conservative federal government in 2006. Some of these (such as the gas tax) essentially constitute block transfers, but most are disbursed on a project basis. This gives federal and provincial officials opportunities to involve themselves in the development of infrastructure policy in individual municipalities. For reasons that we will discuss later on, federal and provincial officials often prioritize different infrastructure projects than municipal officials, and in many of our cities, municipal officials complained bitterly that local expertise and preferences are disregarded by decision makers at other levels of government. Nonetheless, the offer of much-needed intergovernmental funding is rarely resisted, and projects that secure provincial and federal funding support typically go ahead regardless of how well they fit with pre-existing municipal priorities. Finally, we should note that the technical and capital-intensive nature of infrastructure tends to marginalize local social forces other than business. If other local social forces do get involved, it is most often through protest against unwanted projects (or against the undesirable side-effects of construction) during the implementation stage.

## FEDERAL PROPERTY

The amount and significance of property owned by the federal government differs greatly across our case cities. Although its property ownership ensures that the federal government plays a central role in all of the cases examined by our authors, two distinct patterns of policy making can be observed in our cases. One pattern – evident in such cities as Halifax, Charlottetown, and Calgary – involves the federal government redeveloping surplus properties, such as decommissioned military bases and surplus office buildings, usually through its property management Crown corporation, the Canada Lands Company (CLC). In these cases, redevelopment is often significantly shaped by questions of financial feasibility (since the CLC is meant to be financially self-sustaining) and may be complicated by the need to transfer property title to the CLC from other federal bodies. The provincial government is largely absent as a policy agent in these cases. By contrast, local agents are often actively involved, and tensions with municipal officials and local societal interests may run high because federal agents are involving themselves in a policy field – property development – that is otherwise a municipal responsibility. Municipal and local societal involvement often takes the form of resistance to some aspect of the federal redevelopment plans, but the degree of federal responsiveness to such advocacy varies significantly from case to case.

A second pattern of policy making in this field – evident in cases such as the Lachine Canal in Montreal and the Toronto waterfront – involves tri-level initiatives to redevelop a major piece of urban land, all or part of which is federally owned. Such initiatives are often strongly advocated by municipal officials and local business leaders, and involve negotiation among multiple levels of government and societal agents. Visions of redevelopment, and models of project financing, are often extensively debated by many agents, including provincial officials. Success, when it comes, tends to involve the institutionalization of collaborative relationships through the development of multilevel governing agreements, or agencies such as Waterfront Toronto.

### EMERGENCY MANAGEMENT

Unlike most of the other policy fields examined in this book, emergency management is a field in which both the functional and the financing responsibilities of various levels of government are well-defined. Municipalities are the first responders in the emergency management system. Their specific responsibilities and funding arrangements are outlined in provincial-level legislation. Federal involvement is largely limited to providing resources for major disaster relief, as well as providing small amounts of money for emergency training and preparedness. At the local level, emergency management involves intensive, ongoing interaction between municipal officials and representatives of key societal agents – be they industrial or commercial enterprises that are subject to significant risk in the case of an emergency, or voluntary organizations that can assist in relief and recovery efforts. Our research suggests that, in general, these local state-society networks function well.

In the intergovernmental realm, the primary nexus of interaction is between municipal officials and the provincial officials who administer province-wide emergency management standards. In contrast, direct interaction between municipal officials and their federal counterparts is rare. One common source of intergovernmental tension arises from the standardization of provincial legislation and funding arrangements.

According to municipal officials in several of our cities, emergency management legislation tends to be tailored primarily towards the needs of smaller municipalities, while both provincial and federal funding parameters fail to acknowledge the specific emergency risks faced by large cities. Given the low day-to-day public profile of emergency management, municipal officials have few opportunities to draw intergovernmental attention to their specific emergency needs. It thus often takes a "focusing event" (Henstra 2003) – such as Quebec's ice storm of 1998, or the SARS crisis of 2003 – to alter established policy and funding patterns in the field.

### IMAGE BUILDING

In recent years, image building has become a major focus for large cities. All of our case cities in this policy field expended significant local resources and effort on building and projecting positive images. In contrast to emergency management, image building is a field where relations among agents are often poorly defined and not regularized. Indeed, the very boundaries of the policy field are unclear, since image building addresses multiple possible audiences – business investors, tourists, and even local residents – and can be pursued through many different kinds of activities. Accordingly, image building in our cities often involves a multitude of different agents; struggles about competing images and imaging initiatives are common. As in the federal property field, two basic patterns of interaction can be identified.

The first pattern of interaction centers on efforts to market a municipality for investment and/or tourism purposes. These involve the development and advertisement of programs to attract target audiences, such as tax breaks and business incubation schemes for investors, or cultural events and visitor services for tourists. They also sometimes involve the development of a formal municipal "brand," such as Saint John's "Loyalist City" brand. While municipal officials are central to such marketing efforts, local societal agents are also key. A range of business agents who have a material interest in attracting investment and/or tourism – Chambers of Commerce, small business associations, sectoral groups such as the hotel industry or major cultural institutions – are actively involved in multiple ways, ranging from advocating for particular images or initiatives, through resource provision, policy development, and implementation. The variety of interests represented leads to frequent disagreement about the substance and governance of imaging campaigns. As a result, the uneasy coexistence of multiple (and some-times conflicting) imaging initiatives in one city is common. In this pat-tern of interaction, multilevel involvement tends to be limited to the provincial level. In some cases (Saint John, St John's), where local image-building agents are strongly connected to provincial counterparts, pro-vincial involvement adds resources to local imaging initiatives. In other cases (Halifax, Toronto), provincial policy priorities and/or imaging campaigns stand in tension with local ones, further exacerbating the conflict over images and imaging priorities that is common in this field.

A different pattern of interaction emerges when image building involves the development of large-scale infrastructure for a "hallmark event," such as the Vancouver Olympics, the Calgary Stampede, or the (unrealized) Halifax Commonwealth Games. In these cases, policy advocacy is again usually led by local agents, but local societal involvement is restricted to the largest and best-resourced interests, such as Chambers of Commerce and major businesses. The need for major intergovernmental funding support in such cases accentuates multilevel involvement, as well as the involvement of politicians, as opposed to administrators. With the pro-vincial and federal governments both involved, the potential for discord over priorities and governance shifts to the intergovernmental arena, and hallmark event projects cannot succeed unless governments agree on sub-stantive priorities and the division of funding responsibilities.

## IMMIGRANT SETTLEMENT

While immigration itself is an area of concurrent federal-provincial juris-diction in Canada, geographically uneven patterns of immigrant settle-ment create a highly diverse landscape of local policy across cities. Broadly speaking, Canadian cities fall into two categories: those that receive few immigrants, and those that receive many. For cities that receive few immi-grants, local immigration challenges are centered on recruitment; for major immigrant gateways, challenges involve the social and economic integration of a large number of newcomers. Our random assignment of policy fields to cities resulted in a relative under-representation of high-immigration cities, so the patterns of multilevel governance described here draw primarily on evidence from lower-immigration cities.[1]

One striking finding of our work concerns the limited involvement of municipal governments in this policy field.[2] In all aspects of the field, municipalities are, at best, minor players; their activity – if they engage in any at all – is largely limited to lobbying other levels of government to develop and fund appropriate policies. This lack of municipal involvement in the field holds even in Calgary and Winnipeg, the two case cities in our sample with relatively high immigration levels. In this context, both recruitment and integration policies are typically developed through the direct interaction of local societal agents with provincial and federal government agents.

In recent years, the federal government has begun to recognize the existence of locally-specific immigrant recruitment and settlement issues by introducing and/or expanding a number of funding programs. These include the Temporary Foreign Workers (TFW) program, designed to address localized labour shortages; the Provincial Nominee Program (PNP), designed to attract skilled, financially self-sufficient immigrants to low-immigration localities; and a variety of settlement funding programs, with a particular emphasis on language training programs. The TFW and PNP programs are both provincially administered, so their rise and growth has led to an increase in provincial involvement in the field, as indicated by the recent establishment of immigration ministries in many provinces. Provincial officials in turn usually collaborate with local businesses and with non-profit community organizations in implementing these programs in individual cities.

As for federal settlement funding, in most of our case cities it bypasses municipal governments and flows directly to local non-governmental agencies that deliver a wide variety of settlement programs in a decentralized way. While such decentralization ensures that programs are tailored to local needs and conditions, the lack of multidimensional, integrated settlement policies in specific cities often leads to fragmentation and duplication in immigrant settlement initiatives at the local level. Among our case cities, the exception to this model is found in Winnipeg. Manitoba is one of three provinces that shoulder full responsibility for immigrant settlement policy; as a result, in Winnipeg it is provincial officials who develop and implement settlement programs in collaboration with local social forces, apparently with great success.

## URBAN ABORIGINAL POLICY

The characteristics of this policy field in many ways parallel those of immigrant settlement. Both fields deal with human services for ethnically and culturally distinct sub-segments of the urban population. Both are fields in which municipalities have no formal jurisdiction, but the federal and provincial governments do. Furthermore, like immigrants, most urban Aboriginal people are concentrated in a small number of cities across Canada. Our research covered the city with the largest urban Aboriginal population in the country – Winnipeg – as well as several cities with very small urban Aboriginal populations. For all these reasons, our findings regarding multilevel dynamics in the two policy fields resemble each other in some ways. However, there are also some significant differences. First, while immigrants are seen by policy makers as people in need of integration assistance, they are also often seen as valued assets for local economies and societies. By contrast, urban Aboriginal peoples tend to be viewed solely as marginal populations in need of assistance, not as valued assets or productive contributors to urban localities. Second, and related, *no* level of government has a well-developed set of policies and programs to address the needs of urban Aboriginal people. The federal government comes closest: it has long provided funding to Native Friendship Centres in many cities, and it now also has an Urban Aboriginal Strategy that provides small-scale funding to local non-profit organizations that serve Aboriginal people in a few selected cities. Yet the scale of this programming is modest, and municipal and provincial governments, for their part, remain largely absent from this field.

The sad but unsurprising outcome of these conditions is that, in most of our case cities, the distinct human services needs of urban Aboriginal people are largely ignored by all levels of government. The needs of urban Aboriginal peoples are served – when they are served at all – by small local non-profit service organizations. At times, these organizations do receive funding from federal programs, but the funding is not tied to any broader place-based policies that assess the overall needs and capacities of Aboriginal people in a particular city. Christopher Leo's chapter on Winnipeg suggests that, even in a city with a large and organizationally vibrant Aboriginal population, governmental support for human services to urban Aboriginals is limited and based in a top-down disbursement of project funds that hinders the development of integrated place-specific policies. In short, in most cases the needs of urban Aboriginal peoples fall through the cracks of the multilevel governance system.

EXPLAINING VARIATION IN MULTILEVEL GOVERNANCE

As we move from description to explanation, we are faced with some challenges in interpreting our evidence. Given the huge variety of forms of multilevel governance, and the many causal factors that may influence these forms (see the introduction to this volume), does our evidence none-theless allow us to develop an overall causal model of influences on the shape of multilevel governance? The short answer is that it does not. The form of multilevel governance that exists in any one policy field, city, or policy initiative is the product of a multiplicity of causal factors – ranging from the distribution of authority and resources to the ideology and stra-tegic leadership skills of politicians, the institutional structure of relevant administrative bodies, and the degree of organization of social forces, among others. These factors often interact in complex ways, and the dynamics of this interaction vary from case to case and field to field.

While the complexity of multilevel governance in big cities militates against the development of an overarching causal model, our evidence does allow a number of more limited, but nonetheless important, causal inferences. The first concerns the relative importance of formal decision-making authority (jurisdiction) versus resources (money, information, and expertise) in shaping patterns of multilevel governance. Here, our evidence viewed as a whole produces a striking insight: resources often trump authority as determinants of who is involved in multilevel gover-nance and how. As might be expected, the distribution of jurisdictional authority does influence who is involved in developing and implement-ing multilevel policy initiatives. If a single level of government has pri-mary authority in a policy field, it usually plays a central role in policy development, and is often involved in implementation too. For example, municipal governments play a central role in the development and imple-mentation of infrastructure policy, whereas the federal government tends to lead on immigrant settlement policy.

However, our evidence suggests that the distribution of resources plays an equally – and sometime more – important role in shaping multilevel governance systems. In many cases, control over financial resources allows agents to insert themselves into (or even to dominate) policy pro-cesses over which they have no formal jurisdiction. For example, through its provision of infrastructure funding the federal government plays a major role in shaping infrastructure policy in many Canadian cities, despite its lack of formal jurisdiction. Policy-relevant knowledge and/or expertise often function in a similar way. In the image-building field, for example, the knowledge and market expertise of dominant private-sector business agents gives them a prominent role in policy develop-ment and policy implementation; in the urban Aboriginal field, the federal government regularly turns to local voluntary organizations to both develop and implement programming using federal funds.

Scholars often assert that multilevel governance is prone to accountability problems (Peters and Pierre 2005), and the insights developed
above support this assertion. In comparison with unitary government
systems, multilevel governance systems tend to increase opportunities
for agents (governmental or societal) who possess relevant resources to
influence policy in a direction that reflects their own particular preferences, rather than the preferences of the broader public as expressed
through elected representatives. We will explore other implications of
resource and authority distribution later on. At this point, however, we
turn to a more fine-grained examination of some causal insights arising
from our work. Our evidence suggests that the behaviour of different
types of agents in multilevel governance settings is shaped by distinct (if
overlapping) configurations of causal factors. We therefore discuss the
behaviour of each type of agent in turn and examine factors (over and
above the distribution of authority and resources) that shape variation
in this behaviour. We begin with local government officials and then
move to other levels of government and to local social forces.

## LOCAL GOVERNMENT

Writing in the early 1990s, Frances Frisken argued that most Canadian
municipalities respond to their weak constitutional standing by adopt-
ing a passive or reactive position in their relationships with other levels
of government (Frisken cited in Siegel 2006, 195). More recently, David
Siegel wrote that most Ontario municipal councils are "comfortable
with possessing limited powers and being able to blame the province ...
for problems or missed opportunities" (Siegel 2006, 194). In other
words, Canadian municipalities have long been seen as policy takers, not
policy makers, on the intergovernmental stage. The evidence presented
in this book suggests that this conclusion is no longer true in a general
sense, if indeed it ever was. Given the constitutional division of jurisdiction in Canada the intergovernmental dealings of municipalities are
more focused on the provincial than the federal level. But with respect
to both provincial and federal governments, our authors have uncovered
a range of municipal behavior across different cities and policy fields.
First, we have cases in which municipalities do behave as policy takers,
implementing policy initiatives developed at other levels of government.
Second, we have cases in which municipalities use multilevel politics to
secure resources that they need to achieve municipal policy aims. Finally,
in some instances municipalities proactively seek to develop multilevel
policy in coordination with other levels of government.

Several factors influence where in this range of responses a municipality is situated in any one policy field. First, as discussed above, the extent to which a municipality has jurisdiction and relevant resources in a particular field clearly matters. However, other factors also play a role. One is the economic and electoral importance of a city to the provincial or federal government. Cities that are seen as pivotal sites of economic production by provincial or federal officials, as well as cities that are strategically important electoral battlegrounds at the provincial or federal level, command more attention and responsiveness to their policy needs and demands at those levels of government. Officials in these cities are thus more likely to achieve their goals on the intergovernmental stage by engaging in proactive policy behaviour, which in turn encourages such behaviour. Thus, it is no surprise that very large cities such as Toronto and Vancouver are particularly proactive in multilevel policy processes.

However, some of our case cities that are very important in the provincial context – such as Halifax and Winnipeg – nonetheless remain largely passive or reactive in their intergovernmental dealings. This points us to the importance of conceptions of local government held by local political leaders. As Leo and his colleagues observe in the chapter on Winnipeg, some local political leaders conceive of municipal government as a minimalist provider of local services, whereas others see it as a comprehensive steward of the economic, social, and cultural well-being of a locality. The "minimalist" conception of local government, which places a premium on efficient, low-cost delivery of core municipal services, limits local political interest and involvement in multilevel politics. The "comprehensive" conception of local government, which calls for municipal leadership in seeking solutions to emerging local problems of all kinds, encourages local politicians to deepen their involvement in multilevel governance. A final factor that may shape municipal involvement in multilevel governance systems is administrative cohesion and capacity in intergovernmental relations. For example, Toronto has a corporate-level intergovernmental relations unit, and, as the Toronto chapter suggests, this unit has played a pivotal role in developing and sustaining a proactive approach to multilevel governance across several policy fields.

## PROVINCIAL GOVERNMENT

The constitutional division of responsibilities in Canada grants broad jurisdictional authority over municipal affairs to provincial governments. Thus, it is no surprise that provinces are heavily involved in multilevel governance in multiple policy fields across all of the cities examined in this book. A closer look, however, reveals a range of provincial approaches. In some policy fields – including urban Aboriginal policy and federal property – provincial governments are not much involved in multilevel governance. In other fields, provincial governments provide project funding to support individual municipal or tri-level policy initiatives, such as building a major piece of infrastructure or mounting a hallmark event. More common than just project funding, however, is systematic provincial involvement in a multilevel policy field, which encompasses the development, funding, and monitoring of a variety of policies and initiatives in that field. Thus, for example, in the fields of municipal infrastructure and emergency management, provinces not only provide funding, but they also develop policies for prioritizing that funding and administer comprehensive regulatory frameworks to which municipalities must conform.

As is the case with municipal involvement, provincial involvement in multilevel governance is strongly affected by the distribution of authority and resources in different policy fields. This is reflected in the varying density of municipal relationships with provincial line departments and agencies in various fields such as infrastructure, immigration, and emergency management. However, the general oversight that provinces have over municipalities means that provincial governments also have a strong concentration of *multipurpose* institutional resources dedicated to municipal affairs. Every Canadian province has a Ministry of Municipal Affairs (or similarly named equivalent) that manages provincial oversight over municipalities and liaises with other provincial bodies in developing and funding policies directed at municipalities. This concentration of institutional resources helps to explain why provincial governments are often involved in multilevel urban governance in a systematic, rather than a project-based manner (in contrast to the federal government).

As mentioned in the previous section, the relative economic and electoral importance of a particular city also influences provincial approaches to multilevel governance in that city. Our studies suggest that the more economically or electorally dominant a city is in its provincial setting, the more dense provincial relations with that city are, and the more likely it is that a provincial government will treat the policy needs of that city separately from the policy needs of other municipalities. The British Columbia government's approach to Vancouver is a good example of the density of intergovernmental connections and the place-tailoring of provincial policy on a number of fronts, such as infrastructure and image building.

Finally, the shape of provincial involvement in multilevel governance is also influenced by the overall character of provincial-municipal relations in a given province. Some provinces – Ontario, Saskatchewan, and Nova Scotia among them – have a tendency to micromanage municipal affairs and see municipalities primarily as implementers of provincial policy directions, whereas others – most notably British Columbia – are less directive (Sancton and Young 2009). In the former cases, provincial officials typically try to retain the upper hand in multilevel policy processes and are reluctant to engage seriously with municipal policy priorities; in the latter cases, they are more likely to treat municipalities as policy partners.

## FEDERAL GOVERNMENT

In contrast to provincial governments, the federal government has no constitutional authority over municipal affairs, and this significantly limits the scope and character of federal involvement in multilevel governance in Canada's big cities. Ever since the 1970s, when the short-lived Ministry of State for Urban Affairs foundered in part on provincial opposition to its initiatives, the federal government has had no administrative unit or political file dedicated specifically and solely to urban affairs. While there was an effort between 2003 and 2006 to develop comprehensive policy capacity in the urban field with the establishment of the Ministry of State for Infrastructure and Communities under the aegis of the Martin government's New Deal for Cities, the Harper years have seen a return to traditional form in this regard.

Nevertheless, the evidence gathered by our authors clearly shows that in recent years the federal government has been, and continues to be, significantly involved in multilevel governance initiatives across a number of policy fields. This activity takes two basic forms: project-based and program-based. Project-based intervention involves the federal government helping to develop and fund a major urban project on a one-off basis. In most cases, project-based intervention usually arises when local elites in a major city team up with provincial officials or local-area federal MPs to lobby the federal government for assistance with a high-profile urban development or mega-event initiative. Our evidence suggests that only very large cities, which have significant lobbying resources and political clout, successfully secure federal support for large-scale one-off projects. The construction of the Canada Line and the preparation for the 2010 Olympics in

Vancouver and the redevelopment of the Lachine Canal in Montreal
are examples of such projects.

Large urban infrastructure and mega-event projects typically involve
all three levels of government working together. Even though the federal
government has no direct jurisdiction over municipal infrastructure, the
scale and visibility of these projects usually compel federal officials to go
beyond funding and to involve themselves in project development and
implementation as well. In addition, there is one category of federal
project-based involvement in cities where federal officials dominate: the
redevelopment of surplus federal property. In these cases, the initiative
for a project often arises at the federal level itself; partly because of this,
the bias towards very large cities is not as evident, and our chapters
reveal federal property redevelopment initiatives in cities of all sizes.

Program-based federal involvement in urban affairs typically arises in
policy fields that are at least partly in federal jurisdiction, but present
policy problems requiring spatially differentiated responses. In these
cases, the federal government develops policy parameters that embody a
number of high-level goals. These are then implemented through the distribution of federal funding to decentralized agents – either to provincial
governments which in turn transfer the funding to local agents on a
project basis, or directly to municipalities or local societal agents whose
projects meet the federal policy goals. The Urban Aboriginal Strategy,
immigrant settlement funding programs, the Provincial Nominee Program,
the gas tax fund, and funding for emergency training are all examples of
program-based involvement.

Perhaps the most prominent form of federal program-based involvement in cities is tri-level infrastructure funding. Programs such as the
Infrastructure Canada Program, the Canada Strategic Infrastructure
Program, and the Building Canada Fund have distributed billons of dollars for local infrastructure projects. But these programs differ from the
other ones listed above in two important ways. First, they do not distribute self-standing federal funding; rather, they require matching contributions from provincial and local agents. Second, their policy goals rather
are vague and underspecified. This often allows federal officials to retain
broad discretion in selecting projects that are eligible for funding. In
other words, while they are "programs" in name, federal infrastructure
funds appear to function more as sources of discretionary project-based
funding than as policy programs in their own right. The legitimacy
conferred by embedding the funding in a "program," combined with
the discretion that allows federal officials to distribute the funding in

politically advantageous ways, make this funding model particularly attractive from the federal point of view.

## POLITICIANS AND ADMINISTRATORS
## IN MULTILEVEL GOVERNANCE

We have thus far treated each level of government as a unitary agent in multilevel governance. This is, of course, not always an accurate representation. Before we turn to local societal actors, then, a few words are in order about political and administrative involvement at all three levels of government. In general, our accumulated evidence reveals that the day-to-day intergovernmental interactions that characterize multilevel governance systems are largely administrative in character. Insofar as a policy field features a stable multilevel division of labour (jurisdiction and funding) and a stable set of programs, politicians rarely stray into it. Emergency management is perhaps the best, though not the only, example of such a policy field. However, while intergovernmental administrative relations are a constant, from time to time politicians also get involved in multilevel governance in all six of the policy fields we have examined.

Our cases suggest that there are several circumstances under which politicians tend to involve themselves in multilevel governance. The first circumstance is when one level of government seeks to clarify or change the multilevel division of labour in a particular policy field. For example, when local officials in a particular city seek a significant change in intergovernmental funding relations, or when they seek to secure broader or better-defined jurisdiction in a policy field, politicians usually lead the effort. A second circumstance is when officials at one level of government seek multilevel support or coordination around a significant new policy initiative, such as Halifax's bid for the Commonwealth Games or Saint John's energy hub development strategy. Both of these circumstances require political leadership for the simple reason that they involve activities that go beyond the scope of authority of administrators and require political authorization in order to take effect. That said, changing the architecture of multilevel governance through new divisions of labour or new policy initiatives often takes a lot of time, and our studies suggest that politicians sometimes lose interest in these processes well before they are complete, leaving administrators to work out the difficult details.

While political involvement in multilevel governance is at times necessary for the reasons noted above, political leaders also engage in multilevel politics for reasons that have little to do with the functional requirements of multilevel governance. As Miller and Smart note in their chapter on Calgary, the multilevel realm is attractive territory for political "posturing and strutting," since it can be used to shift blame for failures or to appropriate credit for successes. Thus, it is not uncommon to see municipal politicians blaming local policy failures on a lack of intergovernmental support; nor is it uncommon to see provincial and federal officials using announcements of intergovernmental funding for local projects as an opportunity to appropriate credit for those projects. In other words, because multilevel politics offers opportunities for shifting blame and accumulating credit across levels of government, it is prone to forms of political involvement that do little to address concrete policy problems, and may even be functionally counterproductive.

## LOCAL SOCIAL FORCES I: THE BUSINESS COMMUNITY

In the previous section of this chapter, we grouped all local social forces in a single analytical category. However, evidence presented throughout the book suggests that local business elites are involved in multilevel governance systems in systematically distinct ways, so we will treat them separately here. The literature on urban politics in Canada suggests that local business agents – especially large employers and those involved in property development – significantly influence, and at times even dominate, local political agendas (Leo and Anderson 2006). One question that animates our work is whether this influence transfers to the realm of multilevel urban politics, or whether local business influence is attenuated there. The short answer is that multilevel governance does not, by and large, attenuate business influence over urban policy issues.

Our cases show a remarkable degree of involvement by local business elites in multilevel governance processes across multiple policy fields and cities. With the exception of urban Aboriginal policy, every policy field examined in this book displayed significant local business involvement. Furthermore, local business agents are often involved in multiple ways in a policy field, from advocacy through policy development to implementation, and in the process, they shape the content of multilevel policy initiatives to a significant extent.

The most obvious reason for such business influence is that business agents have significant material resources and often relevant knowledge and expertise. If multilevel governance is – as posited above – a governance form in which resources matter at least as much as jurisdiction, the concentration of resources that business elites possess places them in a position to strongly influence governance processes, if they so desire. In addition to possessing substantive resources, local business agents also tend to be well organized, which makes them all the more attractive as governance partners. In all of our case cities, local businesses have a peak organization, the Chamber of Commerce; in many cases they also have strong sectoral organizations in fields such as tourism, construction, and emergency management. Such groups often act as effective partners to local government in its intergovernmental lobbying, and they can coordinate business input into policy processes and help to organize the implementation of policy initiatives.

Yet, the relative cohesion of the business community – and thus its ability to exert coordinated influence in multilevel governance – does vary by city. At one end of the spectrum are cities like Saint John and Calgary, both of which have tightly-knit, organizationally integrated business elites; at the other end are cities like Vancouver and Montreal, whose business communities are more heterogeneous and organizationally fragmented. In addition, in some cities (often the same ones that have highly cohesive business elites) the business community exerts a dominant influence on city hall, while in other cities (often those with more fragmented business communities) the relationship between business and local government is more complex. Given that business agents often exert multilevel policy influence in coordination with local government, this relationship between business elites and city hall also has an effect on the voice of business in multilevel politics.

Can we identify any policy fields or cases in which multilevel politics does attenuate the influence of business? There are a handful of cases, such as the Garrison Woods redevelopment of federal property in Calgary, in which policy outcomes clashed directly with the preferences of local business elites, but they are few and far between. There are also some policy fields in which business is not heavily involved – most notably, urban Aboriginal policy and immigrant settlement (as opposed to immigrant recruitment) – but this lack of involvement is not evidence of attenuated influence; instead, it appears to stem from a lack of acute interest in these policy fields on the part of business agents. While it would be an exaggeration to say that business elites in our cities dominate multilevel governance processes – in general, they certainly do not – it is clear that they are major players in many fields, whose interests and resources governmental policymakers ignore at their peril.

LOCAL SOCIAL FORCES II

Aside from the business community, a wide variety of other local social forces are involved in multilevel governance processes across the fields examined in this book. They include immigrant settlement agencies, Aboriginal social service organizations, residents' groups, local arts organizations, and local environmental groups, to name but a few. We do not have the space (or, indeed, enough accumulated evidence) to discuss all of these types of agents individually. But we can make some more general statements about how their engagement in multilevel governance differs from that of business elites, and what explains these differences. First, while business elites in any one city often engage across multiple policy fields, most other social forces are more specialized in their mandate and focus. Second, while business agents sometimes engage directly with provincial and even federal government agents, other social forces tend to channel their participation in multilevel governance *through* local government, unless other levels of government approach them. Third, while business agents are often involved in policy development (in addition to advocacy and implementation), such involvement is not as common for other local social forces, although it does occur in some cases.

These differences reflect, in part, the fact that non-business social forces usually have fewer resources to bring to the multilevel governance table. In particular, the financial resources available to most local societal groups are very limited, and indeed, many of them – such as local arts groups and human service agencies – are themselves financially dependent on governments. That said, local societal organizations often have resources other than money that they can use to engage in multilevel governance. First, these groups often have local knowledge and expertise in a particular policy sector, which makes them attractive vehicles for policy implementation and, on occasion, potential participants in policy development. In human services fields such as immigrant settlement and urban Aboriginal policy, all levels of government rely extensively on local social forces for on-the-ground policy implementation.

Second, local societal organizations may represent significant constituencies, especially for local politicians, and this can give these organizations influence even if they lack other resources. For example, the resident associations that lobbied to halt the redevelopment of two large pieces of federal land in Charlottetown had few policy-relevant resources to offer government agents, but they did represent significant numbers of local residents, and so they garnered support from municipal politicians. This potential for political clout, however, rarely extends beyond the local level. Indeed, while we anticipated that the search for political influence might lead local social forces to "scale up" their activity to other levels of government by forming alliances with social forces in other locations, we found little evidence of such activity, which appears to be hampered not only by the limited organizational capacity of many local groups, but also by divergent policy foci and interests across different municipalities. In this light, it is not surprising that most social forces access multilevel governance primarily through local government. As a result, the degree of multilevel involvement and influence that local social forces have is strongly influenced by local relations between state and society. Thus, the unresponsiveness of Halifax's local government to local social forces works to exclude these social forces from multilevel governance mechanisms in that city; conversely, Saskatoon's more responsive and inclusive local government opens the door for multilevel policy participation by local social forces.

## MULTILEVEL GOVERNANCE AND THE QUALITY OF PUBLIC POLICY IN CANADA'S BIG CITIES

Policy evaluation is rarely far from the surface in academic work on multilevel governance. A pioneering article on multilevel governance by Hooghe and Marks asserts that, "according to many, [contemporary governance] *should* be dispersed across multiple centers of authority" (2003, 233, emphasis added). Indeed, multilevel governance is often said to have advantages over the exercise of authority by one level of government because it allows for a pooling of authority and resources, because it is sensitive to the scale of different policy problems, and because it allows policy to be tailored to local conditions and needs (Hooghe and Marks 2004, 16). In the Canadian context at least, such claims have not been tested in any systematic way. Accordingly, a key objective of our work is to assess the quality of policy produced by multilevel processes operating in Canada's big cities and to draw inferences about factors that affect the quality of multilevel policy outputs.

In order to assess the quality of policy outputs across the cities and fields surveyed in this book, we need to establish clear assessment criteria. Yet many common criteria for evaluating outputs, such as equity (i.e., distributional consequences) or efficiency (i.e., "value for money"), are difficult to assess comparably across the broad range of policy fields, cities, and individual policy initiatives that our authors engage with. Nevertheless, several of the chapters in this book engage in explicit policy evaluation, and these evaluations tend to converge around two criteria that *can* be assessed across a broad range of cases: effectiveness and responsiveness. An "effective" policy, as we will use the term, is one that meets the stated objectives of those who developed it; a "responsive" policy is one that is built on the preferences of local agents – the local officials and societal stakeholders active in a policy field. These evaluation standards are, of course, not the only ones that we could use, and they are open to contestation; but they do align with the justifications for multilevel governance cited above, and as such, they allow us to assess the outputs of multilevel governance against the normative claims for multilevel governance advanced by its proponents.

Even a cursory overview of our evidence from twelve cities suggests that the quality of multilevel policy outputs varies tremendously. Thus, we cannot generalize to say that multilevel governance mechanisms are functioning well in Canada's big cities; neither, however, can we conclude that multilevel governance in Canada's big cities systematically fails to deliver on its promise. Instead, in every policy field that we have surveyed, we find examples of both success and failure. In image building, for example, we find Vancouver pursuing a coherent strategy to position itself as an emerging Asia-Pacific global city, while agents in Toronto struggle to define a strategic policy direction. In the federal property field, the successful and locally supported Lachine Canal redevelopment in Montreal stands in contrast with ongoing conflict over the redevelopment of federal lands in Halifax. In the urban Aboriginal field, Saskatoon's success in developing an urban reserve stands in contrast to the marginalization of urban Aboriginal needs in many of our other cities. Similar contrasts can be found in the other policy fields as well.

Given this wide variation, what factors shape the relative success or failure of multilevel policy making in Canada's big cities? Once again, the variety and complexity of multilevel governance processes across our cases militates against the development of a universal causal model, yet we can draw a number of important causal inferences. The quality of multilevel policy outputs examined in this book clearly varies by both policy field and city. Multilevel governance is more commonly subject to policy failure in some fields than in others. Urban Aboriginal policy and image building are the two fields in which poor policy outputs are particularly common in our cities. Likewise, some cities have a stronger overall record in multilevel policy making than others. In Vancouver, for example, multilevel policy initiatives often achieve the objectives of those who launched them, while in Halifax, multilevel policy initiatives often fall apart due to conflict over priorities among agents. This varia- tion by policy field and city in turn points to systematic variation in underlying causal factors. In the sections that follow, we will explore these underlying factors, examining each of our evaluative criteria – effectiveness and responsiveness – in turn.

## EXPLAINING VARIATION IN THE EFFECTIVENESS OF MULTILEVEL POLICY OUTPUTS

Multilevel governance arises in situations where policy authority and resources are fragmented among multiple actors who operate at differ- ent spatial scales. As a result, achieving desired policy objectives – our measure of "effectiveness" – usually requires coordination among mul- tiple agents. Such coordination can be difficult to achieve, however. Our city studies suggest that the degree of coordination varies greatly across policy fields and cities. For example, in some cases, such as image build- ing in many of our cities, multilevel policy activity is characterized by a proliferation of uncoordinated initiatives; in other cases, we see agents attempting to coordinate with others, but failing to do so. Without coordination under conditions of authority and resource fragmentation, all but the most limited of policy initiatives are not achievable, and even these may be undermined by other, competing initiatives.

The challenge of effective multilevel policy making is thus, to a signifi- cant extent, a challenge of coordination. What factors affect the pros- pects for multilevel policy coordination? One factor is the difficulty of the coordination challenge itself. As noted in the Toronto chapter, two basic things need to be coordinated in multilevel policy making: policy power (that is, authority and resources), and policy agendas. Each of these can be more or less fragmented in relation to a given set of policy objectives. In some cases, one level of government possesses the bulk of formal authority and resources and only requires limited support from other agents to achieve a given set of policy objectives; in other cases, the authority and resources necessary to achieve given objectives are widely dispersed among governmental and societal agents. Likewise, in some cases there is broad agreement among agents regarding policy objectives, while in other cases agents encounter the distinct (and possibly incom- patible) policy agendas of others. The Toronto chapter argues that the more fragmented power and agendas are, the more difficult, costly, and time-consuming it is to achieve multilevel policy coordination. Our broader evidence supports this conclusion, but with an important qualification: agenda fragmentation appears to be a particularly strong predictor of policy failure. In other words, whereas even a complex multilevel constellation of agents can successfully coordinate activity if those agents share an overriding policy objective (such as bringing the 2010 winter Olympic Games to Vancouver), ostensibly simpler multilevel initiatives involving fewer agents (such as the proposed redevelopment of the Shearwater Base in Halifax) may fail if the agents involved espouse policy objectives that are incompatible.

While power and agenda fragmentation among agents influence the prospects for effective multilevel policy coordination, they are not the only relevant factors. One of the most striking correlates of effective policy outputs in our cases is the cohesiveness of administration *within* a single level of government. In most cases, multilevel policy initiatives begin when one level of government chooses to advocate for a multilevel response to a policy problem. But if the relevant administrative bodies at that level of government do not share the same policy objectives, coordination with other levels of government and with social forces is very difficult. For example, numerous federal efforts to redevelop surplus lands in Halifax have been stymied by conflict between the Canada Lands Company and the Department of National Defence, both of which are federal agencies; the development of a cohesive image-building campaign in Montreal has been hampered by the different priorities of municipal tourism, cultural development, and economic development officials. Conversely, the existence of cohesive administrative capacity at one level of government can provide the expertise and long-range outlook needed to sustain a complex multilevel policy coordination effort. Thus, for example, our Vancouver chapter notes that the city has become a major player in intergovernmental relations due in part to its highly professional bureaucracy, which has built sustained links with counterparts at other levels of government. Toronto has recently gone one step further, developing a corporate-level intergovernmental office that has contributed to the success of several significant multilevel policy initiatives.

As we noted earlier, political (as opposed to administrative) involvement in multilevel governance tends to be episodic, not sustained, in character. Yet multilevel policy making is often a lengthy process, and the more complex the coordination, the more time the policy process tends to take. While this lengthy work is often undertaken by administrators, multilevel policy coordination benefits from sustained political support, when available. In a number of the multilevel initiatives discussed in this book – ranging from the Lachine Canal redevelopment in Montreal to tourism promotion in St John's – consistent support over a period of years from politicians at one or more levels of government was critical to the achievement of policy objectives. Conversely, some other multilevel initiatives documented in this book – such as Winnipeg's effort to develop a municipally-led urban Aboriginal strategy – failed because politicians changed their policy priorities before objectives had been achieved.

This brings us to a final observation – one about the importance of institutionalization. Since different levels of government are each subject to distinct electoral dynamics and issue pressures, even thoroughly harmonized policy agendas will have a tendency to diverge over time. And since multilevel coordination often takes a great deal of time, the potential for a change in agenda at any one level of government presents a significant threat to the achievement of multilevel policy objectives. This threat can, however, be mitigated if multilevel governance becomes institutionalized – in other words, if the sharing of resources and authority among agents is regularized through the establishment of a formal agreement or the development of a multilevel governing agency or body. Our evidence provides many examples of such institutionalization, ranging from the settlement services agreement in Winnipeg and the tri-level gas tax sharing agreements developed across Canada under the federal government of Paul Martin to the tri-level Agreement for the Downtown East Side in Vancouver and the Waterfront Revitalization Corporation in Toronto. Such initiatives to institutionalize multilevel governance help to insulate complex, long-range policy initiatives from changes in political agendas at one or another level of government; in this way, institutionalization can play a key role in facilitating effective policy output.

### EXPLAINING VARIATION IN THE RESPONSIVENESS OF MULTILEVEL POLICY OUTPUTS

Proponents of multilevel governance often assert that it enables policy responses that are tailored to local preferences. Local responsiveness is, however, by no means a universal feature of multilevel governance in Canada's big cities. In addition, effectiveness and responsiveness do not necessarily go hand in hand; rather, effective multilevel coordination is a necessary but not sufficient condition for multilevel policies that respond to local preferences. Our authors discuss many multilevel policy initiatives that achieved their goals, but that were not built around the preferences of local stakeholders. The development and operation of the Winnipeg Airports Authority and the use of tri-level infrastructure funding to fund federal or provincial priority projects in numerous cities are but two examples.

What factors, then, influence the degree to which multilevel policy initiatives respond to distinct local preferences? Our evidence suggests that local responsiveness usually (though not always) requires that local agents be actively involved in multilevel policy development, as opposed to just advocacy or implementation. And involvement in multilevel policy development is in turn strongly influenced by the jurisdictional authority and/or the resources – money, expertise, potential electoral impact – that agents possess. Thus, in general, the more the multilevel balance of authority and resources tilts in favour of local agents, the more responsive to local preferences multilevel policy making will tend to be. Before we elaborate on this point and develop our analysis further, however, an important caveat is in order: despite its widespread currency in the literature, the concept of "local preferences" is, in fact, an oversimplified construct, because more often than not, local preferences in any one policy field and city are heterogeneous. While we cannot examine this heterogeneity in full here, the analysis that follows will acknowledge it by treating separately responsiveness to local government and responsiveness to local social forces.

The degree to which multilevel policy initiatives are built around the preferences of local government officials varies widely from case to case. This chapter has identified a number of sources of this variation, which we will review here. First, whether or not a particular policy field or initiative is within local government jurisdiction clearly matters, since having primary jurisdiction over a policy field (such as local infrastructure development) allows local officials to be involved *de jure* in the policy development process. But even when municipal officials have jurisdiction in a particular policy field, their access to tri-level (as opposed to provincial-municipal) policy processes may be blocked by provincial officials, if the latter are intent on defending their own jurisdiction over municipal affairs.

Second, we have seen that the distribution of resources of various kinds is key to multilevel policy influence. On the financial front, local governments are often relatively resource-poor and seek support from other levels of government in multilevel policy fields, which significantly weakens their influence over multilevel policy processes. The tendency of multilevel infrastructure projects to privilege the priorities of other levels of government is one example of this. By contrast, in part because of their formal jurisdiction in a number of multilevel policy fields, local governments often have significant locally-grounded expertise, and this can act as a counterweight to a lack of financial resources in giving municipalities a voice in multilevel policy processes.

A number of other factors – discussed in the above section entitled "Local Government" – also shape the policy influence of local governments in multilevel processes. One is the relative economic or electoral importance of a city in intergovernmental context, which affects the inclination of provincial and federal governments to treat seriously local preferences in that city. Another is the conception of local government – minimalist or comprehensive – held by local officials, which affects their inclination to engage proactively in the intergovernmental arena in the first place. A final factor is the administrative capacity of municipal government in intergovernmental affairs, which affects the ability of municipal officials to articulate and pursue their own priorities on the intergovernmental stage. All three of these factors work together in shaping municipal influence over multilevel policy processes; thus, very large municipalities with a comprehensive conception of local government and strong intergovernmental relations capacity – perhaps most notably Vancouver and Toronto – tend to be most successful in ensuring that multilevel policy processes are responsive to their own municipal interests across multiple policy fields.

The preferences of local officials in multilevel policy processes sometimes coincide with those of local social forces, but at other times they do not. Local business agents often have the necessary financial resources and organizational capacity to articulate their own preferences in the multilevel arena; indeed, the intergovernmental policy agendas of municipal officials are often strongly influenced by those of local business elites. By contrast, other local social forces rarely have such resources and capacity at their disposal. What factors influence multilevel responsiveness to their preferences? The above section entitled "Local Social Forces II" notes two important factors that bear some further discussion here.

The first factor is the pre-existing relationship between local government and local social forces in a given policy field and city. Because most local social forces have limited organizational capacity and are used to interacting primarily with local government, municipal governments often function as "gateways" through which local social forces can access multilevel policy processes. If municipal government has a history of systematically excluding or marginalizing certain social forces (as is the case, for example, in Saint John, Halifax, and Calgary), this important gateway remains closed. In most cases, this in turn decreases the responsiveness of multilevel governance to local social forces, although our chapters present a few cases – such as immigrant settlement in Winnipeg – in which provincial or federal officials choose to bypass local government in order to engage directly with local social forces. The second factor is the degree of policy-relevant expertise that local societal agents can offer to governmental agents. Particularly in human services fields such as immigrant settlement and urban Aboriginal policy, such policy expertise can give otherwise marginal local social forces a voice in policy development. In general, however, multilevel governance as documented in this volume tends to be limited in its responsiveness to local social forces other than business. Enthusiastic promoters of multilevel governance as a responsive mode of policy making would do well to keep this rather sobering conclusion in mind.

## TOWARDS BETTER MULTILEVEL GOVERNANCE IN CANADA'S BIG CITIES

What overall picture of multilevel governance in Canada's big cities emerges from our investigation? It is a picture of contrasts, of tremendous variety in form, in process, and in output. At its best, multilevel governance in Canada's cities does live up to its promise, pooling the resources and authority of multiple agents in the service of constructing locally grounded solutions to complex policy problems. At its worst, it is a quicksand of unaccountable policy making, inter-agency fighting, and wasted resources, laced with ample doses of political opportunism and blame-shifting. Yet, the omnipresence of multilevel governance in Canada's big cities suggests that, for all its potential pitfalls, it cannot and should not be avoided as a mode of policy making. Our cities have too many complex policy files, too many policy problems that cannot be addressed by one level of government acting alone. Although our research suggests that the devolution of some resources and authority to municipalities might produce better policy outputs in some fields, large-scale decentralization to the municipal level, as advocated by numerous recent commentators (see Broadbent 2008), is a chimeric alternative. It comes with its own significant risks, such as the emergence of an American-style gulf in policy capacity between "have" and "have-not" cities, and, more importantly, it is simply not a politically viable option in Canada today.

If multilevel urban governance is here to stay, what do our cases tell us about how the quality of multilevel policy outputs in Canada's cities might be improved? Our body of evidence is sufficiently broad and deep to allow a number of insights and recommendations. Let us begin at the local level. Municipal leaders and academics alike often complain (with some justification) that Canada's constitutional order marginalizes municipalities. Our evidence makes clear that municipal governments nonetheless play a pivotal role in multilevel urban governance. Their influence is as evident in what they do *not* do as in what they actually do. Where municipal officials are uninterested in multilevel coordination or lack the capacity to pursue multilevel policy, multilevel governance tends to be difficult and subject to frequent failure; where municipal officials engage actively and systematically with their counterparts at other levels of government, multilevel policy initiatives are much more likely to succeed. Yet, only a few of our case cities have actively developed their corporate-level intergovernmental relations capacity. A focus on building local capacity to engage cohesively and strategically with other levels of government would significantly enhance the prospects for successful multilevel policy making in many of the cities we have examined in this volume.

Local governments also act as crucial gateways to multilevel policy making for many local social forces, especially those outside the business sphere. As a result, the involvement of social forces in multilevel policy making is often a reflection of pre-existing state-society relations at the local level, and opening up municipal policy processes to a broader range of social forces can enhance their limited influence in multilevel policy processes. Multilevel policy responsiveness, in other words, begins at the local level. It is also clear that local social forces would, in many of our cases, benefit from "scaling up" their activity – for example, by forging issue-specific alliances with their counterparts in other municipalities, or by lobbying provincial or federal officials through broad umbrella organizations. Our research found surprisingly little evidence of such activity, which is likely hampered in many cases by the low organizational capacity and location-specific concerns of local societal groups. Nonetheless, such "scaling up" strategies offer an alternative to the dependence of many social forces on sometimes reluctant municipal interlocutors.[3]

Provincial governments, with their comprehensive jurisdiction over municipal matters, also strongly influence the prospects for good multilevel governance. The key lesson here has to do with the way in which provincial officials conceive of their role in multilevel policy systems. Where provincial officials jealously guard their jurisdiction over municipal affairs and micromanage their relationship with cities, local officials are less likely to be proactive in the intergovernmental arena, and federal officials are less likely to seek direct contact with their municipal counterparts. Where, by contrast, provincial officials see themselves as partners in a tri-level system of relationships, a wide field of possibilities for multilevel collaboration opens up.

As for the federal government, we have noted that its involvement in multilevel urban affairs is often project-based, rather than program-based. This in turn heightens the prospects that short-term political or electoral goals will drive federal urban initiatives, lowers the prospects for sustained collaboration across levels of government, and – as many municipal officials in our case cities complained – produces an unstable multilevel policy environment. Thus, the federal government could contribute significantly to improving the quality of multilevel governance if it further developed its program-based involvement in urban affairs. Of course, the current federal government has steered away from just such an approach, tentatively embraced by its predecessor, so the prospects for federal leadership on strategic urban policy appear dim at present.

All of these insights point in the direction of another observation: the functional requirements of multilevel governance in Canada's big cities are at odds with the current constitutional division of authority in the country. It is not so much the specific division of responsibility among levels of government that is the problem; rather, as Hooghe and Marks (2003) observe, the problem is the very notion that governance consists of nested layers of authority, each with its own separate sphere of policy concerns. Multilevel governance as it has emerged in Canada's big cities rests on the opposite premise: that the policy concerns of nested layers of authority in the Canadian federal system are interdependent and thus require ongoing multilevel coordination. It is highly unlikely that we will see a *de jure* unraveling of Canada's constitutional division of powers in response to this multilevel governance imperative, but the most successful examples of multilevel governance in the preceding pages suggest that this is not required. Rather, what is required is the willingness of governmental agents at various levels to institutionalize multilevel governance *de facto*. Many of the multilevel policy successes documented in this volume hinge on the development of collaboration agreements or collaborative institutions that limit inter-agent transaction costs and help to manage the agenda instability that so often threatens the sustainability of multilevel policy initiatives. To paraphrase American urban politics theorist Clarence Stone (1993), learning to let go of "power over" other agents and replace it with a collective "power to" address complex policy challenges is key to unlocking the positive potential of multilevel governance in Canada's big cities.

## NOTES

1  Detailed discussions of immigrant settlement policy Vancouver, Montreal, and Toronto can be found in Tolley and Young (2011).
2  Good (2009) demonstrates that some major municipalities not covered by our immigrant settlement sampling, such as Vancouver and Toronto, are quite active on immigrant settlement policy. The studies in Tolley and Young (2011) also suggest that large, high-immigration municipalities in Canada are more involved in immigrant settlement than the data sample in the current volume would suggest.
3  Other research has found evidence of "scaling up" among local social forces in some of the policy fields discussed in this book. See for example Boudreau, Keil, and Young 2009.

## REFERENCES

Boudreau, Julie-Anne, Roger Keil, and Douglas Young. 2009. *Changing Toronto: Governing Urban Neoliberalism*. Toronto: University of Toronto Press.

Bradford, Neil. 2005. *Place-based Public Policy: Towards a New Urban and Community Agenda for Canada*. Ottawa: Canadian Policy Research Networks.

Broadbent, Alan. 2008. *Urban Nation: Why We Need to Give Power Back to the Cities to Make Canada Strong*. Toronto: HarperCollins.

Good, Kristin. 2009. *Municipalities and Multiculturalism: The Politics of Immigration in Toronto and Vancouver*. Toronto: University of Toronto Press.

Henstra, Daniel. 2003. "Federal Emergency Management in Canada and the United States after September 11, 2001." *Canadian Public Administration* 46 (1):103–16.

Hooghe, Liesbet, and Gary Marks. 2003. "Unravelling the Central State, but How? Types of Multi-level Governance." *American Political Science Review* 97 (2):233–43.

Leo, Christopher, and Katie Anderson. 2006. "Being Realistic about Urban Growth." *Journal of Urban Affairs* 28 (2):169–89.

Peters, B. Guy, and Jon Pierre. 2005. "Multi-Level Governance and Democracy: A Faustian Bargain?" In *Multi-level Governance*, edited by Ian Bache and Matthew Flinders, 75–90. Oxford: Oxford University Press.

Sancton, Andrew, and Robert Young, eds. 2009. *Foundations of Governance: Municipal Government in Canada's Provinces*. Toronto: University of Toronto Press.

Sellers, Jefferey. 2005. "Re-Placing the Nation: An Agenda for Comparative Urban Politics." *Urban Affairs Review* 40 (4):419–45.

Siegel, David. 2006. "Recent Changes in Provincial-Municipal Relations in Ontario: A New Era or a Missed Opportunity?" In *Municipal-Federal-Provincial Relations in Canada*, edited by Robert Young and Christian Leuprecht, 181–97. Kingston: Institute of Intergovernmental Relations.

Smith, Ralph, and Sherri Torjman. 2004. *Policy Development and Implementation in Complex Files*. Ottawa: Canada School of Public Service.

Stone, Clarence. 1993. "Urban Regimes and the Capacity to Govern: A Political Economy Approach." *Journal of Urban Affairs* 15 (1):1–28.

Tolley, Erin, and Robert Young, eds. 2011. *Immigrant Settlement Policy in Canadian Municipalities*. Montreal and Kingston: McGill-Queen's University Press.

# Contributors

LAURENCE BHERER is associate professor of political science at Université de Montréal. Her research and publications focus on participatory democracy and urban politics.

DAVID BULGER taught political science and law at the University of Prince Edward Island for many years. He is a keen observer of politics on and off the Island, and an aficionado of PEI history.

CHRISTOPHER DUNN is professor of political science at Memorial University, specializing in Canadian public administration and the politics of Newfoundland and Labrador. He has edited *The Handbook of Canadian Public Administration* (2010), and has co-written *Democracy, Diversity and Good Government: An Introduction to Politics in Canada* (2011).

ROBERT FINBOW is professor and chair of political science at Dalhousie University. A recipient of SSHRC and Fulbright fellowships, he has published books and articles on trade, labour, and environmental policies in NAFTA and the EU, comparative political cultures, health care, and social policy in North America and regionalism in Atlantic Canada.

JOSEPH GARCEA is associate professor in the Department of Political Studies at the University of Saskatchewan. His teaching and research focus on Canadian governance and politics, public policy, public management, federalism, multilevel governance, local governance, urban Indian reserves, multiculturalism, immigration, and citizenship.

PIERRE HAMEL is professor of sociology at Université de Montréal. He is also the editor of the journal *Sociologie et sociétés*. He is the author of *Ville et débat public* (2008) and co-author of *Un modèle québécois? Gouvernance et participation dans la gestion publique* (2006).

MARTIN HORAK is associate professor of political science at the University of Western Ontario. His research focuses on comparative urban political institutions and urban policy processes; recent publications include *Governing the Post-Communist City: Institutions and Democratic Development in Prague* (2007).

TOM HUTTON is professor in the Centre for Human Settlements at the University of British Columbia. He specializes in studies of the urban economy and its role in the multiscalar transformation of cities, with recent work including *The New Economy of the Inner City* (2008).

CHRISTOPHER LEO, professor of politics at the University of Winnipeg and adjunct professor of city planning at the University of Manitoba, blogs at christopherleo.wordpress.com/ and makes brief comments at twitter.com/passingscene. He has been researching, teaching, writing, and publishing about urban political and administrative problems for more than thirty years.

GREG MARQUIS, professor in the Department of History and Politics at the University of New Brunswick Saint John, teaches Canadian and North American history. His research interests include urban studies, social history, and the history of popular culture.

BYRON MILLER is associate professor of geography at the University of Calgary. His research, which has been published in a number of leading journals, focuses on the spatial constitution of social movements, urban governance and governmentality, urban growth and change, and the politics of sustainability.

CECILY PANTIN is a policy analyst currently working for the Department of National Defence in Ottawa. She has an MA in Political Science from Memorial University of Newfoundland, where she completed the work for this project as a research assistant for Dr Christopher Dunn.

ALAN SMART is professor at the Department of Anthropology, University of Calgary. His research has focused on urban issues, housing, foreign investment, social change, food safety, zoonotic diseases, and agriculture in Hong Kong, China, and Canada.

DONALD C. STORY is an associate professor in the Department of Political Studies at the University of Saskatchewan. His major areas of current research are governance and management in the nonprofit sector and the relationship between the nonprofit, private and public sectors in Canada.

ROBERT YOUNG is professor of political science at the University of Western Ontario, where he holds the Canada Research Chair in Multilevel Governance. He is the editor of the Fields of Governance series.

# Index

Aboriginal Business Services Network, 92

Aboriginal Council of Manitoba, 306

Aboriginal Friendship Centre Program, 122, 348

Acadians, 54, 76

Affordable Housing Association of Nova Scotia, 80

African-Canadians, 84, 95

Africville, 76

Air Inuit, 123

Alberta Federal Council, 30, 38

Alberta Federation of Labour, 34

Alberta Lottery Board, 45

Allum, James, 304

amalgamation, 73–4, 76–8, 82, 86, 94–5, 108, 231–2, 241, 245

Arsenault, Kevin, 67

Art Gallery of Newfoundland and Labrador, 218

Asia Pacific, 13, 267–8, 270–2, 279–81, 294–5, 360

Assemblée Fransaskoise, SK, 168

Assembly of First Nations of Quebec and Labrador, 123

Assembly of Manitoba Chiefs, 306

Association for New Canadians, NL, 209–12

Association of Municipalities of Ontario, 236–7

Association of Newcomers to PEI, 67–9

Atlantic Accord, 213

Atlantic Canada Opportunities Agency, 70, 92, 143, 146, 149–50, 155, 211

Atlantic Gateway Fund, 206

Atlantic Health Sciences Corporation, 152

Atlantic Institute of Market Studies, 154

Atlantic Mayors Congress, 212

Atlantica Centre for Energy, NB, 138, 156

Atomic Energy of Canada Limited, 139

Augustine, Patrick, 69–70

Basrur, Sheela, 246

Bedford, NS, 75–6

Bell Canada, 110

Bernard, Charles Patrick, 68

Bertram, Carolyn, 62
Big Cities Mayors' Caucus, 170, 271
Binns, Pat, 64
Border Infrastructure Fund, 204
Bourque, Pierre, 126
British Columbia Coalition for
    Immigrant Integration, 318
British Columbia Teachers'
    Federation, 288
Bronconnier, David, 31, 36, 39
Building Canada Fund, 41, 185, 204–
    5, 207, 354
Bureau of International Exhibitions,
    281
Burin Peninsula, NL, 201
business. *See* social forces
Business Council of Manitoba, 320

Calgary, AB, 4, 9–10, 26–52, 178,
    212, 283, 294, 347, 356–7, 366;
    Calgary Catholic Immigration
    Society, 36; Calgary Chamber of
    Commerce, 29, 33, 36, 41, 46;
    Calgary Economic Development,
    33, 40; Calgary Expo Bid 2005, 39,
    42–3; Calgary Homeless
    Foundation, 30; Calgary Housing
    Authority, 45; Calgary Stampede,
    40–3, 346; Calgary Stampede
    Board, 41–3; Calgary Stampede
    Park, 39, 41–3; Calgary Vital Signs
    Survey, 28, 34
Callbeck, Phillips, 54
Calvert, Lorne, 183–4
Campbell, Gordon, 270, 283
Campbell, Larry, 283–4, 288, 291
Canada-Alberta Agreement for
    Cooperation on Immigration, 34
Canada-Alberta Municipal Rural
    Infrastructure Fund, 38

Canada-Manitoba Immigration
    Agreement, 316
Canada-New Brunswick
    Infrastructure Program, 150
Canada-New Brunswick Municipal
    Rural Infrastructure Fund, 150
Canada-Newfoundland and Labrador
    Business Service Network, 213
Canada-Newfoundland Infrastructure
    Program, 202
Canada-Ontario Immigration
    Agreement, 34
Canada-PEI Immigration Agreement,
    67
Canada-Quebec Accord (on immigra-
    tion), 34
Canada-Quebec Agreement (St
    Lawrence Action Plan), 125
Canada-Saskatchewan Immigration
    Agreement, 166
Canada Infrastructure Stimulus Fund,
    204–6
Canada Lands Company, 44–6, 63–6,
    79–80, 238–9, 343, 362
Canada Mortgage and Housing
    Corporation, 45, 80, 289
Canada Strategic Infrastructure Fund,
    38, 83, 150, 184, 202–4, 235–6,
    257, 354
Canada West Foundation, 37
Canada's Economic Action Plan, 204,
    207
Canadian Air Transport Security
    Authority, 181
Canadian Broadcasting Corporation,
    234
Canadian Environmental Assessment
    Agency, 84
Canadian Forces, 44, 309, 313, 330
Canadian Pacific Railroad, 273

Canadian Red Cross, 62–3, 111, 152, 328

Cannon, Lawrence, 65

Cartier, Sir George-Étienne, 53, 56

Champlain Bridge, 124

Charlottetown, PE, 8–10, 22, 53–72, 200, 219, 343, 358; Charlottetown Accord, 57; Charlottetown Airport, 54, 63; Charlottetown Area Development Corporation, 63; Charlottetown City Council, 60, 65, 71; Charlottetown *Guardian* newspaper, 62, 68; Charlottetown Harbour Authority, 63; Charlottetown Metropolitan Area, 57; Emergency Measures Committee, 61

Chrétien, Jean, 183, 235, 239, 291

Christian Reformed World Relief Committee, MB, 328

Cities of New Brunswick Association, 142

Citizenship and Immigration Canada, 34–5, 167–8, 210–11, 314–15, 318–19

Civil Security Act, QC, 108, 111

Clark, Glen, 282, 288

Clyde River, PE, 57

CN Rail, 125

College of the North Atlantic, 207

Collenette, David, 238–9

Commission of Government, NL, 199

Committee of Progressive Electors, BC, 283, 288

Commonwealth Games Canada, 74, 87

Conference Board of Canada, 136

Connaught Bridge, BC, 295

Conservative Party of Canada, 7, 16, 29–30, 88, 137–9, 149–51, 180, 185, 207, 237–8, 240, 316, 343

Coordinating Committee on Newcomer Integration, NL, 211

Corman Park, SK, 178–9

Cornwall, PE, 57–8, 69

Court, Ivan, 157

Covehead, PE, 57

Cruise Association of Newfoundland and Labrador, 216

Cullen, Jake, 68

Cultural Capitals of Canada program, 215

CUPE, 83

Curry Barracks, AB, 10, 44

Cyprus Green, AB, 44–5

Day, Jim, 68

Dartmouth, NS, 75–6, 79–80

De Forest Baldwin, Henry, 29

Delta, BC, 4, 272

Department of Agriculture Canada, 63–5

Department of Canadian Heritage, 211, 219, 221

Department of Indian and Northern Affairs Canada, 64, 90, 92, 219

Department of Labrador and Aboriginal Affairs, 219

Department of National Defence Canada, 79, 238–40, 312, 362

Department of Transport, Infrastructure and Communities, 39

Digby, NS, 149

Disaster Financial Assistance Arrangements, 247, 324–5

Drapeau, Jean, 113

Edmonton, AB, 30–2, 38, 40, 304, 312

Emera Brunswick Pipeline Company, 142

Emergency management, 7, 9, 344–5, 352, 354–5; Charlottetown, 10, 53, 61–3, 71; Montreal, 104–5, 108–13; Saint John, 136, 151–3; Saskatoon, 162, 171–7, 189; Toronto, 13, 228–30, 244–7, 253–4, 257; Winnipeg, 301, 303, 323–9
Energy Council of Canada, 214
Environment Canada, 85, 157
environmental groups. See social forces

Falcon, Kevin, 275–6
Fanning, Edmund, 55
federal property, 7, 10, 343–4, 352, 354; Calgary, 44–5, 357; Charlottetown, 53, 60, 63–6, 71, 343; Halifax, 10, 73–4, 78–81, 87, 360, 362; Montreal, 104–5, 124–30, 360, 363; Saskatoon, 162, 177–82, 189–90; Toronto, 13, 228–30, 238–41, 248–53, 255; Winnipeg, 302, 309–14, 323, 329
Federation of Canadian Municipalities, 37, 170, 235, 271
First Nations, 64, 120, 285, 288; Cree First Nation, 120; Innu Nation, 219–20; Inuit, 120, 219, 221; Métis Nation, 219; Miawpukek First Nation, 219; Mi'kmaq First Nation, 64, 76, 80, 90–1, 219; Mohawk First Nations, 120; Treaty 7 First Nations, 41. See also urban Aboriginal policy
Fisheries and Oceans Canada, 85
Florida, Richard, 18
Ford, Rob, 257
Fredericton, NB, 138, 146, 150, 155–6
Friends of the Home Farm, PE, 64–5
Friends of Upton Farm, PE, 65

Front d'action populaire en réaménagement urbain, QC, 123
Frost, Robert, 68
Furlong, John, 284

Garrison Green, AB, 44–5
Garrison Woods, AB, 44–6, 357
Gas Tax Fund, 150, 157, 204–6, 235–7, 343, 354, 363
Genstar Development Company, 301
George Brown College, 251
Government Services Canada, 118
Graham, Shawn, 140, 144, 150, 155
Green Transit Incentives Program, AB, 39
Griffiths, Arthur, 282

Habitat Métis du Nord, QC, 123
Halifax, NS, 4, 9–10, 54, 61, 73–103, 150, 155, 200, 343, 346, 351, 359–62, 366; Commonwealth Games bid, 10, 74, 81, 87, 346, 355; Commonwealth Park, 81, 87; Community Integration Fund, 84; Friendship Centre, 91–2; G7 Summit, 86; Greater Halifax Partnership, 86, 94; Greenwood, 79; Halifax Chamber of Commerce, 82–3, 94; Halifax County, 76; Halifax Harbour, 74–5, 82–6; Halifax Regional Development Agency, 94; Halifax Regional Environmental Partnership, 83–4; Halifax Regional Municipality, 11, 73–4, 77–97; HRMbyDesign, 90, 95; Nations in a Circle, 91; Shannon Park, 80–1, 87
Hamm, John, 83
Happy Valley-Goose Bay, NL, 219–20
Harcourt, Michael, 270, 281–2, 295

Harper, Stephen, 31, 88, 139, 150, 204, 207, 238, 240, 353

Health Canada, 220–1

Heathrow Airport, 275

Hebron-Nevis Oil Field, NL, 209, 213

Helgason, Wayne, 303

Hibernia Oil Field, NL, 213

Hogan, Bill, 61–3

Holland, Captain Samuel, 54–5

The Home Farm (Ravenwood Farm), PE, 54, 63–5, 69–70

Homelessness Partnership Initiative, 90, 121

Hopedale, NL, 219

Human Resources and Skills Development Canada, 35

Hurricane Juan, 61

Hurricane Katrina, 327

Hydro-Québec, 110

Ice Storm of 1998, 108–9, 111, 345

image building, 7–9, 345–6, 349, 360–1; Calgary, 10, 39–43; Charlottetown, 22, 53; Halifax, 73–4, 80, 85–90, 346; Montreal, 11, 104–5, 113–19, 129, 362; Saint John, 12, 140–5, 153, 345–6; St John's, 13, 200, 212–18, 223, 363; Toronto, 13, 228–30, 241–4, 346, 360; Vancouver, 13, 264–5, 278–90, 360

immigrant settlement, 7, 9, 17, 346–7, 349, 352, 354, 357–8; Calgary, 32–6, 47; Charlottetown, 10, 53, 58, 60, 66–8, 71; Halifax, 73, 76, 86; Montreal, 107, 369; Saint John, 136, 145–8, 153, 156, 314; Saskatoon, 162–3, 165–71, 188–90; St John's, 13, 198, 200,

208–12, 223; Toronto, 33, 228, 233–4, 255–6, 315, 369; Vancouver, 263, 265, 267–8, 279–80, 295, 314, 322, 707; Winnipeg, 32, 302, 314–23, 329–30, 363, 366

infrastructure 7–8, 342–43, 349, 352, 354, 364; Calgary, 10, 28, 31–3, 36–41, 46–7; Halifax, 10, 73–4, 78, 80–5, 87, 94, 96; Saint John, 12, 140, 148–51, 155; Saskatoon, 162, 164, 173, 178, 181–8; St John's, 198–207, 214, 223; Toronto, 13, 228–30, 234–48, 250–1, 257; Vancouver, 13, 263–5, 271–7, 281–2, 291, 295

Infrastructure Canada, 38, 202–3, 206, 235, 257, 354

intergovernmental relations, 4–8, 18, 21, 26, 104, 153–4, 162, 165, 167–71, 210, 264–5, 271–3, 279, 284–7, 290–3, 339, 362; accountability, 73–4, 78, 95–7, 349; conflict, 31, 39, 46, 66, 74, 77–8, 80, 82–4, 93, 108, 118, 185, 248, 266, 272, 274, 344, 356, 362; coordination, 13, 81, 87, 93, 112, 119, 121, 168, 171–83, 188–91, 202, 211, 219, 229–32, 242–7, 249, 252–6, 282, 324–7, 361–3, 368; federal-municipal, 5, 14, 30, 38, 45, 60, 73, 75, 84, 92–3, 96, 121–2, 124–6, 136, 146, 149, 233, 234–8, 301, 330, 354–5, 368; federal-provincial, 34, 92, 120, 125, 156–7, 165–6, 176–7, 190, 221, 300; jurisdiction, 4, 8, 15–16, 20, 69, 73, 91, 93–4, 96, 112, 119–20, 130, 141, 221, 269, 272, 295, 321–3, 341, 347, 349–51, 354–5, 364, 368; provincial-municipal,

11–12, 14, 31–2, 60, 62, 71, 89, 97, 107, 111, 122, 138, 143, 151, 202, 352–3; tripartite relationships, 5, 7, 21, 44, 70, 81, 92, 126–9, 149, 151, 169–70, 177, 184, 190, 203–5, 235–6, 251, 271–2, 292, 295, 305, 342, 352, 354, 363–4

Irving Family, 12, 138–40, 143–5, 156–7

Irving Oil, 155

Itzkow, Martin, 328

Jacobs, Jane, 299

Jacques Cartier Bridge, 124–5

Jewish Child and Family Services, MB, 318

Joint Emergency Preparedness Program, 152, 173–4, 176, 247, 324

Kahnawake Reserve, QC, 120

Kanesatake Reserve, QC, 120

Karma Dzong Buddhists, 76

Katz, Sam, 302, 310, 314, 322, 329

Kelly, Peter, 83

Kennebecasis Valley, NB, 153

Koolhaas, Rem, 239

La Tuque, QC, 120

Labrador Institute, 222

Lachine Canal, 11, 114, 124–9, 344, 354, 360, 363

Ladco Company, Ltd, 301

Lake Placid River Landing Incorporated, 187

Lastman, Mel, 228, 257

Laval, QC, 106, 108, 116

Layton, Jack, 237

Lee, Clifford, 67

Leslie Harris Centre of Regional Policy and Development, NL, 211, 222

Liberal Party of Canada, 16, 30, 76, 88, 137–41, 146, 149–51, 153, 156, 180, 183–5, 235–8, 283, 287

Local Government Act, NL, 199

London, England, 275

Longueuil, QC, 106, 108, 116

Lord, Bernard, 139, 156–7

Macdonald, Sir John A., 53

MacDougall, Gary, 68

MacFadyen, Stu, 60

MacMillan Bloedel, Ltd, 266

Main, Roy, 63, 66

Makkovik, NL, 219

Manitoba Home Builders' Association, 300

Manitoba Immigration Council, 318

Manitoba Labour and Immigration, 317

Manitoba Métis Federation, 306

Manitoba Transportation, 313

Maritime Electric, 61

Maritimes, 10, 74, 76, 140, 146–7

Martin, Paul, 7, 15, 30, 38, 127, 146, 150, 183, 203, 205, 235–7, 249, 300, 342–3, 353, 363

Mary's Harbour, NL, 219

Mau, Bruce, 239

McFarlane, Norman, 153

McGee, Thomas D'Arcy, 53

McKenna, Frank, 142

Meewasin Valley Authority, 183–4, 187–8

Memorial University, 211, 221–2

Mennonite Disaster Service, 328

Mihevc, Joe, 300

Miller, David, 228, 233, 236, 242–3, 247, 249, 254, 257

Mills, Dennis, 248

Miltonvale Park, PE, 57, 59

Ministry for the Public Safety of Quebec, 111
Ministry of State for Infrastructure and Communities, 353
Ministry of State for Urban Affairs, 15, 353
Moncton, NB, 138, 146, 155–6
Montreal, QC, 4, 9, 11, 28, 33, 104–35, 147, 208, 232, 304, 312, 315, 344, 354, 357, 362–3; Board of Trade of Metropolitan Montreal, 116; Cité du commerce électronique, 114; Cité Multimédia, 114; City of Montreal Civil Security Centre, 110, 112; Culture Montréal, 116; Emergency Measures Bureau, 109–10; First Peoples' Festival, 123; Guy Favreau Complex, 124; Island of Montreal, 111–12, 124, 126; Land Insights, 123; Moisson Montréal, 111; Montreal Antiterrorism Advisory Committee, 112; Montreal International, 118; Montreal Metropolitan Community, 106, 116–18; Montreal Urban Community, 109; Native Friendship Centre of Montreal, 119, 122, 131; Old Port, 114, 125–6; Port of Montreal, 112; Société d'habitation de Montréal, 123; Société du Havre, 128–9; Sun Youth Organization, 111; World Trade Centre, 124
Morris, Charles, 55
Mothers of Red Nations, 306–7
Mount Pearl, NL, 203, 206
Mulroney, Brian, 178, 213
Municipal Capital Works Program, 204
Municipal Rural Infrastructure Fund, 204

Murphy, Shawn, 66
Murray, Glen, 300, 302, 304, 322, 329

Nain, NL, 219
National Airports Policy, 178–9
National Association of Friendship Centres, 219
National Energy Board, 152
National Energy Program, 44
National Housing Initiative, 80
National Policy Tariffs, 6
Native Council of PEI, 69–70
Natuashish, NL, 219
New Brunswick Capital Borrowing Board, 150
New Brunswick Community College, 148
New Brunswick Emergency Measures Act, 152
New Brunswick Emergency Measures Organization, 152
New Brunswick Power, 139
New Brunswick Self-Sufficiency Agenda, 146, 156
New Deal for Cities and Communities, 7, 15, 60, 150, 233, 235–6, 299, 342–3, 353
New Democratic Party, 139, 183–5, 237, 282–3, 288, 316
New Public Management, 6
New Westminster, BC, 4
Nicolet Commission, QC, 109, 111
NL Cultural Industries Strategy, 209
NL Department of Human Resources, 209
NL Department of Labour and Employment, 209
NL Department of Municipal and Provincial Affairs, 384
NL Department of Tourism, 215

NL Federation of Municipalities, 211
NL Ocean Technology Sector Strategy,
    214
NL Office of Immigration and
    Multiculturalism, 209
NL Provincial Archives, 218
NL Provincial Innovation Strategy, 209
NL Regional Diversification Strategy,
    209
NL Tourism Development Strategy, 209
NL Tourism Marketing Council, 215
NL Museum, 218
non-profit social agencies. See social
    forces
Noranda Inc., 266
Northeast Avalon, NL, 201
Northumberland Strait, 54
Northwest Territories, 8
Nova Scotia Department of Housing
    and Municipal Affairs, 84
Nova Scotia Framework Agreement
    on Aboriginal Treaty Rights/
    Umbrella Agreement, 90
Nova Scotia Human Rights
    Commission, 84
Nova Scotia Office of Aboriginal
    Affairs, 90, 93
Nova Scotia Utilities and Review
    Board, 78
Nunavut, 8

Ontario Realty Corporation, 250-1
Ottawa, ON, 124, 126-8, 148-9, 173
Olympics, 42; Athens 2004 Olympics,
    282; Barcelona 1992 Olympics,
    282; Beijing 2008 Olympics, 285;
    Calgary 1988 Olympics, 39-43;
    Canadian Olympic Committee,
    284, 293; International Olympic
    Commission, 282-4, 287; Los

Angeles 1984 Olympics, 282;
    Montreal 1976 Olympics, 282;
    Toronto Olympic bid 2008, 249-
    50, 255; Vancouver Olympic
    Village, 288-90, 293; Vancouver
    2010 Olympics, 14, 88, 264, 279,
    281-93, 295-6, 346, 353-4, 362;
    Vancouver Olympics Organizing
    Committee (VANOC), 14, 282,
    284-7, 293
Owen, Philip, 283

Paradise, NL, 203, 206
Parc Downsview Park Inc., 238-40,
    253
Parks Canada, 85, 127-8
Parti Québécois, 108
Partners in Disaster, MB, 328
Partnership BC, 276
Passamaquoddy Bay, NB, 139
Patterson, Walter, 55
Point Lepreau, NB, 138
population growth/decline, 10, 146;
    Calgary, 28, 32-3, 40; Saint John,
    156; Saskatoon, 163, 165; St
    John's, 208; Toronto, 232
Port Hope Simpson, NL, 219
Portugal Cove-St Phillips, NL, 206
Postville, NL, 219
Prairie Ecovillage Development
    Corp., 188
Prince Edward Island Department of
    Agriculture, 63-4
Prince Edward Island Department of
    Health, 63
Prince Edward Island Emergency
    Measures Organization, 63
Prince Edward Island Office of Public
    Safety, 62
Princeton Developments Ltd, SK, 187

Private-Public Partnership Fund, 206
Province House, PE, 53
Provincial Nominee Program, 34, 157, 209, 211, 314–17, 347, 354
Public-private partnerships, 151, 206, 274–8, 293, 296
Public Safety Canada, 62, 173, 247, 325
Public Transit Capital Trust, 137, 204, 206
Public Works Canada, 65, 118
Puil, George, 275

Qualico Developments, MB, 301
Quebec City, 53, 119, 124, 127, 283
Quebec Ministry of Aboriginal Affairs, 121
Quebec Ministry of Culture, Communications, and the Status of Women, 116
Quebec Ministry of Sustainable Development, Environment and Parks, 111
Quebec Public Health Branch, 110
Queen Charlotte of Mecklenberg, 54
Quispamsis, NB, 153

Rathie, William, 273
Recreational Infrastructure Canada Program, 206
Regina, SK, 120, 172–3, 181
Regina Airport Authority, 181
Regroupement des centres d'amitié autochtone du Québec, 123
Remai Ventures Inc., SK, 187
The Resort Municipality, PEI, 22
Richmond, BC, 4, 268, 272, 274–5
Rideau Canal, 128
Rigolet, NL, 219
Robert, Randy, 62
Robinson, Alex, 310

Rogge, Jacques, 284
Rothesay, NB, 153
Royal Canadian Mounted Police (RCMP), 62

SS Queen Victoria, 56
Saint John, NB, 9, 11, 136–61, 342, 345, 357, 366; AIDS Saint John, 151; Atlantic Coastal Action Program Saint John, 150, 157; Board of Trade, 138, 141–3, 145, 148–9, 152, 155–6; Business Community Anti-Poverty Initiative, 141; Central Business District, 140–4; Common Council (City Council), 152–4; Courtenay Bay, 140; energy hub, 12, 138–9, 144–5, 154–5, 355; Enterprise Saint John Inc., 143, 145–6, 148, 154–5; Harbour Passage, 143, 145; Immigrant and Refugee Support Centre, 147; International Longshoremen's Association Local, 144; Market Square, 143; Saint John Chinese Cultural Centre, 148; Saint John Development Corporation, 143; Saint John Emergency Operations Centre, 153; Saint John Energy, 152; Saint John Human Development Council, 141, 148, 156; Saint John Port Authority, 143–4, 152; Saint John Shipbuilding, 137; Saint John Shipyard, 142; Saint John Social Services Council, 156; Saint John Transit Commission, 149; Uptown Saint John Inc., 143, 145, 157; Waterfront Development Partnership, 143–5, 154
Saint Vincent de Paul Society, 111
Salvation Army, 111, 152, 328

Samaranch, Juan Antonio, 283
Saskatchewan Community Share
    Fund, 184
Saskatchewan Emergency
    Management Organization, 172–3
Saskatchewan Emergency Planning
    Act, 171
Saskatchewan Immigrant Nominee
    Program, 166
Saskatchewan Institute of Applied
    Sciences and Technology, 175
Saskatchewan Intercultural
    Association, 168
Saskatoon, SK, 9, 12, 120, 162–97,
    359; Community Development
    Corporation, 185–6; Cultural
    Diversity and Race Relations Com-
    mittee, 169; Emergency Measures
    Organization, 171–5, Emergency
    Operations Centre, 171, 173, 176;
    Emergency Planning Committee,
    172, 174; Emergency Social Services
    Committee, 174–5; Gathercole
    building, 185–8; Immigration
    Community Resource Coordinator,
    168–70; International Women of
    Saskatoon, 168; John G. Diefen-
    baker International Airport, 177–
    82; Newcomer Information Centre,
    168; North Saskatoon Mutual Aid
    Committee, 176; Refugee Coali-
    tion, 168; River Landing Project,
    182–90; Saskatoon Airport Au-
    thority, 177–82, 189; Saskatoon
    Department of Community Servic-
    es, 174–5; Saskatoon Department
    of Fire and Protective Services, 172,
    174–5; Saskatoon Health Region,
    168, 175; Saskatoon Immigration
    Coordinating Committee, 168;

Saskatoon Immigration Project,
    170; Saskatoon Industrial Mutual
    Aid Committee, 174–5; Saskatoon
    Infrastructure Services Department,
    174; Saskatoon Open Door Society,
    168; Saskatoon Public School
    Board, 186; Saskatoon Utility Ser-
    vices Department, 174; TCU Place,
    186; Ukrainian Canadian Congress
    of Saskatoon, 168
Scott, Andy, 150
Senator Sid Buckwold Bridge, SK, 182
Sept-Îles, QC, 120
Service Canada, 167, 211
Severe Acute Respiratory Syndrome
    (SARS), 242, 246–7
Shearwater Airbase, NS, 79–80
Shearwater Development
    Corporation, NS, 79–80
Sheshatshiu, NL, 219
Simon Fraser University, 266
Smith, Richard, 266
social forces, 4–9, 13, 15, 17–21, 26,
    66, 140, 142, 263, 286, 301–3,
    341–2, 349, 358–9, 362, 367, 369;
    business, 6, 11–12, 17–18, 20, 342–
    6, 356–7, 365, 367; Calgary, 27–
    30, 38, 46–7; Charlottetown, 66;
    Halifax, 11, 79, 82–3, 85, 88–90,
    94; Montreal, 106–7, 118, 125,
    129; Saint John, 17, 137–8, 141–
    2, 145–8, 151, 153–5, 156–7;
    Saskatoon, 164, 178, 180, 185–
    7; St John's, 199–200, 212–14,
    217, 223; Toronto, 233, 236,
    239, 251; Vancouver, 273, 277,
    281; Winnipeg, 300, 312, 316,
    320;
    environmental groups, 358;
    Halifax, 82–5, 95; Saint John,

139, 152, 156; Saskatoon, 183;
Vancouver, 277; Winnipeg,
313–14;
non-profit social agencies, 347–9,
358–9, 365; Calgary, 29–30, 35,
43, 46; Charlottetown, 62–3;
Halifax, 80, 91; Montreal, 111,
116, 118, 121–9; Saint John,
141, 145, 147–8, 151–2, 154,
156; Saskatoon, 166–71, 178,
187, 190; St John's, 210, 214;
Toronto, 233, 245; Vancouver,
273, 277, 288–9; Winnipeg,
320–1, 328, 330;
unions; Calgary, 34–5; Halifax, 83;
Saint John, 138, 144–5, 154–6;
Saskatoon, 167
Social Sciences and Humanities
Research Council of Canada, 21
Société franco-manitobaine, 321
Soknacki, David, 240
South Korea, 146, 284
South Saskatchewan River, 184
St Dunstan's University, PE, 54
St John Ambulance, 152, 328
St John's, NL, 12, 150, 198–227; Bay
Bulls Big Pond Water Treatment
Plant, 205–6; Destination St John's,
214–16; Downtown
Development Corporation, 217;
Fort Townshend, 217–18;
Municipal Depot, 206; Petty
Harbour-Long Pond Water
Treatment Plant, 206; Robin Hood
Bay Recycling Facility, 205–6; The
Rooms, 217–18; Scotia Plaza, 217;
Shamrock Field, 217; St John's
Business Information Centre, 213;
St John's Economic Development
Division, 213; St John's Harbour,
203, 217; St John's Native
Friendship Centre, 220–1; St John's
Port Authority, 217; Water Street,
217
St Lawrence River, 106, 124–5, 127
St Lawrence Seaway, 125
St Lewis, NL, 219
St Peter's Bay, PE, 22
Stelmach, ED, 31
Stratford, PE, 57–8, 62, 69
Summerside, PE, 57, 62
Surrey, BC, 4, 268

Taylor, Carole, 278
TD Bank, 40
Temporary Foreign Workers Program,
33–5, 47, 347
Terra Nova Oil Field, NL, 213
Thompson, Susan, 304
Tim Hortons, 35
Toronto, ON, 4, 9, 13, 20, 28, 33,
106, 147, 178, 208, 228–62, 294,
300, 304, 312, 315, 322–3, 346,
351, 360–3, 365; Air Canada Cen-
tre, 245; Build Toronto, 251; CN
Tower, 245; Downsview Park, 13,
229–30, 238–41, 253–5; East Bay-
front, 250–1; Toronto Board of
Trade, 233, 236; Toronto City
Summit Alliance, 233, 236, 257;
Toronto Economic Development
Corporation, 248–52, 257; Toron-
to Economic Development Culture
and Tourism Department, 241,
243; Toronto Emergency Medical
Services, 244; Toronto Emergency
Operations Centre, 245–6; Toronto
Fire Services, 244; Toronto
Harbour Commission, 248–9;
Toronto International, 242–4;

Toronto Island Airport, 249–50, 257; Toronto Office of Emergency Management, 245, 247; Toronto Port Authority, 248–9, 251, 257; Toronto Public Health, 246; Toronto Special Events Unit, 241–4; Toronto Tourism Advisory Committee, 241–2; Toronto Transit Commission, 13, 230, 233–8, 252–5; Toronto Waterfront Revitalization Corporation (Waterfront Toronto), 249–51, 254, 257; Tourism Action Plan, 13, 229–30, 241–4, 253–5; Tourism Toronto, 241–3; Waterfront Revitalization, 230, 248–52, 254, 344; Waterfront Revitalization Task Force, 249; West Don Lands, 250–1
Trans-Canada Highway, 65
Transport Canada, 177–82, 189, 274–5, 277, 310, 312
Tremblay, Gérald, 114

UNESCO City of Design, 117
unions. See social forces
United States of America, 5, 45, 54, 106, 131, 138, 146, 156, 172, 312, 366
United Way, 36, 122, 156, 209
University of British Columbia, 296
University of New Brunswick Saint John, 148
University of Prince Edward Island, 54
University of Saskatchewan, 172, 175
University of Winnipeg, 331
urban Aboriginal policy, 7, 9–10, 13, 17, 347–9, 352, 357–8, 360, 366; Aboriginal Head Start, 122; Charlottetown, 10, 53, 58, 60–1, 68–70; Halifax, 10, 73–4, 80,

90–3, 95–6; Montreal, 104–5, 119–24, 129–30; Saskatoon, 163, 167, 360; St John's, 13, 218–22; urban Aboriginal homelessness, 121; Urban Aboriginal Strategy (federal), 90–1, 121, 219, 348, 354; Urban Multipurpose Aboriginal Youth Centre Initiative, 122; Vancouver, 269, 286; Winnipeg, 301, 303–9, 323, 329–30
Urban Development Agreements, 7, 184–5
Urban Development Institute, AB, 32
Upton Farms, PE, 65–6

Val d'Or, QC, 120
Vancouver, BC, 4, 8–9, 13, 28, 33, 147, 178, 208, 263–98, 300, 304, 312, 314–15, 322–3, 351–2, 357, 360, 362, 365; Cambie Street, 277; Canada Line Transit Project, 13, 264, 274–8, 291–3, 296, 353; Downtown Eastside, 273, 280, 287, 292, 363; Expo '86, 270, 280–1, 295, Gateway Program, 273–4, 277; Granville Island, 289; Metro Vancouver, 264, 269–70, 272; North False Creek, 280, 289; Vancouver Olympics 2010 (see Olympics); SkyTrain, 275, 281, 296; TransLink, 269, 272, 275–7, 295; Vancouver Board of Trade, 273; Vancouver International Airport, 271–5; Vancouver Port, 271
Vandal, Dan, 303, 305
Veterans' Affairs Canada, 58
VIA Rail, 125
Voluntary and Non-Profit Sector Organization of Manitoba, 328

Warren Grove, PE, 57
Wayne, Elsie, 139
Wellington, PE, 22
Wells, Andy, 203
Western Economic Diversification
    Canada, 184, 313
Weyerhaeuser, 266
Whistler, BC, 282, 287–8
White Rose Oil Field, NL, 213
Williams, Danny, 204, 207–9
Winnipeg, MB, 9, 14, 92, 163, 299–
    338, 347–8, 351, 366; Aboriginal
    Council of Winnipeg, 306; Airport
    Advisory Committee on Environ-
    ment, 313; Citizen Equity Commit-
    tee, 322; Community Consultative
    Committee, 313; Core Area Initia-
    tive, 305; Destination Winnipeg,
    313; The Forks, 309, 330; Friends
    of Bruce Park, 313; Friends of
    Omand's Creek, 313; International
    Centre of Winnipeg, 318–19; James
    A. Richardson International Air-
    port, 309–14, 330; Jewish Federa-
    tion of Winnipeg, 321; Kapyong
    Barracks, 309; Municipal Aborigi-
    nal Pathways, 304–5, 308; Social
Planning Council of Winnipeg, 303;
    Welcome Place, 322; Wii Chii Waa
    Ka Nak Indigenous Education Cen-
    tre, 307; Winnipeg Airports Author-
    ity, 309–14, 330; Winnipeg Chamber
    of Commerce, 300, 313, 330; Win-
    nipeg Emergency Control Commit-
    tee, 326–7; Winnipeg Emergency
    Operations Centre, 326–7; Winni-
    peg Emergency Preparedness and
    Coordination Committee, 326–8;
    Winnipeg Mayor's Task Force on
    Diversity, 304, 322; Winnipeg Part-
    nership Agreement, 305–8, 330;
    Winnipeg Private Refugee Sponsor-
    ship Assurance Program, 322; Win-
    nipeg Urban Aboriginal Strategy,
    305–8, 330, 363
Winsloe, PE, 54
World Energy Cities Partnership, 213
World War I, 140
World War II, 57, 75, 200
Wright, Thomas, 55

YM-YWCA, 147–8
Yukon, 8, 204